Learning Data Analysis with Data Desk®

Student Version 6.0

for Windows®

Paul F. Velleman
Cornell University

An imprint of Addison Wesley Longman, Inc.

Reading, Massachusetts • Menlo Park, California • New York • Harlow, England
Don Mills, Ontario • Sydney • Mexico City • Madrid • Amsterdam

Copyright Notice

Reproduced by Addison-Wesley from camera-ready copy supplied by the author.

Library of Congress Cataloging-in-Publication Data

Velleman, Paul F., 1949-
Learning data analysis with the student version of DataDesk,
Windows 6.0 / Paul Velleman.
p. cm.
Includes bibliographical references and index.
ISBN 0-201-25830-7
1. Data desk. 2. Mathematical statistics--Data processing.
I. Data desk. II. Title.
QA276.4.V4455 1998
001.4'22'07855369--dc21
97-16891
CIP

ISBN 0-201-25830-7

1 2 3 4 5 6 7 8 9 10 VG 00999897

Preface

WELCOME TO DATA DESK. The book *Learning Data Analysis with the Student Version of Data Desk 6.0* and the program that goes with it embody a new way to apply statistics to data. The *Data Desk Student Version 6.0* program works graphically so there is no new language to learn. Together, the book and program help you to visualize abstract concepts and to see them applied to real data. Whatever your background and whatever path you are following to learn more about statistics, you will find that it is easier when you can see, touch, and experiment with new concepts and methods. That is what Data Desk and this book are designed to do.

The *Data Desk Student Version 6.0* is a special version of the popular Data Desk statistics program available from Data Description, Inc., of Ithaca, New York. The Student Version is designed to provide the functionality you need to learn statistics with all of the ease and convenience of Data Desk but without multivariate statistics and complex data manipulation that might distract you from learning. When you want to move up from coursework to analyzing research data, you will probably want to upgrade to the full version. Contact Data Description for upgrade details.

The *Data Desk Student Version 6.0* included with this book is based on the 6.0 version of Data Desk. It can open and work with any Data Desk 6.0 datafile that has no more than 1000 cases and 50 variables. The Student Version can also open any Data Desk datafiles created with version 3.0 or later.

The Student Version includes two disks. The first holds the Data Desk program and datafiles. The second disk contains the Help system. These data sets are used in the examples and exercises in the book. You should make a copy of the datafiles to work with. **Never work with the original copy of a datafile.**

Data Desk works on any Macintosh computer with at least one megabyte of memory, and any PC running Windows 95 or Windows NT.

Whatever system you use, your first action should be to make a copy of the disks and put the original disks in a safe place. **Never work with the original disks. Always use a copy.** This precaution will ensure that, when the disk you use for your work fails, becomes damaged, or is lost, you will still have the original and will be able to make a fresh copy. (You read that correctly. I said *when* the disk becomes damaged, not *if* it does. Disks wear out. Disks carried around with your books wear out even faster. Please protect your investment and work with a copy, not with the original disk.)

To the Teacher

This book has been designed to integrate smoothly into almost any basic statistics course. The examples, discussions, and exercises supplement a wide range of texts — from the most traditional to the most modern. Each topic is reviewed and illustrated, providing an additional description that can help students to grasp difficult concepts. The chapters dealing with specific methods can be covered in any reasonable order.

Data Desk can serve two key functions in a statistics course. First, it provides a laboratory that gives students practical, hands-on experience with randomness far beyond what they could gain otherwise without years of analyzing data. Many of the examples and exercises in this book rely on random numbers generated with known properties to illustrate concepts of statistics and probability.

Second, Data Desk is a powerful calculator that enables students to apply even complex methods to real data and then try out alternatives. The hope, of course, is that the student will see past the computer and understand more about how statistics helps to describe the world. I have found in my teaching that seeing a practical application of statistical methods helps students to understand them. But *applying the methods for themselves* helps students to really learn them.

You may find it helpful to have a copy of the full Data Desk 6.0 program so that you can import data from other sources to create new exercises for your students. Data Description can supply this version of the program at special education prices.

Some schools have chosen to establish computer laboratory facilities for students to use and to equip them with software. The *Data Desk Student Version 6.0* is intended for individual student use and *cannot be* licensed for multiple use in a laboratory or library. To equip a laboratory facility or software lending library with Data Desk you must obtain the appropriate licenses from Data Description.

To the Student

I have been teaching statistics for over 20 years, and I know that you may be facing this course with some trepidation. Statistics can be confusing and intimidating at first. If you haven't used a computer before, you may be concerned about the additional burden of learning that new skill. I cannot dispel all of your concerns, but I can assure you from experience with literally thousands of students that Data Desk will actually make it easier for you to understand the concepts of statistics.

If you make the effort early on to become comfortable with the computer and with Data Desk, you will even find that it can be fun to experiment with the concepts and methods of statistics. I realize that in saying this I am risking my credibility with some of you. The thought of a coherent sentence using both the words "statistics" and "fun" strains credulity. Nevertheless, statistics can help you to learn about the world around you, and the computer makes that connection effortless. I can imagine no mysteries more interesting than those of how the world around us works, where the patterns are, and what they look like.

The discussions and examples in this book form a bridge between the basic statistics concepts and methods taught in class and the practical, powerful tool in your computer. The Data Desk program is designed for easy learning in stages. Once you learn basic skills (if you know how to use a Windows or the MacOS you have most of these already), you can learn the rest bit by bit as you need it. Along the way, you will find that Data Desk is consistent — the same actions accomplish the same results in a variety of circumstances — so it is easy to guess what to do even if you don't know for sure.

If you are anxious to start using the program immediately, it is possible to chart a more efficient course through this book. Several chapters provide background material or discuss operations and commands that may not be required by your professor.

• Chapters 3 and 10 provide enlightening information but are not required for the use of the program.

• Chapter 5 discusses data entry and editing. Most of the exercises and examples you will encounter use datafiles that have the data already entered. If you are given an assignment for which data entry or editing is required, you can return to Chapter 5 for guidance.

• Chapter 6 discusses importing and exporting data. Again, most examples and exercises you will encounter use datafiles that have the data already entered, so the tools in this chapter will not usually be needed.

• Chapter 11 discusses transforming data. This is a lengthy chapter and is best approached with a specific question to answer. It might be helpful to read the first section of this chapter to get a general idea of the potential transformation capabilities.

• Chapter 12 discusses data manipulation. For example, the **Transpose** command turns the rows of the datafile into columns and the columns into rows. Most of the datafiles provided to you have the data properly configured so that you will not usually need to use any of the manipulation commands.

• Chapter 13 describes tools to analyze subsets of a datafile. This type of analysis is usually beyond the scope of an introductory statistics course. These features are documented for advanced courses and for incorporation into student projects.

• Chapters 14 and 15 discuss tools for creating reports and presentations. Some students use these features for special projects.

One remark worth making at the start is to remind you that you cannot hurt the computer or the program by any ordinary use and that you can alter a datafile only when you explicitly choose to do so. Ordinary commands, anything you can type at the keyboard, and virtually anything you can do with the mouse can do no real harm. You should feel free to experiment and explore; it is the best way to become comfortable with the computer and with Data Desk.

How Data Desk Came To Be

Data Desk was conceived when the Macintosh was first announced. The design grew out of the author's 15 years of professional experience teaching statistics; writing, using, and evaluating statistics software; and consulting for computer package users. The initial implementation was a program to support teaching, which has been used in classes at Cornell University and elsewhere since 1985.

Data Desk Professional 1.0, released in 1986, extended the student program to a form useful for research and business. Data Desk 2.0, 3.0, 4.0, and 5.0 followed in 1988, 1990, 1992, and 1995 respectively. In 1997 Data Desk 6.0, the program on which this Student Version is based, was released. We built upon our experience with both students and professionals to enhance and refine the design, and to expand the capabilities of the program substantially without sacrificing the natural interface that made Data Desk so easy to learn and use.

We are very proud of our new Student Version. This program is more capable, faster, and easier to use than the original. The book and exercises have benefited from our experience and from the comments and suggestions of others who have used the program.

We will continue to develop and extend Data Desk. We welcome your suggestions, comments, and criticisms. Some of the best features currently in Data Desk were originally suggestions or requests from users.

Contents

CHAPTER 1

Introduction

DATA DESK IS designed for data exploration, data display, and data analysis. Data exploration is the best way to start understanding your data. It helps you to insure that your data are "clean" and ready for further analysis, and gives you an overall idea of the patterns and relationships that may be in the data.

Data display shows you many views of your data but relates all of them together to give you an intuitive overview of what's going on in the data. Data displays are especially effective at showing you what you didn't expect to find — often the most interesting and important aspect of any data analysis.

Data analysis is the process of discovering, describing, and confirming structure or patterns in data. The process itself is often a way to learn about data; one step of an analysis can reveal things about the data that suggest what to do next. Data Desk makes this process convenient, comfortable, and informative. It provides powerful tools, it permits any operation at any point in the analysis, and it is transparent; after a little practice you "see through" the program and feel that you are working directly with the data rather than giving instructions to a computer program to tell *it* to work with the data.

This book is your guide to Data Desk and to both new and traditional methods of looking at data. Even though it is always helpful to understand some statistics theory, it is far more important that you know something about your data — for example, what sort of patterns would be interesting or meaningful to you. Data Desk's natural interface, HyperView menu suggestions, and the tutorial examples in these books can ease you over any gaps in your statistics knowledge, but *you* must supply the understanding of your data.

Data Desk works graphically so there is no new language to learn. Together, the books documenting the program and the program itself help you to visualize abstract concepts and to apply them to real data. Whatever your background and whatever kinds of data you work with, you will find it easier to discover and understand the patterns in your data when you can see and touch the data in a variety of ways.

For example, Data Desk depicts identifiable parts of the data and products of analyses with graphic *icons.* You touch the icons with the mouse to open, select, move, alter, or otherwise work with them. Often you can drag the icon of a variable and "drop" it just where you want it — for example on the axis of a graph or in a table that reports an analysis. Data Desk also makes abstract concepts such as a "cloud of datapoints" into a physical reality that you can touch (with the mouse) and manipulate.

In short, Data Desk offers a unified approach to understanding data.

Although Data Desk is easy to learn, we ask you to read the first two chapters before diving in. This Introduction describes the philosophy behind Data Desk. Chapter 2 defines Data Desk's objects and conventions.

1.1 *What Computing Background Do I Need?*

Data Desk gives you a desktop much like the one you see with Windows or Macintosh. The actions and operations you are already used to are the same ones that specify actions to Data Desk. Specifically, you should know how to:

- Point, select, and drag with the mouse
- Use icons
- Use windows, including moving, resizing, scrolling, and closing windows
- Pull down menus from the menu bar to choose commands

There are a few special definitions, so even if you plan to learn Data Desk by just diving in, you should read the initial chapters to learn about the objects and basic concepts on the Data Desk desktop.

1.2 *Data Analysis*

In the 1970's some statisticians turned their attention from computing isolated calculations to the entire process of analyzing data. They questioned the traditional statistical analysis paradigm in which one first forms a hypothesis, then collects data, and finally tests the hypothesis. Instead, they advocated the open-ended exploration of data with few preconceived assumptions. The father of such "exploratory data analysis" was John W. Tukey of Princeton University and (then) AT&T Bell Labs.

Tukey suggested that we examine our data as a detective would examine the scene of a crime — not with a hypothesis ("I'll bet the butler did it."), but with an open mind and as few assumptions as possible. By letting the data speak to us we hope to learn the truths hidden beneath the random fluctuations, errors, and general confusion seen in real data.

This way of analyzing data is quite different from the traditional paradigm, and traditional statistics packages support it poorly. In his path breaking book, *Exploratory Data Analysis*, Tukey advocates building each step of an analysis upon the knowledge gained from earlier steps. Some traditional statistics packages have added some of the plots Tukey developed to their libraries of procedures, but without the free-form interaction required by modern data analysis they cannot support the full data analysis process.

Recently, growing interest in data mining has helped to fuel interest in ways to view data without preconceived hypotheses. Data Desk has pioneered these methods for over a decade. Data Desk encourages flexible data exploration by letting you move at will among all functions. This consistency and integration make it easy to do what you need to do without having to think about how.

1.3 *Mac and Windows*

Data Desk runs on Windows 95, Windows NT and MacOS. The difference between using the program on Mac and using it on Windows is small, so the same book is supplied with all versions of Data Desk. Any differences in behavior are discussed in the appropriate sections of the book. Operating system-specific discussions of more than one or two sentences are noted in the margin. Specific differences of interest include saving datafiles (Section 4.16) and keyboard shortcuts (Section 1.4).

The default window appearance for each version is slightly different. Section 2.12 discusses the different title bars and close box locations and how they can be customized. The pictures of windows and dialogs in this book alternate between the default Windows appearance and the default Mac appearance.

1.4 *Basic Operations*

This Section defines basic terms and operations.

DESKTOP: Data Desk uses a *Desktop metaphor*. That is, the screen depicts objects as if they were on a large desk. Objects can overlap other objects. Displays can be opened for viewing or put away. Whenever we refer to "the desktop" in these books we mean the Data Desk Desktop.

ICON: An icon is a small picture that represents an object. By touching the icon with the mouse, you can perform operations on the things it represents. For example, a histogram is represented by an icon. You can open it to see the histogram, or drag it to another part of the screen to get it out of your way.

TRASH: To discard an icon (and its contents) drag it into the Trash. The Data Desk trash icon is in the lower right corner of the Data Desk Desktop.

As with other icons, you can open the trash icon. Inside you will find icons that have been dragged into the Trash recently but not yet finally discarded.

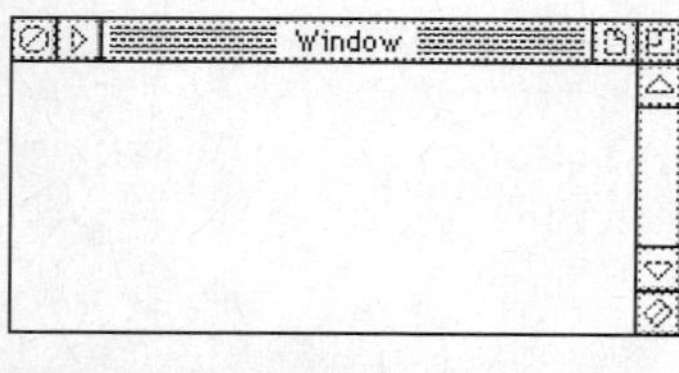

WINDOW: Windows are rectangles on the desktop that can be moved, overlapped, and resized. Windows provide local work environments and thus let you move easily among different tasks. For example, in one window you might edit the contents of a variable while in another you could control the display of a plot.

CLICK: To click an object or click at a particular point on the screen, move the mouse until the cursor (usually an arrow or an I-beam) is at the point you want, press the mouse button and release it.

SELECT: You ordinarily select one or more icons before choosing a command. The command then operates on the selected icons. To select an icon, move the cursor until the tip of the arrow touches the middle of the icon, and click. The icon will highlight.

SHIFT-CLICK: Ordinarily, clicking *de*-selects anything that has already been selected. Shift-clicks on text or data in open variables extend selections inclusively, selecting all cases between the insertion point and the shift-clicked case. Shift-clicking icons selects them specifically as x-variables.

CTRL-CLICK: On Windows, Ctrl-click (Option-click for Mac) in an icon window selects icons as y-variables for a plot or analysis. Like a Shift-click, it extends the selection, leaving already selected icons selected.

COMMAND-CLICK: Click the right mouse button on Windows (command-click on Mac) in a variable window extends a selection *discontinuously*, adding the clicked case to the selection without selecting the intervening cases.

DRAG: To drag, click, hold the mouse button down, and move the mouse If you have clicked an icon, you will drag it with you. Dragging in text selects a range of text. Dragging in a variable editing window selects cases. Dragging in an icon window draws a rectangle around some icons — they are selected when you stop dragging. To stop a drag, release the mouse button.

You can also move icons by selecting them, and then dragging them to a new location or into a plot or analysis.

menu bar

keyboard shortcuts

MENU: Menus are lists of commands. Menu titles appear in the *menu bar* across the top of the screen. To choose a command from a menu, click the menu title and drag down the menu until the command you want is highlighted. Then release the button. Many commands have *keyboard shortcuts* that provide a way to issue the command from the keyboard. The menu item will have "CTRL+letter" on Windows (on Mac: the ⌘ symbol and a letter next to it). Holding down the Ctrl key, or ⌘ key on a Mac, and pressing the letter is the same as choosing the command from the menu.

SUBMENU: Any command with a ▶ to its right in the menu list (where the command key might otherwise be) is the top of a submenu. If you pause over the command a submenu will drop to the right or left of your mouse position. Drag across to the submenu to continue the selection just as you would for a menu. Submenu commands are always grouped according to their type and function.

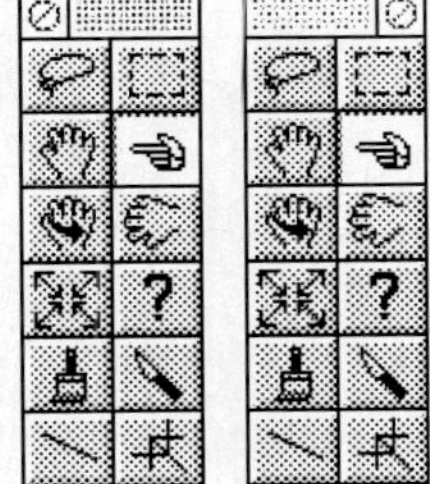

PALETTE: A palette is a special window that stays in front of any other window on the desktop. Typically, palettes hold options or tools (click on a tool to "pick it up"). For example, the Tools palette holds 12 tools for manipulating plots. The Colors palette offers 64 colors; select points and click a color to set the selected points to that color.

DOUBLE-CLICK: One way to open an icon is to select it and then choose the *Open* command from the *Data* menu. Another way is to point to the icon and press the mouse button twice quickly. This is called a double-click.

1.5 *Installing* Data Desk Student Version 6.0

To install *Data Desk Student Version 6.0,* insert the *Program* (Disk 1) floppy disk and copy the *Data Desk Student 6.0* folder and paste it on your local hard drive; eject the floppy disk. Insert the floppy disk *Data Files and Help File* (Disk 2) and copy the enclosed icons and paste them inside the *Data Desk Student 6.0* folder on your local hard drive.

Alternatively, you can launch *Data Desk Student Version 6.0* from the floppy disk drive. Open the *Data Desk Student 6.0* folder. Double-click on the *Data Desk Student* program icon. However, if you want to use the help system you must first install the program and the Help file on your local hard drive.

CHAPTER 2

Basic Concepts

IN THIS CHAPTER we define the basic objects and actions that make Data Desk work. If you are an experienced desktop interface user, Data Desk operations should be familiar and natural to you. Read thjroughj this chapter to learn about concepts, commands, and icons that are special to Data Desk.

2.1 *The Data Desk Desktop*

Basic operations on the *Data Desk desktop* include:

- Selecting icons by touching them with the mouse and clicking the mouse button
- Extending the selection with a "shift-click"
- Selecting several adjacent icons by dragging across them
- Dragging one or more selected icons to another place on the desktop
- Selecting menu commands.

If you are unfamiliar with any of these concepts, you should review the introductory material in your operating system manual.

The Data Desk desktop can be reduced to cover only part of the screen. Click the small white rectangle in the lower right corner and drag it; the top of the desktop automatically drops down from under the menu bar so that you can reposition the desktop as well. The File cabinet icon at the upper right and Data Desk trash icon at the lower right always stay on the Data Desk desktop, moving with the desktop as you resize or reposition it. To resize the Data Desk desktop to full screen, click its title bar to highlight it, then click the zoom box in the upper right corner.

HOW-TO

Data Desk desktop can be resized and repositioned. Click its zoom box to resize to full screen.

2.2 *Menus and Submenus*

Data Desk menus are organized according to function as follows:

MAC OS

The menu holds the **Help** command, which enters Data Desk's on-line help system, and the **About Data Desk** command, which provides information about the datafile and disk space and identifies the program and version number.

File
File commands deal with the file system. They include opening, closing, saving, and deleting datafiles, printing data and results, importing and exporting datafiles, and exiting the program.

Edit
Edit holds commands for editing, searching, replacing data, and setting preferences. Some edit commands also edit plots.

Data
Data commands create, open, close, and duplicate icons on the Data Desk desktop. The **Data** menu is for manipulating Data Desk icons, but

commands in the **Data** menu do not directly affect your datafiles on the disk.

Special
Special functions include commands for controlling selector and group buttons, the Results log, Slide Show, emptying the Trash, and working with Data Desk windows. The **Windows** submenu includes a complete list of all open Data Desk windows to help you find a window that may have become hidden behind other windows on the Data Desk desktop.

Modify
Modify commands manipulate displays. They are grouped into submenus according to the aspect of the display that they affect.

Manip
Manip functions include sorting, ranking, splitting, generating and appending variables. In general, manipulation commands work with variables and produce new, modified variables as results.

Calc
Calc commands compute statistics. They generally work with variables and produce statistics calculations, result variables, and supporting plots.

Plot
Plot commands work with variables and produce displays.

WINDOWS

Help
This menu lets you open the Data Desk online help system (see the MacOS section on the preceding page). The **About Data Desk** command, which provides information about the datafile and disk space, and identifies the program and version number.

submenus

Data Desk *submenus* group related commands. Submenus accommodate more functions than could ever fit in standard menus and organize them so they are easy to find. A submenu is indicated by a ▶ symbol in the right margin of the menu (Fig. 2-1). Position the mouse over that menu item and hold down the mouse button. A new menu automatically drops either to the right or to the left of the main menu. To enter this submenu, slide the mouse to the side, and make your menu selection as usual. You need not slide exactly horizontally, but instead can move diagonally, directly to the subcommand you want.

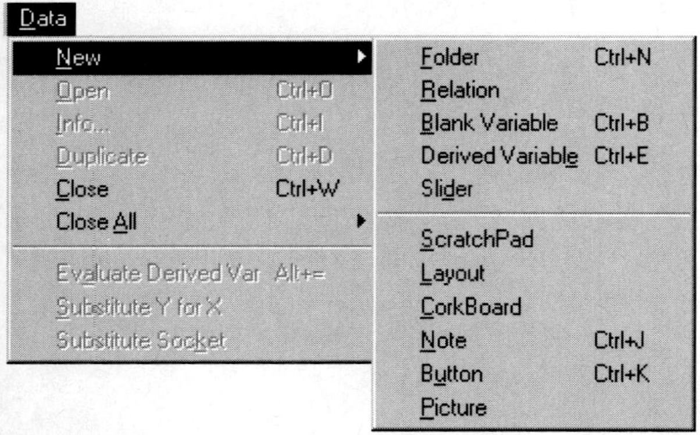

***Figure 2-1**. Submenus drop automatically from menu items with a ▶ on the right. The **New** submenu lists all the icons you can create.*

Data Desk provides menus attached to places other than the main menu bar. When you see a box with a drop shadow, it indicates that a menu will pop up when you click the box. Other pop-up menus are attached to parts of Data Desk tables and plots, and are called HyperView menus.

2.3 Datafiles

Datafiles store data between work sessions on Data Desk. You can start Data Desk by opening a Data Desk datafile. Datafiles contain icons that represent objects such as variables, displays, and tables.

When you quit or exit Data Desk, you can save the entire state of your analysis — including all data and results — in a datafile. Datafiles can be copied to other disks, duplicated, renamed, or discarded.

To open a Data Desk datafile or an ASCII file from within Data Desk, choose **Open Datafile…** from Data Desk's **File** menu.

If you would like to combine the data from an ASCII file or the data and results from an existing Data Desk file, with a currently open datafile, choose **Import...** from the file menu. Data Desk will open the imported file and place all the data and results into a new folder in the *Results* folder.

The **New Datafile** command in the **File** menu closes the current datafile and creates a new, empty datafile named Untitled.

2.4 Data Desk Windows

Data Desk icons open into windows that reveal their contents. These windows can be moved around, overlapped, and resized with the mouse. Some windows contain icons, some contain the text of a variable's values, some contain output from a statistics procedure, and some contain plots. In this manual we sometimes use the terms "icon window," "variable editing window," "output window," and "plot window," respectively, for these four types of windows.

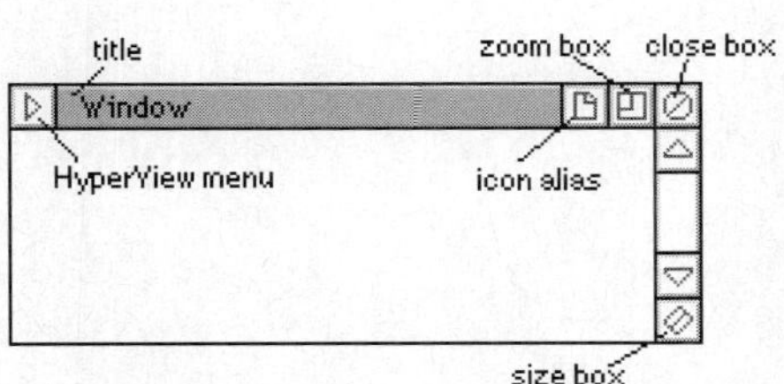

Figure 2-2. The parts of a window.

Each window (Fig. 2-2) has a *title bar* across the top. On Mac, the title bar includes a *close box* on the left, the icon alias and the zoom box on the right. On Windows, the close box, the icon alias, and the zoom box are all in the right corner of the title bar. Clicking the close box closes the window. Click the close box with the right mouse button on Windows, or the ⌘ key on Mac, to bring up a HyperView menu offering the **Throw Away** command. Most windows also have a *size box* in the lower right corner. To resize the window, drag this box until the gray outline of the window is the right size. A *zoom box* in the upper right corner of many windows provides a quick way to expand the window to its maximum size and then shrink it back to its original size. On a Mac, holding down the option key while clicking the zoom box of a window sizes it to match the current page setup specifications, within the constraint of the plot buffer. To rename the window, click the right mouse button (on a Mac, hold down the command key, ⌘, and click) on the title bar and choose the **Rename Window** command.

The small rectangle on the right of the title bar is a miniature icon that behaves like the window's icon. You can select the window's icon by clicking on the *icon alias*. Double-clicking on the icon alias locates the window's icon, making it visible on the desktop and selecting it. A window may also have a small triangle on the left of the title bar (▷). This is the window's

icon alias

HyperView menu

global *HyperView menu*. Section 4.2 discusses HyperView menus.

The {Edit} **Preferences** command offers two options to customize the title bar. When the Close box on right box is checked, the close box is placed in the far right corner of the title bar (the default on Windows). When the box is not checked, the close box is placed in the far left corner of the title bar (the default on Mac).

When the Blue Title Bars box is checked, the title bar is tinted blue and the name of the window is left justified (the default on Windows). When the Blue Title Bars box is not checked, the title bar is decorated with horizontal gray lines and the name of the window is center justified (the default on Mac).

scroll bar

Windows that hold icons only resize horizontally. Resizing some windows, such as a window displaying a scatterplot, alters the way their contents are displayed. Resizing other windows only alters the amount of their contents that is visible. The *scroll bar,* located across the bottom or on the right border of the window, provides a way to slide the window across its contents. A gray scroll bar indicates that some of the contents of the window are beyond the bounds of the window's rectangle and invites you to scroll the window to see them. In addition, dragging a selection rectangle off the right or left edge of an icon window or off the bottom or top of an editing window scrolls the window.

active window

When two windows overlap, one falls in front of the other. The window in front has its title bar highlighted. The front window is called the *active window,* because it is the window that reflects your actions. To bring a window to the front, click any part of it or double-click the (shaded) icon from which it opened.

HOW-TO

Most windows remember their position on the desktop when they are closed and return to that position when reopened.

To move a window to another part of the Data Desk desktop, drag it by its title bar. A window can be dragged so that part of it extends off the screen. By dragging and resizing, you can position windows next to each other on the desktop in any arrangement you want. Windows remember their position on the desktop when they are closed and return to that position when reopened, if possible.

HOW-TO

The {Special ▸ Arrange} **Tile Windows** command resizes and repositions windows so that they fit neatly on the screen.

The **Windows** submenu in the **Special** menu lists all open windows, front to back. When you select the name of a window in this menu, the window is moved to the front. This is a handy way to retrieve a window buried under other windows and therefore not available for clicking. The {Special ▸ Arrange} **Tile Windows** command repositions and resizes variable, plot, and output windows so that they fit neatly on the screen. When many windows are open, the tiled windows may be quite small. You can enlarge any window with its zoom box if you want to examine it more thoroughly, and zoom it back when you are done. The {Special ▸ Arrange} **Stack Windows** command makes each window large and fans them into a stack that shows an identifiable section of each window with just enough room for clicking. The {Special ▸ Arrange} **Send Window Behind** command makes the frontmost window the bottom window without the need to click on another window.

HOW-TO

On Mac and Windows, hold the Shift key while opening a window to forget its previous location.

There is no limit to the number of windows Data Desk can have open at once, but it is a good idea to keep your Data Desk desktop neat by closing unneeded windows.

2.5 *Icons*

Each of the principal objects that Data Desk works with or produces is represented on the desktop by an icon. You can tell what kind of object you have by what its icon looks like.

To do anything with an icon you must first select it by moving the tip of the cursor's arrow on top of the icon and clicking. Selected icons highlight. To move an icon, click on it and drag. You can move several icons by selecting them all and then dragging any one of them. When you drag an icon to the right or left edge of an icon window, the icons in the window scroll to reveal any additional icons located beyond that edge of the window. The speed of scrolling increases as you get closer to the edge of the window. To avoid scrolling, drag icons off the top or bottom of their windows or drag them rapidly across the right or left edge. This feature makes it easier to manage windows with many icons. We recommend that you use folders to group icons logically when there are many icons in a window.

The icons need not be in the same window. You may place icons on the Data Desk desktop, but it is usually more convenient to leave them in the windows that ordinarily hold them.

Icons provide a convenient place to put away data, plots, and analyses so that they don't clutter the screen but are still readily available. Whenever you close a window it will close into an icon. Whenever you open an icon, it will open into a window. To open an icon, select it and choose **Open** from the **Data** menu, or double-click on it.

HOW-TO

You can work with a shaded (open) icon as you would with any other icon.

When an icon is open to show its window, the icon appears shaded. Shaded icons are still active; you can move them, discard them, and use them as you would any other icon.

To rename an icon, click on its current name and edit it as you would any text. Pressing the Tab key selects the name of the next icon to the right in the same window. When you tab off the right edge of the icons' window, the icons scroll to stay in view.

2.6 *Variables*

variable

A *variable* contains data. A typical variable might have numbers recording measurements or observations about some individuals, organized as a column of values. Variables often hold numbers, but they can also hold text or a mixture of numbers and text. To see the contents of a variable, open its icon. The variable opens into a window displaying its contents, and the icon of the variable is shaded to indicate that the variable is open. You can enter new data or alter the data in the window. In Chapter 5 we give details and show examples of how to enter and edit data in variables.

A Variable

The icon for a variable looks like a column of values. Ordinarily you can leave variables closed and work with the icons. After all, statistics is about the relationships among the variables and not about calculations on the numbers, so you rarely need to see the numbers themselves. By leaving the variables closed, you can keep your screen less cluttered.

Each variable has a name. You may use almost any name you can type, including names with punctuation marks, spaces, and numbers. For example, "Wages + Tips", "123", and "Σ{random values}" are all legal variable names. Variable names can have up to 33 characters, but it is a good idea to choose short, evocative names. If a variable name is too long to fit neatly under its icon on the desktop, the name is abbreviated. Click the abbreviated name to see the full name.

variable names

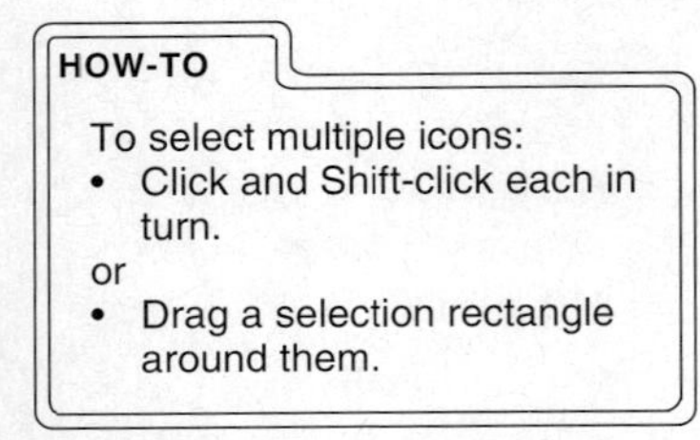

HOW-TO

To select multiple icons:
- Click and Shift-click each in turn.

or
- Drag a selection rectangle around them.

To change the name of a variable (or of any icon) click on the name to select it and type the new name. Press the Tab key to advance to the next icon and rename it as well. To create a new variable choose {Data ▸ New} **Blank Variable**. Chapter 5 discusses data entry and editing in detail.

Most Data Desk operations use one or more variables to plot or compute something. You specify the variables by clicking on their icons to select them. For example, to make the histogram of a variable, click its icon and choose {Plot} **Histograms**. When you select a variable, its icon highlights and it is branded with a "Y" (Fig. 2-3).

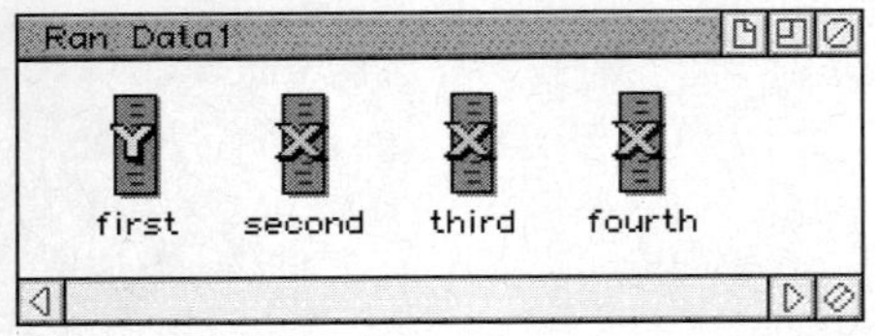

Figure 2-3. *y- and x- highlighted icons.*

To select a second and third variable, hold down the Shift key and click their icons in turn. They will highlight with "X" brands. Alternatively, if variables are adjacent in a window, you can point to one side of them, hold the mouse button down, and *drag* the mouse across the variables. An outline box will follow the mouse. When you release the mouse button, all icons covered by the box are selected. (It is important to start dragging while the tip of the mouse arrow points to the side of a variable. Otherwise, if the arrow touches a variable icon, you will select that variable and drag it with you.) You may select icons from several different windows.

REMEMBER

Mac OS:
Option-click to select y.
Shift-click to select x.
Option-shift-click to de-select.

Windows:
Ctrl-click to select y.
Shift-click to select x.
Ctrl-shift-click to de-select.

Y highlighted variables play a special role for some commands in Data Desk. For example, they are the dependent or predicted variables in a regression and the y-axis in a scatterplot. Typically, the first variable you select is a y-variable and subsequently selected variables are x-variables. You can explicitly select a y-variable at any time by holding down the Option key on Mac or the Ctrl key on Windows while selecting the variable. The mouse cursor changes to Y to indicate y-selection. Similarly, holding the Shift key while selecting variables changes the cursor to X to indicate x-selection. Both of these cursors select with the point of the arrow rather than with the middle of the cursor.

To change an already selected icon from y-highlighting to x-highlighting, Shift-click the icon. To change to y-highlighting, Ctrl-click on Windows (Option-click on Mac). To de-select an icon hold down both the Shift and Ctrl keys (Shift and Option keys on Mac) and click it.

When you *drag* across several variables, they are selected in left-to-right order, so the first will be the one on the left, even if you drag from right to left.

To discard a variable, drag its icon to the Trash. You can retrieve the variable by opening the trash icon and dragging it back out. The {Special} **Empty Trash** command finally discards variables placed in the Trash. The Data Desk Trash icon looks slightly different from the Microsoft Windows' Recycle Bin or the Macintosh Finder's trash icon. If you resize the Data Desk desktop on a Mac, you can see both trash icons.

You can discard a Data Desk icon only in the Data Desk Trash. If the Trash doesn't accept an icon, check that you have dragged the icon to Data Desk's Trash icon and not the operating system's trash icon.

2.7 *Folders*

When using a small number of variables, you may want to arrange them in a single icon window and select them as needed. For more complex analyses or larger collections of data, it is better to organize variables into groups so that you can deal with them easily.

Several icons may belong together because they describe the same individuals or circumstances, because they contain related quantities, because you plan to use them together in an analysis, or because you want to group them to clean up the Data Desk desktop. In Data Desk, icons can be grouped into *folders* for any of these reasons.

HOW-TO

Using folders helps keep the Data Desk desktop uncluttered.
Retrieve a buried folder icon with the **Locate** commands in the **Special** menu.

Folders keep the desktop uncluttered by providing a convenient way to group collections of icons. You may collect any icons — whatever the reason for grouping them — into a folder. Moreover, folders can contain other folders. For example, a folder of economic indicators might include a smaller folder of energy-related variables along with general variables like GNP.

Folder windows resemble relation windows, which we discuss in Section 2.9.

Feel free to make many folders to keep the desktop clear and organized. It is easier to find an icon by opening an aptly named folder than by scrolling a window back and forth. An icon buried several layers down in nested folders can be retrieved with the **Locate** commands in the **Special** menu. In general, each new analysis you perform on a dataset deserves its own folder and an appropriate, descriptive name (for example, *regression on sales*). Each of these folders, in turn, may have several subfolders to hold plots and output icons separately, for example. Data Desk automatically groups the results of many analyses in their own folders.

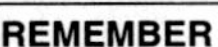

Selecting a folder automatically selects all the icons it contains in left-to-right order.

Data Desk's folders keep icons in a strict left-to-right order. It is always clear which item is the first (the leftmost), which is the second, and so on. This order can be important to the statistics and display operations in Data Desk. So a second reason for using folders is to keep variables in a particular order.

Folders also provide a convenient way to manipulate groups of variables. They can simplify advanced analyses by providing a way to group variables. When you select a folder's icon, Data Desk selects all the icons it contains in left-to-right order.

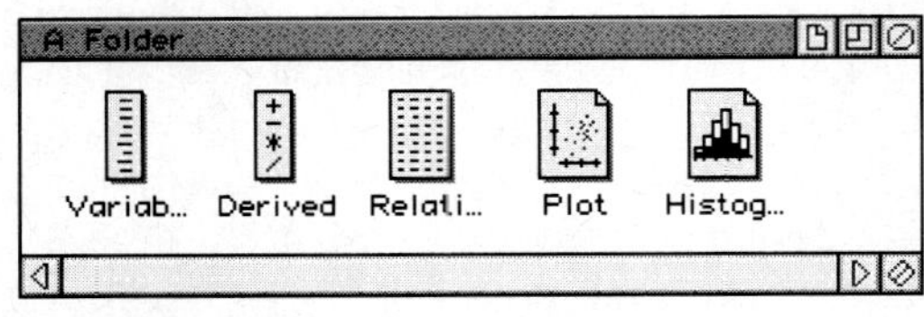

Figure 2-4. A Folder window holds icons.

To create a new folder choose the {Data ▶ New} **Folder** command and provide a name. Typing Ctrl+N (⌘N on Mac) creates a new folder as well. The new folder is added to the frontmost icon window on the right.

An open folder shows a short, wide window that holds a single row of icons (Fig. 2-4).

REMEMBER

Icons dragged into the icon of a folder are appended to the right of the icons in the folder.
This ordering holds even if the folder window is open.

If there are too many icons to fit in the window, its scroll bar across the bottom can move them left and right. If you drag a selection rectangle off the side of a folder, the icons automatically scroll away from you and continue the selection. You can drag the icons to new positions in the window, on the desktop, or to other folders.

Icons dragged into the icon of a folder are appended to the right of the icons in the folder. The folder icon highlights when the dragged icon is over it. Release the mouse button to drop the dragged icons into the folder. You can drop icons into a closed folder icon or into the shaded icon of an open folder.

To discard a folder, drag its icon to the Trash. Every icon in the folder will be discarded; any icons that are open close their windows immediately. Of course, a discarded folder can be retrieved until the Trash is emptied. When the shaded icon of an open folder is dragged into the Trash, the folder's window closes and follows it into the Trash.

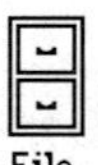

2.8 *Storage folders and the File Cabinet*

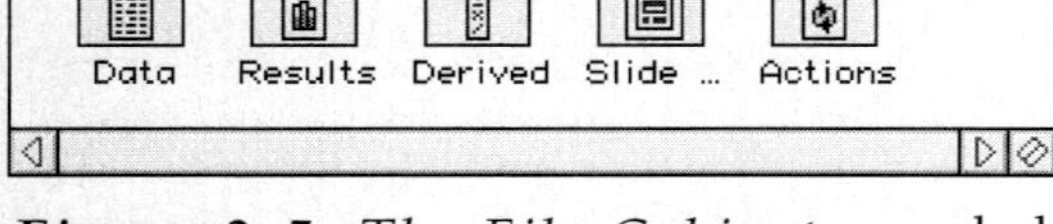

Figure 2-5. *The File Cabinet holds special storage folders.*

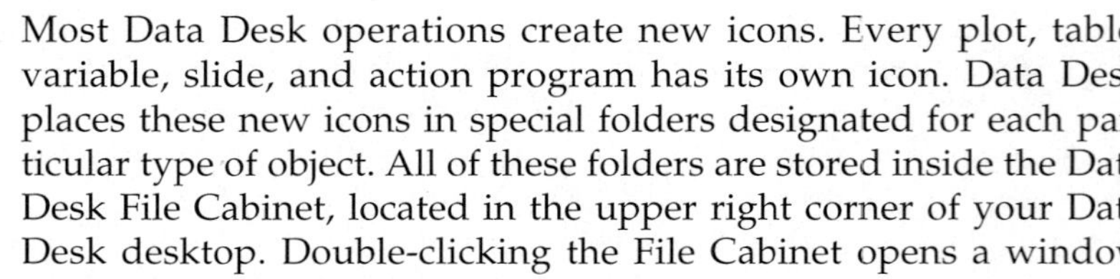

Most Data Desk operations create new icons. Every plot, table, variable, slide, and action program has its own icon. Data Desk places these new icons in special folders designated for each particular type of object. All of these folders are stored inside the Data Desk File Cabinet, located in the upper right corner of your Data Desk desktop. Double-clicking the File Cabinet opens a window holding the special storage folders (Fig. 2-5).

Plots, tables, and special results variables are placed in the *Results* folder. Data relations (see Section 2.9) are placed in the *Data* folder. Derived variables are placed in the *Derived* folder. The slides that make up the slide show are placed in the *Slide* folder. Action programs are placed in the *Action* folder. None of these folders are created until needed. For example, your file will not have a *Results* folder until you create a plot or table. Your File Cabinet may never have an *Action* or *Slide* folder if those types of objects are never created.

The folders inside the File Cabinet and the objects inside the folders are not restricted to their assigned location. Icons can be moved from one folder to another. You can create new folders to organize your icons differently. Any icon can be placed on the Data Desk desktop. The only restriction is that data variables generally may not be moved between data relations because doing so usually makes no sense (see Section 2.9).

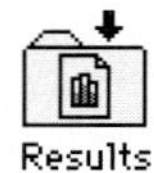

The *Results* folder is the storage folder you will use most frequently. It keeps track of the progress of your analysis by storing the icons of each object you create. Many programs offer a way to record the sequence of commands you have typed so that you can edit and resubmit the commands to repeat the analysis with minor changes. Data Desk has no typed commands to record. Being object-oriented, Data Desk instead records the sequence of objects created in the course of your analysis in the *Results* folder . Because each Data Desk result object can be modified, updated, or used as a template for another analysis, the *Results* folder provides a more direct record of your work as well as a convenient way to try slightly different alternatives.

Any folder can be designated the *Results* folder, so you may want to have separate results folders for different analysis paths. To designate a folder as a new *Results* folder, click the new folder's icon (or the icon alias in the folder's window title bar) and choose {Special ▶ Results Log} **Assign**.

2.9 *Relations*

Figure 2-6. *A relation typically has variables in columns by cases in rows.*

Most datasets are rectangular. There are variables (usually represented as columns) and cases (usually represented as rows). Each case has a value recorded for each variable. The recorded value may be a value defined as "missing" rather than a number or a category name. Because each case has a value for each variable and each variable has a value at each case, the array of data can be shown as a rectangular table of values (Fig 2-6).

Data analyses typically relate two or more variables to each other. However, the variables must hold data for the same cases in the same order. If a variable recording median education in each of the 50 states was arranged in alphabetical order, it would make no sense to plot it against a variable holding median income in each state that was ordered from west to east, or against a variable that recorded income by region rather than by state.

This rectangular structure is known in database theory as a *relation*, and Data Desk adopts this terminology. Formally, each row in a relation must be unique. Accordingly, Data Desk assigns a unique case number to each row in order from top to bottom.

If your dataset is a standard rectangular data table, calling it a relation changes nothing. (Like the *Bourgeois Gentillehomme*, who was pleased to learn that he spoke in prose, you can be assured that you already use relations.) However, if your data include variables recorded for several relations, you will find that Data Desk's relational data management abilities let you structure, enter, and work with your data in more natural ways.

For most datasets, Data Desk uses relations to make your life easier automatically. For example, if your data form a simple relation, Data Desk automatically keeps cases aligned in your variables. Thus, if you cut a case out of one variable, Data Desk offers to delete that case from all variables in the relation to preserve your ability to analyze the variables together.

Most analyses that deal with more than one variable make sense only when the variables are in the same relation. You cannot combine variables from two different relations in the same plot or calculation, but Data Desk provides ways to refer from one relation to another so that the resulting variables are properly matched.

2.10 *Selecting*

The concept of *selecting* is fundamental to Data Desk operations. Icons, cases, and parts of plots can all be selected. Data Desk commands and plot tools operate on these selected objects. To select something ordi-

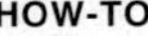

HOW-TO

Dragging on the Data Desk desktop will select the items on the desktop.

HOW-TO

A convenient shortcut for **Select All** is,

for Windows: **Ctrl+A**
for MacOS: **⌘-A**

narily you touch it with the mouse and click. If you hold down the Shift key while clicking, selected objects accumulate; if not, the new selection replaces any previous selection. When selecting cases, hold the Shift key to select the range of cases between the current insertion point and the click. Hold the Ctrl key (Option key on Mac) to add the clicked case to the selection discontinuously.

The {Edit} **Select All** command selects all selectable objects in the frontmost window. That is, it selects all cases in variable editing windows, all icons in icon windows, and all datapoints in plot windows. The Ctrl+A (⌘-A for Mac) combination is a keyboard shortcut for Select All.

Most of the commands in the **Modify** menu work on the active, or frontmost window. A window is made active by clicking anywhere in the window, although it is usually best to click on the window's title bar so that the selection state of the window is not disturbed. Only one window can be active at a time.

2.11 *Result Windows, Plots, and HotResult Variables*

result windows

Most Data Desk commands produce some sort of output — usually one or more icons that open to reveal tables of numbers or plots. Some commands produce variables, which can then be used in other commands. Others produce *result windows.* A result window is a window that contains the results of a command. The icon of a result window looks like a document.

Result

The icon opens into a window containing words and numbers. Although result windows contain text, they cannot be edited like variables. However, you can copy the text with the **Copy Window** command, which is active in the **Edit** menu when the result window is active, and transfer it to a ScratchPad for editing. Tables of results have columns separated by tab characters, so you can reposition them in a word processor or paste them into a spreadsheet program.

Scatterplot

Histogram

Bar Chart

Rotating Plot

Pie Chart

BoxPlot

Data Desk makes many kinds of *plots.* Each plot has a standard result window shape icon with a picture that varies according to the type of plot. In Chapter 8 we describe the various kinds of plots available in Data Desk.

Data Desk plots are interactive tools for the data analyst. Each type of plot provides ways to select and identify datapoints, and to work with or modify the plot. In Chapters 9 and 10 we discuss these methods.

HotResult

Most Data Desk commands that produce variables holding computed results, create a special kind of variable called a *HotResult variable.* HotResult variables can be used exactly like variables except that their values depend upon the analysis that produced them. If you change any of the variables used in that analysis, or change the analysis itself, its HotResult variables update automatically to reflect the new state of the data or analysis. However, you cannot open a HotResult variable icon and edit its values.

HotResult variables behave much like derived variables, which we discuss in Section 4.6. Their ability to remain consistent with the data when you alter or correct it is an example of Data Desk's ability to maintain consistency throughout analyses and plots.

2.12 *Defaults and Preferences*

Data Desk comes with standard defaults for all its manipulation, calculation, plot and smoothing options. You set your own defaults by selecting the desired options from each Options dialog and clicking the Set Defaults box. These changes are saved with the program and are active for analyses generated in the current and any future datafile.

Data Desk has a Preferences... dialog which is accessed from the **Edit** menu. It has four sections. The first section affects your editing actions and is appropriate only if you are working on Mac.

Notation

Significant Digits

Round to Nearest

The second section of the Preferences dialog lets you control the precision and presentation of numbers in any derived variable, generated variable, or scratchpad. The standard setting is for Fixed notation with 8 significant digits. Change the notation to Scientific or Engineering by clicking the ***Notation*** pop-up menu and choosing the desired format. Change the number of digits to be displayed by typing a new value in the *Significant Digits* box. When using scientific or engineering notation, Data Desk provides for the rounding of data to eliminate spurious values close to zero. You control this feature by entering the number of digits to round to in the *Round to Nearest* box. For example, the number 0.1234 displayed with scientific notation, 3 significant digits, and rounded to 0.0001 is displayed as 1.23e-2. The number 0.0001234 with the same parameters is displayed 1.00e-4. Changing the rounding parameter to 0.000001 displays the number as 1.23e-4.

The third section of the Preferences dialog allows you to preset how certain features work and display on the Data Desk desktop.

The Warning dialog warns you if you request a category-based plot or table, such as a bar chart or contingency table, for a variable that has more categories than specified here. The check protects from accidentally specifying a continuous variable for these commands. See Section 15.3 for more information.

Close box on right and *Blue Title Bars* effect the appearance of Data Desk windows. *Close box on right* moves the close box from the upper left corner to the upper right corner. The default setting is the upper left corner for Mac and the upper right corner for Windows.

Blue Title Bars changes the appearance to a left justified title tinted with blue. The default setting is center justified/gray lines on Mac and left justified with blue tint on Windows.

Both platforms can support any combination of these settings.

Put Derived with Relation tells Data Desk to place new derived variables (see Section 4.6) in the same relation as their argument variables. If this option is not selected, derived variables are placed in the *Derived* folder in the File Cabinet.

MAC OS

Faster Save speeds the time and decreases the memory requirements for saving files. It does so by writing directly into the current file during the

MAC OS

save process. If a hardware failure occurs during the Faster Save, the file could become damaged. The default save writes a completely new file, which takes longer and requires more memory, but protects the original datafile from damage due to hardware failures.

Auto Set Plot Tool causes Data Desk to select an appropriate default plot tool each time a new plot is opened. For example, when a rotating plot is opened, the rotation hand is automatically selected because that is the tool most likely to be useful. If this option is not selected, the active plot tool will not change until you choose a new one.

Small Default Plot Symbol option sets the plot symbols to a dot (.) instead of a standard plus symbol (+) for data which is pasted, imported or typed in.

Zoom option lets you set the speed with which the windows open up in Data Desk. The default speed is medium. You may choose to set zoom to fast in which case double clicking on an icon will cause an open window to instantaneously appear on the desktop.

MAC OS

The fourth section of the Preferences... dialog allows you to change the location of the Scratch file, an intermediate working file created during each analysis session on Macintosh computers. Data Desk places the Scratch file in the *System* folder, but you may prefer to move it to another location, — for example to place it on a disk with more room. To change the location of the Scratch file click the **Change** button and select the new location for the file. To put the Scratch file back in its usual location, click the **Automatic** button.

When you use Data Desk on a Powerbook or other battery-powered computer, you may wish to create a RAM Disk and direct the Data Desk Scratch file to that RAM Disk. This will both speed Data Desk operations and reduce the need to "spin up" your hard disk. However, be sure you have enough room. Data Desk's Scratch file can grow larger than 1MB.

2.13 *Leaving Data Desk*

To leave Data Desk, choose **Exit** (**Quit** on Mac) from the **File** menu. This command closes all open windows, saves changes in the main Datafile (if you approve) and returns to the operating system. If the datafile is named Untitled, Data Desk asks for a new datafile name.

CHAPTER 3

Data

BOOKS ABOUT STATISTICS, graphics, and data analysis almost never discuss or define data. Although this isn't the place for a long discourse, an understanding of basic terms and principles can help you analyze data better.

3.1 *Basic Concepts*

Most people think of data as numbers and category names, but if that was all they knew about our data they would be unable to analyze it in a sensible way. Data must be *about* something for any analysis to be meaningful. Analysts who concentrate on the numbers but lose sight of what the data are about can easily go astray, producing impressive but worthless graphs and tables and missing important patterns or exceptions. Indeed, those working with data can only understand what kinds of patterns are important if they know *why* they are looking at the data.

case

Data are values measuring or reporting information about each individual in a group along with details of how the values go together and what they report. The values can be numbers or names, or even a mixture of the two. The individual is called a *case* in Data Desk.

variable

Data values that record the same thing about each case are gathered into a *variable*. In formal statistics, a variable is a particular kind of mathematical entity. In data analysis, a variable is both the data values and the underlying phenomenon they record. Typically, a variable is represented as a column of values, with a row for each case.

relation

In Data Desk, variables holding values about the same cases in the same order are gathered into a *relation*. Because the rows of each variable in a relation hold data about the same cases, the columns representing the variables are often placed side by side to form a rectangular table. The individual cases reported on by these variables can usually be described generally. For example, they may be survey respondents, cars, countries, or months. Because each variable in a relation describes the same individuals, they characterize the relation, so naming relations after them is often useful.

Data values aren't simply numbers or categories. They come from some source and record information about some phenomenon. To analyze the data intelligently, you need to know more about the phenomenon and how it has been recorded. In other words, you need to know the answers to the news reporter's familiar questions: who, what, where, when, and why.

In this case the *who* names the observer, recorder, or source of the information. This information should be part of that report along with your analysis. It can be placed in the information record of a relation or folder.

The what, when, and where define the matter recorded, the time, and the location. You might need one, two, or all three to describe particular data values. Variables are often named with their *what*. Measurements of sales would be in a variable named *Sales*. Sometimes, the *when* or *where* should be part of the variable name, especially when the same matter is recorded for different times or places in related variables. Sales for stores in each of two years (when) might be in variables named *Sales87* and *Sales88*. Sales for stores in each of four regions (where) might be in variables named *SalesNE, SalesSE, SalesNW*, and *SalesSW*.

It is also important to have a sense of *why* the data were recorded. The *why* information may help to guide your analysis toward particular displays or methods or alert you to possible biases. For example, data on smoking and health attributed to a tobacco industry researcher in the 1950s should be interpreted differently than data on the same subject reported by a respected health research institute in the 1980s. It is also important to know whether you are using data for a purpose other than the original intent of the observer.

3.2 *Relations, Variables, Cases, Values, and Data Structure*

Data Desk is a general tool that can work with many kinds of data from a wide variety of sources, so it uses general terminology. Many fields and some kinds of programs use specialized terminology. The following terms are some alternatives:

data tables

rectangular dataset

- RELATIONS are usually represented in statistics programs as rectangular tables of data in which each row represents a case and each column represents a variable. They may be referred to operationally as *data tables* or even (by programs that do not imagine more than a single relation) as *datasets*. Formally, a relation is the set of cases, the set of variables, and the values recorded for each case on each variable. A spreadsheet is a typical representation of a single relation. Some writers in statistics use the term *rectangular dataset* to mean the same thing.

  Most statistics and graphics operations make sense only for values that are related — that is, for values measured on the same individuals in the same order. Data Desk often requires that variables analyzed together be in the same relation.

field
column
variable

- VARIABLES are usually represented as columns of values. In a database program a variable would be a *field*. In a spreadsheet, a variable would commonly be a *column*, although some variables might be rows. The term *variable* is quite standard in statistics and is used throughout the Data Desk books. It suggests that the values gathered together represent some underlying phenomenon and that patterns found in the data values for different variables may tell you something about how these variables are related.

respondent, subject
observation, period

record

rows

- CASES are the individuals to which the data values refer. A case may be called by another name according to the circumstances. Thus we speak of a survey's *respondent*, a psychology experiment's *subject*, a study's *observation*, or a *period* in time-sequenced data as cases. Each of these entities would commonly be a single case in a relation. In a database program a case would be a *record* with values for each field. When variables are represented as columns of values, cases are represented as *rows* across adjacent variables. That's how they appear when you open variables from the same relation in Data Desk.

sample
population

In statistics, the group of cases is often a *sample* drawn from a larger *population.* Data Desk makes no particular assumptions about the sample, except that the inferential statistics it computes assume that the sample is representative of the population and usually that it is drawn at random.

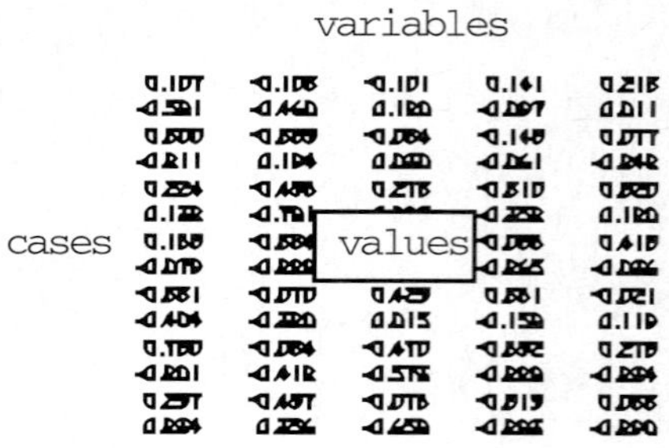

unit

- VALUES are the elements that fill the variable-by-case structure. Each variable in a relation has a value (which may be "missing") for each case, and each case has a value for each variable. Data values are usually recorded in some measurement *unit,* such as dollars, inches, years, and so on. Units can be converted to other units (as when you convert feet to inches), but a standard unit may be used conventionally to record a particular phenomenon. However, even when a particular unit is standard, good data analysis may require that you transform the data, as when you work with the logarithm of the original values or with the difference or quotient of two values, which may alter the unit.

variables

cases

values

3.3 *Missing Data*

missing value

Sometimes we cannot obtain a data value for each case. Values are lost, experiments are ruined, subjects are too subjective, respondents don't respond, observations are not observed, records are not recorded, and so on. You can indicate a missing data value in Data Desk with a blank or with any nonnumeric character. Any data value that isn't a valid number is treated as a *missing value* by any operation that requires numbers. Thus you can label missing values with information about the cause of the omission.

For example, Data Desk considers the following to be missing values in a numeric variable: "missing", "refused to answer", "not at home", "equipment malfunctioned". All behave as missing values in any numeric computation, but show up in the variable's editing window just as they were typed.

Sometimes it is useful to mark a case as missing temporarily to remove it from an analysis. One easy way to do so is to place a nonnumeric character in front of the case value. An "*" makes a good marker that is easy to find and remove when the numeric value is needed again. The data value "*3.4" is treated as missing, but preserves its original numeric value for later reference.

missing category names

When Data Desk opens a variable that resulted from an internal computation, it displays missing values with the "•" symbol. You can type this symbol as Alt-8 on Windows, Option-8 on Mac. Data consisting of category or group names is considered missing only if the case is empty or consists of a •.

NaN (Not a Number)

Data Desk represents missing values internally with a construct called a NaN, which is short for "Not a Number". NaNs also result from calculations that involve missing values, or from calculations that yield a non-numeric result (such as the square root of –1 or the log of 0).

3.4 *Infinities*

infinity

There are two exceptions to the rule that text is treated as missing values in computations: the text "Infinity", and "–Infinity" are interpreted as infinity and negative infinity, respectively. You may want to enter data with infinite values, but you should take care to use only those techniques that can accommodate infinities (for example, by ranking the data first to compute nonparametric statistics). Computations that cannot accommodate infinities treat them as missing values. Any text that begins with the letters "inf" or with a "+" or "–" followed by "inf" (regardless of capitalization) is interpreted as infinity. Thus the words "inference" or "infrastructure" would also be interpreted as infinity.

3.5 *Outliers, Blunders, and Rogues*

Real data are dirty. Errors creep in at almost every step of data collection, recording, and organization. Even correct data describe a world that contains individuals so extraordinary that it may be impossible to understand the ordinary course of events without treating them specially.[1]

outlier

Any case that is far from the body of the data is an *outlier*. Some outliers are clearly extreme. Others are more subtle, being extraordinary in some combination of variables but not extreme in any one variable. The medical patient who is 6'3" and weighs 110 pounds is an example. Neither his height nor his weight alone is extraordinary, but the combination of the two show him to be extraordinarily thin — possibly thin enough to warrant excluding him from a medical experiment.

blunders, rogues

Extraordinary cases are sometimes divided into *blunders* and *rogues*. Blunders are clerical or measurement errors in the data that are not informative about the real world. They should be identified and either corrected or omitted.

Rogues are correctly measured and recorded, but are inherently unusual. Even though a rogue case is correct, you may do well to omit it from your main analysis and treat it specially. A data analysis that describes most of the data well and deals specially with a few exceptions is almost always more useful than an analysis that provides a mediocre fit to all the data but makes no exceptions. In no event should rogues be summarily discarded. A rogue can be worth more to your understanding of the data than all the ordinary cases because it makes a particular aspect of the data clear.

3.6 *Numerals and Numeric Values*

Many Data Desk operations calculate with numeric data values. Some, such as bar charts, tables, and analysis of variance, use data values to define categories. When a variable is used to define categories, its values

[1]The venerable statistical consultant Cuthbert Daniel has referred to such values as "non-missing" values — that is, values that really should have been missing but aren't.

numerals

are interpreted according to their *text* rather than their *numeric* value so that the numbers are seen as sequences of *numerals.*

Some variables can be interpreted reasonably as either numeric or categorical. For example, the *Cylinders* variable in the Cars data counts the number of cylinders (so that the *average number of cylinders per car* is a reasonable statistic). It might just as well be used to partition cars into four groups: 4-cylinder, 5-cylinder (the Audi 5000), 6-cylinder, and 8-cylinder cars for a pie chart.

When numbers are read as numerals, numbers that are written differently but would evaluate to the same numeric value are *not* equal. For example, the data values "1", "1.0", and "+1.0" all have the same numeric value, but specify categories with different labels in procedures that require categories.

Unlike conventional statistics programs, Data Desk doesn't require that the values in a variable be all numbers or all text. Nor is it necessary to specify in advance whether numbers are to be interpreted as categories or as numeric values. Data Desk considers your use of the data and determines from that how to interpret the values.

APPENDIX 3A *Kinds of Data*

Data come in several different kinds. Traditionally, analysts classified data as nominal (category names), ordinal (ordered, but not measured), interval (suitable for addition and subtraction operations), and ratio (suitable for multiplication and division operations). Although these categories can be useful for understanding what can be learned from data, they should not be used to restrict how data are analyzed.[2]

Mosteller and Tukey (1977) suggest seven categories that more closely represent the nature of data values.

AMOUNTS

Amounts are the most common kind of data. They cannot be negative. Amounts include collections of things (for example, amounts of money), measurements ("amount" of height), durations (amounts of time), and so on.

COUNTS

Counts are whole numbers that enumerate things. They cannot be negative.

COUNTED FRACTIONS

Ratios with a fixed base, as in "there are 25 workers in this plant and 5 of them are women, so 5/25 of the workers are women." The most common counted fractions are *percents,* which are counted fractions with a base of 100.

NAMES

Names are categories taken in no particular order.

RANKS

Ranks are integers reporting the order (but not the value) of cases.

GRADES

Grades are categories with a natural order, such as freshman, sophomore, junior, senior. Much survey and testing data are reported as grades because respondents are offered 5 or 7 choices in order from low to high with no indication of spacing or units.

BALANCES

Balances can be positive or negative and may be unbounded in both directions. They are the most general form of data, but may be the least common. Often balances come about as a difference between two amounts (for example, a balance can be used to represent "velocity northward" when a negative value indicates "velocity southward." Alternatively, the amount of northward velocity (bounded by 0) and the amount of southward velocity could be reported, with the original value being their difference. The logarithm of an amount that can be arbitrarily close to zero can be a balance.

These kinds of data have properties that are worth noting because they help to determine the kinds of plots and analyses appropriate for the

[2] See "Nominal, Ordinal, Interval, and Ratio Typology is Misleading." *The American Statistician,* February, 1993.

data. For example, variables that are categorical (names and grades) are often best displayed with pie charts and bar charts.

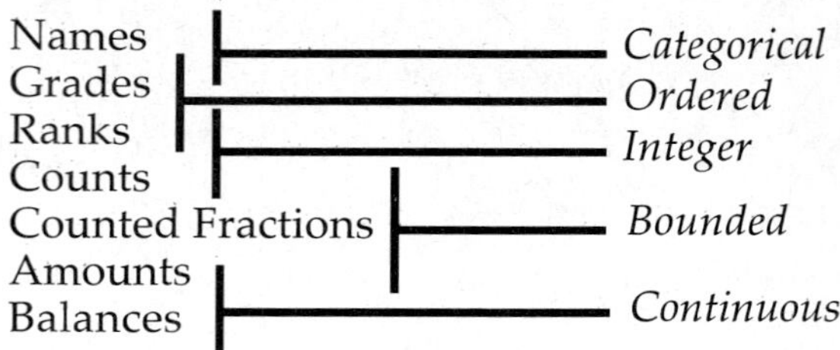

Mosteller and Tukey recommend transformations that can make data analyses simpler based upon the kind of the data.

- Amounts are often better analyzed after taking logs.
- Counts usually benefit from a square root or logarithm transformation. The "Box–Cox" transformation offered in {Manip} **Transform** menu (see Section 11.15) offers powerful ways to find effective transformations for both amounts and counts types of data dynamically.
- Percents almost always are easier to analyze as $\log [p/(1-p)]$, where p is the percent expressed as a fraction between 0 and 1. (Use $\log [p/(100-p)]$ for percents expressed as values between 0 and 100.) The Tukey *lambda* transformation offers powerful ways to find effective transformations for such data dynamically (see Section 11.18).
- The ith rank out of n is often best transformed by $\log [(i-1/3)/(n-i+2/3)]$.
- Balances usually should not be transformed.

APPENDIX 3B *Matrices, Tables, and Relations*

Data analysis requires simple and convenient data manipulation and editing, and powerful numerical computations. A data analysis environment must provide ways to organize, label, manipulate, examine, edit, and compute with data.

matrix

Statisticians often use the mathematical structure called a *matrix* to specify statistics computations. The most common way to do so is to regard each variable as a column of numbers and to append columns side by side in some order to make a matrix. Matrices are powerful tools for specifying and performing statistics calculations, but they are merely mathematical conveniences. They are neither fundamental statistics entities nor appropriate data management structures.

tables

Because most data tables are rectangular, data analysts often array their data in *tables.* The most common form for these tables is as columns of numbers and text placed side by side. Data tables thus look much like data matrices. However, tables are simply ways of arranging data for display and (sometimes) editing. Variable editing windows form a table of data designed for examining and editing data. Because they can be rearranged and resized on the screen they make a more flexible table than the traditional row by column form, but otherwise they can be thought of as a table.

relations

Data Desk keeps variables in icons. The icons look like columns of values and open into windows that show columns of values. *Relations* keep variable icons side-by-side in left-to-right order, and guarantee that when cases are removed, inserted or moved in some variables, the other variables in the relation remain consistent.

folders

Data Desk also provides *folders* to help you organize your icons on the desktop. Folders can hold any Data Desk icons including variables, relations, and other folders. Variables can be grouped into folders to provide a hierarchy in which a single folder icon refers to several related variables.

Data Desk thus assigns the various functions required for data analysis to different views of the data. Variable icons are easy to arrange, organize, and rename. Folders provide a simple structure to make large datafiles more manageable. Variable editing windows open side by side to form a data table. Relations offer a clear structure for data and make sophisticated relationships among several relations possible. Data Desk computations use matrices internally, but matrices are not available as objects on the desktop.

CHAPTER 4

Data Desk Concepts

YOU CAN LEARN Data Desk bit by bit, starting with simple operations and gradually adding more and more powerful skills. In Chapter 2 we discussed the basic concepts that every Data Desk user must understand. In this chapter we go further, introducing powerful concepts and features that will help you become a more efficient and effective Data Desk user.

4.1 *Selecting Variables*

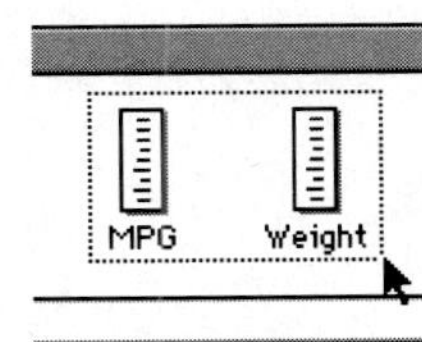

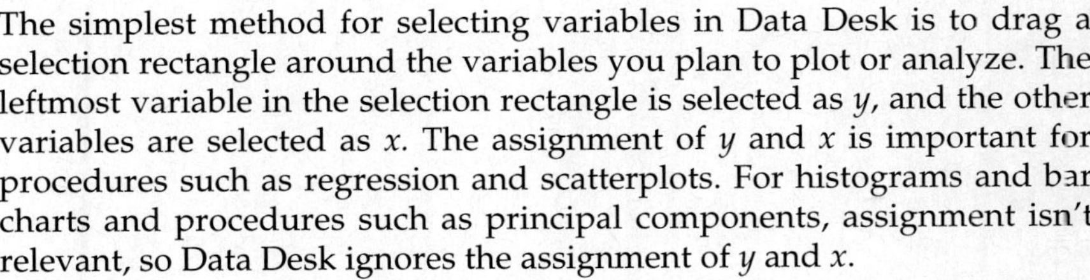

The simplest method for selecting variables in Data Desk is to drag a selection rectangle around the variables you plan to plot or analyze. The leftmost variable in the selection rectangle is selected as y, and the other variables are selected as x. The assignment of y and x is important for procedures such as regression and scatterplots. For histograms and bar charts and procedures such as principal components, assignment isn't relevant, so Data Desk ignores the assignment of y and x.

You can also select y-variables by holding the Ctrl key on Windows, or the Option key on Mac, while clicking, and x-variables by holding the Shift key while clicking. Variables selected with a selection rectangle and those selected by selecting their folder's icon are selected in left-to-right order.

When several y-variables and several x-variables have been selected, Data Desk attempts to work with appropriate combinations of variables as follows:

- All one-variable commands ignore selection type and operate on each variable in turn; y-variables first, followed by x-variables.
- Two-variable commands (such as **Scatterplots**) and two-variable transformations attempt to pair variables:

  If one y-variable and several x-variables are selected, the y-variable is paired with each x-variable in turn, and the command operates on each pair of variables.

  If several y-variables and one x-variable are selected, the x-variable is paired with each y-variable in turn, and the command operates on each pair of variables.

  If an equal number of y-variables and x-variables is selected, the first y-variable is paired with the first x-variable, the second y-variable is paired with the second x-variable, and so on, and the command operates on each pair of variables.

4.2 *HyperView Menus*

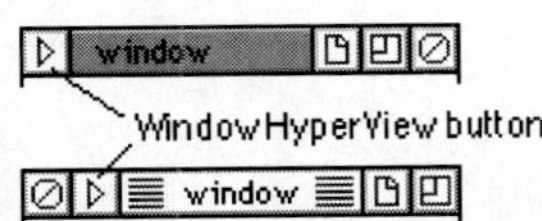

Data Desk is an open environment. At any time you can do almost anything. Data analysis requires such freedom because any plot or calculation may suggest new things to do. The possible connections and paths are endless, but some paths are more common than others. For example it is common to consider both the scatterplot of two variables and their

> **TIP**
> The HyperView menus attached to the axis labels of a scatterplot offer to select the variable plotted on that axis. Before clicking in the HyperView menu, hold the Shift or Option key down to select as *x* or *y* variable.

correlation, so if you are looking at one of them, you might want to see the other.

HyperView menus suggest such next steps in the data analysis. Each Data Desk output window offers direct paths to additional plots or analyses. Parts of the plot or output text are designated as *HyperView buttons*. When the mouse is over a HyperView button, it changes to a button hand, . Pressing the mouse button at that location pops up a menu suggesting related plots or analyses.

data context

The *data context* of your analysis is informed by your knowledge of the world and of your data. If you understand the background of your data so that you can recognize a meaningful pattern, you are likely to learn a great deal more from the *process* of analyzing the data than from reading a table of statistics or just looking at a plot. Data Desk is designed to help you bring your real-world knowledge to bear on your data analyses, even if you are not an expert at advanced statistics.

statistics context

In contrast to the data context, the *statistics context* of a data analysis consists of the properties and relationships among the statistics and graphics methods. Data Desk incorporates this context in HyperView menus. Most Data Desk results windows' HyperView menus suggest additional or alternative analyses or plots. These might be checks on the underlying assumptions of a procedure (such as a histogram to check how a variable is distributed) or they might be naturally related analyses (a frequency breakdown to provide the counts and percentages graphed in a pie chart). For example, when you press the mouse button with the over an axis label in a scatterplot, the HyperView menu that pops up offers to locate the icon, make a histogram, or make a normal probability plot of the variable plotted on that axis. If you press the mouse button with the over a correlation coefficient in the correlation analysis, the HyperView menu suggests a scatterplot of the underlying variables (Fig. 4-1).

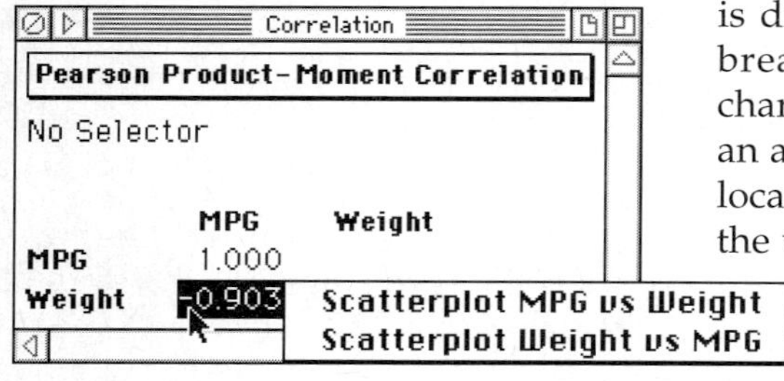

Figure 4-1. *Context-Sensitive HyperView menu.*

HyperView menus neither restrict your choices nor require any action. Most HyperView menu commands could be selected from the desktop menu bar in the ordinary way. HyperView menus are simply suggested steps placed at your fingertips and set apart from the full array of Data Desk capabilities so that you can select among them easily. HyperView menus offer expert guidance, but they are designed to assist you rather than to take control of the analysis.

4.3 *Global and Context-Sentsitive HyperView Menus*

Global HyperView menus are attached to the window as a whole. Most Data Desk windows have a submenu arrow, ▷, located in the upper left corner of the title bar. The HyperView menu attached to that arrow suggests general actions related to the analysis or display in the window (Fig. 4-2).

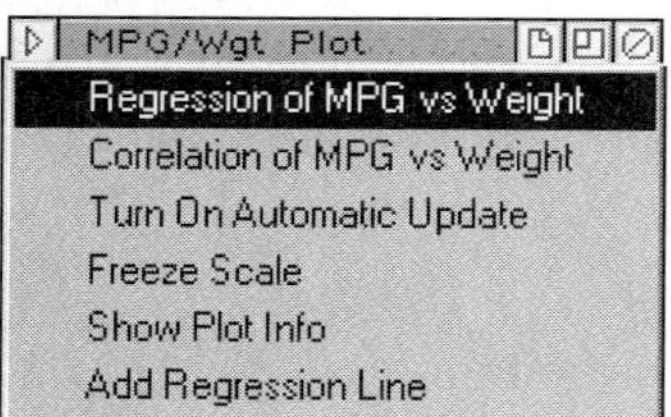

Figure 4-2. *The global HyperView menu is located at the ▷ symbol at the top of a window. It offers actions related to the analysis or display in that window.*

Context-sensitive HyperView menus attached to parts of a display or table offer particularly effective expert suggestions. They can be more context-specific than the global HyperView menus. In plots, for example, the HyperView menus attached to the axis labels usually offer to locate the icon of the displayed variable or to show it in a simple one-

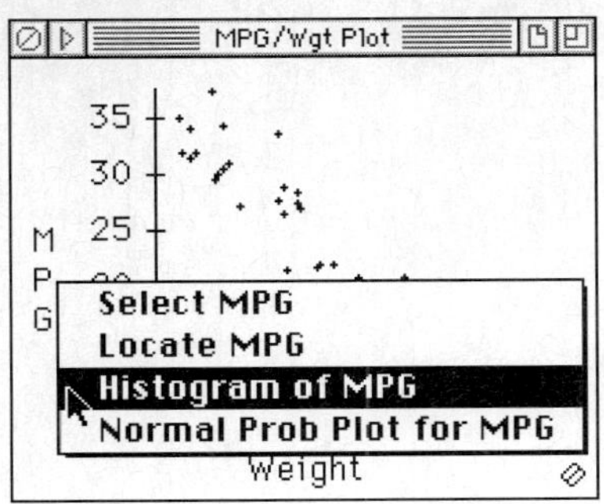

Figure 4-3. One HyperView menu in a scatterplot suggests ways to look at the y-axis variable.

variable display, such as a histogram (Fig. 4-3). In most tables, the HyperView menu attached to the test statistic usually offers a display to check if the assumptions of the test are valid. While not all HyperView menu paths are documented in this book, context-sensitive HyperView menus that embody statistical expertise are discussed in chapters dealing with the specific analyses.

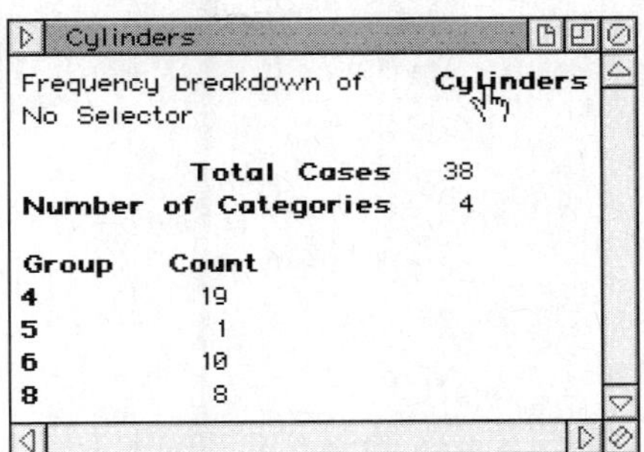

Figure 4-4. *When the mouse cursor changes to press the mouse to see a menu of context related analyses and plots.*

When a part of a plot or table has a context-sensitive HyperView menu underneath, the mouse cursor changes to when it passes over that part. Whenever the cursor looks like this "button presser", you can press the mouse button to see a HyperView menu (Fig. 4-4).

HyperView menus maintain consistency by working with any selector or group variable (see Chapter 13 for a discussion of selector and group variables) that was active when the window contents were first computed. Thus, for example, if you compute an analysis using the **Selector** button to select a subset of cases, any plot generated by a HyperView menu from that analysis uses the same selector variable, so it displays the cases that contributed to that analysis and no others.

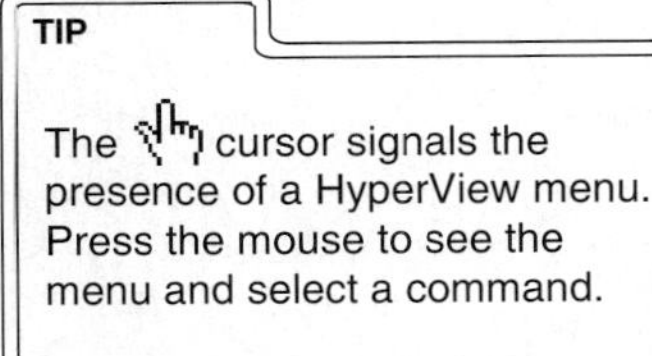

If a selector variable was active when the original analysis was performed, the HyperView menu commands are *not* identical to selecting the named variables' icons and choosing the specified command from the desktop menu bar. These commands are identical to setting the **Selector** button as it was when the original analysis was performed and then selecting variables and choosing a command.

4.4 *Data Analysis Expertise*

No two data analyses are exactly alike. Each analyst has favorite tools and methods and favorite ways to combine them. The HyperView menus in Data Desk are only a selection from all the alternative paths that are possible. This selection embodies the program designer's many years of data analysis and consulting experience and reflects a philosophy of data analysis grounded in the tradition of exploratory data analysis.

4.5 *Updating Windows*

Data change during an analysis. You might transform the data, correct a value, or temporarily eliminate an extraordinary case. During an analysis you might try alternatives: "What would be the prediction if we lowered the price?", or "What if we isolate the Southwest region and repeat the analysis for those cases?" For these reasons and others, you may change your data, either permanently or temporarily. Each change may require that you repeat parts of your analysis to see how they adjust.

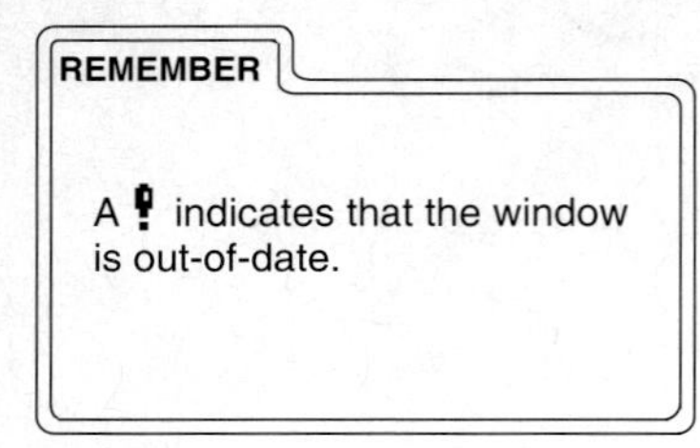

Data Desk's results windows indicate immediately when the variables they use have been changed. The submenu arrow that marked the global HyperView menu ▷ changes immediately to an exclamation mark ! to alert you to the change. A new HyperView menu offers to Redo the analysis in a new window using the updated variables, or to Update the window in place.

Window updates guarantee that HyperView menus reflect the state of the data shown in the plot or analysis. It is often better to redo the plot or computation to a new window than to update the current display in place because it lets you compare "before" and "after" views of the data and keep a history of the analysis.

Figure 4-5. *When you choose* ***Turn On Automatic Update*** *from the window's global HyperView menu, the menu button will turn gray to indicate the change in status.*

Many windows also offer the option of automatic updating. Select **Turn on Automatic Update** from the window's HyperView menu (Fig. 4-5). The window's HyperView menu button, (▷), will turn gray to indicate the change in status. Windows set to automatically update do just that. Whenever they are notified of a change in an underlying variable they immediately recompute. The most common use for automatic updating is to create custom dynamic plots by using sliders. An automatically updating plot of a derived variable that uses a slider changes dynamically as you move the slider. Section 11.14 discusses sliders and gives an example. Choose **Turn Off Automatic Update** from the global HyperView menu to return the window to its original state.

You should use automatic updating only in special situations. Windows that change when you aren't watching them are confusing and may cause you to miss important aspects of your data. We suggest that you set only selected windows to update automatically and then watch them while they change.

4.6 *Derived Variables*

Data Desk variables hold data values for plots and analyses. Ordinarily, variables hold values as numbers or text. Derived variables hold instead the *expression* from which data values are computed. For example, a derived variable might hold the expression *log(income)*. When used as a variable, the derived variable evaluates the logarithm of the values in the variable named *Income* so that they can be used in the display or calculation.

The derived variable icon resembles a variable icon but has arithmetic symbols on it to suggest the algebraic expression. Derived variables can be used anytime as a substitute for ordinary variables.

The most common derived variables are simple transformations of other variables or simple arithmetic combinations. The easiest way to generate these is by selecting the variables to be transformed or combined and choosing a function from the {Manip ▶ Transform} submenus.

Derived variables are especially powerful because changing a value in any of the variables used in its expression changes the value of the derived variable. Thus the value of the derived variable holding *log(income)* is always the logarithm of the income values even if you change some income values.

Derived variables are very much like the HotResult variables created by many Data Desk analyses, except that you can always edit a derived variable expression. You cannot edit a HotResult variable.

In Chapter 11 we discuss derived variables at length and list the functions you can use in derived variable expressions. You will find that derived variables extend Data Desk's capabilities to let you compute many things that might not be built in as menu commands.

4.7 *Following the Links*

Data Desk maintains and follows arbitrarily long links among variables, derived variables, and results windows. For example, changing a variable affects all derived variables that depend upon it, any plots or tables that depend upon those derived variables, any secondary statistics that depend upon the tables, any plots or tables that depend upon the secondary statistics, and so on. All dependent plots and tables can be updated or recomputed after a change. For example, a scatterplot of the *logarithm* of *Assets,* defined with a derived variable, will offer to update when data values in the variable *Assets* are changed.

The exclamation mark appears as soon as you make a change in a variable's editing window. You can open a variable, change values, and immediately update dependent windows without closing the variable's window. Thus you can easily try a number of "what if?" experiments by varying data values, selection criteria, or functions, and then updating results windows. If a dependent window is set to update automatically, click outside the derived variable editing window, or press Enter on Mac to stop editing the derived variable expression and to update the window.

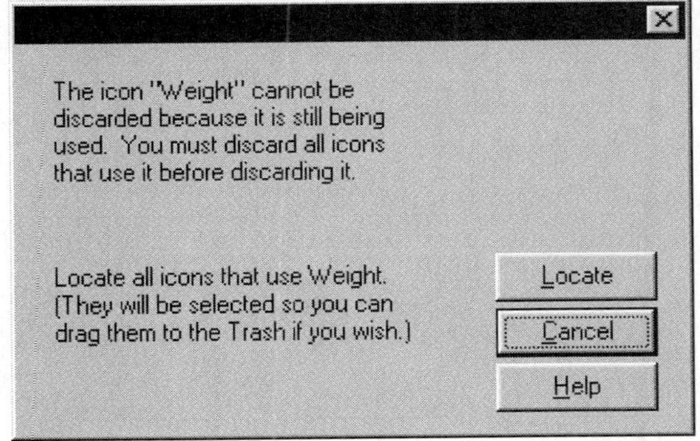

Figure 4-6. *You cannot discard an icon that is still in use. Data Desk offers to locate icons that use the one you wish to discard.*

You may not discard any variable or derived variable that is still being used by a results window. Data Desk alerts you and offers to locate the icons that still use the one you want to discard.

You may discard a variable along with all its dependent windows. If Data Desk cannot empty all of the Trash, it displays an alert (Fig. 4-6). You can locate any dependent icons by pressing the **Locate** button in the dialog. You can then pick up any selected icon and drag it into the Trash. Because all the dependent icons are selected by the **Locate** command, they will all be dragged into the Trash together.

4.8 *The Clipboard*

Text, cases, variables, plots, and tables are placed on the Clipboard by the **Copy** and **Cut** commands in the **Edit** menu. The **Copy** command in the **Edit** menu changes according to the nature of the frontmost window to reflect the kind of object you can copy. For example, it will read **Copy** for text in a single window, **Copy Cases** for cases selected from one or more variable editing windows in a Relation, **Copy Variables** for icon windows, and **Copy Window** when the frontmost window is a plot or output table. The Copy command places the copy on the Clipboard. In Chapters 5 and 6 we discuss **Copy** in more detail.

The **Show Clipboard** command in the **Edit** menu displays the Clipboard window. Resize the window to see more of the Clipboard contents. Ordinarily the Clipboard window displays the contents of the Clipboard automatically. When the Clipboard contains a table of data values copied or cut from several variables, the values may not appear in the Clipboard window. Nevertheless, they are available for **Paste Cases** or **Paste Variables** commands and will be on the Clipboard if you leave Data Desk and enter another program.

4.9 *ScratchPads*

ScratchPads are simple editing windows that close into icons. The {Data ▸ New} **ScratchPad** command creates a ScratchPad and places it in the *Results* folder. You can type any message, or paste any text into a ScratchPad, and edit the text with all the standard editing commands (including **Undo**).

ScratchPads are convenient for a number of uses. You may want to keep a ScratchPad on the desktop to hold information about a datafile, or keep one in each relation to describe the data in that relation. ScratchPads are ideal for noting what you did during an analysis and reminding yourself of what you intend to do. They typically hold notes about the data or analysis at large.

ScratchPads provide a temporary editing environment. For example, the **Copy Window** command in the **Edit** menu copies any output table as text. If you paste the text into a ScratchPad, you then can select and copy numbers from the table easily. Similarly, you can import the entire contents of a text file into a scratchpad. The text file might contain data or could, for example, be a text description of a datafile.

ScratchPads also offer a calculator capability closely related to the calculation abilities of derived variables (see Chapter 11). Type any expression that would be legal in a derived variable, select it, press the right mouse button and type = on Windows (type ⌘ = on Mac) or choose **Evaluate** from the scratchpad's global HyperView menu. (In Section 4.2 we discussed HyperView menus.) The results appear in the ScratchPad just below the expression. (In Chapter 11 we provide more details.)

4.10 *Presentations*

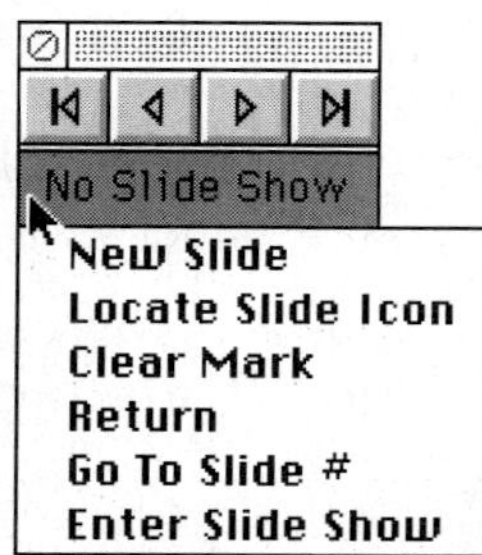

Slide Shows provide a helpful way to guide colleagues or customers through a particular analysis. Each slide in a slide show is a collection of one or more Data Desk displays. To open or create a slide show, choose {Special} **Slide Show**. The Slide Show palette provides tools to navigate through a slide show. The pull-down menu attached to the bottom of the palette provides additional navigation aids and a **New Slide** command, which creates new slides. (In Chapter 15 we discuss Slide Shows in detail.)

Several window types created from the {Data ▸ New} menu are helpful for creating effective Slide Shows as well as Templates and Action programs. *Note windows* are similar to ScratchPads, except they don't display title bars or resize boxes. They are typically placed in corkboard windows to annotate templates. Note windows are also used to put direction and annotation in slide shows when you don't want the viewer of the slide shows to accidentally close the Note window. Note windows close when the slide closes. To reposition a Note window, hold down Ctrl key, Option key on Mac, click anywhere on the window and drag. To resize, hold down the Option key, Ctrl key on Windows, and grab the lower right corner.

To create a Note window, choose {Data ▸ New} **Note**. A blank Note window is created and displayed in the frontmost corkboard window. If no corkboard is open, a new one is created and the Note window is placed inside it. Click on the window and begin to type. A Note window acts like any other text editing program. Cut, Copy, and Paste work for selected text. On a Mac to change font and size, select the desired text, hold down the ⌘ key, click on the window and choose **Text Format...** (Fig. 4-7). Select the desired options and choose **OK** to allow the changes to take effect. (Text format is not available on Windows in this version.)

Text Format...
Lock
Locate Icon
Close
Throw away

Figure 4-7. *To change font and size, select the desired text, hold down the ⌘ key on Mac, click on the window, and choose* ***Text Format....*** *(This option is not available on Windows in this version.)*

Other commands can also be accessed by holding down the right mouse button, or ⌘ key on Mac, and clicking on the window. **Locate Icon** finds and selects the icon of that window. **Close** closes the window. **Throw Away** puts the window in the Data Desk trash.

Picture windows are similar to Note windows except they hold pictures instead of text. Picture windows do not have title bars and can be repositioned and resized by holding down Ctrl key (Option key on Mac) just like Note windows. Picture windows accept bitmaps on Windows and PICTs on Mac.

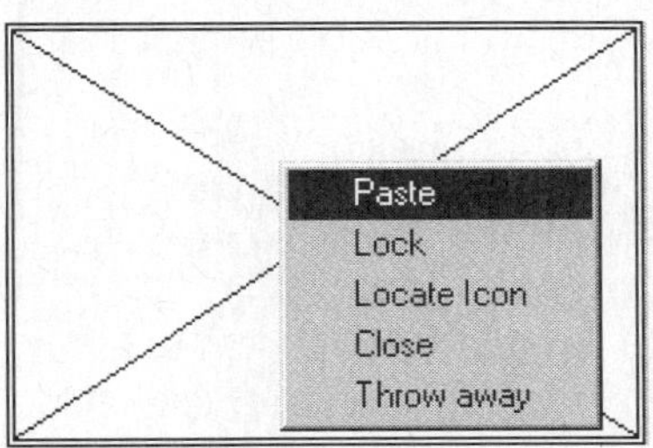

Figure 4-8. *To place a picture inside a picture window, hold down the right mouse button, or ⌘ key on Mac, and click on the picture window. A menu of commands pops up. Choose* ***Paste.***

To create a Picture window, choose {Data ▸ New} **Picture**. A blank Picture window is created and displayed in the frontmost corkboard window. If no corkboard is open, a new one is created and the Picture window is placed inside it. To paste a picture into a Picture window from the clipboard, hold down the right mouse button, or the ⌘ key on Mac, and choose **Paste** (Fig. 4-8).

The special commands accessed by holding down the right mouse button, or ⌘ key on Mac, are the same as the Note window, except that **Paste** replaces **Text Format....**

Button

Buttons provide a convenient method to take you to a specific window, perhaps as a way of branching off the main sequence of the slide show, or instead of a slide show for limited sequence needs. They are also used to initiate Action programs. Buttons are simple to create and use. Choose {Data ▸ New} **Button** to create a button. Data Desk creates an icon, places it in the *Results* folder and asks you to name it. The new button is displayed in the frontmost corkboard window. If no corkboard is open, a new one is created and the button is placed inside it. To link a button to a window, drag the window's icon or icon alias into the button. The button highlights to indicate you are positioned correctly. Now when you press the button, the attached window is opened and placed frontmost.

The techniques used to resize and reposition buttons are the same as those for Note and Picture windows. The commands accessed by the right mouse button, or ⌘ key on Mac, are also the same, except that **Rename Button** replaces **Paste** and **Text Format...** .

Figure 4-9. *Hold down the right mouse button, or the ⌘ key on Mac and click on the button to bring up a menu of commands that operate on that button.*

Corkboards are special windows that allow other windows to be "tacked" to them. They provide a convenient place to keep related windows together. Any Data Desk window can be tacked to a corkboard. Drag the icon alias of the desired window into the Corkboard window. Once the window is attached to the corkboard, it can be removed by dragging the icon alias off the corkboard. Windows "tacked" to corkboards can be resized and repositioned as you would just like any untacked window. You cannot, however, move the tacked window outside the corkboard. When the corkboard is moved or closed, all the windows attached to the corkboard move or close with the corkboard.

TIP

You can drag a selection rectangle across multiple windows inside a corkboard.

NOTE

When a window inside a corkboard is the active window the title bar of the window and the title bar of the corkboard highlight.

To open a new Corkboard window choose {Data ▶ New} **Corkboard**. Data Desk opens the window and places its icon in the *Results* folder. To resize a Corkboard window, grab its lower right corner and proceed as you would with any window.

You might think that Corkboards are the same as Layout windows (see chapter 15). The difference is that you can still work with windows attached to corkboards. Plots and tables recompute and display current states, points can be selected, and HyperView menu commands can be selected, just like any untacked window. There really is no functional difference between windows in corkboards and those on the Data Desk desktop, except for the restriction of staying inside the corkboard. The objects in layout windows are just static pictures of windows.

Another unique characteristic is that icons of windows tacked to a corkboard are contained inside the Corkboard icon (Fig. 4-10). So when you attach a window to a corkboard, the window's icon is no longer visible or available for use. When the window is detached from the corkboard, the icon is put back in the folder where it resided when its window was tacked. The same thing happens to icons of windows attached to slides.

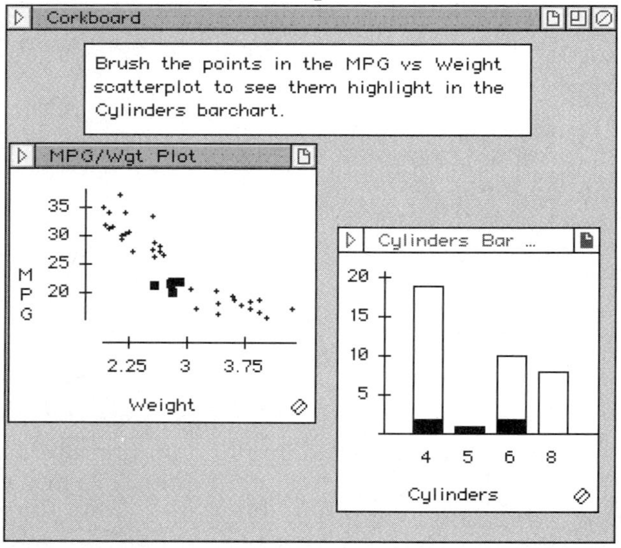

Figure 4-10. *You can tack any Data Desk window inside the Corkboard window. Plots and tables recompute and display current states, points can be selected, and HyperView menu commands can be selected, just like any untacked window.*

Note, Picture, Button, and Corkboard windows are different from other windows in one other important way. If a

Slide Show is open, creating a Note, Picture, Button or Corkboard window automatically adds that window to the active slide. If that happens, the window's icon becomes part of the slide's icon, just like any other window that is added to a slide.

All notes, pictures, buttons, and corkboards can be locked by choosing the **Lock** command from the window's HyperView menu. Locked windows cannot be changed, or have any new objects or text added to them. Choose **Unlock** from the window's HyperView menu to allow changes to the window. Locked windows are helpful for protecting the integrity of template files.

4.11 *Sliders*

Sliders are tools with which you can design your own dynamic displays and computations. A slider window holds a horizontal axis intersected by a hairline (Fig. 4-11). You can grab the axis with the tool and slide it from side to side. As it slides, it displays the value at which the hairline crosses the axis and publishes it as the value associated with the slider's name. If that name is used in a derived variable expression, the derived variable takes on a new value whenever the slider is moved. See Chapter 11 for more discussion of derived variables and sliders.

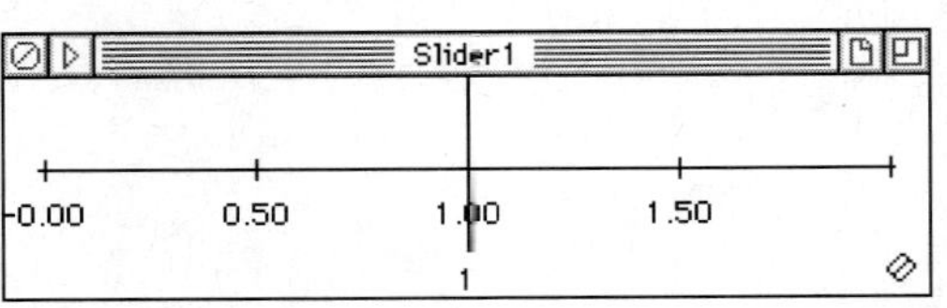

Figure 4-11. *Sliders are building blocks for customized dynamic displays and analyses.*

4.12 *Templates*

A *template* is a predefined collection of text, buttons, and results into which you can drag new data. Templates typically reside in separate files that hold no data. To use a template, first open your datafile. Then Import the template, adding its contents to the datafile.

To put your data into the template drag the icons of variables into the sockets provided.

Template files typically open with an introductory Corkboard window that provides general information and navigation controls. This first corkboard usually contains any or all of the following pieces (Fig. 4-12):

- A note that describes the template's purpose
- A note instructing how to use it
- Sockets into which to drag your variables
- Buttons to navigate through the template

As you work with the template, other windows open. These other windows, which may or may not be corkboards, can hold additional instructions, navigation buttons, output tables, and plots.

Control Panel

This template accepts the assigned variable, determires whether it is categorical or quantatative, and plots it in a "bar plot".

If the variable is categorical, a Bar Chart is created and displayed.

If the variable is quantatative, a Histogram is created and displayed.

Instructions: Drag a variable into the variable socket labeled 'myvar' and press the button labeled 'Plot It'.

myvar | Drag in a variable

Plot It

Figure 4-12. *Introductory Corkboard window.*

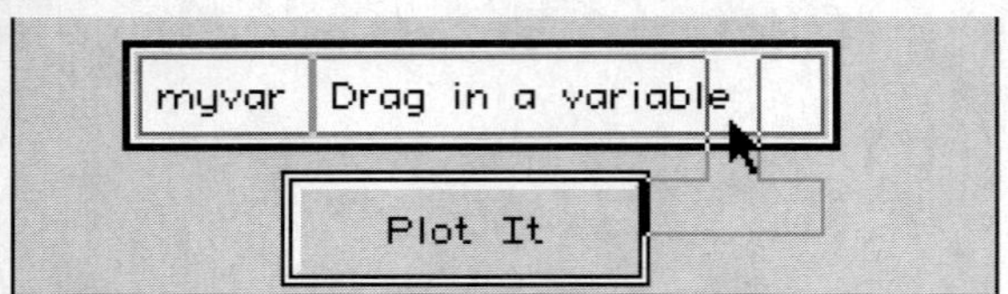

Figure 4-13. The variable socket highlights to indicate the proper positioning of the dragged variable.

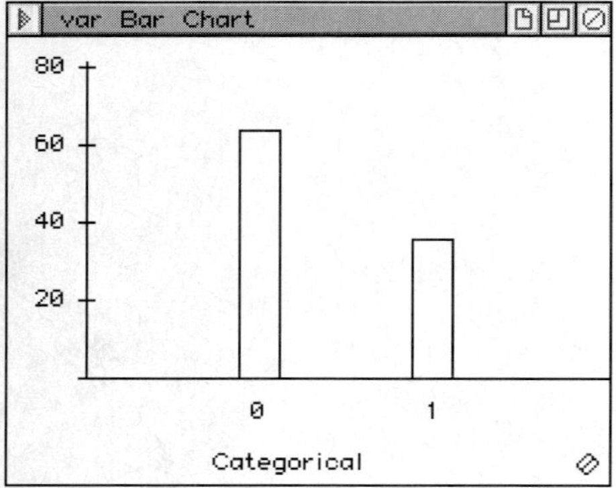

Figure 4-14. A bar chart displays categorical data.

Figure 4-13 shows the proper positioning of a dragged variable. The border of the substitute socket highlights when the dragged variable has been properly positioned.

The *Sample Template* in the *Data Desk Student Datafiles* folder is designed to analyze a variable to determine whether it is categorical (a grouping of categories such as *male / female* or *high / medium / low*) or whether it is quantitative (a range of continuous values such as heights, exam scores, or blood pressure readings). The template then creates the appropriate plot for the assigned variable — a bar chart if the variable is categorical or a histogram if the variable is quantitative. (We discuss histograms in Section 8.3 and bar charts in Section 8.8.)

The first step in using this template is to assign a variable to it. This file includes two example variables that you can use. One is named *Categorical* and the other is named *Quantitative*. Select the variable *Categorical* and drag it into the substitute socket *myvar*. The substitute socket should now read *myvar* | *Categorical*.

Now press the **Plot It** button. The appropriate plot for the assigned variable is displayed — in this case a bar chart (Fig. 4-14). Try it again. Close the bar chart, drag the variable *Quantitative* into the substitute socket and press the **Plot It** button. A histogram should now be displayed on the screen.

4.13 *Dependencies*

Data Desk icons often use other icons. For example, plots use the variables they display. In general, results are computed from some underlying variables. In a scatterplot of income versus age, both of the variables *Income* and *Age* are used by the scatterplot. If either changes (for example, because you change a data value in one of the variables) the scatterplot will show the ❢ symbol and offer to update or redo in a new window.

REMEMBER

The {Special ▶ Locate} **Users of** command finds and selects the icons that directly use the currently selected icons.

Data Desk keeps track of the icons used by other icons so that all windows know whether the icons they use have changed. The {Special ▶ Locate} **Users of** command selects and locates all icons that use the selected icons, opening and scrolling icon windows if necessary to make them visible. Issue the command again to see the next level of use.

Similarly, {Special ▶ Locate} **Arguments of** selects and locates the icons of objects used by the selected icons. Issue the command again to see the next level of dependence. For example, selecting the HotResult variable's icon of regression residuals and choosing **Locate ▶ Arguments of** highlights the summary table of the regression that generated those residuals, and makes its icon visible. Locating arguments again (now for the regression summary table, which was selected) selects and locates the variables used in the regression analysis.

4.14 *Information Records*

Each icon has an *information record* that holds additional information

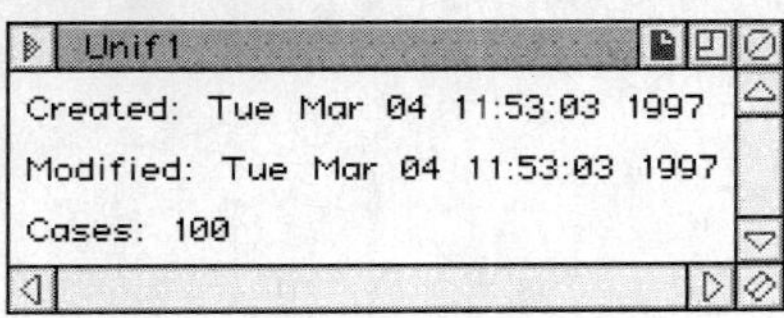

Figure 4-15. *The Info Dialog provides information about an icon in a window associated with that icon.*

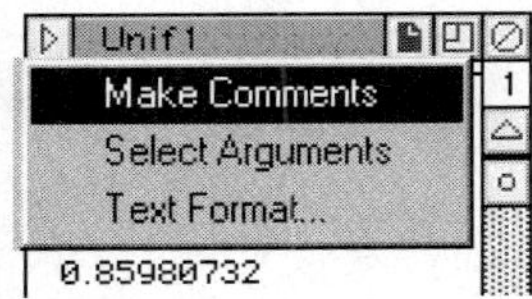

Figure 4-16. *To make notes about a variable, use the* ***Make Comments*** *command from the HyperView menu of the variable's window.*

about the icon. To see or alter the information record, select the icon and choose **Info...** from the **Data** menu. The information record displays information such as the date and time the icon was created, and the date and time its contents were last modified (Fig. 4-15). The date and time information help document the icon's history, but they depend upon the computer's built-in clock. You should be sure that the clock and calendar in your computer are set correctly.

Some icons, such as variables, also offer the opportunity to save comments about the icon. The icon window's global HyperView menu may hold either a **Make Comments** command (Fig. 4-16) or, if comments have already been saved, a **Show Comments** command. (We discussed HyperView menus in Section 4.2.) Comments are a good way to document a variable for future reference, leave a note to yourself or to others about changes, or just jot down a few reminders.

You can view the information for several variables at once by selecting all of their icons before choosing the **Info...** command.

4.15 *Multiple Relations*

A dataset with several relations is most interesting when you can work with them together. Relational database programs allow you to do so in a formal way. Some spreadsheet programs provide ways to link separate spreadsheets each of which can hold a relation. Data Desk performs simple operations on relations as natural point-and-click actions on the desktop.

Generally, variables that record values for the same individuals belong in the same relation. Variables that record values for other individuals belong in a different relation. For example, data on baseball would include several relations: one for hitters (whose batting and fielding performance are recorded), one for pitchers (because the variables reporting earned run average and games won are recorded only for pitchers), and one for data on teams (such as last year's attendance and finishing position in the standings).

We might have kept all the data in a single big relation, but then each hitter would have "missing" recorded for the variables recording pitching performance, and we would have to decide whether a pitcher's hitting performance should be recorded or set to "missing".

Thus, it is more efficient and natural to keep three separate relations and provide ways for one relation to look up data in another. For example, for each player we may want to look up his team's finishing position in the team relation. Data Desk provides basic facilities for looking up values across relations, and uses relations to provide a consistent organization for the data. We discuss these facilities in Chapter 11.

Conventional statistics programs deal with only one relation at a time, so the terminology of relations isn't common in statistics. However, the concepts are fundamental to all data analysis because they center your attention on the basic question, "Who has been sampled?" Data Desk uses relation structure to keep straight the possibly complex relationships among variables.

REMEMBER

Your datafile is vulnerable to errors and power failure only during a **Save** or **Quit.**

4.16 *Saving Datafiles*

Data Desk provides two commands for saving files — {File } **Save Datafile** and {File} **Save Datafile As....** The **Save Datafile As...** command saves the current version of the data, including any changes not yet recorded in the datafile, under a new name. The original datafile (under its original name) remains unchanged. The Save Datafile command has a slightly different behavior on Mac than on Windows.

MAC OS

The {File} **Save Datafile** command updates the open file to reflect any changes made since the last save. On Mac, Data Desk provides two methods for saving files when the **Save** command is chosen. The default method writes a completely new copy of the file, including any changes since the last save, to a new location on your disk. Once the new copy has been created, the old copy is deleted. This process requires space for at least two full copies of the file on your hard drive but protects against hardware failures during the save process. Because the original copy of the file isn't deleted until the new copy is created, Data Desk can always go back to the original file if the save procedure fails.

REMEMBER

The **Faster Save** option is faster and requires less disk space **BUT** IT CAN RESULT IN DAMAGE IF A HARDWARE FAILURE OCCURS DURING THE SAVE PROCESS.

The second **Save** method is called **Faster Save**. This option is selected in the Preferences dialog. If you select **Faster Save**, and the {File} **Save Datafile** command is invoked, Data Desk copies any changes into your datafile immediately. This process is faster and requires less disk space than the default save, *but it can result in damage to your datafile if a hardware failure occurs during the save.* Always be cautious when using the Faster Save option.

On Windows, the Save Datafile command makes changes directly to the file. The Faster Save preference does not change the behavior of the save command

TIP

When closing your datafile, type ⌘ **N** as a shortcut for "Don't Save" on Mac.

*No changes you make to your data or results you produce are saved permanently until you select the **Save Datafile** or **Save Datafile As...** command, or Quit, Exit on Windows, or Close and Save changes in the exit dialog.*

Despite the safety features built into Data Desk, *you should **always** keep a backup copy of any datafile that would take substantial time to recreate.* The safest backup copies are those preserved on another disk that is not in the computer. A disk placed safely on a shelf cannot be harmed by any computer failure. That is the *only* full guarantee against disk damage resulting from power failures, physical shocks, or unanticipated interactions among programs.

REMEMBER

***Always* keep a backup copy of your data.**

4.17 *Compacting Files*

REMEMBER

No changes you make are saved permanently until you **Save Datafile**, **Save Datafile As....**, or **Exit** (**Quit** on Mac) or **Close** (and Save changes).

Data Desk datafiles hold a great deal of information in addition to your data. Data files often hold displays, tables, and other results of analyses, derived variables and other computations, and all the information necessary to link these objects. This linking provides fundamental Data Desk features such as brushing among all displays, updating of analyses and displays when data change, dynamic plot animations in response to sliders, and the propagation of missing values so that subsidiary analyses are computed on appropriate data subsets. Data Desk often saves intermediate information (for example, residuals or other hot results, or the results of evaluating a derived variable expression) that could be reconstructed from the underlying analyses. Saving these intermediate values speeds Data Desk's response to your requests at the expense of increasing the size of the datafile.

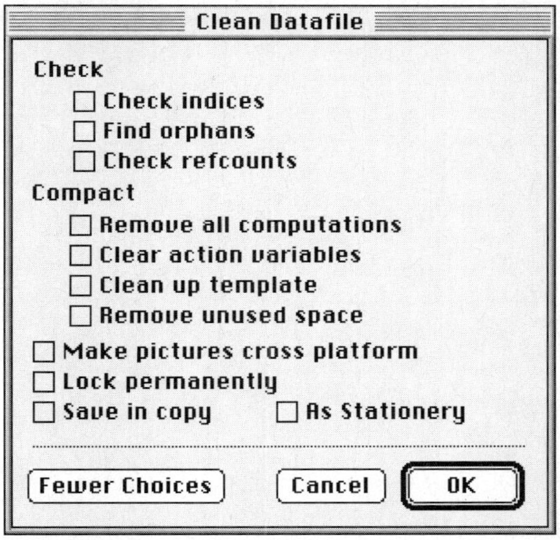

Clean Datafile

Check
- Check indices
- Find orphans
- Check refcounts

Compact
- Remove all computations
- Clear action variables
- Clean up template
- Remove unused space

- Make pictures cross platform
- Lock permanently
- Save in copy
- As Stationery

Fewer Choices | Cancel | OK

Figure 4-17. *The* ***Clean Datafile*** *command offers detailed options. You can select detailed steps rather than the full check and archive.*

Occasionally, errors can arise in the linkages among Data Desk objects. Usually these errors have little consequence, but they should be repaired if possible. The **Clean Datafile** command in the **File** menu offers three options. The first, **Complete Check**, (the default selection), finds and repairs any inconsistencies in the file's data structures. It also finds and deletes any objects that are no longer used by the file. If your datafile seems to be behaving strangely, if you suspect a problem, or if you have an old or especially complex file, it is a good idea to run a **Complete Check**.

Clean Datafile also offers the option of **Save Archived Copy**. **Save Archived Copy** performs a **Complete Check** and then removes information that can be reconstructed. For example, **Save Archived Copy** will remove the computed values of a HotResult or derived variable because these can be reconstructed from their formulas. When the values are needed again, Data Desk will automatically recompute them, which may cause an uncharacteristic delay. Nevertheless, **Save Archived Copy** can compact the size of a datafile dramatically. Some datafiles can be compacted by 50% or more. When an archived file is used, you may notice delays each time you call for values that must be recomputed. As they are computed, they are saved, so Data Desk's responsiveness will soon return to normal (and the file will grow in size). It is a good idea to create an archived copy of a file before distributing it to other Data Desk users, or when you plan to store it for a while without using it and want to save disk space.

You must save the file before creating the archived copy. **Save Archived Copy** saves the archived version in a new file named '<filename> (Archived)' and keeps the original file open.

APPENDIX 4A *Hints and Shortcuts*

In this appendix we discuss ways in which you can improve your efficiency when using Data Desk. It also offers tips for making Data Desk work more efficiently.

KEYBOARD SHORTCUTS

Many commands in Data Desk can be issued by holding down the Ctrl key, command key on Mac (marked with a ⌘) and pressing another key. These keyboard shortcuts appear next to the commands in the menu. For example, the **Undo**, **Cut**, **Copy**, and **Paste** commands in the **Edit** menu can be issued with ⌘-Z, ⌘-X, ⌘-C, and ⌘-V on Mac, respectively, or Ctrl Z, Ctrl X, Ctrl C, and Ctrl V on Windows.

RENAMING AND THROWING AWAY WINDOWS

To rename a window quickly, press the right mouse button, or ⌘ key on Mac, click on the title bar and choose the **Rename Window** command. To throw away a window quickly, press the right mouse button, or the ⌘ key on Mac, click in the Close box and choose the **Throw Away** command.

TAB AND ENTER

Whenever a dialog has an **OK** button or an outlined button, pressing Enter or Return on Mac, is equivalent to pressing that button.

In dialogs that ask you to type something, Tab skips to the next item to be typed, so you need not remove your hands from the keyboard. Tab also advances to the next icon to the right when you are editing icon names on the Data Desk Desktop.

DRAGGING SEVERAL ICONS AT ONCE

To drag several icons at once, select them, pick up any of them, and drag. A gray outline shows the icons gathered under the mouse arrow. You can drag several icons into another icon window, the icon of another window, or the trash icon — even if they come from different windows. You can drag icons into a relation window only if they have the right number of cases to conform to that relation. And don't forget, you can always drag the icons of variables into tables and plots to add or replace variables.

KEEPING DISK FILES SMALL

Disk operations slow down as datafiles grow and as free space on the disk is used up. It is always a good idea to discard unused or unnecessary icons and unneeded files. You must empty the Trash to recover the disk space. Even then, Data Desk will recover the disk space only if it seems necessary. Doing a **Save Datafile As...** or **Save Datafile** and then a **Close Datafile** forces space recovery. The **Clean Datafile** command, discussed in Section 4.17, provides significant data compaction.

PROGRESS REPORTING

When commands show a rotating cursor while they compute, you can press the Esc key, or ⌘-period on Mac, to abort the operation. Pressing the Esc key, or ⌘-period on Mac, also aborts some other operations even when no rotating cursor is visible.

Several of the more time-consuming commands provide visual feedback in the form of a count-down "clock" or "thermometer" that appears below the File Cabinet icon on the Data Desk Desktop.

Stopping Plot Animation

To stop a rotating plot or a slider that has been pushed while the Shift key is held down and is thus continuing to slide, press the Space bar or click anywhere in the window.

Important Warnings

Never work with the original Data Desk disk. *Always* copy the disk first and work with the copy. It is very tempting to "just try out the program once," but please take the time to protect your investment by making a backup copy.

Never work with the original copy of any important datafile. *Always* copy the datafile first and work with the copy. Despite the precautions taken by Data Desk, there is always a risk, as with any program, that a failure could damage your datafile. The only safe datafile is one that is on a disk in a safe location (that is, not in the computer). For additional safety, you should keep two or three copies of any important datafile (the latest version, the one before that, and the one before *that*) on separate disks.

Appendix 4B *Hot, Warm, and Cold Objects*

Some Data Desk objects and windows change instantly to reflect changes in other windows, such as changes in data values, changes in expressions, or changes in a plot. Others offer to update, but do not change until you specifically request the change. Still other objects change only when you change them directly. In common computer interface parlance, these are *hot*, *warm*, and *cold* responses to changes, respectively.

Data Desk balances among hot, warm, and cold responses to give you the greatest flexibility in analyzing your data while minimizing the chance that you will inadvertently analyze the wrong version of the data. This appendix discusses the specific assignment of updating methods.

Cold Objects

Cold objects are the bedrock of your analysis. In many ways they define what you are working with. In Data Desk, the fundamental cold objects are variables and expressions. The only way to change your data is to edit it explicitly. No format changes to plots or tables can affect the underlying data.

Similarly, the expressions in derived variables that define their structure can be changed only by explicitly editing them. There is a distinction between the defining *expression*, which is an algebraic formula, and the *values* generated by evaluating the expression, which are numbers or text for each case.

Hot Objects

Hot updating is common in spreadsheets, where a change in one cell instantly changes others. It has the advantage that the relationship between two objects with a hot connection appears to be almost a physical link. It has the disadvantage that the updating can occur before you have a chance to look at it, so you may miss seeing the change and lose the ability to compare "before" and "after" views or the freedom to decide not to make the change.

In Data Desk, derived variable *values* are always hot. Any change in the values of variables used in a derived variable expression immediately changes the values generated by the derived variable. This action reflects the basic concept of a derived variable as a function of other variables. For example, it is hard to conceive of changing an income value without instantly changing the corresponding value of *log* (*Income*).

By maintaining a hot link between the basic underlying data values and the values generated by evaluating derived variable expressions, Data Desk reduces the chance that you might correct a data value but forget to correct calculations that depend upon it.

Several operations on plots are hot. For example, the selection of data points immediately selects those points in all other plots and editing windows, which makes brushing and slicing possible. (In Chapter 9 we discuss ways to work with plots.) The assignment of plot symbols or colors immediately changes the plot symbol or color of the corresponding points in all plots. Hot links such as these help to preserve the impression that different plots are showing different views of the same data.

Warm Objects

Data Desk extends the usual dichotomy of hot or cold links to include warm links. Warm links *offer* to recompute as soon as you change the underlying data or expressions, but they actually recompute only when you tell them to. Warm links are primarily part of the HyperView menu links among windows. Changing data values in a variable or the formula in a derived variable immediately notifies all analyses and plots that depend upon those values or formulas that they may want to recompute. The analyses and plots then display a ❢ symbol in their windows to alert you that they no longer reflect the current state of the data.

Click on the ❢ symbol to see a HyperView menu that offers to update the window in place or to redo the calculation or drawing in another window. Redo is offered so that you can easily compare the "before" and "after" views of the analysis — and is often the best choice.

Warm links have the advantage that you can observe the consequences of editing the data or formulas and that you need not suffer those consequences if you do not choose to. In fact, you may choose to update only some of your plots and tables.

Many windows offer an **Automatic Update** command in the HyperView menu to allow you to change from warm linking to hot linking. When a window is hot, its global HyperView menu is gray.

APPENDIX 4D *Data Desk Limits*

Data Desk adapts dynamically to the size and configuration of the computer on which it is running. As a result, it is difficult to define the limits of the program exactly. In this technical appendix, we describe some of these limits as precisely as possible. The guides given here should be taken as "rules of thumb" rather than as absolute limits, unless a specific limit is specified.

MEMORY

Data Desk requires at least 1MB of RAM. Data Desk manages memory dynamically, trading space among program, data, and results. If you are working with large datafiles - especially one with many cases, you may want to increase Data Desk's memory allocation to more than 1 MB. On the Mac, to allocate additional memory, select Data Desk's icon on the Finder's desktop, choose {File} **Get Info**, and type a larger number into the "Preferred size" box. Data Desk tries to alert you when memory is tight.

If you notice that your disk drive is very active during a Data Desk calculation, that is a sign that Data Desk lacks sufficient room in memory for all of your data and is moving data in and out of memory. You can speed up calculations by giving Data Desk more memory.

VARIABLES

Each *Data Desk Student Version 6.0* datafile is limited to 50 variables. The limit is imposed when saving the file. During a session you may generate and use any number of variables.

CASES

Variables created in the *Data Desk Student Version 6.0* can have up to 1000 cases.

WINDOWS

Data Desk can open as many windows as memory allows. However, it is a good idea to clean up your desktop occasionally.

CHAPTER 5

Entering and Editing Data

DATA DESK'S VARIABLES are always immediately available. You can read, type, copy, or paste new data values at any time. In this chapter we discuss data entry and editing. In Data Desk there is no difference between the two. You view, edit, alter, and correct data in exactly the same way as you type in new data. These methods closely resemble the methods you probably already know for entering and editing text in a text processor or numbers and equations in a spreadsheet.

Most statistics are computed on numbers, but variables may hold ordinary text as well. For example, a variable might hold the name of each respondent in a survey or the name of each sales region in a set of sales data. Some data are best represented as words; for example "male" and "female" for a variable recording gender. Data Desk lets you mix numbers and text freely in a variable.

Many of Data Desk's commands operate only on numbers and expect variables to hold numbers. For example, it is impossible to average "rich," "middle class," and "poor," but it is natural to average incomes recorded in dollars. Other commands recognize text — usually to identify different groups or categories of cases. Commands that expect numbers treat nonnumeric data values as if they were missing observations.

Although Data Desk's full data editing capabilities are very powerful, basic data entry and editing are quite simple. If you are just beginning to learn Data Desk, you may want to read only selected sections of this chapter and then work with data imported from other sources (see Chapter 6) or with the example datasets. You can learn basic skills easily and add to them as you go.

At the beginning of this chapter we describe data entry and editing operations. In the final two sections we present examples. You may want to turn to the example as you read the descriptive sections, and even work through parts of the example to see how the operations work.

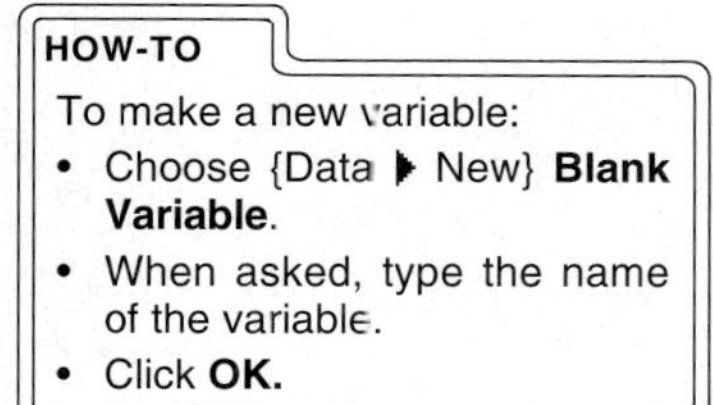

5.1 *Entering Data for One Variable*

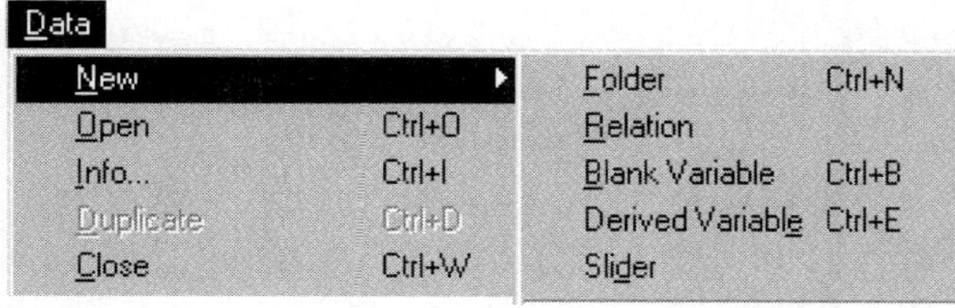

Figure 5-1. *To create a variable choose {Data ▸ New}* ***Blank Variable.***

To create a variable, choose {Data ▸New} **Blank Variable** (Fig. 5-1.). Data Desk displays a dialog requesting a name for the variable.

Type a name for the variable and click the **OK** button. You can rename the variable at any time. Data Desk appends the icon of the new variable to the frontmost relation window and opens it to show an editing window. The new blank variable has as many cases as are in its relation, but each case is blank. If there is no open relation window, Data Desk creates a new relation that has no cases, names it *Data,* puts its icon in the *Data* folder in the File Cabinet, and puts the new variable's icon in that relation.

To enter data, type values one row at a time, ending each row by pressing the Enter key (on Mac the Return key also works). You can make the

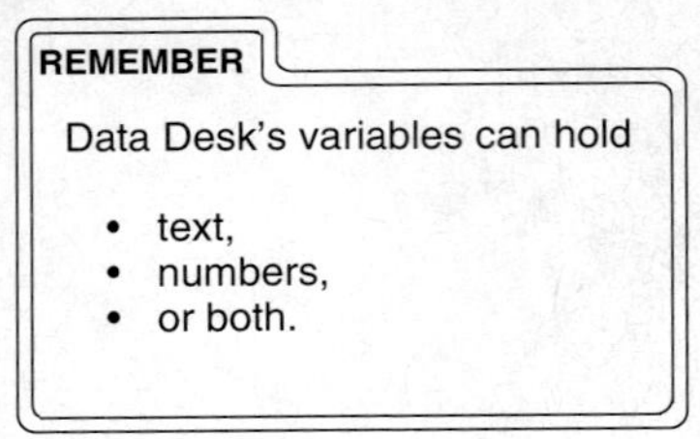

window wider by dragging the Size box to the right, or make it longer by dragging the Size box downward or by clicking the Zoom box. As you type, you replace the old blank cases or, if you're at the bottom of the variable window, you append new cases to the relation.

When you are done typing, click the Close box or choose {Data} **Close Window**. The editing window closes into the variable's icon.

5.2 *Editing a Variable*

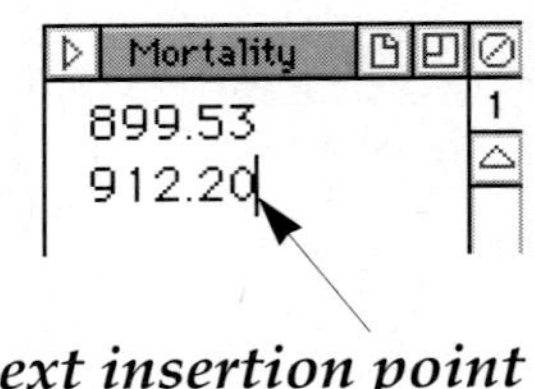

text insertion point

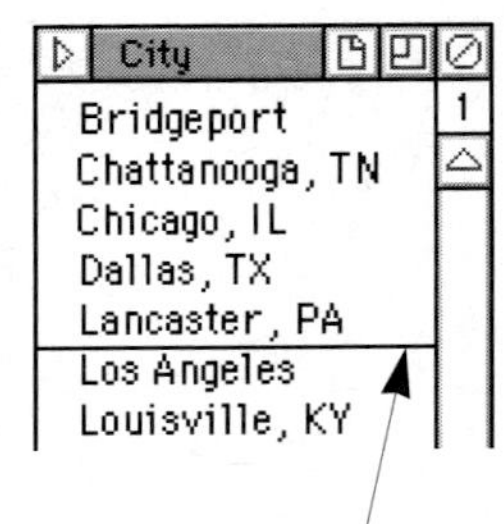

case insertion point

Whenever a text editing window is frontmost, anything typed is either inserted in the window at the vertical blinking *text insertion point* or replaces text that is selected. The Backspace key deletes the character before the insertion point or the entire highlighted selection.

To alter a single value in a variable, edit it with the standard data editing methods. Click between two characters in the text of a case to place a text insertion point between them or drag across characters to select them. Type or paste to insert text at the blinking cursor or to replace the selected text.

Data Desk extends these conventions to data cases. Thus, to insert a case between two other cases, click between the cases to place a horizontal blinking *case insertion point* ⟝⟞ between those cases. Type or paste text to start a new case at that point.

You can drag up or down across several cases to select them. If you drag off the top or bottom of a window, it scrolls automatically and selects cases as they become visible. Type or paste text to replace all the selected cases and begin inserting new cases at that point. Press Enter to begin a new case.

You can tell whether a click will place a vertical or horizontal insertion point by the orientation of the mouse cursor. A vertical "I-beam" (I) places the vertical text insertion point, and a horizontal "cross-beam" (⟝⟞) places a horizontal case insertion point. As you move the mouse up and down along the cases in a variable, the cursor alternates between these two shapes.

5.3 *Extended and Discontinuous Selection*

To select a range of text, click at one end of the text and then hold down the Shift key and click at the other end of the text. Shift-clicks extend text selections in editing windows in the same way that they extend icon selection in an icon window.

You can also extend a selection of cases with a shift-click. Click at one end of the range of cases and then shift-click at the other end. All the cases between the two clicks will be selected.

discontinuous selection

Data Desk offers an additional case editing feature that is not commonly available for text but is available in some spreadsheets. Press the right mouse button on windows, or the ⌘ key on Mac, then click on any case to add it to the set of selected cases. The intervening cases don't get selected. This type of *discontinuous selection* provides many powerful

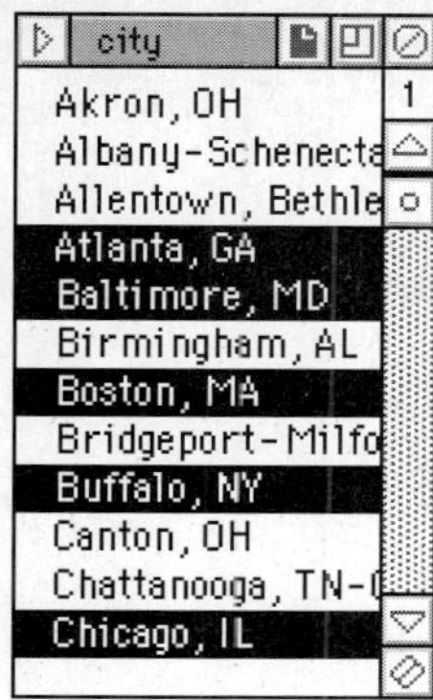

Figure 5-2. *Discontinuous selection.*

capabilities. Discontinuous selections can also arise from a **Find** command (see Section 5.13) or from selecting cases in plots (see Section 9.4).

Discontinuous case selections do not correspond directly to standard text editing. When you edit text, there can be only one continuous selection, so you always know exactly which parts of the text will change when you type or paste. When cases are selected discontinuously (Fig. 5-2), you no longer know where typed or pasted text should go. Consequently, you may not type or paste. A discontinuous selection may spread across many cases, so that some of the selected cases have scrolled out of view. If you cannot type or paste into your variable editing windows, it might be because what appears to be a simple continuous case selection is in fact part of a discontinuous selection with other selected cases scrolled beyond the screen. Try again to select the cases you wish to replace.

You can cut, copy, or clear discontinuous cases, *but you can't undo the operation.* Cut or copied cases form a data table on the clipboard and can be pasted elsewhere in the variable windows, pasted directly into an icon window as variables, or moved to another program from the clipboard. (In Chapter 6 we describe importing, exporting, and data tables.)

5.4 *Editing Several Variables*

You may want to edit several variables together. You can open variables from different relations at the same time, but it makes sense only to edit together variables from the same relation. Because all the variables in a relation refer to the same cases, if your editing deletes, adds, or changes the order of any cases, those changes affect the entire relation — both the variables that are open and those that are not.

> **TIP**
>
> Windows "remember" where they were before.
>
> Hold the Shift key down while opening variable windows to make them align.

Usually, when you open two or more variables they are arrayed neatly across the screen. You can force variable windows to align in such a table by holding down the Shift key while opening them. Editing windows for variables in the same relation scroll together so that the same case number is at the top of each window. As long as the windows are aligned, each row across all open windows in the relation represents a case in that relation. You can align data editing windows that are already open with the {Special ▶Arrange} **Align Editing Windows** command, but the command only shifts windows up and down, so you must first place them in the desired horizontal position.

5.5 *Entering Several Variables*

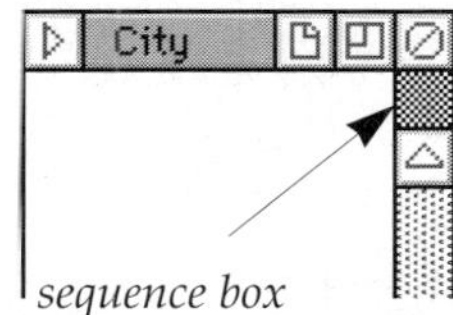

editing sequence

It is best to enter data one case at a time, moving along a row extending across several variables. You can create or open as many variables as you want Their windows may overlap, and you may resize them as necessary.

The Tab key moves the text insertion point to the next variable. The *Sequence box* in the upper right corner of the window, at the top of the scroll bar, specifies the order of the variables in the *editing sequence.* A variable whose Sequence box is gray is not in the editing sequence, and will be skipped over by the Tab key. If the sequence box holds a num-

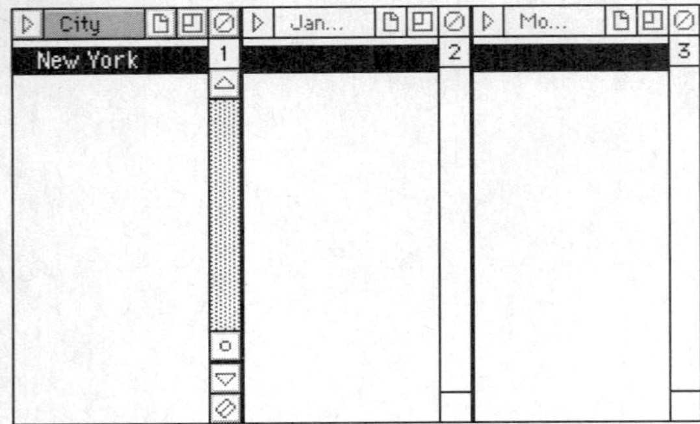

Figure 5-3. Sequenced variable editing windows.

ber, this number specifies the place of the window in the editing sequence (Fig. 5-3.). To add an editing window to the end of the sequence, click that variable window's sequence box.

If none of your variable windows have a number on the Sequence box, you need to create an editing sequence before you can begin to edit or enter data. Click the Sequence box of each variable window that you want to include in the sequence in the order you want them included in the sequence.

Ordinarily, Data Desk adds newly opened editing windows to the end of the editing sequence. To remove a window from the editing sequence, click on the Sequence box; it will turn gray. The {Special ▶ Sequence} **Clear Editing Sequence** command clears the entire editing sequence. The {Special ▶ Sequence} **Remove From Sequence** command removes the frontmost window from the editing sequence.

All variables in the editing sequence must be in the same relation. If a newly opened variable isn't added to the editing sequence, check to be sure that it is in the same relation as the variables in the editing sequence. Data Desk objects if you try to add a variable from a different relation to the existing editing sequence.

HOW-TO

To move to the next variable in the editing sequence,

- press Tab.

To start a new case,

- press Enter.

When variable editing windows are sequenced, the Tab key advances to the next window in the sequence at the current case. You can always tell which variable you are editing because its window is active. Thus you can type a value in the first variable, press Tab, and type the value for the same case in the second variable, press Tab, and type the value for the third variable, and so on.

Variable editing windows that aren't in the editing sequence are skipped over by the Tab key. If they are in the same relation, they still scroll with the other variable windows and are still affected by copying, cutting, clearing, and pasting cases.

TIP

If variables don't join the editing sequence, look for an open variable from another relation, establishing *that* relation as the one with the editing sequence. Close the other variable to make a new sequence in another relation.

You can also enter data values one variable at a time. Create each variable in turn by choosing {Data ▶ New} **Blank Variable.** *Be sure that the cursor is at the top of the variable and is flashing vertically, I, before you begin typing.* If you don't, your cases may become unaligned. After you enter a value, you can press the Enter or Return key, or use the down arrow, to move to the next entry. If you use the Enter or Return key on a Mac, be sure to define the actions of these keys in the Preferences dialog, found in the **Edit** menu, to replace the next row.

5.6 *Moving Around*

Pressing the Enter key, and on Mac, the Return key, returns the cursor to the first variable of the editing sequence and makes its window active. These keys either select the next case for editing or place a case insertion point after the current case. The **Preferences...** command in the **Edit** menu lets you choose which it should do.

The Tab key always moves to the next variable in the editing sequence. Usually, it selects the value at the same case for editing. However, if the text entry point is in the last variable of the editing sequence or in an unsequenced variable window, Tab "beeps" and then behaves like Return.

Mac OS

On a Mac, in addition to Tab and Return, you may want to use the Enter key, which is on the numeric keypad. The {Edit} **Preferences...** command lets you specify whether the Enter key should work like the Tab key or like the Return key.

In addition to using Tab, Return and Enter as editing keys, Data Desk supports the cursor control (arrow) keys found on many keyboards. The ↑ and ↓ keys move to the previous and subsequent *case* in the current editing window, respectively, selecting the entire case for editing. The ← and → keys move to the previous and subsequent *variable* in the editing sequence, respectively, and stays at the same case.

Of course, you can always place an insertion point anywhere by simply pointing and clicking or by selecting an entire value by pointing and double-clicking.

5.7 *Cutting, Copying, and Pasting*

The **Cut**, **Copy**, and **Paste** commands in the **Edit** menu work the way they do in most applications, except that they also operate on selected cases in variable windows. When operating on cases rather than on characters in text, these commands read **Cut Cases**, **Copy Cases**, and **Paste Cases**.

HOW-TO

To move cases from one place to another:

- Select the cases to be moved. They may be discontinuous.
- **Copy cases**.
- Click between two cases.
- **Paste Cases**.

The **Cut Cases** and **Paste Cases** commands operate on the entire relation. If you cut cases from one or more variables, those cases are removed from the entire relation. If you paste cases into one or more variables, extra cases (filled with blanks) are created in the other variables in the relation. It is easy to move cases around in a relation by cutting them from one place and pasting them into another. You can work in a single variable; when you do, cases in the entire relation will be reordered.

The Cut Cases and Copy Cases commands can also be used to place selected cases from Data Desk onto the clipboard. Only cases from variables in the editing sequence are placed on the clipboard. The editing sequence serves to specify the order of the cases. The case values form a data table and are separated by the *data table delimiter.* In Section 6.3 we discuss this delimiter and show how to set it.

5.8 *Details of Editing*

To edit variables, you must first open them. To correct a case, scroll the variable windows until the case appears. The vertical scroll bar in a variable window moves the text up and down to reveal other cases. Data Desk keeps rows aligned across all variables in the relation. Whenever one variable scrolls up or down, all variables in the relation scroll together. Even if some windows are short and squat and others are tall and thin, the *top* line of every variable window in the relation always displays data for the same case in each variable.

If you know the case number, the {Edit ▸ Go To...} **Case #...** command will get you there quickly. If you know the data value, the {Edit} **Find...** commands may help. If you selected the case in a plot the {Edit ▸ Go

To...} **Top Selected Case** scrolls the window to show the case. Select the value that you want to change and type the correct value. To alter only a few characters, backspace over them or drag across them and type their replacement. To insert new characters, click where they should be inserted and type. To correct more than one data item in the case, press Tab to move the insertion point to the next variable at the same case.

If you select text in one variable, the corresponding cases in all the other opened variables are selected. To replace a value in any open variable, make that variable active (frontmost) and type the new value. To deselect them, click anywhere in a variable or a plot window.

To delete one or more cases, select them by dragging the cross-beam cursor, ⟼, in any variable editing window; the cases highlight in all linked variable editing windows. Press the Delete or Backspace key to delete the cases.

To insert a new case in the middle of the data, click in the first variable editing window in the editing sequence between the two cases where the new case should be inserted. Type the first value of the new case and press the Tab key. Type the new value for the second variable and press the Tab key to proceed to the third variable.

To continue inserting new cases conveniently, use the **Preferences...** command to set the Enter key, and the Return key on a Mac, to start a new case rather than moving to the next case. Then pressing Enter (or Tab at the end of the case) will start a new case.

5.9 *Undo*

Most of Data Desk's editing operations can be reversed with the **Undo** command in the **Edit** menu. This includes reversing the deletion of cases across several variables. You can undo only the previous operation. The **Undo** command changes to indicate the kind of operation that can be undone or to report that it **Can't Undo**.

If you choose **Undo**, you can then choose to **Redo**. The menu will specify the action that can be taken. The **Undo** command works even if some windows have been closed since the original operation.

5.10 *Managing Windows*

active window

When many variables are open at once, the screen can become cluttered. The *active window* — that is, the one that will be affected by typing — is the one with a darkened title bar. It is in front of any other windows that may overlap it (except palette windows) and usually has an insertion point in it or some text highlighted for replacement.

Often variable editing windows are positioned neatly on the screen and the top left one is the first in the editing sequence. However, you may reposition and resize editing windows as you like. For example, you may have variable editing windows large enough to cover most of the screen. You might then position them as a stack of windows and use Tab to move to the next window in the stack.

REMEMBER

Variable editing windows must be in the editing sequence for the Tab key to move from one to the next. To add a window to the editing sequence click its sequence box.

No matter what the actual position of variable editing windows on the screen, the editing sequence (see Section 5.5), not the windows' positions, defines the actions of Tab and Return.

A window that is in the current relation but is not part of the editing sequence can be very useful. Such a window might hold case identifiers such as the names of the individuals in the dataset or simply the sequence numbers from one to the total number of data values. Case identification windows help you to be certain that the data you are typing is correct for the case in which you are typing. Because Tab skips over windows not in the editing sequence, you can enter or edit data without having to work past the identification window.

5.11 *Shifting Cases*

TIP

To make a lagged variable:
- Duplicate a variable.
- Open the duplicate.
- Select same number of cases that you want to lag.
- Choose **Shift Cases Down** from the **Edit** menu.

TIP

You can also lag a variable with the *Lag* function in a derived variable expression.

See Chapter 11 for information about derived variables.

You can alter the case alignment across variables with the **Shift Cases Up** and **Shift Cases Down** commands in the **Edit** menu. **Shift Cases Up** and **Shift Cases Down** shift the cases in the variable editing windows in the editing sequence. If the frontmost window isn't in the editing sequence, it alone is shifted. Shifting realigns variables that may have become misaligned and can create "lagged" variables. Both shift commands expect a continuous range of cases to be selected.

Shift Cases Up deletes the selected cases in the frontmost window and shifts the remaining cases up to fill the hole. Blank cases are appended to the end of the variable to preserve its length.

Shift Cases Down shifts downward all cases from the first selected case through the last case in the data, opening a gap of blank cases in the variable. You indicate how large a gap you want by *the number of cases that you select*. Thus, to open a gap of two blank cases, select two cases and choose **Shift Cases Down**. The two blank cases are inserted just above the selected cases. Cases shifted past the end of the variable are deleted from the bottom to preserve its length. (To make a variable longer relative to other open variables, put it in its own new relation and insert new cases by typing or pasting.)

5.12 *More on Linking*

Data Desk is a highly integrated data analysis environment. One important aspect of this integration is that case selection operates simultaneously in all plot and variable editing windows in a relation. That is, selecting a case in a variable editing window highlights corresponding parts of plots. Selecting a point in a plot selects the corresponding case in any variable editing windows. You can work with both plots and variable editing windows together to identify and edit cases.

For example, to find out more about a plotted point, select it in the plot and open an appropriate variable. The case will be selected for editing. (The {Edit ▸ Go To...} **Next Selected Case** command gets you there quickly.) If one of your variables holds names or other case identifiers, you can open it, select cases in a plot, and {Edit} **Copy Cases** from the identifying variable to place a list of the case names on the clipboard.

You can then paste this list into a ScratchPad or into a report you may be writing with another program.

For example, you might select the best performers on some measure in a plot, open the variable holding case names, copy cases, type in a ScratchPad "The best performers are:", and paste their names into your text.

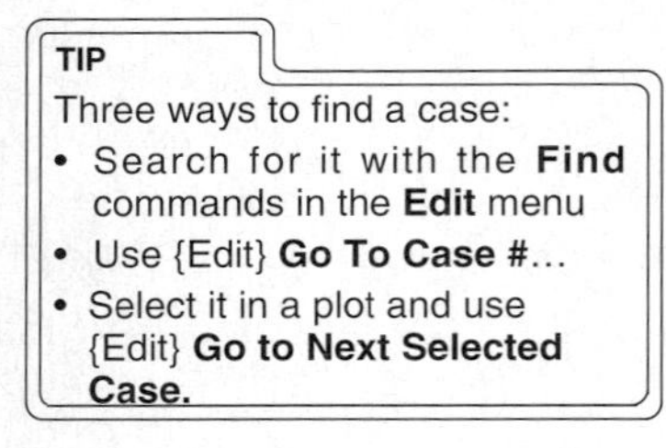
TIP

Three ways to find a case:

- Search for it with the **Find** commands in the **Edit** menu
- Use {Edit} **Go To Case #...**
- Select it in a plot and use {Edit} **Go to Next Selected Case.**

You can use variable windows to identify points selected in a plot. Select a group of points in a scatterplot (see Chapter 9 for details on selection in plots) and see them highlighted in a variable containing case identifiers. You can also use the {Edit} **Find** command to select cases that match particular text in a variable; they will highlight in all plots as well.

5.13 *Finding and Replacing Cases*

The **Find...** and **Go To...** commands in the **Edit** menu (Fig. 5-4) locate cases in the frontmost open variable editing window. The **Find...** and **Go To...** commands are grouped into submenus of related commands. Together they offer elementary data management and editing functions to help you work with your data.

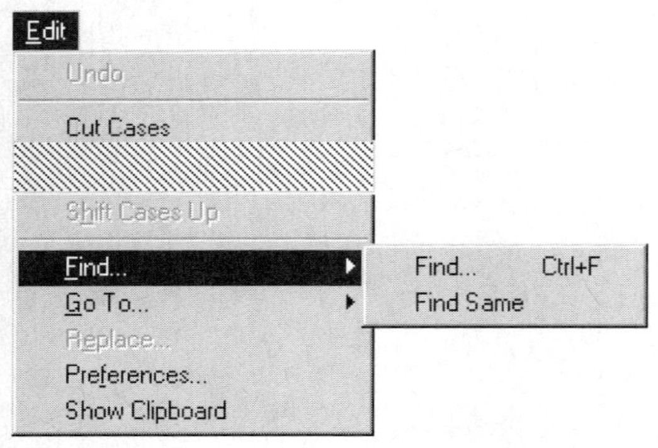

*Figure 5-4. The **Find** commands are in the **Find** submenu*

Find... prompts for the text to find (Fig. 5-5). According to the setting in the dialog, it either finds all occurrences of the specified text or finds the first occurrence of the text *after the current insertion point.* It selects either any occurrence of the text string in each cell or restricts itself to looking for the whole word in each cell.

The **Find next nonnumeric case** option locates cases that are not numbers and would be treated as missing values in a calculation. It is particularly helpful for finding typographical errors.

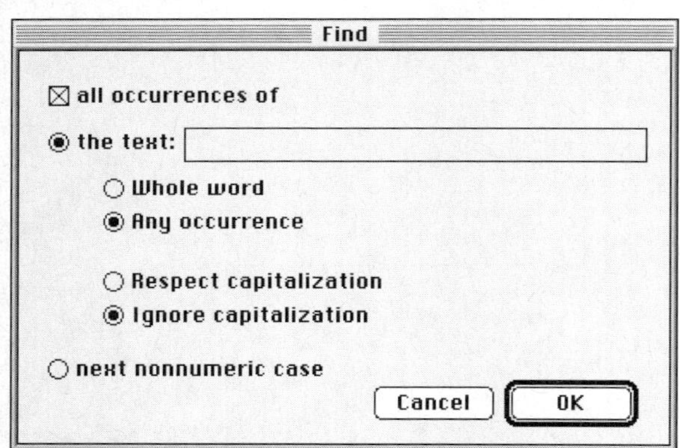

*Figure 5-5. The **Find** dialog offers several searching options.*

Find Same moves to the next case that matches the search criteria most recently specified, but does not prompt for new text or settings. It remains active only while there is text to find.

The **Go To...** submenu contains commands that help you step through cases.

Because cases can be selected easily in any plot or editing window, it is common to have many discontinuous cases selected. Most of the **Go To...** commands help you to look through the selected cases. The **Go To...** commands are:

- **Go To Next Selected Case**
- **Go To Previous Selected Case**
- **Go To Top Selected Case**
- **Go To Bottom Selected Case**
- **Go To Case #...**

The **Go To Case #...** command locates a case by its case or row number. The other Go To... commands step through selected cases either forward or backward.

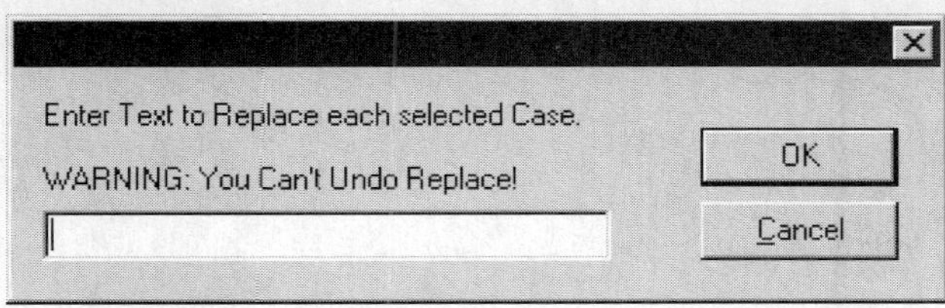

Figure 5-6. *The Replace dialog asks for text that will replace each selected case in the front editing window.*

The **Replace...** command in the **Edit** menu prompts for text and replaces *each* selected case in the frontmost window with that text (Fig. 5-6).

Replace overwrites entire cases, not parts of the text in cases. The **Replace** command isn't active unless at least one case is selected. It isn't active if you have selected only some of the text of a case. Drag vertically across a case to be sure that it is selected.

Because the **Replace** command replaces all selected cases in the frontmost window, it provides a way to *recode* data. You can find all cases satisfying some criteria and then replace them with the new value. You can also recode by identifying cases in a suitable plot and replacing them in a variable. Alternatively, you can create a new variable and use **Replace** to recode its (empty) cases to the codes you choose. Another alternative is to recode data with the IF, THEN, ELSE commands and logical operators of derived variables (see Chapter 11).

5.14 *Printing Variables*

To print a variable's contents, select its icon and choose {Manip} **Make Variable Table.** Data Desk displays variables in a Table with each variable's name at the top of its column Now choose {File} **Print**. Choose landscape orientation with the {File} **Page Setup** command to fit more columns on a page.

You must have a printer driver installed for these commands to work. (Refer to the operating manuals for your printer.)

In Chapter 6 we discuss other ways of printing and saving windows in Data Desk.

5.15 *Example: Entering Data*

Data entry and editing are easy to learn by example. If you know how to edit text using a text editor, you will find that editing data in Data Desk uses all the standard text editing conventions and extends them to include the editing of cases across several variable editing windows and the manipulation of discontinuous case selections.

The step-by-step example given here shows a data entry and editing session. You can work along with the example doing each of the things suggested and matching the figures against how your screen looks.

At any step in the example you can save your work. The first time you save (with the {File} **Save Datafile...** command) Data Desk will ask you to name the datafile. To resume work at a later time, open the saved datafile. The windows on the desktop will reopen automatically to the places they occupied when you saved the file.

(1) To start the example, open Data Desk. Choose {Data ▶ New} **Blank Variable**.

Data Desk asks you to name the first variable (Fig. 5-7). Name it *City*.

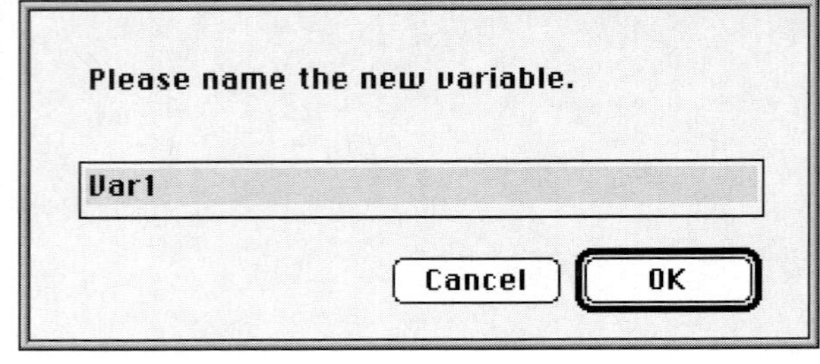

Figure 5-7. Data Desk asks you to name the new variable.

Data Desk creates a new relation, names it Data, places the icon of the new variable in the relation, and opens it for editing (Fig. 5-8).

Figure 5-8*. The variable* City *is opened and becomes the frontmost window.*

(2) Create more variables to hold the data. Choose {Data ▸New} **Blank Variable** and name it *Jan Temp*. Data Desk places *Jan Temp* in the same relation, next to *City*.

(3) Press Ctrl+B (⌘–B on a Mac) to create another new blank variable. Name this variable *Mortality*.

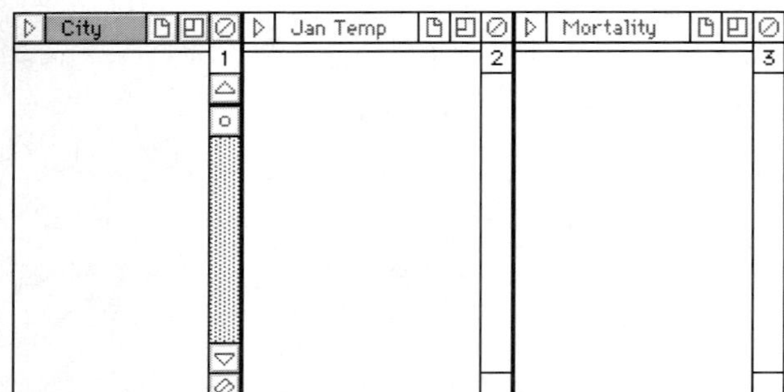

Figure 5-9. *The* Jan Temp *and* Mortality *variables.*

The editing windows should now look like those shown in Fig. 5-9.

As each variable is created it is automatically added to the editing sequence. The editing sequence numbers at the top of the vertical scroll bars specify the order of the windows for the Tab key and for copying or pasting cases.

(4) Point to *City* and click anywhere in the window. The title bar of the City window highlights, and a flashing horizontal case insertion point appears at the top of the window to indicate that this position is where the new case will appear.

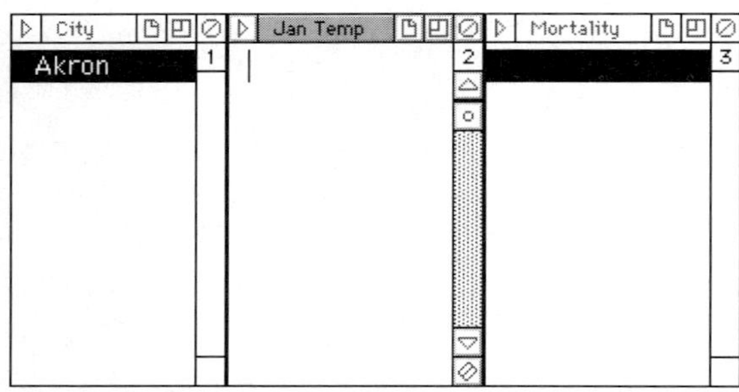

Figure 5-10. *Akron highlighted with insertion point at second window.*

(5) Type the name of the first city: Akron. If you make a mistake, backspace and correct it. As soon as you start typing, Data Desk creates a new case in these three variables and makes room for it in the windows. The new case is highlighted across all three windows and the cursor changes to a vertical blinking bar where you are typing (Fig. 5-10).

(6) Press Tab to move the insertion point to the second window, which now becomes active. Its title bar highlights and the flashing bar indicates that you can type its first case.

(7) Type Akron's January temperature: –2.78. (The temperatures are in degrees Celsius.)

(8) Press Tab to move to the *Mortality* window, and type Akron's age-adjusted mortality rate: 921.87.

(9) Press Enter, or Return on a Mac, to return to the City window to place a case insertion point after the case just typed. When you start typ-

City	Jan...	Mo...
Akron	-2.78	921.87
Albany	-5.00	997.87
Allentown	-1.67	962.35
Atlanta	7.22	982.29
Baltimore	1.67	1071.29
Birmingham	7.22	1030.38
Boston	-1.11	934.70
Bridgeport	-1.11	899.53
Chatinooga	5.56	1017.61
Chicago	-3.33	1024.89

Figure 5-11. *Data for 10 cities.*

ing the name of the second city, Albany, Data Desk inserts the new case. Continue entering data for the first 10 cities (Fig. 5-11).

(10) Now, when you press Enter and type, the cases scroll up to make room for the new case. You can use the scroll bar to move up or down through the rows of data. Continue entering the next several rows of data. The scroll bar moves with you so that it is always in the active window. The next seven cases are shown (Fig. 5-12).

City	Jan...	Mo...
Chatinooga	5.56	1017.61
Chicago	-3.33	1024.89
Dallas	7.78	860.10
Lancaster	0.0	844.05
Los Angeles	11.67	861.83
Miami	19.44	861.44
New York	0.56	944.65
Philadelphia	0.0	1015.02
Syracuse	-4.44	950.67

Figure 5-12*. The next seven cases.*

(11) Scroll the windows up and down.

5.16 *Example: Editing Data*

(12) If you have followed along *exactly,* then you copied the misspelling of Chattanooga. Click in the City window and drag across the incorrect characters (Fig. 5-13).

City	Jan...	Mo...
Chatinooga	5.56	1017.61
Chicago	-3.33	1024.89
Dallas	7.78	860.10
Lancaster	0.0	844.05
Los Angeles	11.67	861.83
Miami	19.44	861.44
New York	0.56	944.65
Philadelphia	0.0	1015.02
Syracuse	-4.44	950.67

Figure 5-13. *Chattanooga misspelled.*

City	Jan...	Mo...
Chattanooga	5.56	1017.61
Chicago	-3.33	1024.89
Dallas	7.78	860.10
Lancaster	0.0	844.05
Los Angeles	11.67	861.83
Miami	19.44	861.44
New York	0.56	944.65
Philadelphia	0.0	1015.02
Syracuse	-4.44	950.67

Figure 5-14. *A case insertion point after Miami.*

(13) Type the correct characters. They will replace the highlighted ones (Fig. 5-14).

(14) Insert a new case after Miami.

- Click the City window to make it frontmost.
- Move the mouse between "Miami" and "New York" until it shows a cross-bar cursor: ⟩—⟨.
- Click between the Miami case and the New York case to identify the place to insert a new case. You should now see a blinking horizontal case insertion point.

(15) Type "New Orleans". As soon as you start to type, Data Desk makes room for the new case and selects it for editing. Inserting cases in variable editing windows is analogous to inserting characters in text; click where you want to insert, and type.

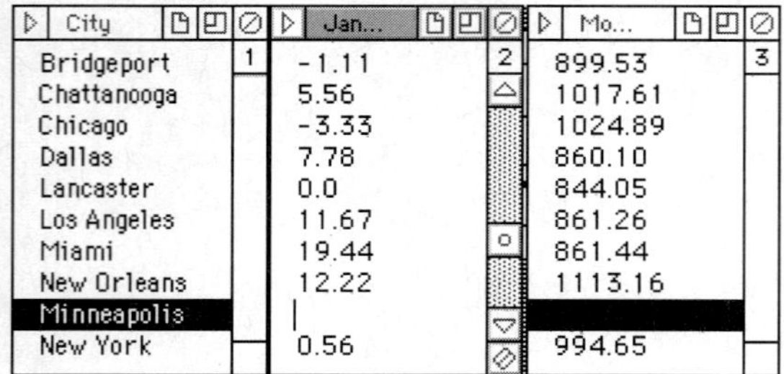

Figure 5-15. Adding new cases.

(16) Press Tab to move to Jan Temp and type 12.22. Press Tab again to enter New Orleans' mortality rate, 1113.16.

(17) Press Return to start another case, and enter the data for Minneapolis: Jan temp, –11.1, Mortality, 857.62 (Fig 5-15).

(18) Select Minneapolis. Click above "Minneapolis" with a cross-bar cursor and drag down across the case. The entire case is selected and highlights (Fig. 5-16).

City	Jan...	Mo...
Bridgeport	-1.11	899.53
Chattanooga	5.56	1017.61
Chicago	-3.33	1024.89
Dallas	7.78	860.10
Lancaster	0.0	844.05
Los Angeles	11.67	861.26
Miami	19.44	861.44
New Orleans	12.22	1113.16
Minneapolis	-11.1	857.62
New York	0.56	994.65

Figure 5-16. Minneapolis selected.

(19) The **Cut** command in the **Edit** menu now reads **Cut Cases**, indicating that you have selected an entire case rather than characters in text. Choose **Cut Cases** to remove Minneapolis from the open variables.

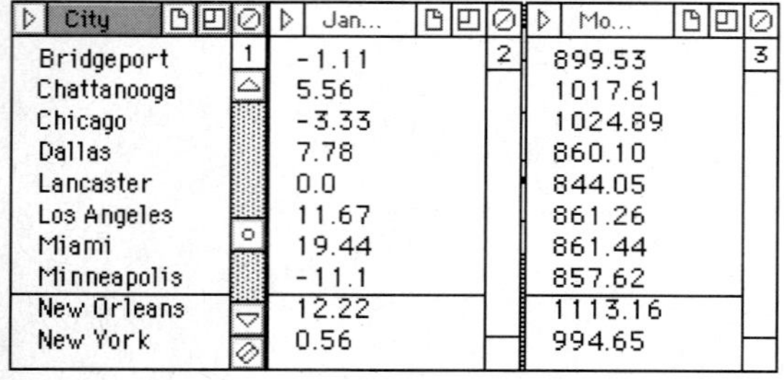

Figure 5-17. Minneapolis case moved.

(20) Most editing operations can be undone. The **Undo** command in the **Edit** menu changes to indicate the previous operation. Choose **Undo** to restore Minneapolis to all three windows.

(21) Cut Minneapolis again to move it to its proper alphabetical location before New Orleans:

- Repeat steps 18 and 19.
- Click above New Orleans with the cross-bar cursor and choose **Paste Cases** from the **Edit** menu. The entire Minneapolis case appears at the case insertion point (Fig 5-17).

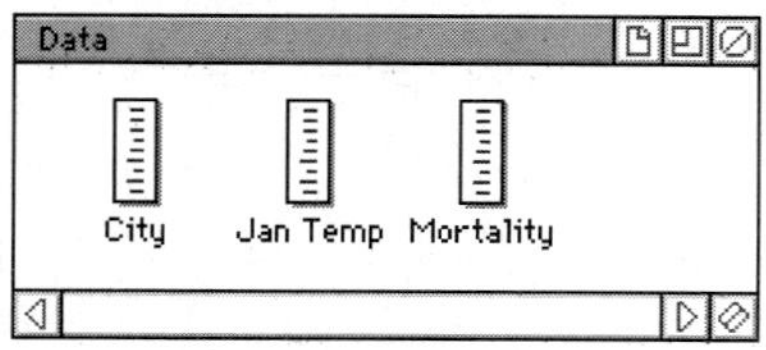

Figure 5-18. Variables closed into their icons and arranged in the datafile window.

(22) Close Mortality. To do so, click in the Mortality window to make it the active window. Then click the Close box. The window zooms back into its icon.

(23) Choose {Data ▸ Close All...} **Variables**. Alternatively, select the icons for each window (for example, by selecting their icon aliases) hold the Shift key, and Choose {Data} **Close**. The datafile window should now look like that shown in Fig. 5-18.

CHAPTER 6

Importing and Exporting

DATA DESK IS DESIGNED to work along with the other programs you use. Data Desk accepts data in standard text file forms from files and from the Clipboard. You can open a new file for the data or import it into an existing datafile. Data Desk accepts the text forms created by standard spreadsheet and database programs as well as nondelimited datafiles used by many mainframe statistics programs. You can export data and numeric results from Data Desk in forms that are accepted by all major statistics programs, spreadsheets, database programs, word processors, and presentation graphics programs. You can export any Data Desk display as a graphic that can be pasted into a word processor or manipulated further in a graphics program.

6.1 Opening Files

There are several methods for opening files in Data Desk. Choosing {File} **Open** command opens the standard open dialog from which you can choose the file you wish to open. Data Desk closes your currently open file (offering to save changes if necessary), and opens the selected file. The **Open** command opens files saved in Data Desk version 3, 4, 5, and 6 and files saved in text (sometimes called ASCII) form. When opening a text file, Data Desk offers the dialog in Fig. 6-1. Data Desk expects text files to hold delimited data tables, which are discussed in Section 6.2.

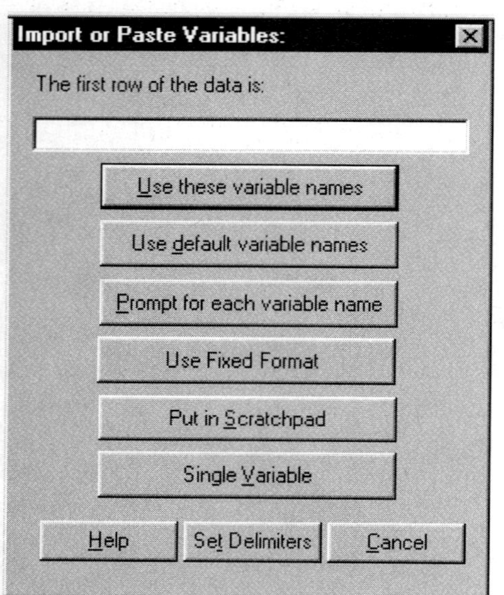

Figure 6-1. *Data Desk opens an import dialog when the file you choose to open is a text file.*

Double-clicking on the icon of a file or dragging its icon over the Data Desk icon opens the file. If no file is currently open, Data Desk simply opens the selected file. If the double-clicked file is a Stationery pad file (Mac only, see Section 6.8), Data Desk imports the contents of the new file into the open file. Double-clicking on a Stationery pad file is a quick way to bring a Template into an open file.

6.2 Data Tables

Data Desk ordinarily transports variables by placing them in a *data table*. A data table is a table of data values with tab marks delimiting each successive data value in a case and a return delimiting the cases themselves. A data table looks like this:

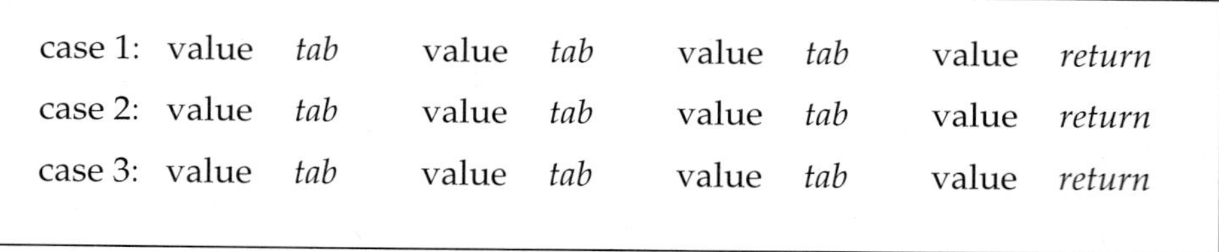

case 1:	value	*tab*	value	*tab*	value	*tab*	value	*return*
case 2:	value	*tab*	value	*tab*	value	*tab*	value	*return*
case 3:	value	*tab*	value	*tab*	value	*tab*	value	*return*

rectangular datasets

Many programs read and write data tables either to text files saved on a disk or to the Clipboard. In Data Desk, each column of a data table is a variable and each row is a case. Data tables are always rectangular. That is, all variables have the same number of cases and every case must have a value (numeric, text, or missing) for each variable. Relations have exactly this structure.

The first row of a data table may hold the names of the variables. You can think of these names as column labels — indeed, they may be column headings on a spreadsheet or on a table in a text document.

Data Desk offers to place variable names in the first row of data tables that it exports, and can read variable names from the first row of data tables that it opens or imports. This can be particularly helpful, for example, when exchanging data with a spreadsheet. Select the column titles in the spreadsheet along with the data. When you paste or open the resulting table, the column titles will automatically become variable names. Conversely, moving data from Data Desk to a spreadsheet, the variable names can become column headings automatically.

The {Manip} **Make Variable Table** command combines selected variables into a data table in a window on the desktop so you can scroll up and down in it to view variables together.

6.3 *Opening Delimited Text Files*

When you Open or Import a text file, Data Desk presents a dialog from which to choose the file. Text files typically contain either a data table with each row holding a case and columns (variables) separated by a delimiting character, or a single column of data. If the text file holds a delimited data table, select the desired file and press the **Open** button.

Data Desk shows you the first row of the data table and offers a choice among six alternatives:

- Use the displayed text as variable names. The variables' values then start with the second row of the data table.
- Automatically generate the default variable names *Var1, Var2, ...* . You can, of course, rename the variables later.
- Prompt for a name as each variable is created. The prompt displays the first case in each variable to remind you of its contents, but this case remains part of the data. The prompt also allows you to enter background information for each variable.
- Place the contents of the file in a new Scratchpad. This alternative is particularly useful if you wish to examine the contents of the file first or if you have opened an ordinary text file (for example, a description of the data) rather than a data table. Scratchpads are a good place for simple editing. For example, you can easily delete lines of introduction or program listing that sometimes precede the actual data. Then just Copy the part of the file you want, click on an icon window, and Paste.
- Place the entire data table into a single variable. This alternative can be useful if you wish to edit the data table further and want to work with the case-aware capabilities of Data Desk's data editing commands or string function derived variable commands.
- Cancel the Open command.

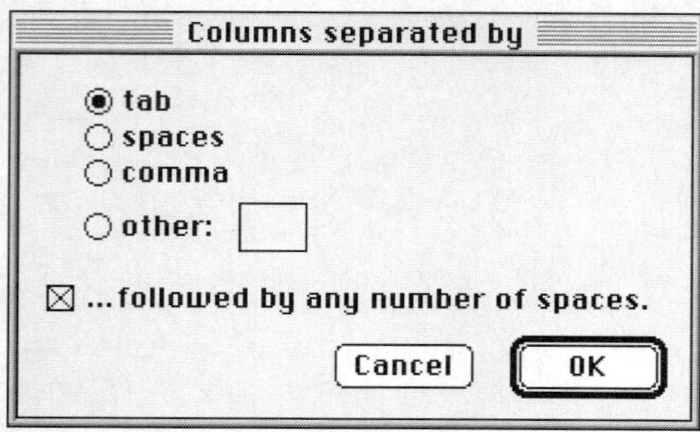

Figure 6-2. *You can specify an alternative delimiter for data tables.*

While data tables ordinarily have a Tab character between each column, you can specify another choice of column delimiter. Press the Set Delimiters button to display another dialog that lets you specify alternative column delimiters (Fig. 6-2).

You can substitute another character, such as a space, comma, or anything you can type, for the Tab character in the standard data table. You can also specify whether spaces following the delimiter should be removed or left in the data. Ordinarily, extra spaces are removed.

Changing the delimiter affects opening, importing and exporting files and copying and pasting variables. The delimiter you specify is used to find the column separators for the **Import**, **Paste Variables** and **Paste Cases** commands. The specified delimiter is also inserted between columns in output tables exported to a text file or placed on the Clipboard with the **Export**, **Copy Variables** and **Copy Cases** commands.

If you change the delimiter, the new delimiter remains in effect until you change it again or Exit (Quit on Mac) Data Desk.

After the delimiters are defined and the desired variable naming alternative is selected, Data Desk creates a new relation, giving it the same name as the datafile. Each column of the data table in the text file is placed in a variable and named according to the instructions provided earlier.

6.4 *Importing Files*

Data Desk's **Import** command adds the contents of the imported file to the currently open file. The program can import text files and Data Desk version 6 files, but not earlier Data Desk files. (To import files saved by earlier versions of Data Desk, first Open them individually and Save them as Data Desk 6 files.) The Import command is also used to bring templates into files.

To import a file choose {File} **Import**. Data Desk offers the standard Open dialog from which you select the file to be imported. If the selected file is a Data Desk file, both the variables and the results in that file are added to the open file and placed in a folder. The new folder is placed in the Results folder and given the same name as the file from which the contents were imported.

If the file is a text file, the steps are the same as those for opening a text file. (See Section 6.3). Data Desk presents the first row of the data table and asks you to choose the method for naming the variables. The delimiter used to separate the variables can be defined in the Set Delimiters dialog (Fig. 6-2).

Data Desk places the imported variables in a new relation, gives it the same name as the datafile from which the text was imported and places the relation in the Data folder. You can drag imported variables from this new relation into existing relations, but it is your responsibility to insure that the new variables are measured on the same individuals as those in the old relation; Data Desk can only check that the variables have the right number of cases.

If the file does not contain a data table, you can place the file's contents into a scratchpad or a single variable. In this way you can import a text file and edit it in a scratchpad, or use it to document a datafile.

6.5 *Copying Variables to a Data Table*

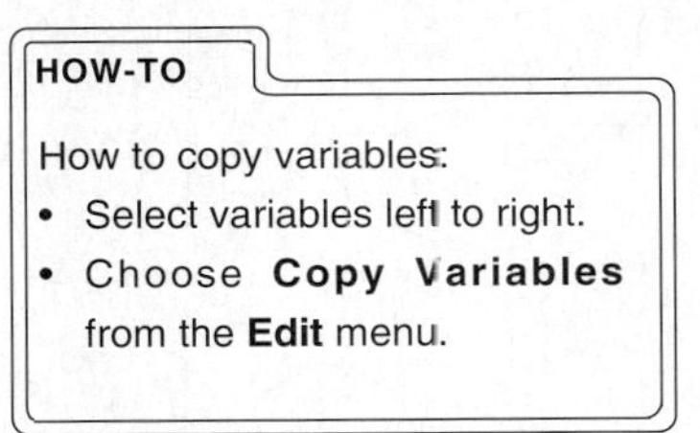
HOW-TO

How to copy variables:

- Select variables left to right.
- Choose **Copy Variables** from the **Edit** menu.

To copy variables to a data table in the Clipboard, select the variables *in the order in which they should appear in the table (left-to-right).* Recall that when you drag across icons to select them, they are ordered left-to-right, and that when you select a folder or relation icon, its contents are selected left-to-right. When you have selected variables, the **Copy** command in the **Edit** menu changes to **Copy Variables**. Choose it to copy the entire contents of the selected variables onto the Clipboard.

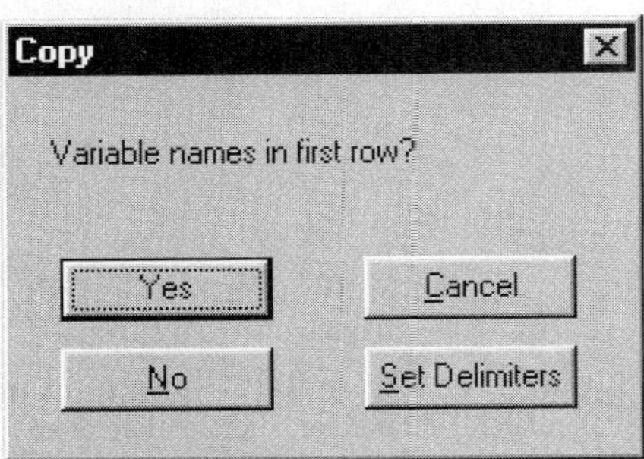

Figure 6-3. *The Copy Variables dialog.*

Data Desk asks if you wish to place variable names in the first row of the data table. If you are moving the data to a word processor or a spreadsheet, you may want to have the variable names at the top of the columns. Other programs may be confused by nonnumeric information in the first row, so you need to know something about the program to which you are moving the data. You can also substitute a different character for the Tab delimiter. (See Section 6.3.)

You now have a data table on the Clipboard. You can move to another program, and paste the data table into that program.

While the Clipboard is a convenient way to move data, it is not designed to handle large amounts of data. If the Clipboard cannot do the job, try exporting selected variables to a text file to be read by the other program (see Section 6.7), or move smaller amounts of data in several operations, switching between applications.

6.6 *Pasting Variables from the Clipboard*

When the Clipboard contains text and the frontmost window is an icon window, the **Paste** command in the **Edit** menu changes to **Paste Variables**. Choose it to paste each column of the data table into the datafile as a variable. Pasting variables follows the same steps as those for opening or importing text files. Data Desk presents the first row of the data table and asks how to name the variables. The delimiter separating the variables can be specified in the Set Delimiters dialog.

Data Desk creates a new relation named *Clipboard* to hold the new variables. Data Desk always gives new relations the name of the data's source for data imported or pasted. You may drag the variables into other existing relations if they have the correct number of cases, but you are then responsible to see that the new variables are indeed measured on the same individuals as those in the old relation.

Important — ***do not open new variables to paste into***. Data Desk automatically creates the variables it needs for the data on the clipboard based on the delimiters defined in the Set Delimiters dialog.

6.7 *Writing a Data Table to a Text File*

You write a data table as a text file in much the same way you copy variables to the Clipboard. Select the variables you want in left-to-right order. Then choose {File} **Export**. Data Desk offers the option of placing variable names in the first row. It then asks you to name the new file and to specify where in the file system you would like the file placed. Choose **Save** and Data Desk writes the data into that file in data table form. Most programs that work with data can read text files.

6.8 *Appending Cases in Data Desk*

The **Parallel Append** command appends the cases in one group of variables to the end of the cases in a second group of variables, appending the first variable in the first set to the first in the second, the second variable to the second, and so on. This can be especially helpful when importing additional data to be added to an existing relation. Newly imported (or pasted) variables are given their own relation. To append them to an existing group of variables, select the variables to be appended as *x*'s (holding the Shift key while selecting them) and the variables to which they should be appended as *y*'s (holding the Option key on Mac, or the Ctrl key on Windows, while selecting them), and choose {Manip} **Parallel Append**. Data Desk creates a new relation labeled *Parallel Append* with the variables labeled as they were in the first group. The relation also holds an additional variable labeled *Groups*, which labels the cases according to whether they were selected as "x" or "y".

Data Desk can perform **Parallel Append** even on datasets too large to fit into memory all at once. It is thus practical to import a particularly large datafile in pieces and "stick" it back together again in Data Desk.

Parallel Append is also helpful for datasets to which additional data is added regularly, for example, as new reports are completed each quarter.

6.9 *Copying Selected Cases*

To copy selected cases from variables:

- Open the variables.
- Select the cases you wish to copy by clicking, dragging, and shift-clicking to select ranges of cases, or discontinuous sets of cases. Alternatively, open a display along with the variables and select cases in the display rather than in the variables' editing windows. The selected cases highlight in *all* windows including the variable editing windows. Another way to select cases is with the **Find...** commands in the **Edit** menu.
- After you have selected cases, click on the title bar of a variable editing window to make it frontmost. The **Copy** command in the **Edit** menu will then read **Copy Cases**.
- Choose **Copy Cases** from the **Edit** menu. You can also choose **Cut Cases** if you wish to remove the cases from all variable editing win-

dows. Note that the cases are only copied to the local clipboard of each window by this step. The subsequent steps transfer the data to the Clipboard for export to other programs.

- Make sure that the *sequence boxes* in the upper right of each window above the scroll bar show numbers *in the order in which you want the data columns arranged on the Clipboard*. Data Desk builds a data table on the Clipboard with *only values from variables in the editing sequence at the time the data table is needed*. This method allows you to open additional variables to identify the cases to be selected without having to copy their values as well. For example, you might open the variable *Sex* along with several others, use the **Find** command to select all subjects coded "Female" on *Sex*, and then copy the selected cases. If you did not want to copy a column that simply reads "Female" in the data table, you would omit *Sex* from the editing sequence at this step by clicking its sequence box to turn it gray.
- Leave open the editing windows from which you want to copy so that the full editing sequence is defined.
- If you now quit Data Desk or transfer to another program, Data Desk puts the copied cases on the Clipboard as a data table in the order specified by the editing sequence.

Another way to copy selected cases from variables is to construct a selector variable (see Section 13.1). When the selector is active, **Copy Variables** copies only the selected cases.

When editing variables, Data Desk keeps a separate internal clipboard for *each* open variable. This makes it possible to copy cases from one part of some variables and paste them in another part regardless of the order or position of the variable windows when you paste. Data Desk also remembers any rows that are moved so that it can keep the entire relation consistent.

When you leave Data Desk or transfer to another program, Data Desk creates a data table on the operating system's Clipboard from each of Data Desk's separate clipboards belonging to variables in the editing sequence. The editing sequence order specifies the order in which variables are arranged in the table.

Because the data table is only created when it is actually needed, it only contains data from variables that are open and in the editing sequence *at that time*. This has several consequences that could be confusing.

- Copy Cases does not alter the Clipboard window displayed by the **Show Clipboard** command in the **Edit** menu. You can confirm that the cases are ready to form a data table by opening a ScratchPad and pasting into it.
- If you close a variable or remove it from the editing sequence, its values will not be included in data tables formed later. Unlike other Copy and Cut commands, **Copy Cases** does not complete its operation immediately, but only when the Clipboard is needed.
- You can resequence the variable editing windows at any time before actually taking the Clipboard to another program.

- Only variables from a single relation can be in the same editing sequence, so a copied data table will always be for a single relation.

6.10 *Copying Data Desk Results*

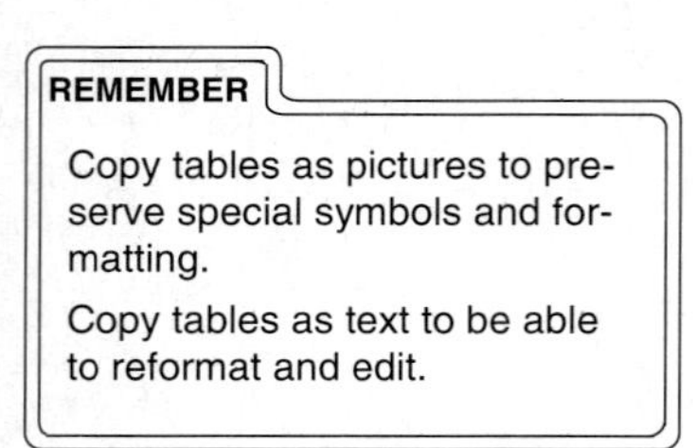

Data Desk presents statistical results (summary reports, regression summary tables, correlation tables, ANOVA tables, contingency tables, etc.) using boldface, italics, and special symbols to enhance readability. You can copy these tables as pictures to preserve this formatting.

Data Desk can also copy statistical output as text with a tab mark separating each of the columns. This lets you move tables to a word processor or page formatting program, insert your own tab-stops, and reformat the text however you would like. For example, you might change the column headings to another font or to a bigger size.

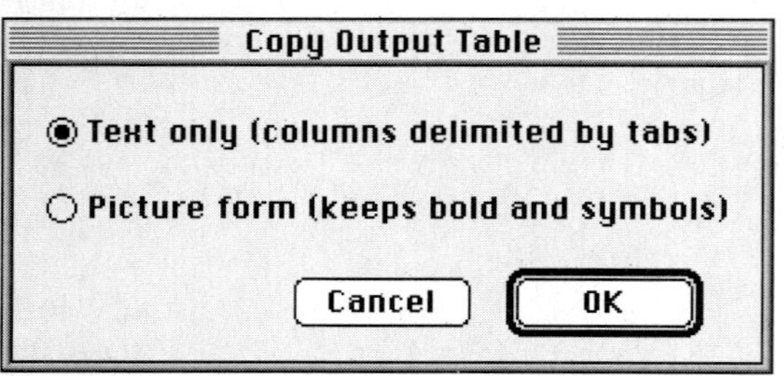

Figure 6-5. *Data Desk offers to copy tables as tab-delimited text or as a picture.*

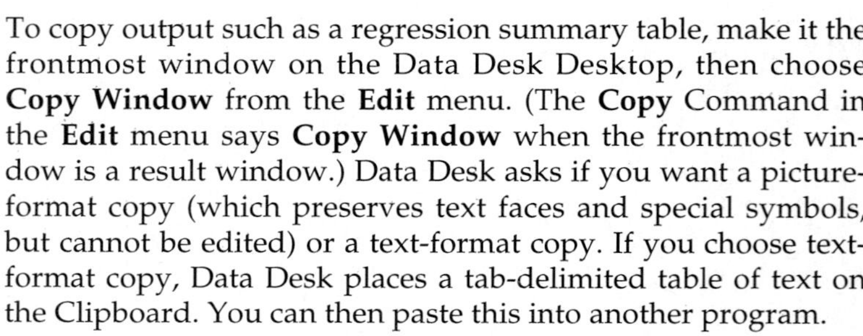

To copy output such as a regression summary table, make it the frontmost window on the Data Desk Desktop, then choose **Copy Window** from the **Edit** menu. (The **Copy** Command in the **Edit** menu says **Copy Window** when the frontmost window is a result window.) Data Desk asks if you want a picture-format copy (which preserves text faces and special symbols, but cannot be edited) or a text-format copy. If you choose text-format copy, Data Desk places a tab-delimited table of text on the Clipboard. You can then paste this into another program.

You can copy plots in exactly the same way. Plots copied onto the Clipboard are in PICT2 format on Mac and bitmap format on Windows. Each element of a PICT2 file is recorded as a graphic object. You can paste the picture of the plot into virtually any graphics editing program and modify any element of the plot easily. If you print the plot from a graphics editor, a word processor, or from a page composition program it will print with the full precision of your printer rather than with the limited precision of the screen.

6.11 *Printing from Data Desk*

Data Desk supports all standard printers. The **Page Setup** command in the **File** menu presents printer setup options according to the printer you have selected from your operating system's or network software. Please refer to your operating system or network software documentation for details.

You can print any window with the **Print...** command in the **File** menu. It prints the contents of the frontmost window in PICT form on Mac (bitmap on Windows) to take greatest advantage of the resolution of your printer. Plots usually look better printed black (or colors)-on-white rather than the screen standard white (or colors)-on-black, and Data Desk defaults to this choice. You can change the default with the {Plot ▸ Plot Options} **Print White-on-Black** command.

Layout windows are output formatting windows into which you can paste or drag pictures of other Data Desk windows and add text annotations. You can then position the pictures and text boxes as you please and then print it with the {File} **Print...** command. Layout windows are useful for printing multiple displays on the same page. They are described in detail in Chapter 14. To print multiple windows at the same time, select the windows to be printed, hold down the shift key and choose {File} **Print...**.

APPENDIX 6A *Examples of Importing and Exporting*

The following examples illustrate data transfer between Data Desk and several kinds of programs. In most cases, the descriptions given here apply to other similar programs.

from a terminal program

- TO COPY A DATA TABLE FROM A TELECOMMUNICATION PROGRAM OR ELECTRONIC MAIL, select the text you wish to copy from the recorded terminal session, and choose the **Copy Table** command (usually) from the **Edit** menu. Most terminal emulation programs and electronic mail programs provide this command, or one like it. It replaces consecutive spaces with a tab character and copies the resulting table to the Clipboard as a data table that you can paste into Data Desk.

You can use the same method to send data through a terminal program or by electronic mail, but the details depend upon the program you are using.

from a spreadsheet

- TO COPY A DATA TABLE FROM A SPREADSHEET to Data Desk, select the rectangle of cells to copy. Remember that Data Desk can read the first row of a data table as variable names, so you can include column captions if you wish. Choose **Copy** from the **Edit** menu. You can now paste the resulting data table into Data Desk with the **Paste Variables** command.

> TIP
>
> When transferring data from spreadsheets or databases to Data Desk, first reformat to remove currency symbols, commas, or date formats.

Data formatted in a spreadsheet with $ symbols, commas, or in special date formats looks like text to Data Desk. You must convert the format of a column to general numeric form before copying it for export to Data Desk if you want Data Desk to work with the numeric values rather than the text. Some programs offer a spreadsheet-like interface, but often they do not support copying and pasting operations in spreadsheet style, so you may need other methods for them.

to a spreadsheet

- TO COPY VARIABLES FROM DATA DESK TO A SPREADSHEET, select the icons of the variables, folders, or relations, and choose **Copy Variables** from the **Edit** menu. Move to the spreadsheet program, indicate where the table should be placed by clicking the upper left cell to fill, and **Paste.** If you select derived variables (see Chapter 11), Data Desk computes their values for export. If a Selector variable is active, Data Desk selects the specified cases.

to a word processor

- TO COPY VARIABLES AND DISPLAYS TO A WORD PROCESSOR, use any of the copying methods discussed in this chapter. Data tables are ordinary text with a Tab between columns and a Return at the end of lines. If you have not defined tab stops in your word processing document, the data table will probably look wrong at first. To format a Data Desk output table that has been copied as text, you may need to define tab stops for different parts of the table. For example, in a regression summary table the tab stops for the ANOVA table may be different from the tab stops for the table of coefficients.

from a word processor

- TO MOVE DATA FROM A WORD PROCESSOR TO DATA DESK, edit the data to have the form of a data table. The data must contain a unique delimiter between each column. The most common delimiter is the tab character (which is usually convenient in word processors because it helps to format the data into columns for display and editing.) Each row of data must end with a return. (For most word processors this means that each line is a new paragraph.)

Copy the data table by selecting it in the word processor and choosing **Copy**. Paste the table into Data Desk. If the delimiter between columns is not the Tab character, then press the Set Delimiter button and specify the delimiter. Each column of the original table becomes a variable in Data Desk. Alternatively, you can save your file in "Text Only" form and then read it with either the **Open** or **Import** command in Data Desk. If the delimiter is not a Tab character, you must set the delimiter in Data Desk first. Be sure to remove extraneous text, or your variables will not be read correctly.

Whenever you move data from text-based programs, take care that there is no extraneous text. Data Desk expects the data to form a rectangle in which each row has data for exactly the same number of variables. It is especially important that the first row has the correct number of data elements because it is from the first row that Data Desk learns the number of variables.

It is also important that the delimiter be unique. One common error is to use the Space character as a delimiter when spaces may appear in some of the data (between first and last names, for example). The delimiter separating variables must be a unique character that appears nowhere else in the data.

between Data Desk and other statistics and graphics programs

- TO MOVE VARIABLES BETWEEN DATA DESK AND OTHER STATISTICS AND GRAPHICS PACKAGES, use text files. Most programs that deal with data can read and write data tables as text files. You must check whether the other package can accept or place variable names in the first row of the data table, and choose the appropriate alternative in Data Desk. Many packages impose restrictions on variable names such as limiting their length or requiring special symbols. Data Desk imposes no such restrictions, so you may need to rename some Data Desk variables before exporting them. You should also check that the other program can work with nonnumeric values and with variables that mix numeric and nonnumeric values before including such variables.

  Virtually every program with a verbal command language requires that variable names be unique. Data Desk does not have that restriction, so you may need to rename variables to make the names unique.

APPENDIX 6B *Moving Files Between Mac and Windows*

Data Desk 6.0 can open any Data Desk 6.0 files regardless of which operating system the file was saved on. This appendix offers some hints to make the process of moving files across systems smoother.

• Data Desk files saved on the Mac for use on Windows need to be saved with the ".dsk" extension. For example the file Cars, needs to be saved as Cars.dsk.

• Data Desk files saved on Windows for use on Mac are typically transferred via network or translation software like PC MACLAN Connect or PC Exchange. Your translation software needs to be customized to recognize and translate Data Desk files. For example, with PC Exchange, a new record needs to be added that maps the DOS suffix ".dsk" to the Mac document type "DFil". With PC MACLAN Connect, a new record needs to be added that maps the DOS extension ".dsk" to the Mac Creator "DDSK" and the document Type "DFil".

If you have Data Desk files that are transferred to Mac without going through a translator, launch the DD Translation Utility program. (This program is supplied with all Macintosh versions of Data Desk.) When the program launches it opens a dialog which allows you to select the file. Press the Translate button to create the file which can be opened by Data Desk on the Macintosh.

7

Simple Summaries

univariate statistics

SUMMARY STATISTICS PROVIDE concise descriptions of the numbers in a variable and permit simple comparisons of the variable to others or to external standards. Many different summary statistics are common, but they describe only a few different characteristics of data. Because summary statistics summarize a single variable at a time, they are sometimes called *univariate statistics.*

Data Desk computes many summary statistics and offers them in several ways. Rather than asking you which statistics you want each time you request summary statistics, Data Desk expects you to establish a default selection of statistics. It then computes these summaries each time you ask for summaries and offers ways to modify your default choices afterward. This method is faster than stopping to choose statistics because usually your default choices are what you wanted.

The {Calc ▶ Calculation Options} **Select Summary Statistics...** command offers a dialog with choices of default summary statistics. Click in the check boxes to select (or deselect) the corresponding statistics. The Select Summary Statistics dialog does not compute statistics; it merely defines the default selection of summary statistics to be computed with any future summary statistics commands.

When a Summary output table is frontmost, you can access the Select Summary Statistics dialog from the table's global HyperView menu to modify your selection of statistics in that window. Ordinarily, you would choose this command to modify your selection of statistics for the table itself. However, this version of the dialog also lets you change the default settings directly by pressing the Set Defaults button. Your new selection of summary statistics will then become the default selection for all future summary statistics commands.

Weight

Summary of **Weight**
No Selector

Count 38
Mean 2.86289
StdDev 0.706870

Figure 7-1. Default Summary report of Weight *in the Cars data.*

Percentile 25

☐ **Lower Percentile**
☐ **Upper Percentile**
☐ **Mid Percentile**
☐ **Percentile Range**

Some of the statistics (for example, the *Upper Percentile*) require a number as well. For these, click the check box to the left of the statistic and type the number into the appropriate text box. The default summary statistics options are the sample mean, the standard deviation, and the number of numeric values. You can set new defaults by selecting the boxes for the desired statistics and then selecting the Set Defaults box. The latter sections of this chapter provide descriptions of each statistic.

7.1 Summary Reports

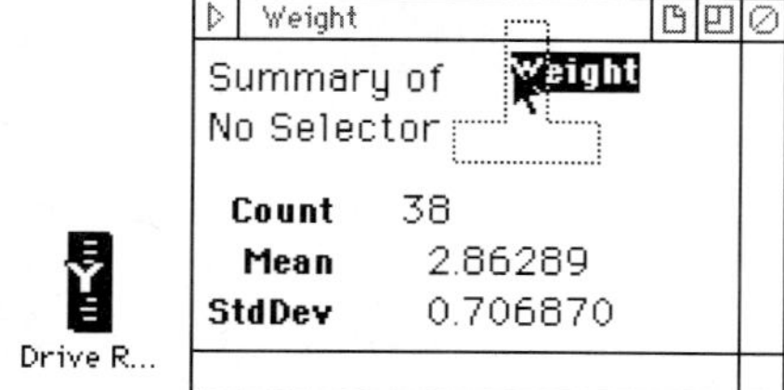

Figure 7-2. Drag the icon of a new variable on top of the name of the current variable to recompute the summary table for the new variable.

The simplest summary command creates a table for each requested statistic for the selected variable (Fig. 7-1). Select the variable of interest and choose {Calc ▶ Summaries} **Reports.** If more than one variable is selected, a separate window is created for each variable. It's easy to change the variable in the table. Just pick up the icon of the new variable and drag it on top of the name of the current variable (Fig. 7-2). The table updates using the new variable.

Wgt/Cyl

Summary of **Weight**
For categories in **Cylinders**
No Selector

Group	Count	Mean	StdDev
4	19	2.29479	0.288270
5	1	2.83000	•
6	10	3.10500	0.345704
8	8	3.91362	0.228225

Figure 7-3. *Summary reports by group.*

Wgt/Cyl

Summary of **Weight**
For categories in **Cross**
No Selector

Group	Count	Mean	StdDev
France,4	0	•	•
France,5	0	•	•
France,6	1	3.41000	•
France,8	0	•	•
Germany,4	4	2.17625	0.304176
Germany,5	1	2.83000	•
Germany,6	0	•	•
Germany,8	0	•	•
Italy,4	1	2.13000	•

Figure 7-4. *Reports by Groups table where* Group *is defined as the crossed variable of both* Country *and* Cylinder *variables.*

7.2 *Summaries by Groups*

To compute summary statistics for cases categorized into groups, select the variable to summarize as *y*, select the variable holding the group names as *x*, and choose {Calc ▶ Summaries} **Reports by Groups**. Data Desk places the summary statistics in a table with a row for each category in the grouping variable and a column for each requested statistic (Fig. 7-3). Reports by Groups tables display statistics for one continuous variable and one grouping variable. Either of these variables can be replaced by dragging the new variable's icon on top of the name of the variable to be replaced.

Sometimes it is important to display statistics for the intersection of two or more grouping variables. For example with the Cars dataset, you might be interested in statistics for each country of manufacture broken down by cylinder type. To create a table for these categories, first combine the grouping variables by using the **Cross** command. Select your grouping variables and choose {Manip ▶ Transform ▶ Misc} **Cross**. The new crossed variable is placed at the end of the original data relation. This variable can now be used as a grouping variable in the **Reports by Groups** command (Fig. 7-4).

Summaries for multiple group variables are a valuable adjunct to factorial Analyses of Variance (See Chapter 21). Select the ANOVA dependent variable as *y* and the crossed factor variables as *x*. The summary statistics will report summaries for each cell of the experiment design.

The **Generate Hot Variables** command in the global HyperView menu of the Reports by Group table creates HotResult variables and places them in the Derived folder. The first set of variables hold the row labels of the Reports by Groups table with the categories from each original crossed variable in a separate variable. The other variables hold the values for each column. Once these variables have been created, you can use them in any plot or table, just like regular variables. The difference is that HotResult variables update automatically in response to changes in the table. Thus, if the data underlying the table change and you update the table window, the values in the HotResult variables update and so will any plots or tables built with these variables. If you want to generate HotResult variables for specific columns, select the HyperView menu under the column heading and choose **Locate** or **Select**. All **Reports by Groups** HotResult variable icons are placed in the Derived folder in the File Cabinet.

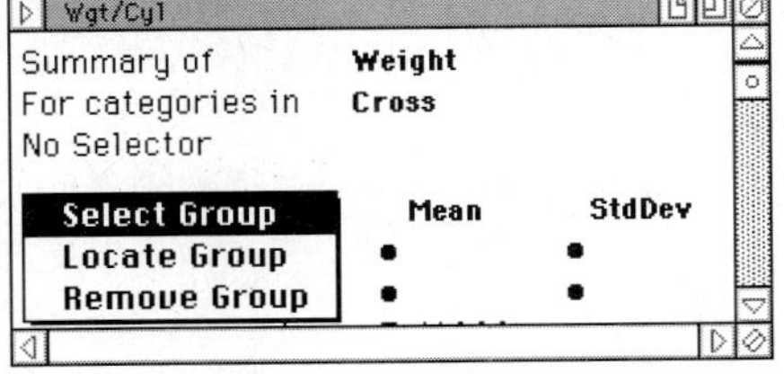

7.3 *Summaries for Multiple Variables*

You may want to compute summary statistics that make it easy to compare the values of each summary statistic across several variables. For example, a scatterplot of standard deviations versus means is an effective way to look for increasing variance with increasing level — a violation of assumptions for some analyses.

Data Desk provides three commands to compute summary statistics for more than one variable at a time: **Reports Multiple**, **Reports Multivariate,** and **As Variables**. The main difference between these commands is that **Reports Multivariate** employs casewise (sometimes called listwise) deletion. This means that any case that has a missing or nonnumeric value in any of the variables is omitted from the computation of all the statistics. (We discuss casewise deletion in Appendix 13A). The **Reports Multiple** and **As Variables** commands restrict the deletion of cases to the individual variables. For example, if case 3 in variable 1 is missing, **Reports Multivariate** excludes case 3 from the calculation of all the variables. **Reports Multiple** and **As Variables** includes case 3 in the calculation of the other variables, as long as case 3 is not missing in those other variables.

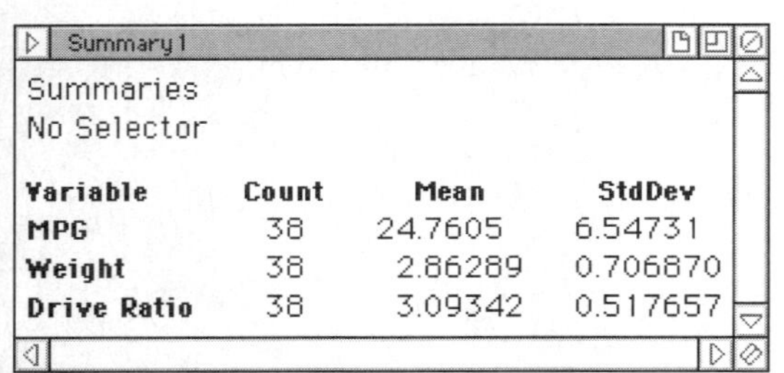

Summary 1

Summaries
No Selector

Variable	Count	Mean	StdDev
MPG	38	24.7605	6.54731
Weight	38	2.86289	0.706870
Drive Ratio	38	3.09342	0.517657

Figure 7-5. *Summary statistics generated with the* ***Reports Multiple*** *command.*

Select the variables for which you want to compute summary statistics and choose {Calc ▶ Summaries} **Reports Multiple** or choose {Calc ▶ Summaries} **Reports Multivariate** if you desire casewise deletion. These commands generate a table with a column for each summary statistic selected from the Select Summary Statistics dialog and a row for each selected variable (Fig. 7-5).

The label for each column in the table holds a HyperView menu that contains the commands **Select, Locate,** and **Remove**. The **Select** and **Locate** commands create and make active a HotResult variable holding the values from that column. If the variable already exists, the **Locate** command selects the variable icon as a y-variable, and brings it to the front. The **Select** command just selects the variable, although its icon may remain hidden. As with all icon selection in Data Desk, simple selection selects the icon as a y-variable; hold the Shift key down while choosing the command to select as x. The **Remove** command deletes the column from the table.

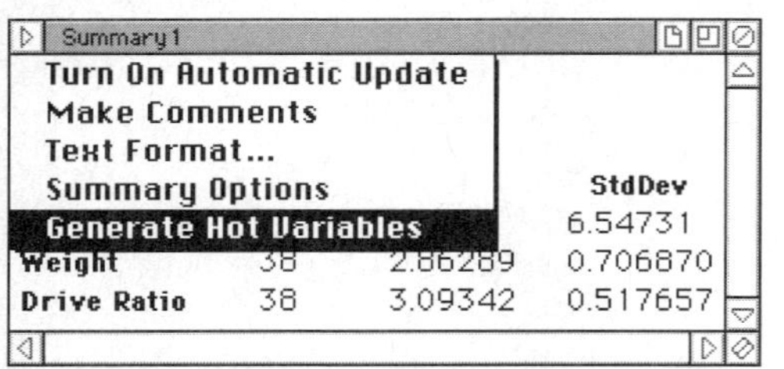

Figure 7-6. Generate Hot Variables *command creates HotResult variables that hold the values reported in each column of the summary report table.*

To drop all the columns of the table into HotResult variables, choose **Generate Hot Variables** from the table's global HyperView menu (Fig. 7-6).

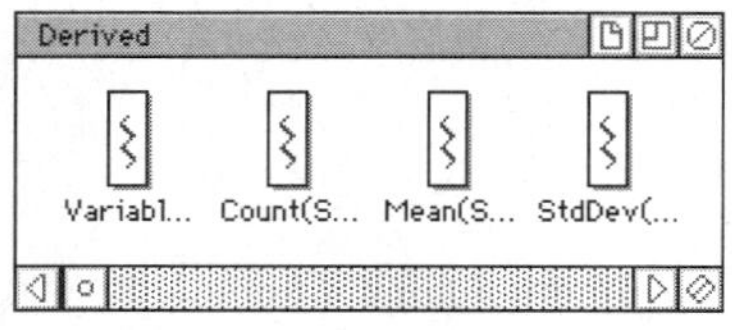

Figure 7-7. *The {Calc ▶Summaries}* ***As Variables*** *command places the statistics as Hot Result variables in a* Summaries *folder.*

To generate the HotResult variables directly without making the table, select the original variables to be summarized and choose {Calc ▶ Summaries} **As Variables**. Data Desk creates a folder called Summaries which holds the icons for all the HotResult variables and an icon for the **Reports Multiple** table (Fig. 7-7).

Once they are created, you can use these HotResult variables in any plot or table, just like regular variables. The difference is that HotResult variables update automatically in response to changes in the underlying data. Thus, if a value changes in one of the underlying variables, the values in the HotResult variables update and so will any plots or tables built with these variables.

7.4 HyperView Menus

Summary reports offer an excellent opportunity to use HyperView menus. In addition to the commands relating to HotResult variables just discussed, additional Data Desk HyperView menus suggest other analyses or plots that tell you more about your data. For example, summary statistics treat each variable individually, summarizing the center of the values, their spread, and other aspects of how they are distributed. Histograms (see Section 8.3) convey much of the same information graphically, so it is often helpful to see a histogram along with a summary report.

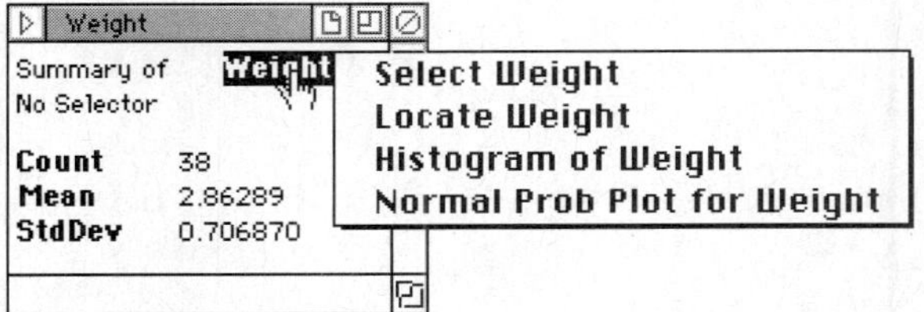

Figure 7-8. The HyperView menu offers you to look at a graphical display of the variable being summarized.

When you move the mouse over the name of the variable in a summary report, the cursor changes to a cursor (Fig. 7-8). This change indicates that a HyperView menu exists at this location. When you click at that point a short menu of suggested plots and analyses pops up. For variables in summary reports tables and those selected as *y* in summary by groups tables, the HyperView menu includes the suggestion of a histogram and a normal probability plot. The **Select** command selects the variable so that it can be used with the next command. The **Locate** command finds the icon of the summarized variable in case you want to examine its values. HyperView menus attached to *grouping* variables in the reports by groups table suggest plots and tables appropriate for category variables, like bar charts, pie charts and frequency tables.

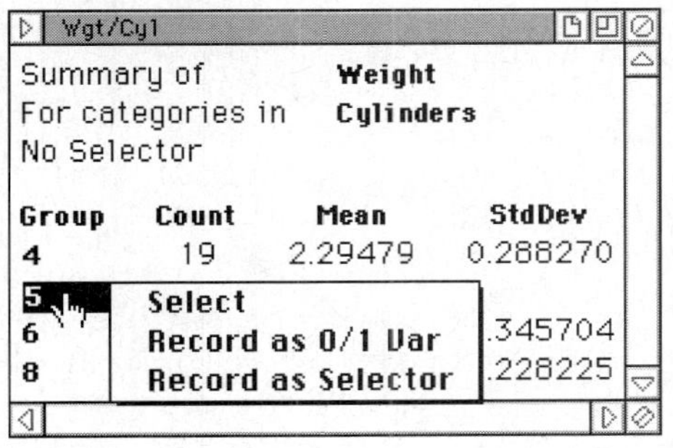

Figure 7-9. The HyperView menu attached to each row of the summary table allows you to select that category and record your selection using the selector variable.

The values in each row of the reports by groups table hold a HyperView menu that allows you to isolate and work with the cases from a specific category. The **Select** command selects the cases from the specified category and highlights those points in any open plot (Fig. 7-9). The **Record as 0/1** command creates a new variable that holds 1's for all the cases in the specified category and 0's for all the others. Data Desk asks you to name the new variable and places its icon at the end of the relation window. The **Record as Selector** command does everything the **Record as 0/1** command does and then assigns the new 0/1 variable to a selector button. (See Chapter 13 for a discussion of selector buttons and subset analysis.)

7.5 Measures of Center

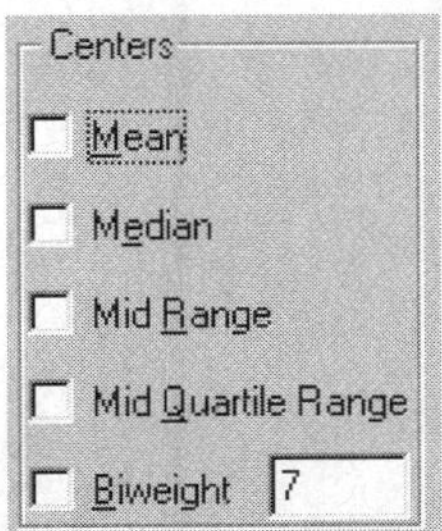

The center is the most common single numeric description of a batch of values. Measures of center are so common in ordinary speech that it is easy to forget that they have precise mathematical definitions.

The center goes by many names. It is often called the *level*, the *middle*, or the *mean* (*average*). Many statistics texts refer to centers as *measures of location* or *measures of central tendency*. Whatever the name, all centers obey two rules:

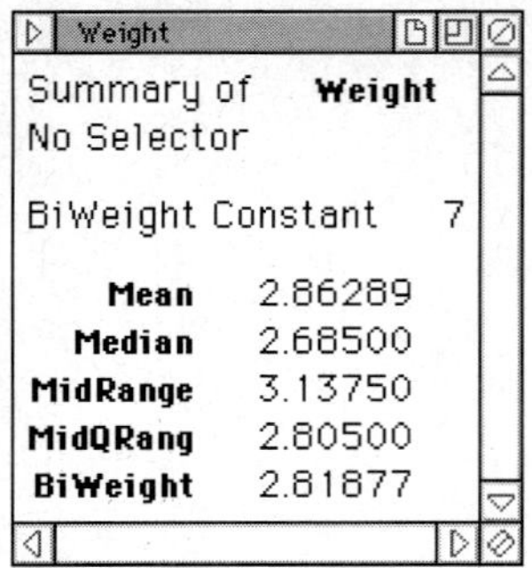

Figure 7-10. *Five centers computed for Weight.*

- If every value in a variable is incremented by a value, *a*, then the center increments by the value *a*.
- If every value in a variable is multiplied by a value, *b*, then the center is also multiplied by the value *b*.

7.6 *An Example*

The Cars dataset contains information about 38 automobiles. A summary report of five centers computed for car weight is shown in Fig. 7-10.

Each center measure satisfies the two rules, but they differ in value because they are computed differently.

mean (average)

The sample *mean* or *average* (in the example, 2.86289) is the most commonly used measure of center. It sums the numbers and divides by the total number of values summed.

The sample mean is the basis for many statistical methods. It is easy to compute, but it can be misleading if the variable contains any extraordinarily large or small numbers. For example, consider the difficulty faced by a student who tries to salvage his grade average following a zero exam grade.

median

The *median* (2.68500) is the middle value. That is, half of the numbers in the variable are less than or equal to the median and half are greater than or equal to it. The median is used less often than the mean because it is harder to compute and more difficult to deal with mathematically. Nevertheless, it has some advantages. For example, the median isn't affected by occasional extraordinary data values.

midrange

The *midrange* (3.13750) is the mean of the largest and smallest data values. It is useful primarily when the overall extent, or *range*, of the data is of particular interest.

midquartile range

The *midquartile range* (2.80500) is the mean of the second and third quartiles.

biweight

The *biweight* (2.81877) is a *robust* center, which means that it isn't unduly affected when the data have extreme values. The biweight is not as common a measure of center as the others discussed here. We define it in detail in Appendix 7A.

7.7 *Measures of Spread*

Spreads
- ☐ Stan. Dev.
- ☐ Range
- ☐ Variance
- ☐ InterQuartile Range
- ☐ Standard Error
- ☐ Pop. Stan. Dev.

Measures of spread describe the extent to which individual values cluster around a particular center. Like centers, measures of spread go by several names. Terms such as *variability*, *variation*, and *dispersion* are common synonyms for *spread.*

Measures of spread obey two rules:

- If every value in a variable is incremented by the value, *c*, then the spread remains unchanged.
- If every value in a variable is multiplied by a value, *d*, the spread is multiplied by the *absolute value* of *d*.

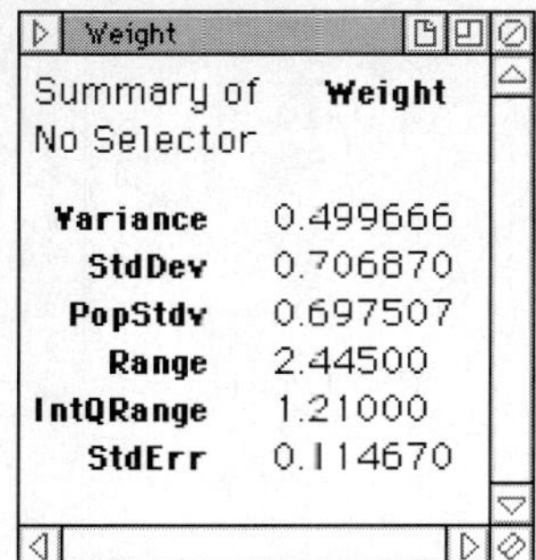

Figure 7-11. *Measures of spread computed for Weight.*

Measures of spread computed for car weight are shown in Fig. 7-11.

Each of these spreads (except the Variance) satisfies the two rules, they differ in value because each is defined and calculated differently.

The *standard deviation* (0.706870) is the most frequently used measure of spread. It is a natural companion to the sample mean because it describes the extent to which the collection of data values scatter around the sample mean. Like the sample mean, the standard deviation can be affected by extreme data values.

Standard deviations can be calculated in several different ways. For n values, $y1, y2, ..., yn$, Data Desk first computes the sample mean, y, and then calculates the standard deviation as:

$$s = \sqrt{\frac{\sum(y_i - \bar{y})^2}{n-1}}$$

range

The *range* (2.44500) is the absolute difference between the largest and smallest data values. It summarizes the overall extent of the data and is a natural companion to the midrange.

variance

The *variance* (0.499666), which is the square of the standard deviation, is often thought of as a measure of spread. Although the variance grows with increasing dispersion and shrinks when the data values cluster closely about the mean, it isn't a true measure of spread because it doesn't obey the second rule for spreads. Specifically, multiplying a variable by a value d has the effect of multiplying its variance by d^2.

interquartile range
quartiles

The *interquartile range* (1.21000) measures the range of the middle half of the data. It is the absolute difference between the data *quartiles*. (Quartiles are discussed along with other percentiles in the Section 7.8.) The interquartile range is related to the median in the sense that both are found by ordering the data values and then counting in from the ends.

standard error

The *standard error* (0.114670) is the standard deviation divided by the square root of the number of cases. It is the standard deviation of the sampling distribution of the mean.

population standard deviation

The *population standard deviation (0.697507)* is the square root of (the sum of squared deviations from the mean divided by the number of cases). This statistic is used when the cases constitute the entire population.

7.8 *Order Statistics*

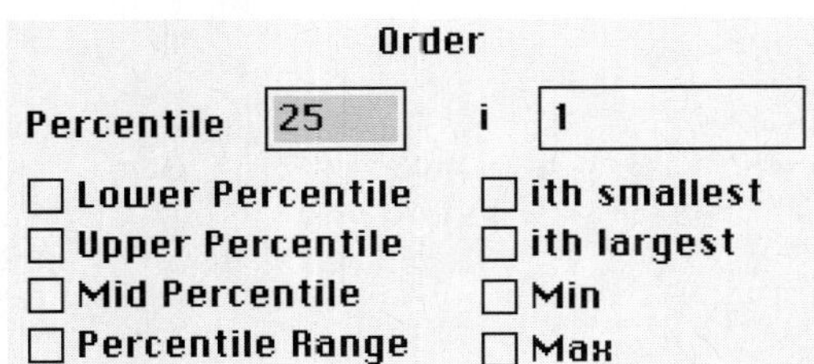

Many summary statistics, including some of those discussed so far, order the data values from lowest to highest and then select values based on their position in the ordered list. For example, the *minimum* and *maximum* values are common order statistics.

Because order-based statistics depend only upon the relative ranking of values, they resist being unduly influenced by extraordinary values. An extreme value that might render the mean or standard deviation misleading will have only a slight effect on the median, mid-25th percentile, or interquartile range. Because order statistics deal with infinities gracefully, Data Desk doesn't ignore infinities when computing order statistics. Other summary statistics treat infinities as missing values. (As with any value, you can search for infinities (∞ is typed with Alt-5 on Windows and Option-5 on Mac) with {Edit ▶ Find} **Find** and replace them with a nonnumeric value such as * to omit them from the ranking.)

percentiles

Percentiles specify relative position in an ordering of the values in a variable. A percentile is the ordered data value falling a specified fraction of the distance between the minimum and the maximum. Generally, the kth percentile (where k is between 0 and 100) in a variable of size n is the value that is the $(k/100) \times n$ smallest. The minimum is the 0th percentile and the maximum is the 100th percentile. The median is the 50th percentile and the lower and upper quartiles are the 25th and 75th percentiles, respectively. If the k% value falls between two data values, Data Desk interpolates the adjacent data values.

To specify which percentiles to compute, click in the Percentile box and type a number between 0 and 100. All percentile statistics are computed from this value.

lower percentile

The *Lower Percentile* is the value falling the specified fraction of the distance from the minimum. It is the statistic you would calculate if you desired the kth percentile.

upper percentile

The *Upper Percentile* is the value falling the specified fraction of the distance from the maximum. For example, if 30 is entered into the Percentile box, the upper percentile reports the 70th percentile (100–30). It is often useful to compare symmetric percentiles, and the upper and lower percentile statistics make doing so easy.

mid percentile

The *Mid Percentile* defines a general family of order-based centers. It is the average of the value at the specified kth percentile and the value at the symmetrically placed (100–k)th percentile. For example, a mid percentile of 0 is the midrange. The mid percentile of 25 is the average of the two quartiles.

percentile range

The *Percentile Range* defines a general family of order-based spreads. It is the difference between the value at the specified kth percentile and the value at the symmetrically placed $(100–k)$th percentile. Thus, the percentile range of 0 is the range. The Percentile Range of 25 is the interquartile range. The percentile range of 50 is always 0 because it is the difference between the median and itself.

rank

minimum
maximum

Another way to specify relative position in a variable is by the ordered position or *rank*. Percentiles do not depend directly on the number of values in a variable. Ranks count individual values from 1 to n — either counting up from the *minimum* (to obtain the ith smallest) or counting down from the *maximum* (to obtain the ith largest). The 1st largest value is the maximum. The nth largest value is the minimum. The 1st smallest value is the minimum. The nth smallest value is the maximum.

To specify which ordered positions to calculate, type a value between 1 and n in the i box. If i isn't an integer, Data Desk interpolates to find the appropriate value

7.9 *General Summaries*

Data Desk provides information fundamental to interpreting other statistics.

Group Names

The *Group Names* displays the names of the grouping categories for reports by groups tables.

Counts

Counts, usually denoted by n in formulas, sums those cases in a variable that are numbers. It doesn't count missing values, infinities, or cases with non-numeric text.

Total Cases

The *Total Cases* is the sum of Counts and the NonNumeric Cases. Because Data Desk permits both text and numbers in variables, the count of numeric values may be different from the total number of cases. Most formulas in statistics texts are written for an ideal world in which a numeric value is recorded for every case. As a result, many texts use n to denote the number of cases rather than the number of numeric values.

Non Numeric (Cases)

The *Non Numeric Cases* is the number of cases that don't contain numbers. Any case that isn't numeric is treated as missing by Data Desk in any operation requiring numbers, so the number of nonnumeric cases is also the number of missing values. (You can make a numeric case missing simply by editing its value to be nonnumeric — for example, by putting a "*" or a ">" next to it.)

Sum

The *Sum* is the sum of all values in the selected variable. NonNumeric or missing cases are not included in the calculation.

Sum of Squares

The *Sum of Squares* takes the square of each value in the selected variable and sums them.

7.10 *Moments*

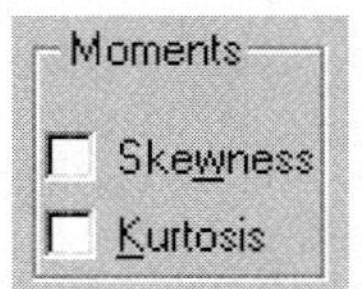

Moments summarize numerically the characteristics of data distributions observed in histograms by summarizing the shape of a data distribution. Moments should be used with caution, however, because they are easily affected by extraordinary values.

coefficient of skewness

The *Coefficient of Skewness* is a moment-based summary that describes deviation of a distribution from symmetry. A symmetric distribution has a skewness coefficient of zero. Positive skewness indicates a longer tail stretching into higher values. Negative skewness indicates that the longer tail stretches into lower values.

coefficient of kurtosis

The *Coefficient of Kurtosis* describes the degree of peakedness in the distribution's shape. Distributions with positive kurtosis have long tails and a narrow, peaked, central hump. Distributions with negative kurtosis have short tails and a wide, flat, central hump. Data Desk adjusts the kurtosis so that the Normal (or Gaussian) distribution has a kurtosis coefficient of zero.

coefficient of excess

This adjusted form is sometimes called the *coefficient of excess*.

Appendix 7.B gives the formulas for skewness and kurtosis.

APPENDIX 7A *The Biweight, A Robust Center*

biweight

The *biweight* is a center that is said to be *robust* because it is relatively unaffected by extreme values and yet behaves like the mean for well-behaved data. The biweight is a *weighted mean* in which the weights are computed *adaptively*, depending on the data values themselves. Specifically, the biweight is computed as follows:

1) For each data value, x_i, compute: $u_i = \dfrac{x_i - median(x)}{cMAD(x)}$

where median(x) and MAD(x) are the median and median absolute deviation from the median of the x-values, respectively, and c is a tuning constant that you may specify. Constants smaller than 6.0 are dangerous, and larger constants give less robust results; 7.0 is often a good choice and is the default choice given in the **Select Summary Statistics...** dialog.

2) For each u_i, compute an associated value, w_i:

$$w_i = (1 - u_i^2)^2 \qquad u_i^2 \le 1$$

$$w_i = 0 \qquad u_i^2 > 1$$

3) Compute the biweight by taking the weighted average of the data values, using the collection of w's as the weights:

$$biweight = \frac{\sum w_i x_i}{\sum w_i}$$

See Mosteller and Tukey (1977) for more information about the biweight.

APPENDIX 7B *Coefficients of Skewness and Kurtosis*

The coefficient of skewness describes deviation of a distribution from symmetry. It is calculated from the following formula:

Skewness = $M_3 / M_2^{\,3/2}$, where

$$M_2 = \sum (y_i - \bar{y})^2 / n \quad \text{and} \quad M_3 = \sum (y_i - \bar{y})^3 / n$$

The coefficient of kurtosis is a moment-based summary that describes the degree of peakedness in the distribution's shape. It is calculated from the following formula:

Kurtosis = $(M_4 / M_2^2) - 3$, where

$$M_2 = \sum (y_i - \bar{y})^2 / n \quad \text{and} \quad M_4 = \sum (y_i - \bar{y})^4 / n$$

Subtracting 3 makes the kurtosis = 0 for the normal distribution. This form is sometimes called the *coefficient of excess.*

EXERCISES

1. (a) Retrieve the Singers dataset. Create boxplots comparing the heights of all four voice parts. Use **Summary Reports** in the **Calc** menu to obtain the statistics, and record them in the table.

	Mean	**Median**	**Standard Deviation**	**Interquartile Range**	**Upper Quartile**	**Lower Quartile**
Soprano	______	______	______	______	______	______
Alto	______	______	______	______	______	______
Tenor	______	______	______	______	______	______
Bass	______	______	______	______	______	______

(b) Sketch the boxplot of the Altos and indicate on it the values of the median, upper and lower quartiles, maximum, and minimum.

2. Some of the order statistic summaries are in fact measures of center or spread. Find each of these values for the Altos and enter it in the appropriate column.

	Center	**Spread**
Mid-25th percentile	_____	_____
33% difference	_____	_____
50th percentile	_____	_____

3. (a) One of the Altos is 72 inches tall. Change her value to a missing value. (Open Alto and insert a * before the 72.) Recompute the statistics for Altos. Report the following numbers.

Mean ________ Median ________ St. dev.________ Interquartile range________

(b) Considering the effect that removing the 72-inch Alto has on the mean and median values, which statistic would you use to describe the typical height of Altos? Explain your choice.

(Don't forget to return the 72-inch measurement to its nonmissing status.)

4. Using the Cars dataset, compute the mean, median, midrange, and mid-25% percentile of the Displacement variable. Write them below.

Mean _______ Median _______ Midrange _______ Mid-25% point _______

All of these statistics are measures of center. Why do they differ so much?
(*Hint:* Make a histogram and mark on it the median, 25%, and 75% points.)

5. The data in the Cars dataset are recorded in U.S. units. Thus, for example, Weight is in thousands of pounds, Displacement is in cubic inches, and MPG is in miles/gallon. Suppose we wish to convert some of these variables to other units. First, compute the statistics for these variables as they have been recorded in the dataset.

	Unit	**Mean**	**Standard Deviation**	**Interquartile Range**	**Maximum**
Weight	1000 lb	_______	_______	_______	_______
Displacement	in^3	_______	_______	_______	_______
Horsepower	hp	_______	_______	_______	_______
MPG	mi/gal	_______	_______	_______	_______
Cylinders	# cylinders	_______	_______	_______	_______

6. Fill in the corresponding statistics for the new units. You should be able to find these values with no more than a calculator and the information from Exercise 5. You can also use the calculator ability of Data Desk's ScratchPad.

	New Unit	Conversion Factor	Mean	Standard Deviation	Interquartile Range	Maximum
Horsepower	watts	1 watt =746 hp	______	______	______	______
Displacement	cubic cm	1 cc = 1 in^3/16.4	______	______	______	______
MPG	furlongs/day	1fg/dy = mpg/52	______	______	______	______
Weight	long ton	1 ton = 2240 lb	______	______	______	______
Cylinders	excess of 4	# cyl – 4	______	______	______	______

What principles did you apply in arriving at your answers?

7. On the following histograms, mark the approximate locations of the mean, median, and mode.

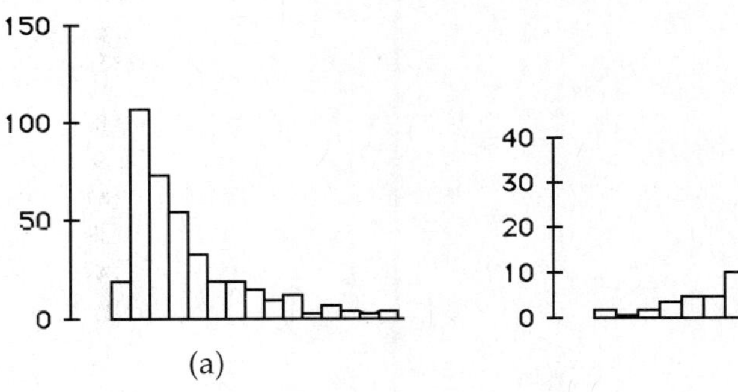

(a) (b)

8. Which of the histograms in Exercise 7 shows a skewed distribution? Would you expect the coefficient of skewness to be positive or negative?

9. Suppose that the data in the histograms of Exercise 7 were shifted by adding 100 to each value and were rescaled by multiplying each value by 10. What would the histograms of these new variables look like (compared, for example, with the histograms shown)?

CHAPTER 8

Displaying Data

DATA ANALYSIS DISPLAYS are powerful tools for finding patterns in data. Innocent looking data can reveal remarkable and unanticipated structure when plotted in the right way. Pictures naturally convey general trends and patterns and let extraordinary values or unexpected behavior stand out. When plots work together even complex relationships among several variables are easy to see and understand.

- *DATA DESK'S DISPLAYS ARE INTERACTIVE.*

To get the full benefit of a display, you need to be able to work with it while analyzing your data. In Data Desk, you aren't limited to simply reading a static display. Instead, you identify subgroups and create new variables based on them, learn about special cases, record projections, or trace sequences. You can even drag a new variable onto an axis and watch the display change.

- *DATA DESK'S DISPLAYS ARE DYNAMIC.*

Data Desk displays use animation to reveal aspects of your data that static plots can't show. Some dynamic displays, such as rotating plots, are built in. Or, you can build your own dynamic displays with sliders. And all Data Desk displays are fully integrated with other analysis methods, so you can save projections and newly found structure for further analysis.

- *DATA DESK'S DISPLAYS ARE LINKED.*

Linking highlights points that are selected in one display in *all other* displays — including variable editing windows. Thus you can see relationships among several variables at once. Data Desk also links assigned plot symbols and colors so that the representation of a case is consistent across plots.

- *DATA DESK'S DISPLAYS ACTIVELY GUIDE YOU TO NEW ANALYSES.*

Data Desk's displays feature HyperView menus, which suggest additional analyses that build on your progress. HyperView menus put new ideas for analyzing data at your fingertips.

- *DATA DESK'S DISPLAYS INCORPORATE NEW INFORMATION.*

When one of the underlying variables or functions in a display is modified, Data Desk offers to update the display to incorporate the new information. This feature significantly simplifies the analysis process by keeping track of when displays could be updated — and then doing it when you want. "Before" and "after" comparisons are easy when you redo a plot and place the versions side by side.

In this chapter we describe the displays available in Data Desk. In Chapter 9 we discuss tools and commands for working with displays and show you how to use them. Chapter 10 discusses dynamic graphics in detail.

8.1 *Data Analysis Displays*

area principle

Data Desk displays obey the *area principle*, which says that the visual impact of a part of a display is proportional to the area it occupies. Displays that observe the area principle are more likely to reveal patterns in data and less likely to create optical illusions that might lead to false conclusions. Data Desk doesn't use a false impression of depth for decoration, because that can leave the illusion that equal *volumes* represent equal amounts.[1]

Data displays can be grouped into two broad classes:

data analysis displays

versus

presentation displays

- *Data analysis displays* address the question, "What do I want to *know* about the data?" They help you discover patterns and avoid unwarranted conclusions. Data analysis displays are usually as plain as possible because excess clutter and irrelevant changes of pattern or color distract the eye from the data.
- *Presentation displays* address the question, "What do I want to *show* about the data?" They depict conclusions already reached and try to convince the viewer to believe them. They often incorporate shading, patterns, or color to improve the artistic appeal of the display.

Both kinds of displays are useful, but it is best to use them in proper order. First, understand your data with data analysis displays and then explain your insights to others with presentation displays. Data Desk is designed to analyze data and thus concentrates on data analysis displays.

Of course, many of Data Desk's plots are excellent presentation displays. You can enhance any display by adding captions and labels in a Layout window. For greater artistic control, you should use one of the many graphics programs. To transfer a Data Desk display to another program, copy the display onto the Clipboard with the **Copy Window** command in the **Edit** menu (active when the frontmost window is an output window).

8.2 *Plotting Conventions*

Most of Data Desk's displays are requested from the **Plot** menu, or from HyperView menus. Each plot command creates an icon that holds the plot, and then opens it to show the plot. Data Desk constructs a name for the plot by abbreviating the names of the variables depicted. To rename an open display, hold down the right mouse button on Windows or the ⌘ key on Mac, click on its titlebar and choose **Rename Window.** Both the display and its icon name change. Alternatively, you can rename the display's icon in the usual way.

Data Desk initially arranges displays so that four or more are visible at once on the screen. You can often see more in your data by comparing several plots to each other when each shows a different view of the data. By integrating these views into a coherent whole (perhaps with the aid of selecting parts of one display to see the corresponding parts of the other highlight), you can see far more in the data than any one display can show.

You can arrange and resize display windows to suit your particular needs. You may also use the {Special ▸ Arrange} **Tile Windows** or **Stack Windows** commands to reshape and reposition all displays. **Tile Windows** arranges all open displays so that all are visible (Fig. 8-1). **Stack Windows** arranges the displays in large format in a stack, fanning their title bars so that you can select any display with a single mouse click (Fig. 8-2).

[1]For an amusing and informative discussion of these concepts, see the classic book *How to Lie with Statistics* by Darrell Huff.

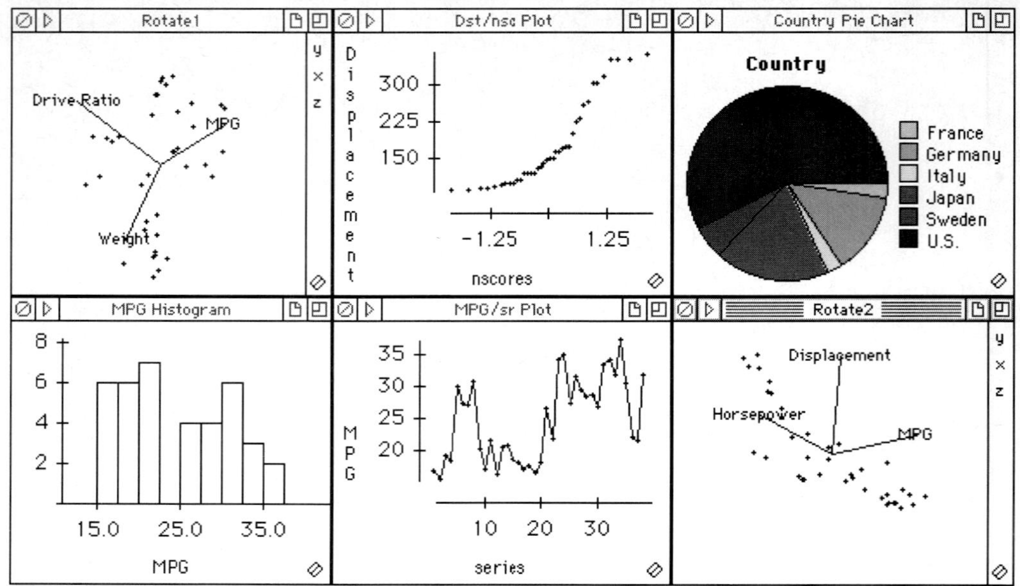

Figure 8-1. *Tiled windows cover the screen. Click a plot's zoom box to see it full-size.*

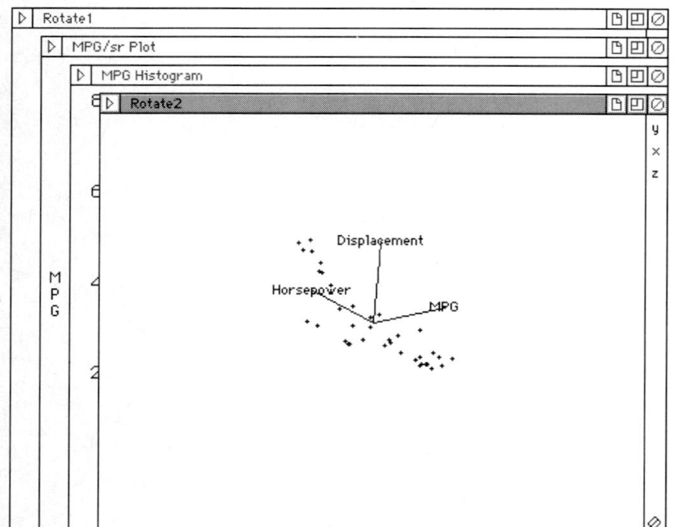

Figure 8-2*. Stacked windows.*

The **Close All ▶ Displays** command in the **Data** menu provides a convenient way to close all open display windows into their icons. To close selected displays, select their icons (or icon aliases), hold the Shift key, and choose {Data} **Close.**

Most **Plot** commands can generate several plots at once. Commands that are plural (for example, **Histograms**, **Scatterplots**, and the like) generate a separate display for each icon selected or for each pair of *x*- and *y*-variables.

Data Desk draws most plots in white on a black background and prints all plots in black on a white background. Black on white is generally better for printing but is less effective for interactive displays. Points plotted white-on-black look like stars on a black background and seem to glow on the screen, making them easier to see. You can change displays to plot black-on-white with the {Plot ▶ Plot Options} **Black on White** command. Holding down the option key while clicking the zoom box of a plot window sizes it to match the current page setup specifications within the constraint of the plot buffer.

MAC OS

All plots in Data Desk have an option to Set Plot Scale in the plot window's HyperView menu. You can also match the scale and size of plots. Drag the icon or icon alias of one plot into the window of another. The second plot will rescale to the same scale as the first and resize to the same physical dimensions. You can then easily overlay the two plots in a layout window.

If the drawing of a plot is aborted (for example, because Data Desk alerts you that a variable may have the wrong structure and you cancel the command or because you aborted plotting by pressing Esc button on

Windows or the ⌘-period on Mac), Data Desk may create an empty plot. You can discard the plot (drag its icon alias to the trash), or substitute new variables in it as described in Section 9.11.

HOW-TO

Histograms depict the distribution of values in a *numeric* variable.

Bar Charts depict the number of cases in each group of a *categorical* variable.

Plots to Depict Distributions

The plots discussed in the following section depict the distribution of a variable or compare the distributions of several variables or groups. By understanding a variable's distribution you can be aware of extraordinary cases, of clumping, or of asymmetries that might alter your conclusions about the data.

8.3 *Histograms*

histograms

Data Desk makes two kinds of displays that show data in bars. Bar charts (Section 8.8) display variables that contain category names or identifiers. Each bar depicts the number of cases in a category. Histograms display variables that hold numeric values. Each data value is represented by an equal amount of area in the display, and these little bits of area are collected into bars placed side by side. Thus histograms depict the overall distribution of data values.

HOW-TO

How to make histograms:

- Select the variable(s) to display.
- Choose **Histograms** from the **Plot** menu.

Histograms show:

- The range of values covered by the data
- Where the values concentrate
- Whether the values are distributed symmetrically around the center or trail off to one side
- Whether there are gaps where no values were observed
- Whether any values stray markedly from the rest

Histograms show the distribution of numeric values. The division into bars is arbitrary and can be changed to adjust the display. (By contrast, bar charts show counts of cases in predefined groups.) Often the first questions asked about a numeric variable can be answered by a histogram. For example: How big are the values? Are they spread out or compact? Are they symmetrically distributed about the middle or skewed? Do they cluster into two or more groups?

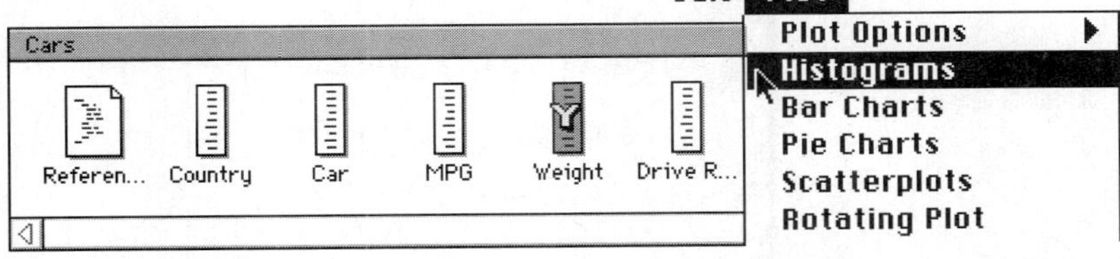

*Figure 8-3. To make a histogram, select the variable to display and choose **Histograms** from the **Plot** menu.*

To make histograms, select the variables to be displayed and choose {Plot} **Histograms** (Fig. 8-3). The first histogram opens in the upper left corner so that you can drag its size box down and right. Or you can click its zoom box to fill the screen if you want to. Histograms take the name of the variable they display.

Fig. 8-4 shows the weights (in thousands of pounds) of the cars in the Cars dataset. The height of each bar shows the number of cars whose weights fall in a given range. The range

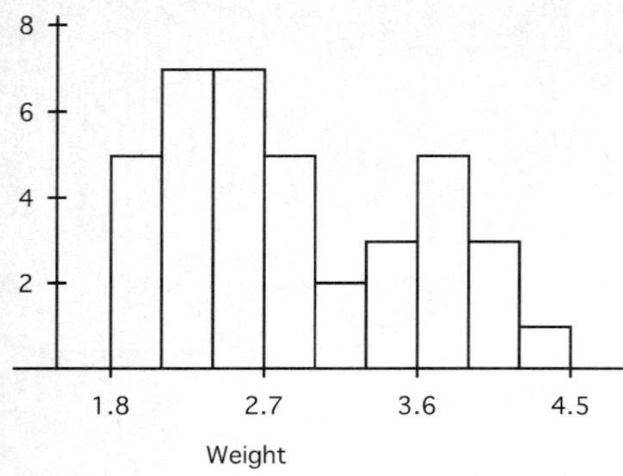

Figure 8-4. *Histogram of car weights.*

covered by a bar starts at the value labeled at its left edge and extends up to, but not including, the value at the next tick mark to the right. Thus in Fig. 8-4 each bar depicts a range of 300 pounds. The cars weigh between 1800 pounds and 4500 pounds. If you look carefully, you can see that there is one car between 4200 and 4500 pounds, three between 3900 and 4200, and so on.[2]

The shape of the histogram reveals whether the data distribution is generally *symmetric*. Symmetrically distributed data are usually easier to work with and are more likely to satisfy the assumptions required by most statistics. If a histogram isn't symmetric, it is said to be *skewed* toward the side that is more stretched out. The *tails* of a distribution contain the extreme largest and extreme smallest values in the data.

A histogram may have a single central hump, or *mode*, or it may have more than one mode. *Unimodal* (single-hump) data distributions are usually easier to work with and more likely to satisfy the assumptions of common statistical methods. *Bimodal* (two-hump) and *multimodal* (many-hump) distributions may indicate subgroups in the data. For example, a histogram of heights of people will usually have two modes — one consisting mostly of men and one mostly of women. Statisticians generally do not think that ordinary bar-to-bar variation in a histogram identifies modes, but rather they look at the overall shape of the histogram to see whether it shows large-scale humps.

The histogram of car weights is interesting because it is bimodal. This distribution probably represents a division between compact cars and larger cars, but it is remarkable to see such a strong split into groups rather than a smooth distribution including both large and small cars.

The **Compute Bar Counts** command in the histogram's HyperView menu creates three HotResult variables and places them in a folder called *Derived,* which is located inside the File cabinet. The *Levels* variable contains the values at the left edge of each bar, the *Count* variable contains the number of cases assigned to each bin, and the *CumulativeCounts* variable contains the number of cases assigned to each bin plus the cases for all of the bins to the left of it. These HotResult variables update automatically in response to changes in the histogram. Thus, if the data underlying the histogram change or you change the scale of the histogram, the values in the HotResult variables update, and any analyses built using the HotResult variables offer to update to reflect these changes.

[2]The plot tool, discussed in Chapter 9, will grab the histogram and slide it side to side, so you can position any bar directly over the vertical axis to read its height easily.

8.4 *Recentering and Rescaling Histograms*

With all that you can learn from a histogram it is important to keep in mind what you *cannot* learn. When a histogram is drawn, the data values are grouped and each group is graphed with a bar. Histograms of the same data drawn at different scales or with different group boundaries can look quite different. For example, if you drag the histogram window's size box to the right, the histogram gives the impression of an almost flat distribution of weights (Fig. 8-5).

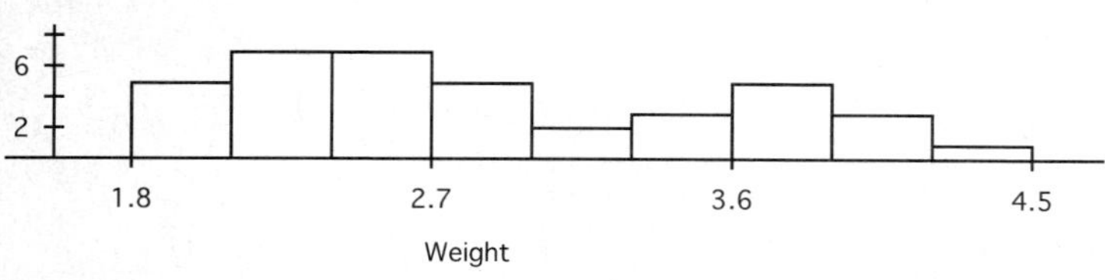

Figure 8-5. *Drag the Size box to the right to make a histogram that gives the impression of a flat distribution.*

If you drag the size box down and left to make the histogram tall and thin, it gives the impression of greater variation from bar to bar (Fig. 8-6).

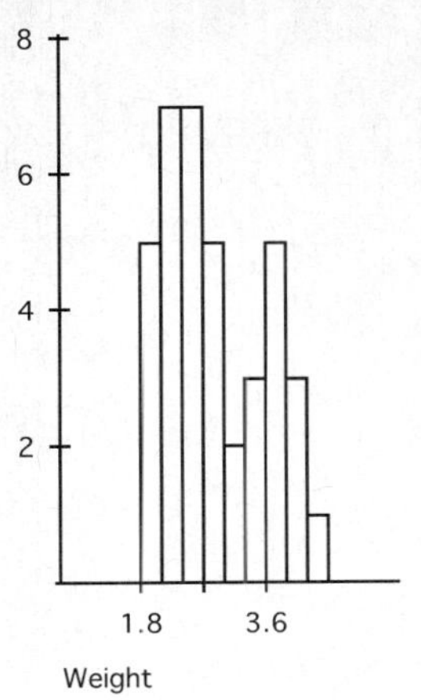

Figure 8-6. A tall histogram gives the impression of greater variability.

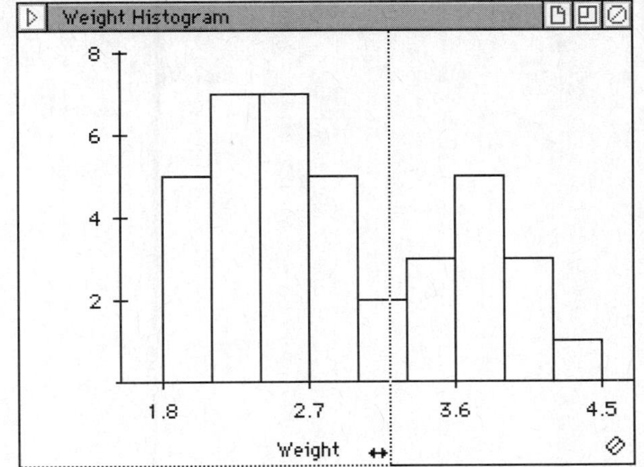

***Figure 8-7.** Hold down the **Ctrl** key on Windows, or the **Option** key on Mac, and resize the window to specify more or fewer bars.*

The bars of a resized histogram adjust proportionately to the changes in the window dimensions but ordinarily don't change in number.

If you press and hold the **Ctrl** key on Windows, or the **Option** key on Mac, while resizing the window, the histogram bars remain about the same size but the number of bars changes to fill the new window. For example, you can rescale the car weights histogram so that each bar represents a weight range of 1000 pounds instead of 300. Hold down the **Ctrl** key on Windows, or the **Option** key on Mac, (the cursor will change to a left-right arrow when it is placed in the grow box) and drag the window smaller to leave room for slightly more than four bars (Fig. 8-7). When you release the mouse button, the data are redistributed into four bars (Fig. 8-8). This scaling hides the bimodal pattern — a good example of the importance of finding the right scale for a display.

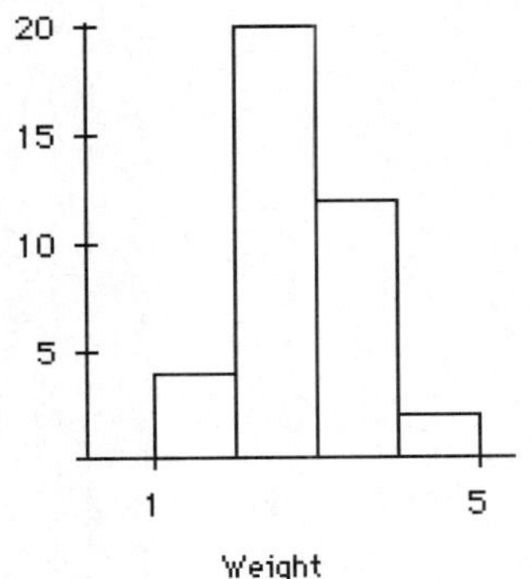

***Figure 8-8.** The histogram of Figure 8-7 resized to four bars.*

These two rescaling methods make it easy to adjust a histogram to have bars of any size and to have roughly the number of bars that makes the display look best. For example, to make the bars smaller, make the histogram window smaller. To increase the number of bars, hold down **Ctrl** key on Windows, or the **Option** key on Mac, and make the window wider. At one extreme, you can make a histogram with very few bars. At the other extreme, many of the bars are empty, so the filled bars appear to be separated. For example, the car weights were recorded to the nearest hundred pounds, so a histogram with bars representing ranges smaller than that may have empty bars (Fig. 8-9). As you rescale the histogram, the HotResult variables that record bar counts will automatically update (see Section 8.3).

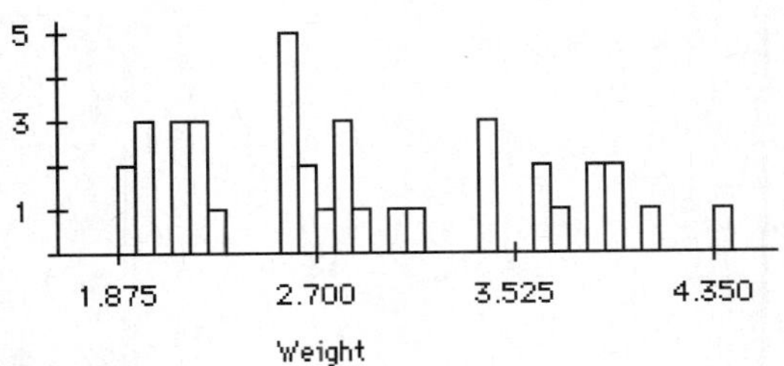

***Figure 8-9.** Requesting too many bars leaves empty bars.*

Because differently scaled histograms of the same data can look remarkably different, it is a good idea to rescale a histogram a few times to get a sense of what it *doesn't* say about the data.

The **Plot Scale...** command in the Histogram's global HyperView menu offers another way to rescale a histogram. You can specify the starting bar, bar width, and bars per tick interval. The **Plot Scale...** command is also available from the {Modify ▶ Scale} submenu.

The dialog initially displays the current values for the frontmost histogram. Type in new values and press **OK**. Keep in mind that these val-

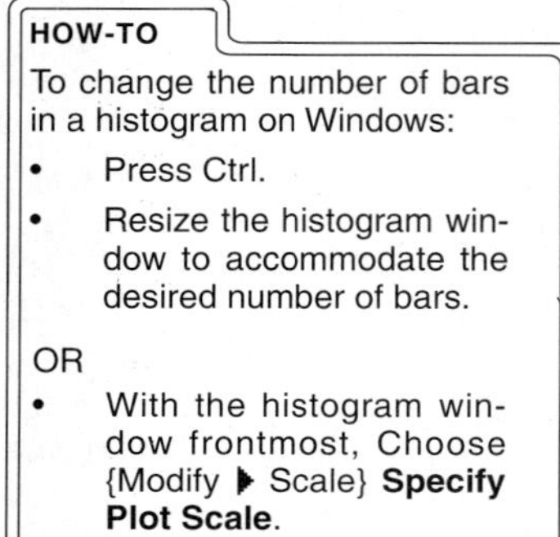
HOW-TO

To change the number of bars in a histogram on Windows:

- Press Ctrl.
- Resize the histogram window to accommodate the desired number of bars.

OR

- With the histogram window frontmost, Choose {Modify ▶ Scale} **Specify Plot Scale**.

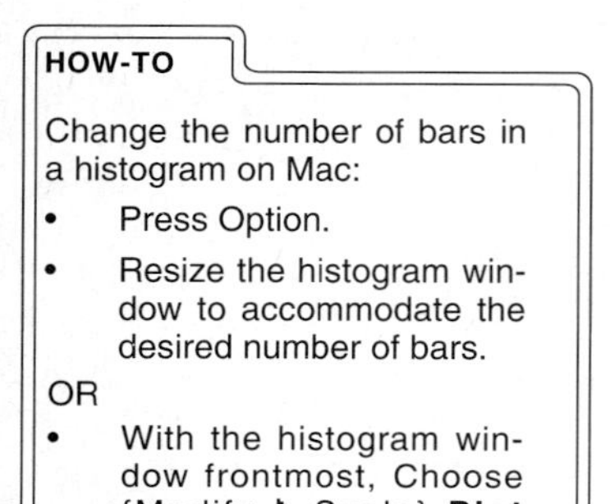
HOW-TO

Change the number of bars in a histogram on Mac:

- Press Option.
- Resize the histogram window to accommodate the desired number of bars.

OR

- With the histogram window frontmost, Choose {Modify ▶ Scale} **Plot Scale**.

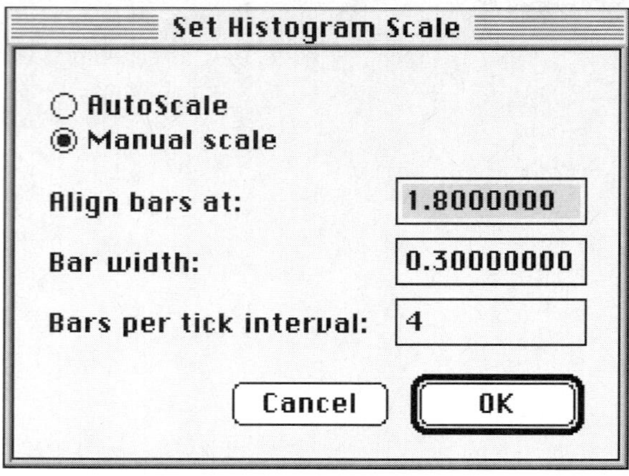

Figure 8-10. ***Plot Scale*** *lets you control histogram scaling in detail.*

ues are in the same units as the data being plotted, in this case thousands of pounds (Fig. 8-10).

Data Desk sets the histogram to **Manual Scale** when the histogram scale has been changed. To return to automatic scaling, click the **AutoScale** radio button in the Scale Histogram dialog.

You can apply the scale of a histogram to any other histogram by dragging the icon alias of the source histogram into the center of the target histogram.

To slide a histogram side to side, grab it with the Grabber, ☝, from the Plot Tools palette and slide it to the desired location (see Section 9.8).

Choose {Modify ▶ Scale} **Home** to return the histogram to its original scale.

8.5 Dotplots

Histograms display the distribution of all the values in a variable. Dotplots compare the distributions of values in each of several groups. For example, the data in the Cars dataset include the grouping variable *Country,* which specifies the group (country) in which each car was manufactured (Fig. 8-11).

Car	Country	MPG	Weight
Buick Estate Wagon	U.S.	16.9	4.360
Ford Country Squire Wagon	U.S.	15.5	4.054
Chevy Malibu Wagon	U.S.	19.2	3.605
Chrysler LeBaron Wagon	U.S.	18.5	3.940
Chevette	U.S.	30.0	2.155
Toyota Corona	Japan	27.5	2.560
Datsun 510	Japan	27.2	2.300
Dodge Omni	U.S.	30.9	2.230
Audi 5000	Germany	20.3	2.830
Volvo 240 GL	Sweden	17.0	3.140
Saab 99 GLE	Sweden	21.6	2.795
Peugeot 694 SL	France	16.2	3.410
Buick Century Special	U.S.	20.6	3.380

Figure 8-11. *The variable* Country *can be a group variable.*

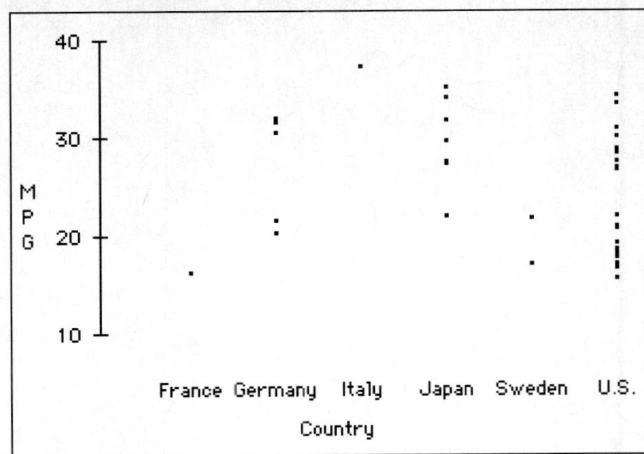

Figure 8-12. Dotplot y by x of MPG *by* Country.

To compare miles per gallon for the cars according to their country of origin, select the variable *MPG*, containing the mpg of the cars, as the *y*-variable, and the variable *Country*, containing the name of the country of origin, as the *x*-variable, and then choose {Plot} **Dotplot y by x**.

A dotplot displays each group as a thin vertical strip and each value as a single dot in its strip You can see where the dots clump together and how the groups compare in location and range (Fig. 8-12).

For each group, the dotplot shows:

- The overall level of values
- The range of the data
- Any clumping of values in the variable

In addition, the collection of dotplots together shows:

- How the levels of the groups compare
- How the ranges of the groups compare
- Whether clumpings are similar across groups

If there is no room to put the full name of a group under its strip of dots, Data Desk abbreviates the name, first to three characters then to just the initial letter. If you resize the window to make it quite small, there may be no room for any labels.

Dotplots can be converted into boxplots (see Section 8.7) by choosing the **Add Boxes** command from the dotplot's global HyperView menu. When the plot is displayed as a boxplot, the command changes to **Remove Boxes**. You can switch the plot back to a dotplot by choosing the **Remove Boxes** command.

8.6 *Dotplots of Separate Variables*

Sometimes you may want to compare several variables in the same relation. They might, for example, be measurements of the same quantity taken at different times or places. The **Dotplot Side by Side** command offers a way to display variables from the same relation side by side. Select the variables to be plotted and choose {Plot} **Dotplot Side by Side** (Fig. 8-13). Dotplots Side by Side use casewise deletion for missing values, so if there is a missing value in one of the variables the entire case will be omitted from the plot.

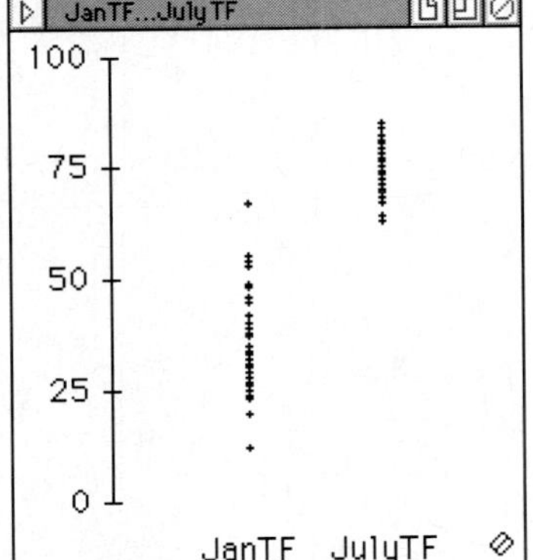

Figure 8-13. Use of the **Dotplot Side by Side** *command plots* January *and* July *temperatures.*

Dotplots provide a convenient way to display the relationship between data values and color when you assign colors according to the values in a variable (see Section 9.13 for details). A dotplot of the variable from which colors were assigned shows the colors and the values that go with them and can serve as a key for the color assignment in other displays.

8.7 *Boxplots*

Boxplots display much of the same information as dotplots, but hide value-by-value detail to show more summary information. To make a boxplot, select a variable holding the values to be displayed as *y* and a variable holding the group identities as x and choose {Plot} **Boxplot y by x**. To compare several variables in a relation, select the variables to display and choose {Plot} **Boxplot Side by Side**.

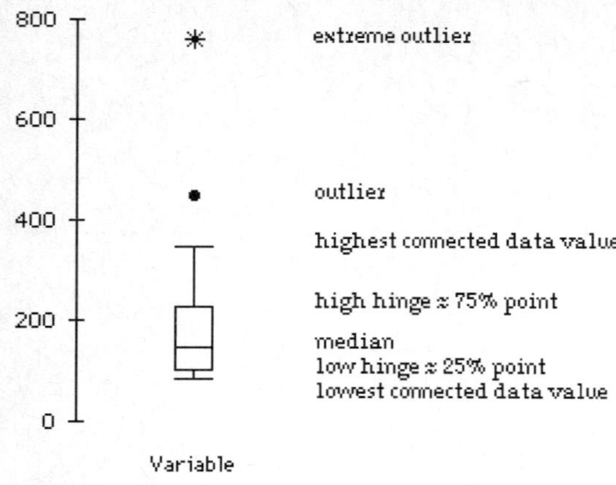

Figure 8-14. Components of a Boxplot.

Boxplots have four components (Fig. 8-14):

- The outlined central box depicts the middle half of the data between the 25th and the 75th percentiles.
- The horizontal line across the box marks the median.
- The *whiskers* extend from the top and bottom of the box to depict the extent of the main body of the data.
- In addition, extreme data values are plotted individually, usually with a circle. Very extreme values are plotted with a starburst (see Fig. 8-14).

In Appendix 8A we define the components of a boxplot precisely.

Boxplots comparing several variables show patterns in level and spread, and possible outlying values. For each variable selected, the boxplot shows:

- The overall level of values
- The overall variability or spread of the data
- Whether the main body of data values is distributed symmetrically around the median
- Any values that stray markedly from the rest

> **REMEMBER**
> The **Boxplot Side by Side and the Dotplot Side by Side** commands operate casewise, so if there is a missing value in one of the variables the entire case will be omitted from the plot.

In addition, the collection of boxplots shows:

- How the levels of the variables compare
- How the spreads of the variables compare
- Relationships between the levels and spread. For example, do variables with a higher overall level tend to be more variable as well?

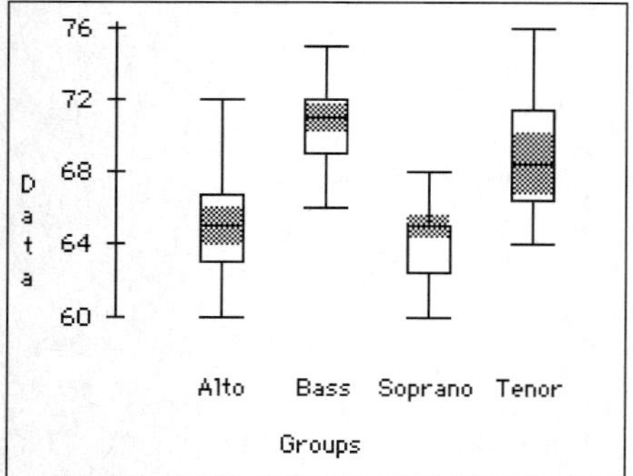

Figure 8-15. Boxplots of singers' heights by part. The median soprano height overlaps the upper edge of the box.

Fig. 8-15 shows that the tenors and basses are generally taller than the sopranos and altos, which isn't surprising. All four groups seem to be comparably variable.

Resizing a boxplot window changes the heights and horizontal locations of the boxes but not their widths. If the window is too narrow, the boxes may overlap and the box labels are abbreviated as for dotplots.

Boxplots can be converted into dotplots (see Section 8.5) by choosing the **Remove Boxes** command from the boxplot's global HyperView menu. When the plot is displayed as a dotplot, the command changes to **Add Boxes**. You can switch the plot back to a boxplot by choosing the **Add Boxes** command.

Boxplots and Inference

It is tempting to think that, when two boxplot boxes do not overlap, the difference between their medians is statistically significant. However, although inferential statistics usually take into account sample size, boxplot boxes don't. Boxplots display confidence intervals to indicate whether the difference between any two of the group medians is statistically significant. The {Plot ▶ Plot Options} **Boxplot Options** command offers to remove these confidence intervals. You can also set boxplot options from the global HyperView menu of any Boxplot window.

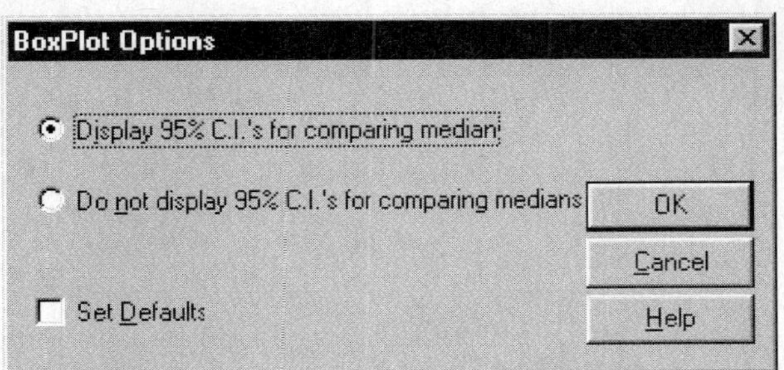

Figure 8-16. *Boxplot options offer to display confidence intervals for comparing medians of two boxes.*

The *Display 95% C.I.'s for comparing medians* option superimposes a shaded area on each box, indicating confidence interval bounds around its median (Fig. 8-16). These are not individual confidence intervals, but rather are constructed so that if two gray boxes fail to overlap, the corresponding medians are discernably different at approximately the 5% significance level. (See Appendix 8A for Boxplot definitions.)

For the singers' heights, the tenors and basses appear to be significantly taller than the sopranos and altos because the shaded areas of the boxes don't overlap (see Fig. 8-15). It isn't clear whether the basses are significantly taller than the tenors. We may want to look into this question more carefully with more powerful inferential methods. (See Chapters 18 and 19 for a discussion of hypothesis testing and confidence intervals.)

Plots to Compare Categories

category variables

Variables that classify cases into *categories* rather than reporting measurements or values require special displays. Data Desk offers two displays for such *discrete* data: bar charts and pie charts.

> **REMEMBER**
>
> Histograms show the distribution of a variable that holds numbers.
>
> Bar charts show the counts in each category of a variable that names groups.

8.8 *Bar Charts*

Bar charts are sometimes confused with histograms because the two displays look very similar. The difference between them is in the kind of data they display. Bar charts display variables that contain category names or identifiers. Histograms display variables that hold numeric values. A bar chart depicts each category with a bar whose length is proportional to the number of cases in the category. Unlike histogram bars, the left-to-right order of bar chart bars is arbitrary, so the overall shape of a bar chart is meaningless.

> **HOW-TO**
>
> How to make a bar chart:
>
> - Select the variable that identifies the groups.
> - Choose **Bar Charts** from the **Plot** menu.

To make a bar chart, select the variable that identifies the groups and choose {Plot} **Bar Charts**. For example, a bar chart of *Country* from the Cars data is shown in Fig. 8-17.

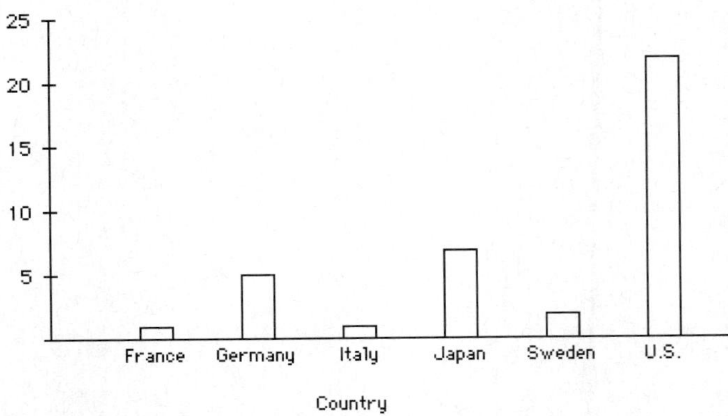

Figure 8-17. *Bar chart of* Country *for the Cars data.*

Bar charts make it particularly easy to compare categories because most people can discern differences in the lengths of two bars set on a common baseline quite well, and even (somewhat less precisely) the ratios of the lengths. For example, Fig. 8-17 clearly shows that there are slightly more Japanese cars than German cars in this sample and that U.S. cars dominate the sample with three or four times as many cars.

However, bar charts don't emphasize the relationship of category size to the whole sample, so they usually are used when the relative sizes of the groups are of greater interest than the division of the whole into subgroups.

A bar chart shows:

- How many categories there are
- The relative size of each category
- Whether any category is particularly dominant or particularly sparse

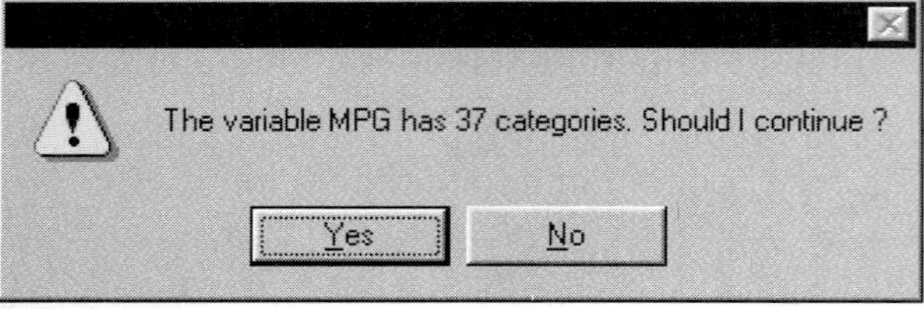

Figure 8-18. *Data Desk posts an alert if you choose a possibly inappropriate variable for a bar chart.*

Group names are abbreviated if necessary. Groups can be identified with numbers as well as names. Data Desk assumes that the variable selected for a bar chart contains names and interprets the contents of that variable according to their *text* values. Thus the values "1" and "1.0" would not be placed in the same category because their text values differ, even though they are equal numerically. If Data Desk suspects that a variable is not a group variable (for example, if it has many categories, each of them with only one case) it checks with you before proceeding (Fig. 8-18).

The **Compute Bar Counts** command in the bar chart's HyperView menu creates three HotResult variables and places them in the *Derived* folder, inside the File cabinet. The variable *Levels* contains the name of each category, the *Count* variable contains the number of cases assigned to each category and the *CumulativeCounts* variable contains the number of cases assigned to each category plus the cases for all the categories preceding it. These HotResult variables update automatically in response to changes in the bar chart. Thus, if the data underlying the bar chart change, the values in the HotResults update, and any analyses built on the HotResult variables offer to update to reflect these changes.

8.9 Pie Charts

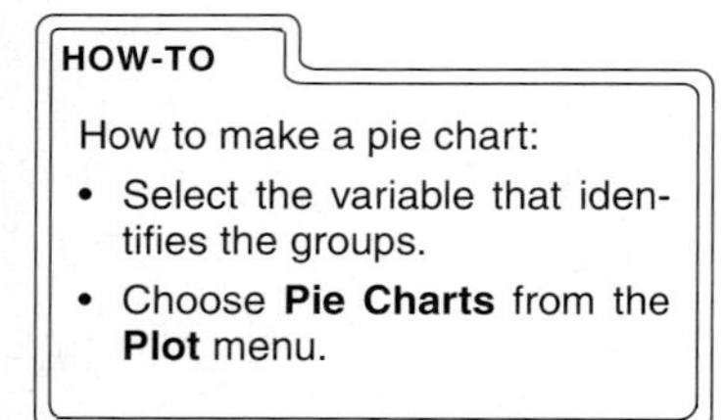
HOW-TO

How to make a pie chart:

- Select the variable that identifies the groups.
- Choose **Pie Charts** from the **Plot** menu.

Traditionally, pie charts have been thought of as presentation displays. A pie chart depicts a variable that contains category names or identifiers. The "pie" represents the whole population, which has been partitioned into categories or groups, each represented by a slice or wedge. The area of each wedge of the pie is proportional to the number of cases in its category. Pie charts are thus particularly suited for displaying the division of a whole into several subgroups.

To make a pie chart, select a variable containing category identifiers and choose {Plot} **Pie Charts**. To change the variable being displayed in an existing pie chart, drag a new variable containing category identifiers into the pie chart window.

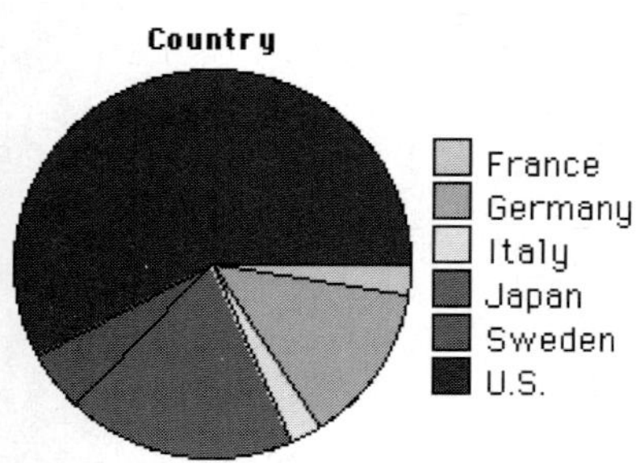

Figure 8-19. *Pie chart of* Country *in the Cars data.*

For example, the pie chart of *Country* from the Cars data (Fig. 8-19) highlights the *relative fraction* of cars from each country. By contrast, the bar chart shown in Fig. 8-17, emphasizes the *number* of cars from each country.

Although pie charts are based on the area principle, they have been criticized because many people can't discern small differences in the angles of pie wedges and thus may misjudge what a pie chart displays. Nevertheless, pie charts are intuitively easy to understand and are used widely.

Pie charts show:

- How many categories there are
- The partitioning of the whole into fractions
- Whether any category is particularly dominant or particularly small

Pie charts are colored by default. Each slice takes on the color that would be assigned to its category if the displayed variable were used to assign colors by group (see Section 9.13). If you are using Data Desk on a Mac, you can choose to fill the slices of the pie chart with patterns by choosing the **Use Patterns** command from the plot's HyperView menu. The **Use Patterns** command changes to **Use Colors** when the pie chart is displayed with patterns.

Plots to Depict Relationships

Many of Data Desk's displays show the relationships among two or more variables, or the relationship between a single variable and a standard. These plots depict each case as a point in the display. The points can be plotted with different symbols, connected with lines, moved on the display, and otherwise modified by using the plot tools and commands discussed in Chapter 9.

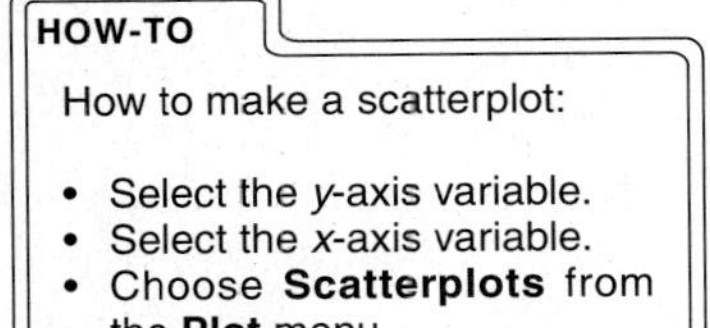
HOW-TO

How to make a scatterplot:

- Select the *y*-axis variable.
- Select the *x*-axis variable.
- Choose **Scatterplots** from the **Plot** menu.

8.10 *Scatterplots*

Scatterplots show relationships between pairs of variables. In Data Desk, values in the same row of each variable in a relation refer to the same case and thus are paired suitably for a scatterplot. Every case plotted in a scatterplot has two data values — one for each of the two variables graphed. By convention, the variable whose values are plotted vertically is denoted y, and the variable whose values are plotted horizontally is denoted x. The distinction between y and x variables persists throughout much of statistical analysis and is reflected in the different ways that Data Desk highlights icons designated y or x.

To make a scatterplot, first select the variable to plot on the vertical (y) axis. Then, hold down the Shift key (to extend the selection and get the cursor), and select the variable to plot on the horizontal (x) axis. Finally, choose {Plot} **Scatterplots**.

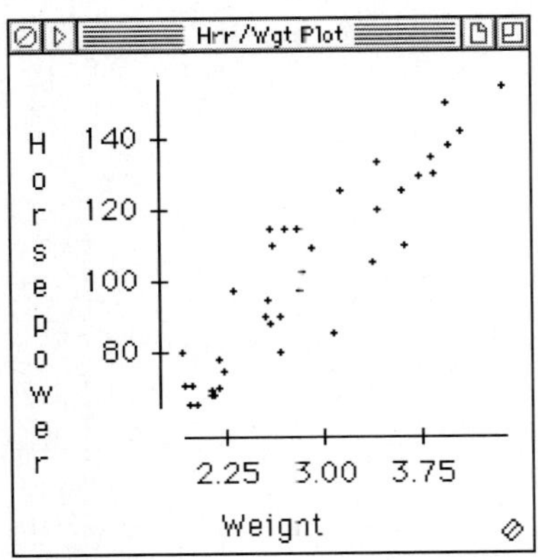

Figure 8-20. *Scatterplots show the relationship between two variables.*

For example, in the Cars dataset, a scatterplot of *Horsepower* versus *Weight* shows that heavier cars have more powerful engines, as you might expect (Figs 8-20 and 8-21).

Scatterplots show:

- Trends between y-values and x-values
- Whether a trend is straight or curved
- Clustering of data points
- Changes in the spread of y-values as x-values increase
- Extraordinary data points far from the rest of the data

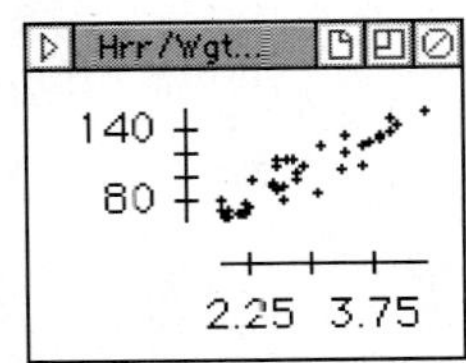

Figure 8-21. *A compact version of Figure 8-20 shows much the same information.*

Trends in a scatterplot are often interesting statistically. Straight-line relationships may be approximated numerically with regression analysis, which we discuss in Chapter 22. Simple curved relationships can be described similarly with the use of transformations, such as those that we discuss in Chapter 11.

Two commands in the scatterplot's global HyperView menu help you find interesting linear trends. The **Add Regression Line** calculates a best fit line by minimizing the sum of squared residuals and displays the line on the plot. If you have colored the points in your plot (see Section 9.13), the **Add Color Regression Lines** command displays a separate regression line for each color. This feature helps you compare groups and identify outliers. To remove any point from the calculation of color regression lines, change the point's color to white. (To color a point, select it and click on the desired color in the colors palette.)

As with histograms, the visual impression of trends in a scatterplot is altered if the size and shape of its window is changed. However, a scatterplot can become too large. A plot with only a small number of data points (around 20 or 30) often is easier to read when drawn in a window about 2 inches square than drawn to fill the entire screen. See Section 9.15 for a discussion of manipulating the scale with the **Plot Scale...** command.

You can select several *y*-variables (press the Ctrl key on Windows, or the Option key on Mac, to get the Y cursor) and one *x*-variable, or one *y*-variable and several *x*-variables to request several plots at once. For example, you might plot the dependent variable in a multiple regression as *y* against each of the predictors in the regression equation.

You can replace either variable in a scatterplot simply by dragging the icon of the new variable on top of the axis labels of the variable to be replaced (Fig. 8-22). To replace both variables, select the new *y*-axis variable as *y* (Ctrl-click on Windows or Option-click on Mac) and the new *x*-axis variable as *x* (Shift-click) and drag them both into the center of the plot.

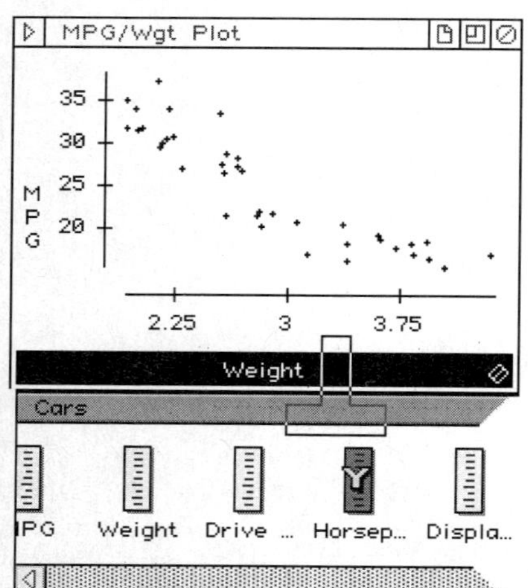

Figure 8-22. *Drag the icon of the variable on top of the axis label to replace the variable in the plot.*

Overlaying Plots

You can overlay scatterplots of other variables over any scatterplot. The points plotted in an overlay layer cannot be selected; only the original, "base" layer of points can be selected. However, points in overlays are still linked to other plots and analyses, so they will highlight, change color, and change symbol to reflect corresponding changes in other plots.

The **Show Plot Info** command in a scatterplot's HyperView menu opens a window that displays the elements of the plot and allows you to modify these elements (Fig. 8-23). For example, next to the keyword *Scatterplot* you will find the names of the variables plotted. You can drag and drop a variable's icon over either of these names to change the scatterplot. Next to the keyword *Selector* you will find the name of the selector variable (see Chapter 13) currently applied to the plot (if any). Drag a new selector variable here to apply it to the plot. Following the keyword *Overlays,* is a list of y–x pairs displayed as overlays in the plot. Of course, you can drag new variable icons over any of these variable names to substitute the new variable for the old ones. Any parts of this window that aren't currently used by the scatterplot show the placeholder word "Value" to indicate where to drag the icon of a variable.

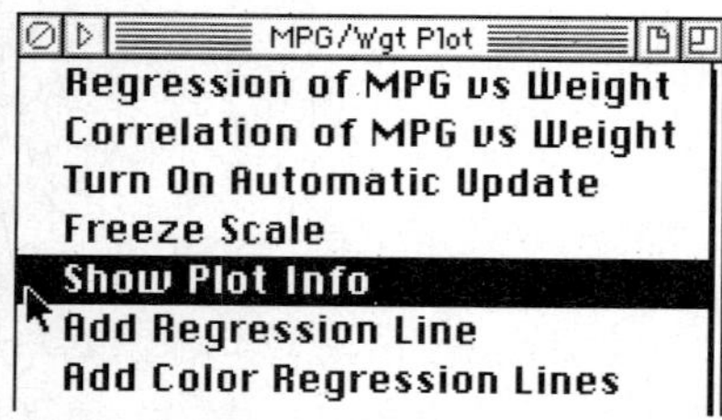

Figure 8-23. *Choose* ***Show Plot Info*** *command in the HyperView menu to display the elements of the scatterplot.*

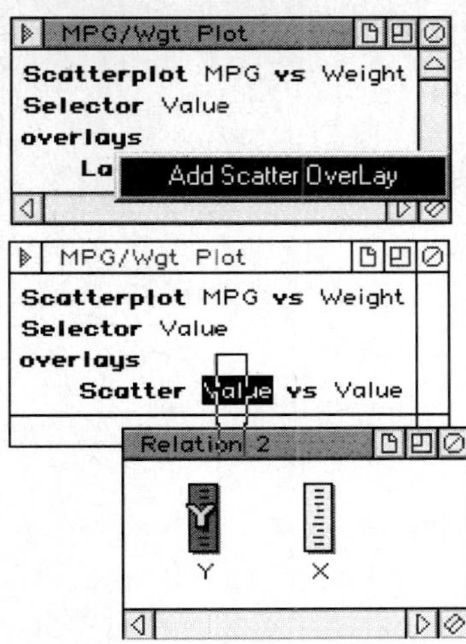

Figure 8-24. Drag the variables over the Value label in the design window to add a layer of data to the scatterplot.

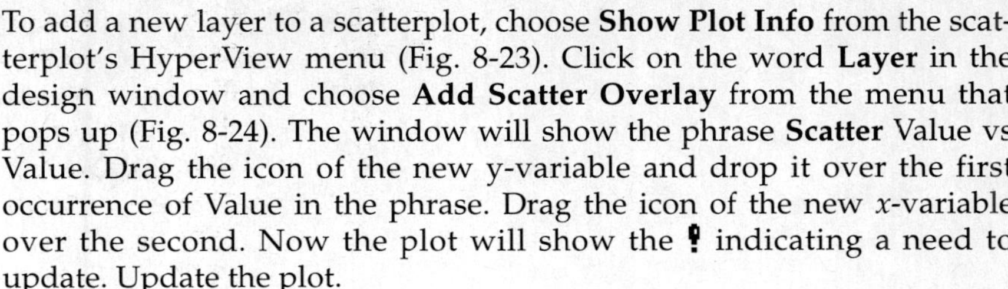

To add a new layer to a scatterplot, choose **Show Plot Info** from the scatterplot's HyperView menu (Fig. 8-23). Click on the word **Layer** in the design window and choose **Add Scatter Overlay** from the menu that pops up (Fig. 8-24). The window will show the phrase **Scatter** Value vs Value. Drag the icon of the new y-variable and drop it over the first occurrence of Value in the phrase. Drag the icon of the new x-variable over the second. Now the plot will show the ! indicating a need to update. Update the plot.

Now the word "Scatter" in the design window holds a HyperView menu that offers to remove the layer or to insert another layer. You can follow the same procedure to add more layers.

Plot layers work best if the overlaid plots are from a relation other than the base plot. If the overlaid plot is from the same relation, the color, symbol, and selection state of the points in both the base and overlay layers must be the same. This condition can make it difficult to tell which layer of points you are looking at. It also may be confusing when you select a point and also see another, apparently unrelated point highlight as well (because it plots the same case in the relation in terms of two other variables).

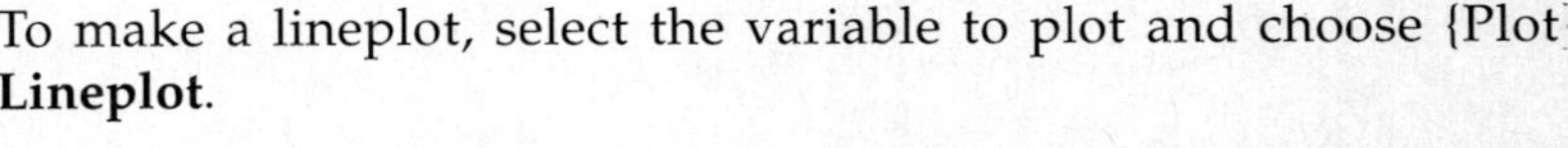

8.11 *Lineplots*

A lineplot graphs a variable in case order and connects the successive points with lines. It is like a scatterplot of a variable against another that counts from 1 to n.

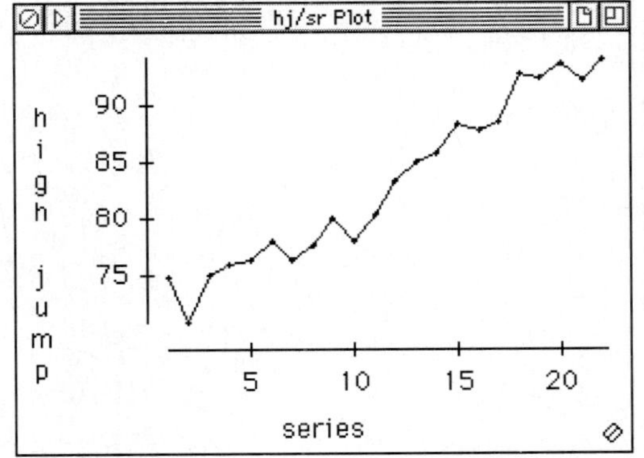

Figure 8-25. A sequence plot of Olympic high jump gold medal performance since 1900 shows a consistent trend of improvement.

To make a lineplot, select the variable to plot and choose {Plot} **Lineplot**.

The line connecting successive points helps your eye to follow any trends, so lineplots are often used for data recorded over time (Fig. 8-25). However, it is a good idea to make a lineplot of any variable just to check for unexpected trends related to the sequence order in which the data are recorded. This is especially true if the cases are recorded in the order in which they were collected.

Lineplots space the datapoints evenly across the x-axis. If your data were measured in order but at unequal intervals, you may get a more appropriate picture of your data by adding lines to a scatterplot of the data against an x-variable that specifies the correct spacing.

The **Multiple Lineplot** command plots several variables, against a common sequence axis. If you are working without a color display, each variable is plotted with a different symbol (up to eight symbols). If color is available, Data Desk plots each line in a different color. Multiple lineplots show how several sequences move together. They do require, however, that all of the sequences be measured on the same scale or the y-axis of the plot is meaningless. Thus, for example, a multiple line plot of the price of Apple Stock (measured in dollars) and the number of Macintosh apples sold annually (in millions of bushels) might show related trends but would arbitrarily equate 100,000,000 bushels to $100.00. It is important to keep in mind that this equivalence is an artifact of the display and has no meaning for the data.

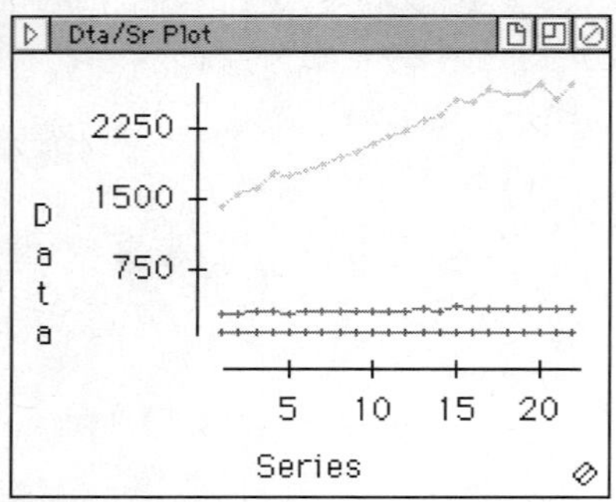

Figure 8-26. DISCUS THROW PERFORMANCE LEAPS AHEAD OF OTHER FIELD SPORTS.

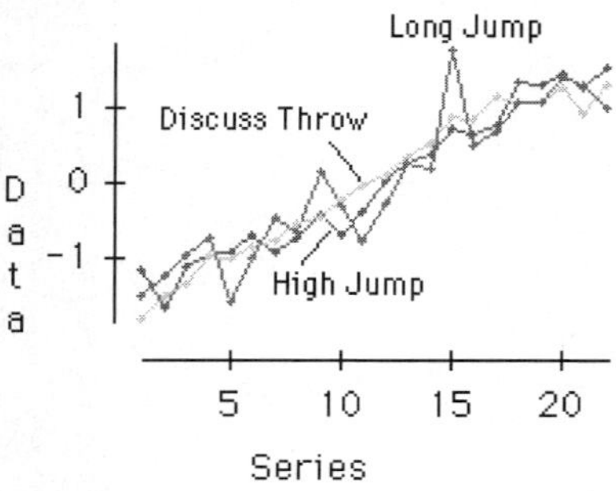

Figure 8-27 Multiple line plot of the Olympic gold medal performances after the variables were rescaled.

A similar, but more insidious, problem is that, when variables displayed together are measured in different units, both their absolute magnitude and their scale are arbitrary. Thus we could decide to represent the Apple stock prices in pennies. To do so we would multiply all the stock values by 100 which wouldn't make the multiple line plot wrong in any formal statistical sense. Multiplication by a large factor will, however, inflate every small fluctuation in stock price into a huge swing, while making the changes in fruit sales seem trivial because they cover only a few million bushels.

For example, the Olympic gold dataset holds three sequences of gold medal performances. Even though all are measured in inches, that doesn't make them comparable. A typical discus throw is much longer than a typical high jump is high. A simple multiple line plot of the three series is shown in Fig. 8-26.

We could caption it "discus throw performance soars while other track and field sports languish." But a simple standardization of all three results produces the equally valid plot in Fig. 8-27, which clearly demonstrates that all sports event performances are improving at the same rate.

Multiple line plots must thus be used (if at all) with great care. They are most trustworthy when the sequences plotted are directly comparable, measured in the same units, and of the same general magnitude and range.

Multiple lineplots create a new relation holding three intermediate variables needed to construct the plot. The first of these appends the selected variables together. The other two provide the x-axis and group names. Because Multiple lineplots work in this separate relation they do not link to the relation of the original data. Initially, the relation is hidden. To make it visible, choose the **Locate** *variable name* command from the HyperView menu attached to either the x-axis or y-axis.

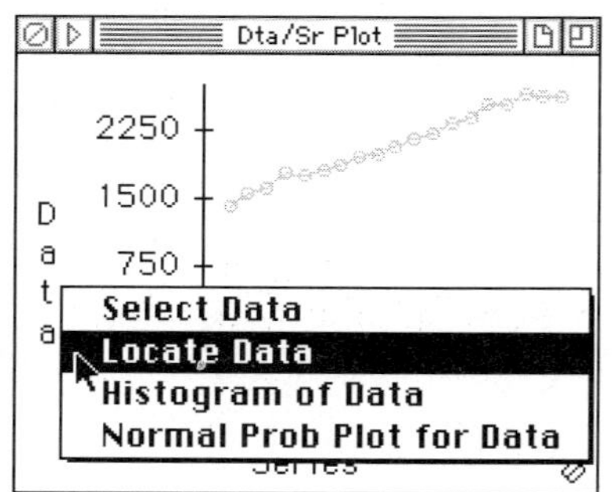

8.13 Normal Probability Plots

A Normal probability plot provides a simple way to tell whether the numbers in a variable are approximately normally distributed. Many statistics are based on the assumption that data or residuals follow a *normal distribution*, so checks of normality help to determine the applicability of some methods.

normal distribution

Data Desk sorts the values in the variable and then, starting with the smallest value, poses the question: "If this were a sample from the standard normal distribution (that is, the normal distribution with zero mean and unit variance), what would I expect the smallest value to be?" The answer is the first *normal score*. It depends only on the number of cases in the variable, and can be estimated with the NScores function available in derived variables (see Chapter 11). The probability plot graphs the observed smallest value against the value expected under the assumption of a normal distribution.

normal score

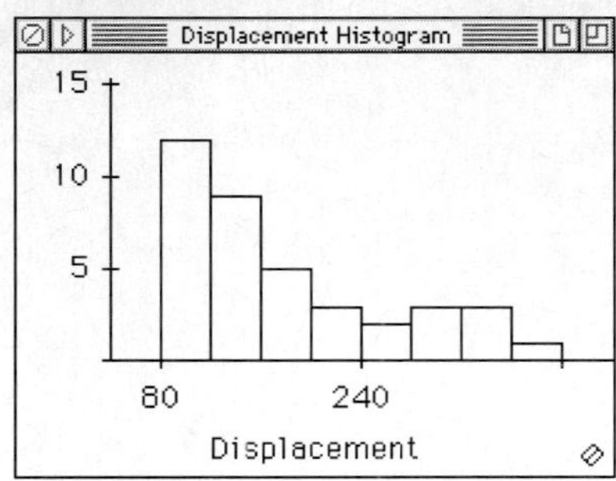

Figure 8-28. A histogram of car engine Displacement *does not look normal.*

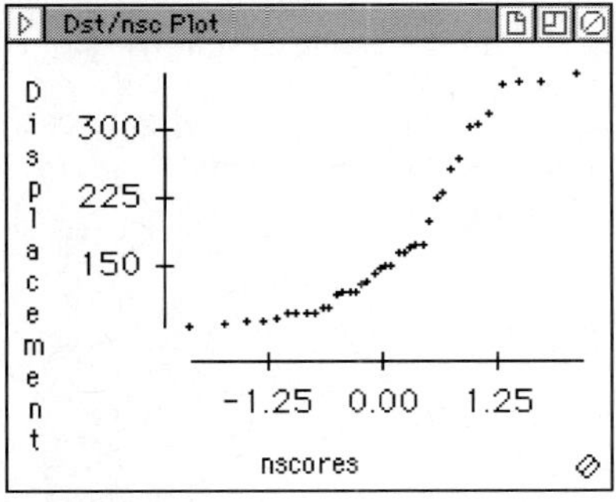

Figure 8-29. Normal probability plot of Displacement *in Cars data.*

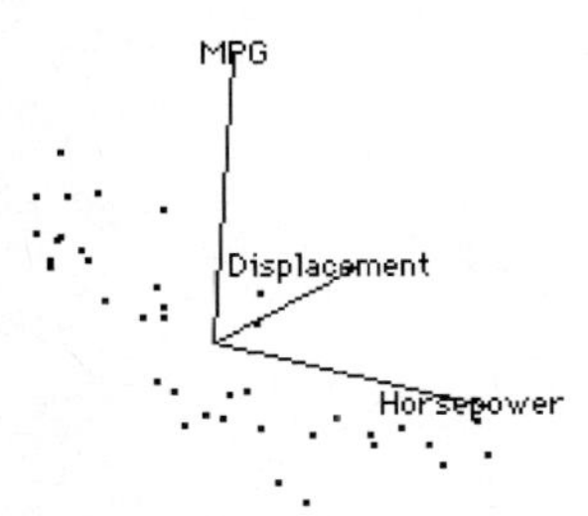

Figure 8-30. Rotating plot of MPG *versus* Displacement *versus* Horsepower *in the Cars data.*

The question is repeated for the second smallest value: "If this were a sample from the standard normal distribution what would I expect the *second* smallest value to be?" The observed second smallest value is plotted against the expected second smallest value.

The corresponding questions are posed and calculations determined for each data value, and the resulting plot graphs the observed value as y versus the calculated *normal score* as x for each case.

To make a normal probability plot, select the variable to plot and choose {Plot} **Normal Prob Plots**. Normal probability plots are also available from HyperView menus in several procedures in which the assumption of normality is important.

For example, the *Displacement* variable in the Cars dataset is very nonnormal. In fact, the histogram shown in Fig. 8-28 has a dip in the middle. Its normal probability plot shown in Fig. 8-29, shows the strong deviation from normality.

Probability plots always show a nondecreasing trend from lower left to upper right. If the plot is straight or nearly straight, the distribution of the variable is nearly normal, and the slope of the line estimates the standard deviation of the variable. If the plot is S-shaped, with the right and left parts pointing up and down, the variable's distribution is more stretched out, or long-tailed, than the normal. If the plot is S-shaped, with the right and left parts pointing right and left, the variable's distribution is more compact, or short-tailed, than the normal. If only one side of the plot bends away from the line, the variable has a skewed distribution.

The correlation of a variable and its normal scores are sometimes used to measure how near the variable's distribution is to the normal distribution. The normal scores are available as the NScores function in derived variables. Appendix 8B provides details about the calculation of normal scores.

8.14 *Rotating Plots*

Plot rotation is an extraordinarily powerful tool for understanding relationships among three or more variables. As you work with rotating plots, you will find that, although plot rotation is a simple and natural way to view data, it has great depth and power for multivariate data analysis. In this section we present the basics of plot rotation so that you can make and use rotating plots. In Chapter 9 we discuss many plot tools and commands that work with rotating plots. In Chapter 10 we discuss rotation as a data analysis tool and demonstrate some advanced rotating plot features.

Rotating plots depict relationships among three or more variables by showing a three-dimensional structure. The impression of three dimensions is vivid but requires that the plotted points move on the screen, so you may want to make a few rotating plots just to see how they look.

To make a rotating plot, select the y- (up–down axis), x- (left–right axis), and z- (in–out axis) variables in order and choose {Plot} **Rotating Plot** (Fig. 8-30).

APPENDIX 8A *Boxplot Definitions*

Boxplots are defined in terms of the median and *hinges* of a collection of numbers. The hinges are the medians of the data from the minimum to the median (like a 25th percentile) and of the data from the median to the maximum (like a 75th percentile). The median is included in both half-variables if it is one of the data values, but it isn't included if it is the average of two data values.

The "box" in a boxplot extends from the low hinge (roughly, the 25% point) to the high hinge (roughly, the 75% point). The horizontal bar is at the median. The *whiskers* extend from the box to the highest data value not above the

high hinge + 1.5(high hinge – low hinge)

and from the box to the lowest data value not below the

low hinge – 1.5(high hinge – low hinge).

Any data value beyond these limits is plotted with a circle unless it exceeds either the

high hinge + 3.0(high hinge – low hinge)

or the

low hinge – 3.0(high hinge – low hinge),

in which case, it is plotted with a starburst.

The shaded intervals for comparing medians are placed symmetrically around the median at

$$\text{median} \pm 1.58(\text{high hinge} - \text{low hinge})/\sqrt{n}.$$

See Chapter 3 in Velleman and Hoaglin (1981) for a complete discussion of boxplots and the derivation of the shaded interval formulas.

APPENDIX 8B *Probability Plots*

Probability plots (sometimes called quantile-quantile or q–q plots) provide information about how well the distribution of a variable matches some theoretical distribution by plotting the observed values (on the y-axis) against their normal scores (on the x-axis).

Traditionally, the ith normal score for a sample of size n has been the mean of the *sampling distribution* of the ith order statistic (that is, the ith ordered value) in a sample of n values drawn from a standard normal distribution. Data Desk instead approximates the *medians* of the sampling distributions of the order statistics of the standard normal distribution. This approach has the advantage of being more resistant to the inherent skewness of the sampling distributions belonging to the extreme order statistics. The ith median order statistic of a sample of size n is approximated by

$$\text{Gau}^{-1}((i - 1/3) \,/\, (n + 1/3)$$

where Gau^{-1} is the inverse normal (or Gaussian) cumulative distribution function. This formula is also used by the NScores function in derived variables.

EXERCISES

1. Sketch a distribution that is:

(a) Bimodal

(b) Skewed to the left

(c) Skewed to the right

(d) Multimodal

2. Make a histogram of the *Altos* variable in the Singers dataset. Which of the descriptions in Exercise 1 apply to this histogram?

3. Make a histogram of soprano heights, keeping the window containing the histogram of alto heights open. Now, resize both windows so that they can be viewed side by side. Describe how they compare with respect to:

(a) Modality

(b) Skewness

4. Make histograms of the heights of tenor and bass singers. State how these groups behave with respect to:

(a) Modality

(b) Skewness

5. Close the histogram windows and create a boxplot comparing all four parts (soprano, alto, tenor, and base).

(a) How do the centers compare among the parts? How can you tell that from the boxplots? Which measures of center are the boxplots informative about? Use a sketch to indicate how to compare centers with boxplots.

(b) How does skewness compare among the parts? How can you tell that from the boxplots? Sketch boxplots to indicate symmetry or skewness.

6. Open the Michelson dataset. It contains measurements of the speed of light recorded in several experimental trials. Display boxplots of the first five trials. The boxplots suggest that the first and third trials may be skewed. Construct histograms of the first and third trials and examine the tails of the distributions. Try various scalings for the histograms. Pick scalings that accentuate the skewness in the distributions. Sketch the distributions as they appear on your screen.

7. The values reported in the Michelson data are measurements of the speed of light in air (adjusted to make them more convenient for computation). The results are reported in sets of 20 trials. At the time of Michelson's work, measuring the speed of light was near the limits of scientific ability. What explanations can you suggest for the patterns you see here? Sketch any plots that may be helpful to your explanation.

8. (a) Open the Clouds dataset. It contains results from an experiment to determine whether seeding clouds increases rainfall. In this experiment, clouds were randomly assigned to be seeded or not and the amount of rain they generated was measured. Make side-by-side boxplots of unseeded and seeded clouds. Sketch the boxplots.

(b) The y-axis of the boxplot is inches of rainfall. Do you see evidence that seeding increases rainfall? Explain your answer.

(c) You could make a scatterplot of seeded versus unseeded clouds. (Feel free to do so.) Explain why such a scatterplot tells you very little about the data. In what ways is it actually misleading to graph these data in this way? (*Hint:* Do you think that these numbers were recorded in the order given here?)

9. (a) Open the Cars dataset. Draw a scatterplot of MPG (y-axis) versus weight (x-axis).

(b) Describe in words the relationship between MPG and weight.

(c) Try stretching the plot by dragging the size box to the right. Does it still give the same impression?

10. Open the SMSAs dataset and make normal probability plots of the populations and July temperatures of the cities represented. Sketch the plots and indicate the shape you expect the distributions to show, based on what the probability plots show. If you want to, make the corresponding histograms and compare what they show with what the probability plots show.

11. For comparison, open the Random Normals dataset. This dataset contains five samples of 250 numbers from a standard normal distribution. Make normal probability plots of at least two of the samples. In what ways do these plots seem to differ from the ideal normal probability plot of data drawn from a normal distribution? Sketch the patterns you are discussing.

CHAPTER 9

Working with Displays

DATA DESK'S PLOTS can display your data in many ways. The true power of these plots comes from touching them and watching them change dynamically in response to your actions. In this chapter we discuss the elements of making and modifying data analysis graphics, and show how various methods and plot tools can help you see more in your data.

Data Desk's plots will help you discover unexpected patterns and relationships, identify groups and clusters, and spot extraordinary cases. Some plots show the distribution of a single variable (for example, histograms) or compare the distributions of several groups (for example, dotplots and boxplots). Some plots show information about category data by depicting relative proportions of the data in each category (for example, bar charts and pie charts). Other displays depict relationships. The relationships can be between a single variable and some standard, such as the sequence order of its cases (for example, lineplots) or expected values from a standard distribution (for example, probability plots), between two variables (for example, scatterplots), comparing several sequences (multiple line plots), or among several variables (for example, scatterplot matrices and rotating plots).

9.1 *Chapter Organization*

Data Desk offers a highly integrated system of data analysis graphics capabilities. Some of the graphics techniques in Data Desk may be new to you, but they are designed to let you work intuitively and to have consistent controls. An action that modifies a plot in some way will modify other plots in much the same way. For example, the tool always repositions the contents of a plot within its window. The related tool rotates points in a rotating plot but behaves (and looks) like the tool in other plots for which rotation isn't appropriate.

It's easy to start working with Data Desk's plots. As you work with them you will learn more and more ways to combine the tools, commands, and options to see more in your data. The combination of graphic views and ways of working with them is far too rich to be able to document every possible combination. Instead, we present the basic principles of dynamic interactive graphics and discuss the corresponding Data Desk tools and commands.

We divide graphics concepts into *actions* (Sections 9.3–9.11) and *aspects* (Sections 9.12–9.20). Actions include all the ways in which you can move, highlight, inquire, or otherwise act on a plot to see a new view, learn more about the data, or record information for further analysis. Many actions are accomplished through the plot tools, but some work in other ways. Aspects of plots specify how the plot looks and works. Most plot aspects are controlled with commands, although some are controlled by tools in special palettes.

9.2 *Organization of Features and Commands in Data Desk*

HOW-TO

The **Plot** and **Modify** menus hold the features and commands that control displays.

In Data Desk, you control displays with the features and commands in the **Plot** and **Modify** menus. Together, they provide many simple and natural ways to work with plots. As with most of Data Desk's features, you should get started with the basic commands and learn as you work.

The **Plot** menu holds the basic plot commands and the basic plot options. Plot options are controlled by the **Plot Options** submenu in the **Plot** menu. Plot options usually specify the default operation of plots. As with other options in Data Desk, plot options specify how the plots you are about to make work or look.

Commands in the **Modify** menu alter or work with the frontmost plot. They are grouped into submenus according to the aspect of the plot affected. Thus commands that alter plot scaling are grouped under the **Scale** submenu. Commands that affect the axes appear in the **Axes** submenu.

The **Modify** menu also holds four palettes; the Tools palette, the Symbols palette, the Colors palette, and the Selection Mode palette. All palettes can be placed on the desktop from menus or submenus. Palettes left on the desktop float above other Data Desk windows so that they are always visible. To select an item from a palette when it is on the desktop, simply click one of the rectangles in the palette. The **Palettes** command (Ctrl-**M** on Windows or ⌘**M** on Mac) places all four palettes on the Data Desk desktop. To hide the palettes choose the **Palettes** command again, type Ctrl-**M** on Windows or ⌘**M** on Mac, or close individual palettes by clicking their Close box. Data Desk opens the palettes to their position on the desktop when they were last closed.

Figure 9-1. *The Tools palette.*

The Tools palette holds 12 tools for manipulating, moving, and using displays (Fig. 9-1), each of which is discussed in the context of its function throughout this chapter. Because plot characteristics differ, a particular tool may act differently on different plots. However, each tool's basic function and behavior is consistent across all plots. Choose {Modify} **Tools** to place the Tools palette on the desktop.

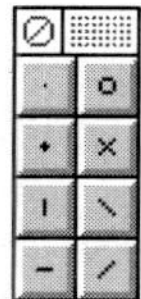

Figure 9-2. *The Symbols palette.*

The Symbols palette shows the eight available plot symbols (Fig 9-2). All points are initially represented by a "+". To change the symbol for a case or a group of cases, select the cases to change and click on a plot symbol in the palette. Those points will then be displayed using the new symbol in all plots that represent individual cases, such as a scatterplot, rotating plot, or dotplot. Choose {Modify ▶ Symbols} **Show As** to place the Symbols palette on the desktop.

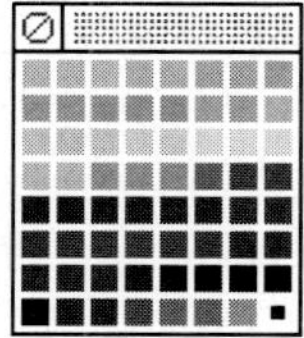

Figure 9-3. *The Colors palette.*

The Colors palette is active only on systems with color. It has 64 squares showing the 64 colors available in a Data Desk display (Fig. 9-3). Select cases and click on any color to display those cases with that color in any plot that represents individual cases. Data Desk works with all color depths, however, it is optimized for a monitor setting of 256 colors. Choose {Modify ▶ Colors} **Show As** to place the Colors palette on the desktop.

Figure 9-4. *The Selection Modes palette.*

The Selection Modes palette offers five special selection options that alter the way in which selection tools work (Fig. 9-4). Click on a selection tool (such as the , , , or) and then click a selection mode to modify the tool's behavior. We discuss selection modes more fully in Appendix 9B. Choose {Modify ▶ Selection} **Mode** to place the Selection Modes palette on the desktop.

ACTIONS

9.3 *Basic Plot Actions*

The basic plot actions are:

- *SELECT*
  Selected points or parts of displays highlight to stand out from the rest of the plot and are available for separate analysis or modification. Many commands operate specifically on the selected cases.
- *LINK*
  Data Desk links plots so that parts of plots in the same relation that represent the same cases show them consistently. For example, selecting a point (and, thereby, a case) in one plot highlights the parts of other plots that display that case.
- *BRUSH AND SLICE*
  You can view relationships among several plots at once by brushing or slicing a plot to select points and seeing the corresponding cases highlight in other plots.
- *IDENTIFY*
  Data Desk can tell you the identity of any individual case in plots that display cases individually.
- *MOVE*
  Motion, such as rotation and repositioning, turns the abstract concept of a "point cloud" into a physical reality that you can touch and manipulate.
- *ISOLATE*
  You can refocus plots to ignore extreme points or to concentrate on interesting subsets of the data.
- *RESIZE*
  You can control the size of the plot contents independently of the size of the plot window.
- *SUBSTITUTE*
  Any plot can serve as a template for new plots. You can substitute a new variable for one in the plot simply by dragging the icon of the new variable over the name of the old one on an axis.

We discuss each of these actions in the following sections.

9.4 *Select*

Selecting is a fundamental operation both because selected points stand out from the background of other points, and because a variety of other commands can operate on the selected points. For example, you can choose to display selected points with any of the eight plot symbols, color them in any of the 64 available colors, or hide them from view to see the remaining points more clearly.

Selected points and regions highlight by becoming brighter, by becoming slightly larger, by changing color, or by filling in open spaces. In some plots (for example, pie charts, bar charts, and histograms) you can't select individual cases, but you can select collections of cases (for example, an entire pie chart wedge or histogram bar).

Several plot tools perform selections.

POINTER

This tool operates on all plots. When you press the mouse button, it selects the datapoint or the part of the plot it is pointing to (Fig. 9-5). The tool selects individual points in scatterplots and rotating plots but selects entire bars in histograms and entire pie wedges in pie charts. As you move the , with the mouse button pressed down, new points (bars or wedges) are selected, and the previously selected points are deselected. Hold down the Shift key to extend the selection, adding unselected points, bars, and wedges to the selection or to deselect parts that have already been selected.

Figure 9-5. *Selected parts of a plot highlight.*

You can get the tool immediately in any plot by holding down Ctrl-right mouse button on Windows or ⌘-Option on Mac.

To select points with the Lasso, draw a line around them (Fig. 9-6). When you release the button, the shape you have drawn is automatically closed, and all enclosed points are selected.

RECTANGLE

To select points with the Rectangle, hold down the mouse button (the cursor is the arrow,) and drag out a rectangle on the plot. When you release the button, all enclosed points are selected.

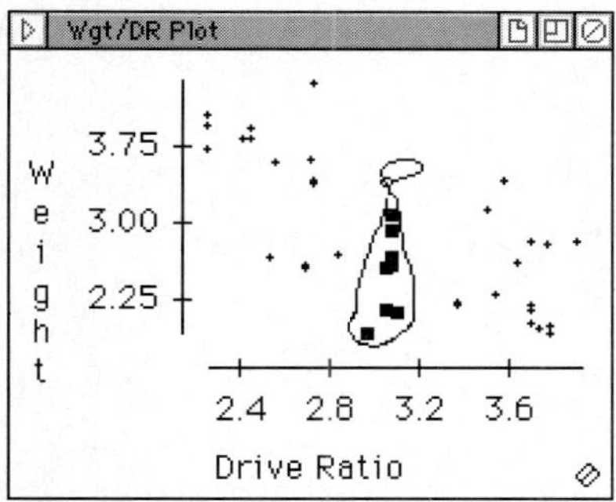

Figure 9-6. *The Lasso selects the points it encircles.*

You can also select with the brush and slice tools discussed in Section 9.6.

EDIT MENU SELECTIONS

The **Select All, Find...**, and **Go To...** commands in the **Edit** menu operate on plots as well. To select all points in a plot choose **Select All** or use its keyboard shortcut, Ctrl-A on Windows or ⌘-A on Mac. To select a case by its case number, choose **Go To...** ▸ **Case #** and specify the case number.

The cases selected in data displays are often important in some way. They may be the cases that stand out in each of several displays of different aspects of the data or an identifiable subgroup of the data. It is natural to select such points with one of the selection tools so that you can examine them more easily and see them in each of several displays. Once you do so, you may want to record the selection for further use. The **Selection** submenu in the **Modify** menu holds commands that record or restore the highlighted selection. The {Modify ▸Selection} **Record** command creates a variable whose values are set to 0 for unselected cases and 1 for selected cases. Such *indicator variables* have many uses in statistics (see Chapter 13). Alternatively, an indicator variable can be used to highlight a set of points. Select an indicator variable, select a plot, and choose {Modify ▸ Selection} **Add**. All the points coded as ones in the indicator variable highlight.

indicator variables

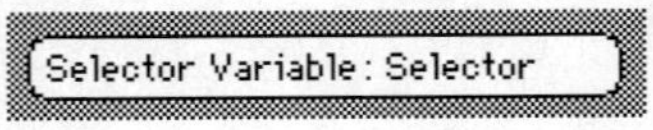

Figure 9-7. The ***Selector*** *button is placed in the lower left corner of the Data Desk desktop.*

Often the selected cases deserve further attention. You can restrict any Data Desk command to work on a subset of cases by creating a 0/1 indicator variable and assigning that indicator variable to an analysis. (In Chapter 13 we discuss this topic at length.) The {Modify ▶ Selection} **Assign Selector** command provides a quick way to create an indicator variable and assign it to restrict an analysis. Highlight the points that define the restricted set and choose {Modify ▶ Selection} **Assign Selector**. Data Desk creates a new variable, asks you to name it, sets its values to 0 for unselected cases and 1 for selected cases, places it in the **Selector** button, and highlights the **Selector** button (Fig. 9-7). The subsequent Data Desk command operates only on the selected cases.

{Modify ▶Selection} **Clear** deselects all cases. {Modify ▶Selection} **Toggle** selects cases currently not selected and deselects those that are selected. {Modify ▶Selection} **Show Identifying Text** displays the labels for selected points on the plot that was frontmost when the command was issued.

{Modify ▶Selection} **Record As Indicators** creates a 0/1 variable for each selected point. The 0/1 variable can be used as a Selector variable (see Chapter 13) or in a regression analysis (see Chapter 25).

{Modify ▶Selection} **Record HotSet** and {Modify ▶Selection} **Assign Hot Selector** are commands to create dynamic indicator variables (see Chapter 13).

9.5 *Link*

Each kind of plot shows a different view of your data, but within a relation the underlying cases are the same. A particular case may be a point in a scatterplot or rotating plot, part of a bar in a histogram or bar chart, or all of these at once. And, of course, each case also corresponds to a row of values in any open variable editing windows.

Data Desk preserves the individuality of cases so that each view of the data shows each case consistently. For example, when you select a case in one plot or editing window, all views of that case are selected immediately and highlight so you can see the selection (Fig. 9-8). The case stands out from the other cases in each window, so its relationship to them becomes clearer. You can select groups of points to see whether they appear as a group in other views of the data or whether the observed grouping is a local feature.

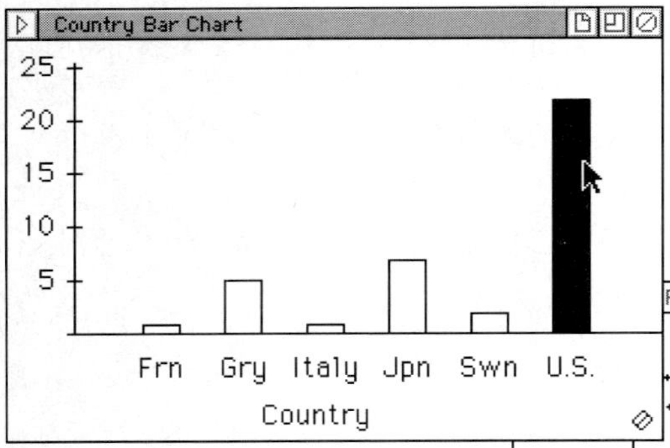

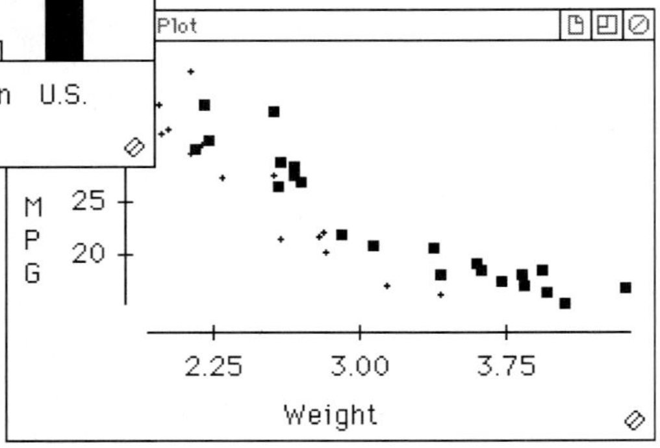

Figure 9-8. The bar chart and scatterplot are linked, so clicking a bar of the bar chart selects the same points in the scatterplot. Note that U.S. cars get better gas mileage for their weight than other cars.

Linking makes it easy to answer questions such as:

- Is this extreme point also extreme in any other view of the data?
- Do the points in this part of the histogram cluster on other variables?
- Is the relationship between these two variables the same for each of the groups in this pie chart?

- Does the pattern shown in this rotating plot correspond to any patterns shown in other views of the data?

These questions require sophisticated and complex statistics calculations to answer numerically but are easy to investigate with linked plots.

Data Desk displays also link plot symbols and colors for plots that show individual cases (such as scatterplots, rotating plots, and dotplots). Each case appears in all of the plots with the same symbol and with the same color.

Only windows displaying data for the same relation can link. If two of your windows won't link, they may be from different relations.

Linking also makes possible the interactive actions *brush* and *slice*.[1]

[1]The term "brushing" has become standard in statistical graphics in the way in which we use it here, but usually refers to the restricted application of brushing scatterplot matrices. The term "slicing" is our own coinage.

9.6 *Brush and Slice*

Brushing and slicing can reveal joint patterns and relationships among many variables. Thus they are actions appropriate for multivariate analysis. In Chapter 10, we discuss brushing in detail.

BRUSH

The brush tool is a rectangle. As you brush the rectangle across a plot, the points it covers are temporarily highlighted, as are the corresponding points in all open, linked displays. By brushing a part of one display you can see how the corresponding cases look in other displays.

To resize the brush, hold down the ⌘ key on Mac or the right mouse button on Windows. The brush rectangle will resize as you drag it larger or smaller. For example, you can make the brush a tall, thin rectangle to look at small, local parts of an x-axis variable. The highlighted points in other plots show the patterns and distributions "conditional" on the selected slice of points.

You can locate points on plots by combining brushing with the Exclusive OR selection mode. With Exclusive OR mode selected, place the Brush tool over the points and press the mouse button. The points will flash on and off in every plot, making them easy to see.

KNIFE

The Knife tool selects points in vertical or horizontal slices of a plot. The knife slices right to left, left to right, top to bottom, or bottom to top, according to its initial direction. Points are selected as the tool passes their position and remain selected unless you reverse direction and drag back over them (Fig. 9-9).

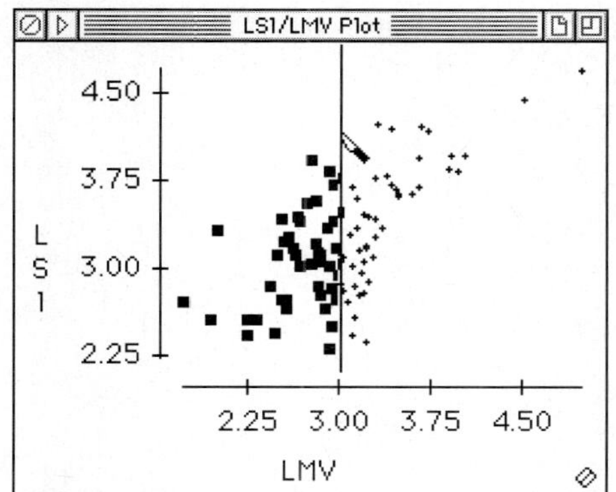

Figure 9-9. *Slicing across a scatterplot. The selection links immediately to other open plots and editing windows.*

Brushing and slicing help you answer questions such as:

- Do the same cases seem to be in roughly the same places in each plot?
- Is there any trend in sales from east to west?
- Which variables change systematically as I move along this principal dimension in a rotating plot?
- How does the relationship between the gas mileage and weight of cars change as drive ratio increases? (Plot *MPG* versus *Weight* in a

scatterplot, plot *Drive Ratio* in a dotplot, and brush or slice *Drive Ratio* while watching the *MPG* versus *Weight* display. See which points highlight as you move from low to high *Drive Ratio*.)

9.7 *Identify*

Data analysis displays help you discover patterns and relationships in your data. However, it isn't enough to see a general pattern or trend. You usually want to know which cases make up each of the groups, which cases form the heart of the trend, and which cases fail to follow the pattern established by the others. For this, you need to be able to identify datapoints on a plot easily.

? IDENTIFIER

The identifier tool provides a crosshair cursor that looks like a bomb sight (Fig. 9-10). Place it over a plotted point and press the mouse button to highlight the point and display its case number.

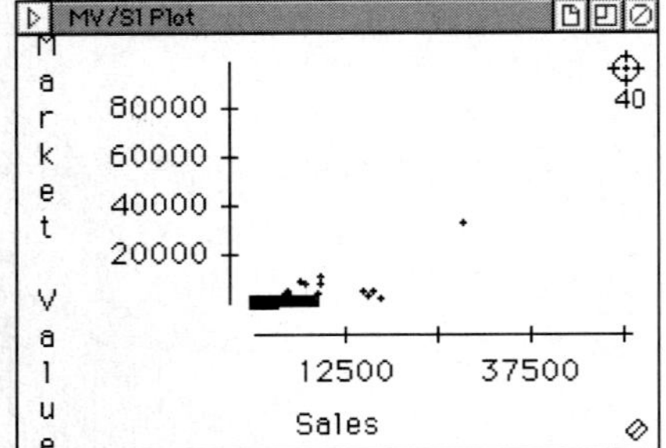

Figure 9-10. When no variables are open, the **?** *tool shows the case number of a datapoint.*

To display identifying text such as a name rather than a case number, open a variable in the same relation as the plotted variables that contains identifying text for each case. The **?** tool then identifies each point on the plot with the text of the corresponding case in the identifying variable (Fig. 9-11). If two or more variables are open, the frontmost window becomes the identifying variable. The identifying variable's window may be completely covered by other windows, but it must be in the right relation. On Mac, to see the case number rather than text when a variable window is open, press the ⌘ key. If you're using Data Desk on Windows, hold down the Ctrl and Shift keys (Option and Shift keys on Mac) while using the **?** tool, and Data Desk displays the text from the five frontmost variable windows.

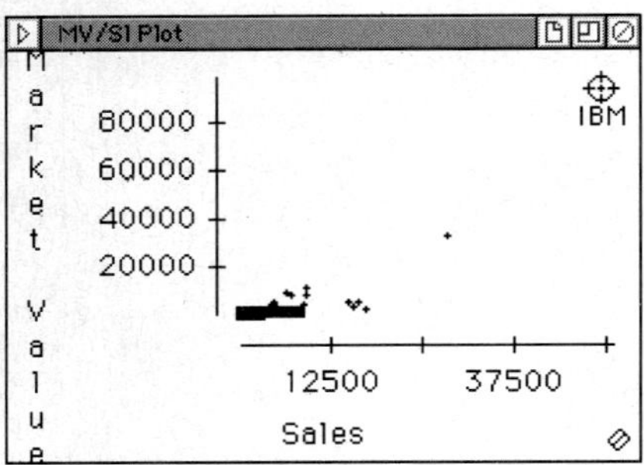

Figure 9-11. When an identifying variable is open and frontmost among open variable windows, the **?** *tool displays the case name found in that variable.*

For example, a scatterplot of *Market Value* versus *Sales* for the Companies data shows an extreme value. We can identify it with **?**. First open the variable *Company* so that the company names are available as identifying text. Then click on the extreme point with **?**. Note that you could have opened the variable *Sector* instead of *Company* if you had wanted to identify points only by their market sector, or the variable *Profit* to see companies' profits.

If several cases have the same coordinates so that they appear at the same point on the plot, the query tool informs you that the identification it is displaying is "1 of k", where "k" is the number of cases at that point. Click the mouse again to see information for the second case plotted at that point. Keep clicking to see the information for each point in turn and then back to the first. (We discussed an alternative way to deal with this problem in Appendix 8C .)

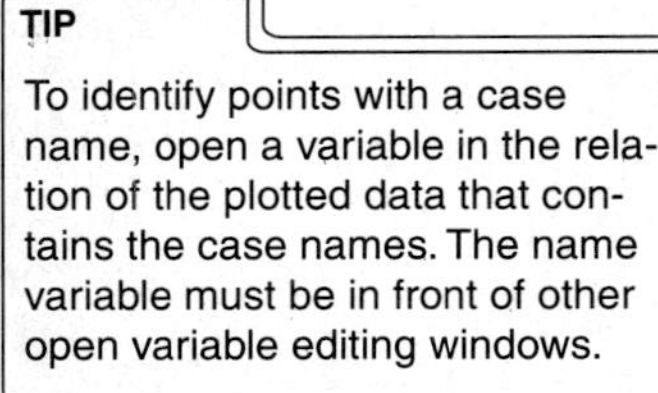
TIP

To identify points with a case name, open a variable in the relation of the plotted data that contains the case names. The name variable must be in front of other open variable editing windows.

Pressing Ctrl and the right mouse button on Windows, or ⌘-Option on Mac, gives you the tool to make it convenient to select points in a plot after you have identified them.

The **Go To...** commands in the **Edit** menu find cases by number, and step through the selected cases to identify them.

Sometimes you want the identifying text of certain points to "stick" to the screen. This is particularly useful for printing or copying plots. Highlight the points you want identified, select the plot where you want the text displayed, and choose {Modify ▶Selection} **Show Identifying Text.** The information displayed is the text contained in the frontmost variable, just like the query tool. Be careful not to use this feature more than necessary. Too many plots with text being displayed slows Data Desk's interactive features.

9.8 Move

Movement provides a natural way to adjust displays. It is easier to push or pull to adjust the way a display looks than to type verbal commands or select menu items. Thus movements such as repositioning the display contents or bringing other parts of the display into view are natural manipulations.

GRABBER

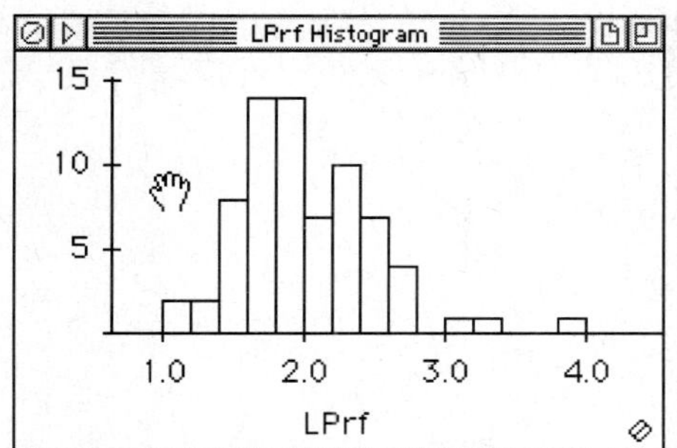

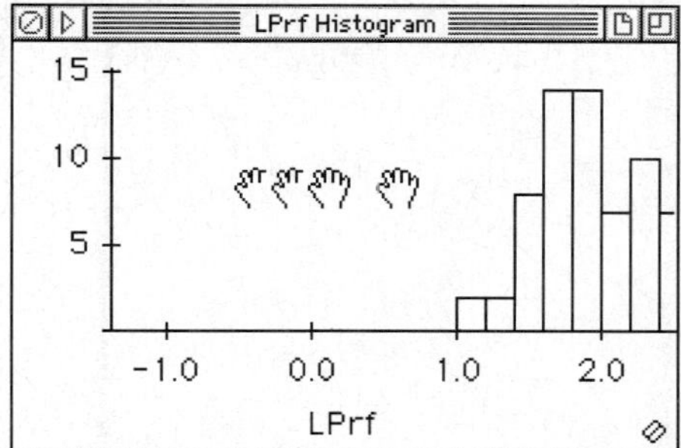

Figure 9-12. *The Grabber tool shifts plot centers.*

The Grabber tool repositions the contents of a plot within its window (Fig. 9-12). This operation is helpful when you need to move a set of points closer to one of the axes. To do so, you slide the display side to side with the Grabber. The Grabber also controls the side-to-side movement of the axis in sliders (see Section 11.14). If you hold the Shift key down while sliding many kinds of plots with the Grabber, the plot will continue to slide when pushed. Click again with the Grabber or press the space bar to halt the slide. The {Modify ▶ Scale} **Home** command returns any plot to its original location and scale and can be a convenient way to retrieve a plot that may have slid too far.

> **TIP**
>
> Hold the Shift key and push a plot with the Grabber tool. It will continue to slide in the direction of the push. Press the Space bar or grab it again to stop the slide.

In rotating plots, the points can be moved away from the center of rotation (where the axes meet). Holding down the right mouse button on Windows or the ⌘ key on Mac changes the cursor to a 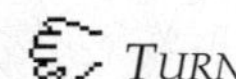 and lets you move both the points *and* the center of rotation for example, to make room for displayed equations.

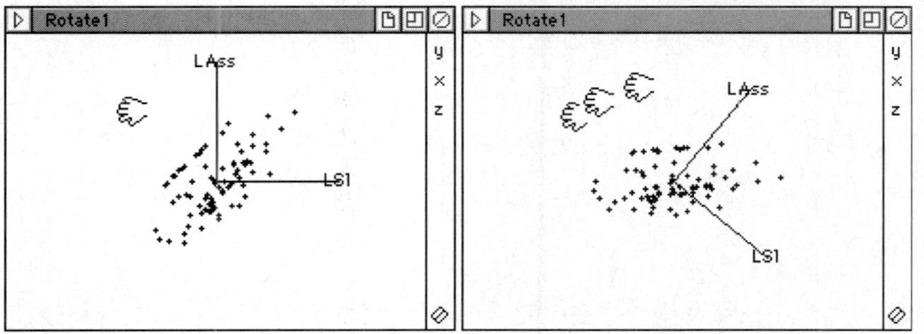

Figure 9-13. *The Turn tool rotates points clockwise or counterclockwise. Here, a plot is rotated approximately 45° clockwise around its z-axis.*

TURN

This tool grabs the points in a rotating plot and turns them around the in–out z-axis of the plot, much like the hands of a clock (Fig. 9-13). The tool is instantly available by holding down both the Ctrl and the right mouse button on Windows, or Option and ⌘ keys on Mac when any plot tool is active on a rotating plot. The M and >

keys can be used to rotate points counterclockwise and clockwise, respectively.

Rotate

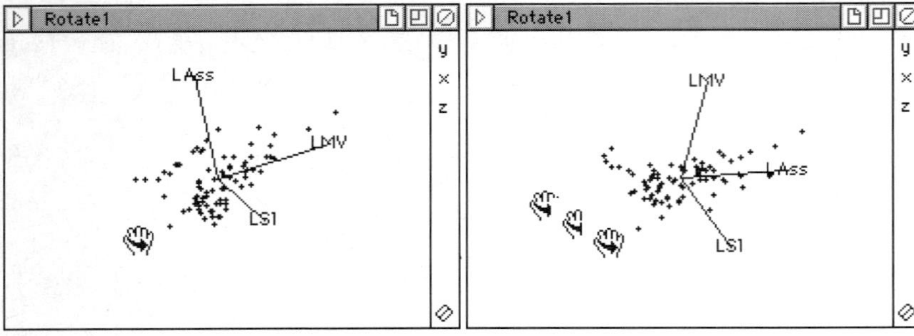

Figure 9-14. The Rotate tool rotates points around an axis that is in the plane of the screen.

The Rotate tool grabs the point cloud in a rotating plot and pushes it around an axis that is in the plane of the screen — for example, around the x- or y- axis (Fig. 9-14). The illusion created is that the points are a three-dimensional cloud that is rotated by pushing it in any direction, much as you might push a world globe that has been mounted to spin around its axis.

You can adjust the sensitivity of the rotate tool. When you press the right mouse button on Windows or the ⌘ key on Mac, the cursor changes to a turning arrow. Press the mouse button to display a circle that represents the size of the sphere that you push with the . Drag the size of the circle to adjust the sensitivity of the tool. A small circle yields a very responsive tool that may spin plots too fast. A very large circle yields a Rotate tool with great sensitivity but without the ability to move the points rapidly.

If you release the mouse button while is active and moving, you push the points so that they continue to rotate in the direction and at the speed of your push. The tool is instantly available by holding down the Ctrl key on Windows or the Option key on Mac when any plot tool is active on a rotating plot.

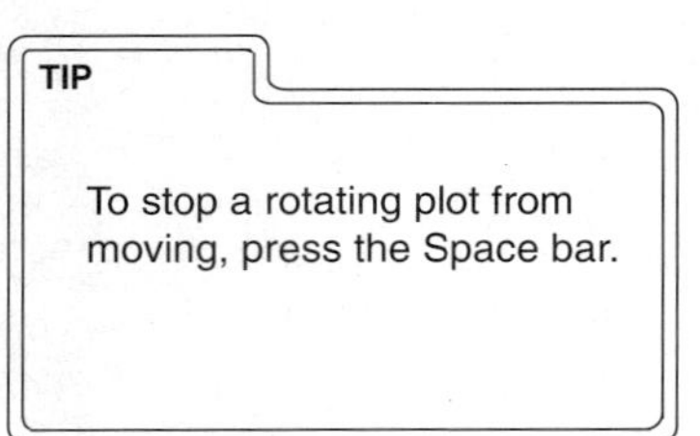

To stop a rotating plot that is spinning on its own, press the Space bar or simply click the plot with any of the movement tools, , , or . You must release the mouse button without moving the mouse to leave the plot stationary.

Arrow Keys

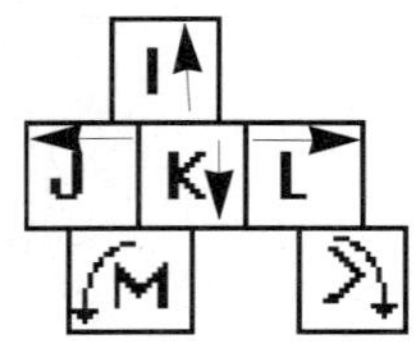

You can also control plot rotation with the arrow keys found on most keyboards and numeric keypads. Hold down an arrow key to rotate the plot in the direction of the arrow. (The plot rotates as long as the key is held down.) The functions of the arrow keys are duplicated on the main keyboard with the I, J, K, and L keys. These keys mimic the layout of the arrow keys: I points up, K points down, and J and L point left and right, respectively.

Each key *adds* its influence to the rotation, so pressing two keys rotates around a 45° line. Pressing both an arrow key and the corresponding letter key rotates the plot twice as fast.

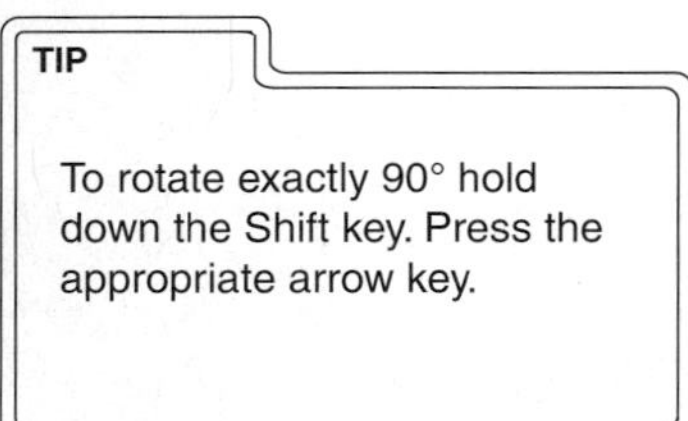

Holding the Shift key and pressing one of the rotation-controlling keys rotates the plot 90° in the indicated direction.

The {Modify ▸ Scale} **Rotate Around Selection** command moves plotted points so that the plot is centered at the mean of the selected points. This operation is especially useful for recentering plots that have been moved away from their original centers. The {Modify ▸ Scale} **Home** command restores the plot to the location and orientation of a newly made rotating plot.

9.9 Isolate

Isolating singles out one part of a display for consideration and hides the other parts of the display. Data that have cases from several groups and data containing extraordinary cases often call for isolation. For example, you might want to eliminate a group or outlier from consideration for the moment or, alternatively, to focus on it.

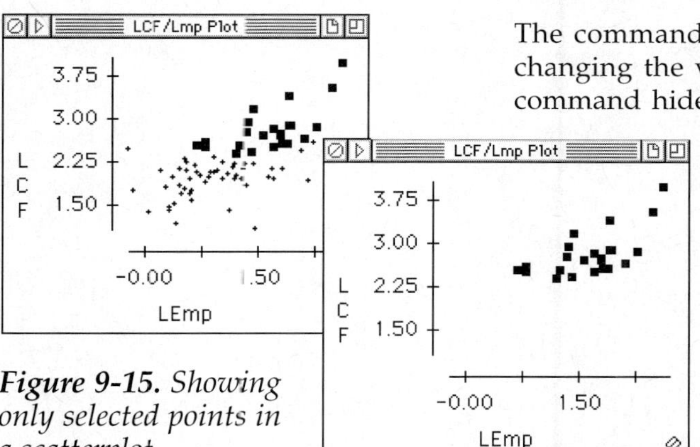

Figure 9-15. Showing only selected points in a scatterplot.

The commands in the {Modify} **Visibility** submenu isolate points by changing the visibility of points in plots. **Show Only Selected Points** command hides all but the selected points in the front plot (Fig. 9-15). You can't select or otherwise work with invisible points. However, visibility is local to the plot; the cases may be visible in other plots in the same relation. If you hold down the Ctrl key on Windows, or the Option key on Mac while selecting the command from the **Visibility** menu, the change in visibility will affect all open plots in the relation.

The **Hide Selected Points** command hides the selected points from the frontmost plot. The **Show All Points** command makes invisible points visible again. **Toggle Hidden Points** hides the visible points and shows the invisible ones.

Refocus

An alternative to isolating points by making others invisible is to isolate them by focusing the plot on them. Other plotted points are still part of the plot but fall outside the plot window, so they aren't seen.

This tool refocuses a plot to display only the part enclosed by the selected rectangle in the plot window. Drag a rectangle on a plot to define the new area to be plotted. The selected rectangle is rescaled to match the plot window. If the rectangle is too small, it will be ignored, so you can start over by collapsing the rectangle to a point before releasing the mouse button. The {Modify ▸ Scale} **Home** command restores a plot to its original scale. The rectangle can extend beyond the plot window, but you must start dragging within the plot window.

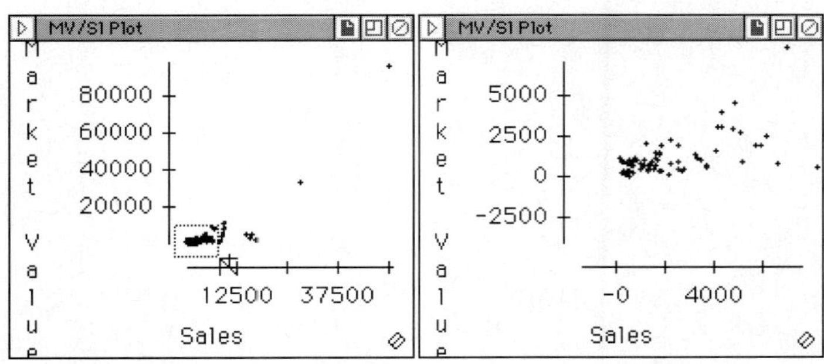

Figure 9-16. Refocus a scatterplot by selecting the desired part of the plot with the tool. The result of the refocus operation is on the right.

For example, in a plot of *Market Value* versus *Sales* for the companies data, we might isolate the mass of points in the lower left from the others. The rescaled display lets us pick out companies (perhaps with the identification tool) whose market value is particularly high or low compared to their sales, without being distracted by the extreme cases (Fig. 9-16).

The {Modify ▸ Scale} **Scale to Selected Points** command performs a similar refocusing of the plot. It redraws the plot with a scale determined as if only the selected points were to be plotted. This method is somewhat different from the tool, which can

TIP

If you accidentally "lose" the points in a plot by shifting them off the screen, choose **Home** to restore the points.

select large amounts of empty space in a plot and include it in the refocused plot. When a plot's scaling has been altered with any of the tools or commands, you can return to the original scaling by selecting all points (**⌘-A** is a good shortcut for **Select All** on Mac; on Windows, use **Ctrl-A**) and choosing {Modify ▶ Scale} **Scale to Selected Points**, or with the {Modify ▶ Scale} **Home** command.

9.10 Resize

Data Desk's plots ordinarily expand or shrink to fit their windows. Many plots resize automatically when you resize their windows, but rotating plots require explicit resizing. You may want to inflate any plot to see details or to concentrate on a part of the plot, even though other parts will no longer fit the window. Or you may want to shrink the plot to see all of it after the refocus tool has dropped points off the edge of the plot window.

RESIZE

to shrink
to expand

To resize the contents of a plot, select the Resize tool and move the mouse cursor inside the plot's window. Near the center of the plot, the cursor looks like . Click the mouse to halve the size of the plot contents. Near the edge of the plot, the cursor looks like . Click the mouse to double the size of the plot contents (Fig. 9-17). The plot window remains the same size, so expanding a plot may push points beyond the edge of the window. These points are still part of the plot; you can see them by sliding the plot with the Grabber, .

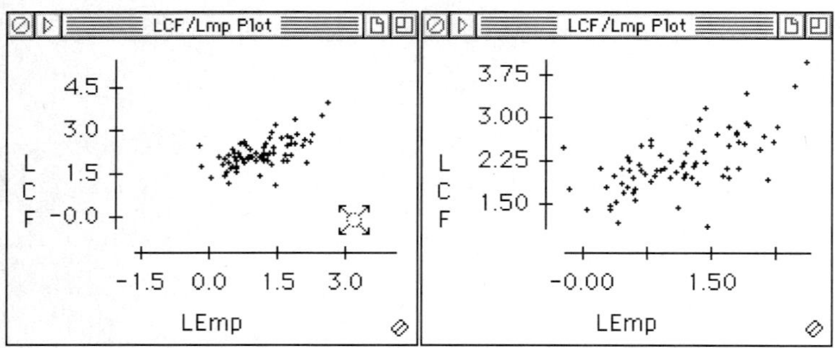

Figure 9-17. *Using the Resize tool doubles (or halves) the scale of the plotted points.*

To perform continuous zooms in scatterplots, lineplots, and dotplots, press the right mouse button on Windows, or the ⌘ on Mac, and the tool at the same time. The plot expands and contracts in a continuous motion.

The tool is available immediately in most plots by pressing Shift-Ctrl-right mouse button on Windows or Shift-Option-⌘ on Mac.

You can also resize plots by changing the scale. To do so use the Plot Scale dialog attached to every plot. You access this dialog from the plot's global HyperView menu or by selecting the plot and choosing {Modify ▶ Scale} **Plot Scale...**. In Section 9.15 we discuss the plot scale dialog in more detail.

9.11 Substitute

You learn more by looking at your data from many different perspectives than by seeing only a single view. Any plot can suggest another that is just slightly different. Many of the actions discussed thus far let you modify a plot slightly to improve the view or clarify an aspect of the display. Data Desk also lets you use some plots as templates for other similar plots. In effect, you can say "I now want a plot just like this one

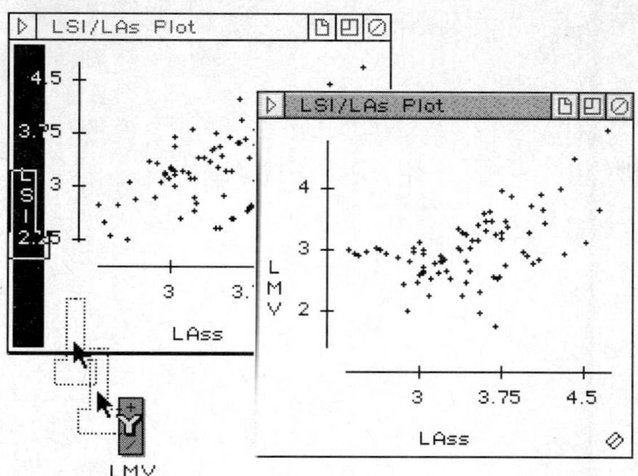

Figure 9-18. Substi-tution by dragging an icon over the axes label of the old plot.

except for the following change."

A typical example is the ability to substitute one variable for another in a plot. To do so, simply drag the icon of the new variable over the axis label of the old plot (Fig. 9-18). Because the plot will change in place, you may want to duplicate the plot first. (Select its icon alias and choose {Data} **Duplicate**.) The duplicate plot opens on top of the original. You might need to move the new plot to see the old one.)

Ordinarily, substituting a new variable on a plot axis rescales the plot to suit the new variable. However, if you first choose **Freeze Scale** from the plot's HyperView menu, the axis scales will remain unchanged. You can easily compare two plots on identical axes by duplicating the first, selecting **Freeze Scale**, and dragging a new variable onto one of the axes. In Section 9.15 we discuss this and other ways to specify plot scales.

An alternative way to substitute is with the template tools, including the {Data} **Substitute Socket** command discussed in Chapter 14. Substitute Socket provides a way to import new data into an existing analysis.

Aspects

Data Desk lets you modify almost any aspect of a plot. Most of the commands that help you do so are in the **Modify** menu, organized into submenus according to the aspect of the plot they modify. Data Desk's plots are data analysis displays rather than presentation displays, so the list of aspects is quite different from the list you might see in a presentation graphics program. The aspects of data analysis plots are chosen to help you understand more about your data.

Unless otherwise specified, in each of the following sections we discuss a submenu of the **Modify** menu. All commands discussed in a section are in that submenu, and all of them operate on the frontmost window and are active if that window is a plot. Some commands have effects that change other linked windows, but they still operate on the front window. Some commands operate on all selected windows if the Ctrl key (the Optionkey on Mac) is depressed.

The **Visibility** and **Selection** submenus relate closely to actions discussed in earlier sections of this chapter.

The basic aspects covered are:

- *Symbols*
  Data Desk can plot points with one of eight symbols. Plot symbols identify groups and mark special points.
- *Colors*
  Data Desk can plot points and lines with one of 64 colors. Plot colors can identify groups, mark special points, or represent a continuous dimension.
- *Axes*
  The axes of a plot describe the relationship between the data values and their graphical representation. However, you can often see the data more clearly without them.

- *Scale*

  Some plots offer control over the scaling of the plot or over the default scale methods.

- *Visibility*

  You can hide some of the points in a plot to focus attention on the others or to show patterns for different groups.

- *Lines*

  You can draw lines between points, add lines from appropriate variables, and save line information in variables.

- *Dimensions and Equations*

  Data Desk's dimensions and equations are appropriate only for rotating plots, and are discussed in Chapter 10.

9.12 *Symbols*

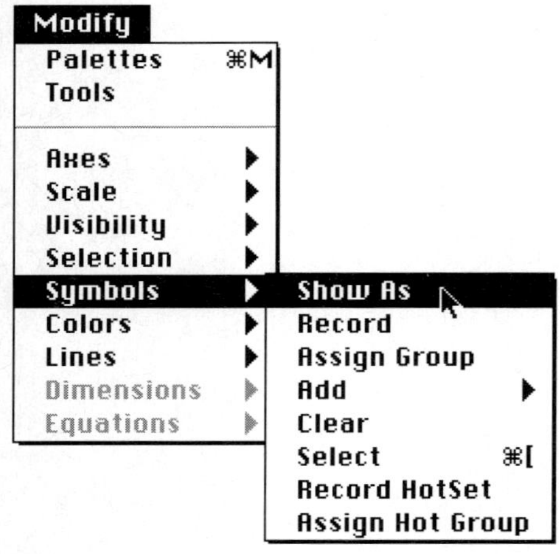

Figure 9-19. *The Symbols Palette can be placed on the desktop by selecting {Modify ▶ Symbols}* ***Show As.***

The **Symbols** submenu of the **Modify** menu holds commands for working with plot symbols (Fig. 9-19). To assign plot symbols to points in a dotplot, scatterplot, lineplot, probability plot, or rotating plot, select the points and choose a symbol from the Symbols palette. If the Symbols palette isn't open, you can place the palette on the Data Desk desktop by choosing {Modify ▶ Symbols} **Show As** command. Symbols are linked immediately to all plot windows; a point assigned a new symbol is immediately plotted with that symbol in all plots that use symbols. You can also assign plot symbols to cases selected in a variable editing window, although you can only see the effect of the assignment in an appropriate plot.

Plot symbols let you mark groups or particular cases. For example, in the Iris dataset introduced by R. A. Fisher, and subsequently used by many writers, measurements are reported for three species of Iris flower. We can plot *Petal Length* versus *Sepal Width* with each species represented by a different symbol. With the scatterplot frontmost, select *Species* and choose {Modify ▶ Symbols ▶ Add} **By Group** (Fig. 9-20).

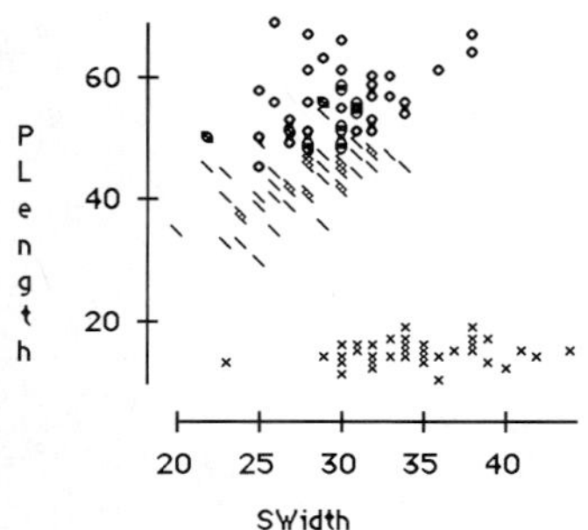

Figure 9-20. *The Iris data. Each species is plotted with a different plot symbol.*

Data Desk's plot symbols have been chosen to look as different from each other as possible and to overlap each other in ways that make it possible to identify the individual symbols. They are not the standard symbols often used in presentation displays. Even if the "o" "/" "\" "|" and "–" symbols all overlap in a plot, it is relatively easy to see each symbol and know that all five points are plotted there.

Plot symbols move easily in rotating plots, but they don't themselves rotate. Thus the "/" symbol always runs from lower left to upper right and never rotates to become the "\" symbol.

The {Modify ▶ Symbols} **Record** command creates a new variable, *Group*, records in it codes corresponding to the symbols of all cases in the front plot, and adds it to the data Relation. To assign symbols from the group identities, select the group variable, click on a plot, and choose {Modify ▶ Symbols ▶ Add} **By Indices**.

{Modify ▶ Symbols} **Assign Group** creates a new variable recording the groups, places it in the **Groups** button (see Section 13.5), and selects that button for the next command.

To assign symbols so that each symbol represents a group, select the variable that holds group names, click on a plot, and choose {Modify ▶ Symbols ▶ Add} **By Group**.

{Modify ▶ Symbols} **Clear** sets all plot symbols to the plus (+).

To select all cases displayed with the same symbol, select at least one point in the group and choose {Modify ▶ Symbols} **Select**. All cases whose plot symbols match the selected cases are selected.

{Modify ▶ Symbols} **Record HotSet** is the same as the **Record** command, except that the variable created is dynamic. The makeup of the variable changes as the symbol assignment changes. {Modify ▶ Symbols} **Assign Hot Group** creates the dynamic HotSet variable and assigns the variable to a **Group** button. We discuss HotSets and HotGroups in detail in Chapter 13.

9.13 *Colors*

Like plot symbols, color is a plot attribute that can convey additional information. All commands dealing with color are in the {Modify ▶ Colors} submenu, which parallels the {Modify ▶ Symbols} submenu almost exactly. The Color palette shows the 64 colors available in Data Desk. The Color palette might already be open. If not, you can place the palette on the desktop by choosing {Modify ▶ Colors} **Show As** command or by opening all the palettes with the {Modify} **Palettes** command.

Color is an attribute of those plots that show individual cases, such as scatterplots, dotplots, and rotating plots. Any plot that can display symbols can display color. When a case is displayed in color, it has the same color in all plots in the same relation that can display color. Color is also used in pie charts, but there it works in a special way (see Section 8.9).

You can assign colors in the same way as you assign symbols: Select cases and click on one of the color squares in the Color palette.

Alternatively, you can {Modify ▶ Colors ▶ Add} **By Group** from a discrete variable, just as you can assign symbols by group. However, colors aren't limited to eight groups as symbols are. Data Desk automatically counts the number of categories and selects colors that are as different from each other as possible to display the categories. Although there are 64 possible colors, it is hard for most people to differentiate more than 10 or so colors.

Alternatively, color can represent a continuous dimension. Adding color from a continuous variable uses a range of colors to represent the range of values in the variable. The range of colors available in Data Desk is circular; the first and last color in the Colors palette are as close to each other as any two adjacent colors in the palette. Data Desk therefore uses only half the color range to represent a continuous variable. The color range represents low values with a pale blue and high values with a deep red, running through green, yellow, and orange for intermediate values.

Data Desk offers several ways to represent values as colors. Often it is best to represent the ranks of the values rather than the values themselves. Many variables follow a humped distribution that groups most values in the middle, so most points are assigned the same color. Ranking spreads the values and thus makes better use of the available color range. The **Add** submenu offers to add colors **By Ranks** or by **Linear** mapping of variable value to the integers 0 to 31 (and then to the first 32 colors).

The **Record**, **Assign Group**, **Record HotSet**, and **Assign Hot Group** commands record colors (as integers between 0 and 63), as the same commands do for Symbols. To restore recorded colors, select the recorded variable and **Add ▶ By Indices**. We discuss HotSets and Hot Groups in detail in Chapter 13.

The **Clear** command sets all colors to the default, white. The **Select** command selects all cases that have the same color as the selected case. (It is hard to tell apart two adjacent colors in the palette.)

A small black square in the center of each color square on the Color palette indicates the colors in use. Ctrl click on Windows, or Option clicking on Mac, on a color or symbol in the palette selects the points matching that color or symbol. Selecting points in any plot that uses color will highlight those colors in the Color palette. This feature allows you to determine the exact colors of points.

9.14 *Axes*

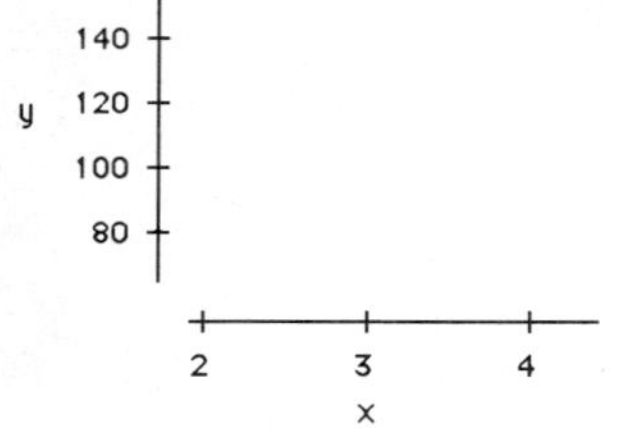

Plot axes tell you what you're looking at and how the plot relates to the data values. The Data Desk commands to modify axes appear in the **Axes** submenu of the **Modify** menu. Axes commands operate on the front window if it is a plot. Alternatively, they work on all selected plots (open or closed) when the Shift key is held down.

Most displays have a vertical y-axis with tick marks, value labels, and the name of the variable plotted in that direction. Many also have a horizontal x-axis with the same features. Boxplots, bar charts, and dotplots have no horizontal axis. Instead, they provide the name of the variable or group displayed in each box or strip. The axes in a rotating plot appear at the center of rotation as lines that point in the direction of the projection of each variable.[2]

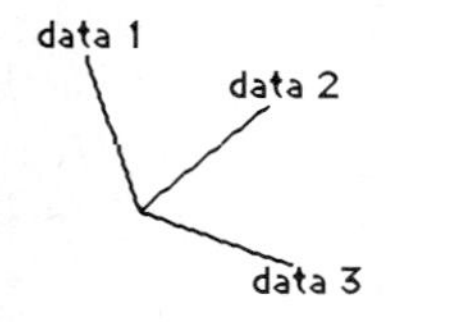

Plot axes serve a different purpose in data analysis displays than they do in presentation displays. Often the numbers underlying a plot are of secondary importance when our goal is to gain insight. You are likely to be more interested in the overall pattern of the data than in the particular values. Many statisticians recommend that data analysis displays have sparse axes. Usually, it is best to show axes in a newly drawn display. However, you may want to hide them later to be able to concentrate more easily on patterns in the data.

The **Hide Axes** command makes axes invisible. Most plots recover the space previously occupied by the axes and use that space for the body of the plot itself. Hiding axes can thus be especially helpful for plots in small windows. In many plots, patterns are easier to see when the axes are out of the way. In rotating plots, hiding the axes also hides the axes' names; it not only gets them out of the way of a central cloud of points,

[2]Formally, rotating plot axes are lines from the origin (0, 0, 0,...) to the points (k1, 0, 0,...), (0, k2, 0,...), (0, 0, k3,...), and so on, with the constants, ki, chosen so that the axis lines will be drawn the same length after plot scaling.

but it also speeds the rotation. The Hide Axes command changes to **Show Axes** for plots in which the axes have been hidden.

Because you might want to toggle between showing and hiding the axes, this command has a keyboard shortcut of Ctrl-Y on Windows or ⌘–Y on Mac. (The "Y" is supposed to remind you of the three axes of a rotating plot.) You can push a rotating plot and then toggle the axes on and off while rotating.

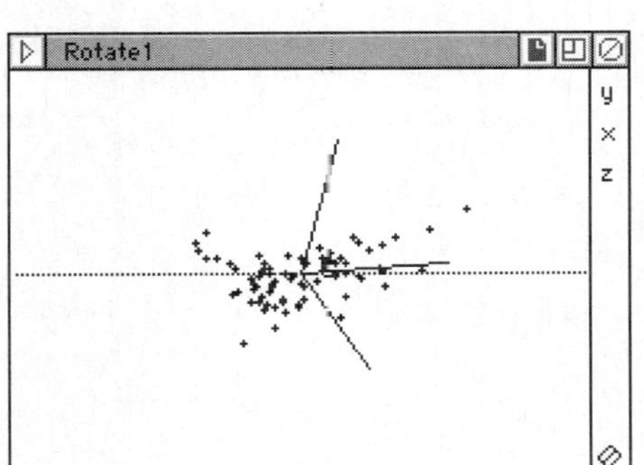

Figure 9-21. Show X-Axis Guide provides a horizontal guideline.

You control the axes and their names separately. Hiding the axes leaves their names. Alternatively, **Hide Axis Names** leaves the lines and tick marks but hides the text of the axis names. That's particularly useful in rotating plots, where the axis names can clutter the plot. It is also used in scatterplot matrices to reduce clutter and to gain plotting area. The command changes to **Show Axis Names** for plots in which axis names have been hidden.

The **Show X-Axis Guide** and **Show Y-Axis Guide** commands place a dotted horizontal or vertical guideline on a scatterplot, lineplot, probability plot, or rotating plot (Fig. 9-21). These guides are especially helpful for seeing whether a pattern deviates from the horizontal (for example, in a scatterplot of residuals) or on rotating plots, for aligning directions of greatest variance.

Show Horizontal Gridlines or **Show Vertical Gridlines** commands place horizontal or vertical grid lines on scatterplots, dotplots, boxplots, and lineplots.

When you hold down the Shift key, the axis commands apply to all windows whose icons are selected.

9.15 Scale

The scale of a plot determines the relationship between the data values and the position of points, bars, lines, and wedges in the plot. The and tools alter the scale of many plots. Alternatively, {Modify ▶ Scale} **Scale to Selected Points** rescales the plot in the front window as if it consisted only of the selected points (but plots all of the visible points). When a plot's scaling has been altered, you can return to the original scaling by selecting all points (**Ctrl-A** on Windows, or **⌘–A** on Mac, is a good shortcut for **Select All**) and choosing **Scale to Selected Points**, or by selecting {Modify ▶ Scale} **Home**.

All plots automatically scale to all points when they are made. Plots rescale whenever they update in response to changes in underlying data or expressions (see Section 4.3). To freeze the scale, choose **Freeze Scale** from the plot window's HyperView menu (Fig.9-22).

LCF/Lmp Plot
Regression of LCF vs LEmp
Correlation of LCF vs LEmp
Turn On Automatic Update
Freeze Scale
Show Plot Info
Add Regression Line
Add Color Regression Lines
Smoothing ▶
Make Comments
Selector ▶
Plot Scale...
Text Format...

*Figure 9-22. Choose **Freeze Scale** from the plot window's HyperView menu to freeze the current scale during Updates.*

Rotating Plots

The {Modify ▶ Scale} **Rotate Around Selection** command recenters rotating plots at the point defined by the means of the selected datapoints along each variable. The {Plot ▶ Plot Options} **Rotating Plot Options** dialog offer other control of scale and center in rotating plots (see Section 10.7).

HISTOGRAMS

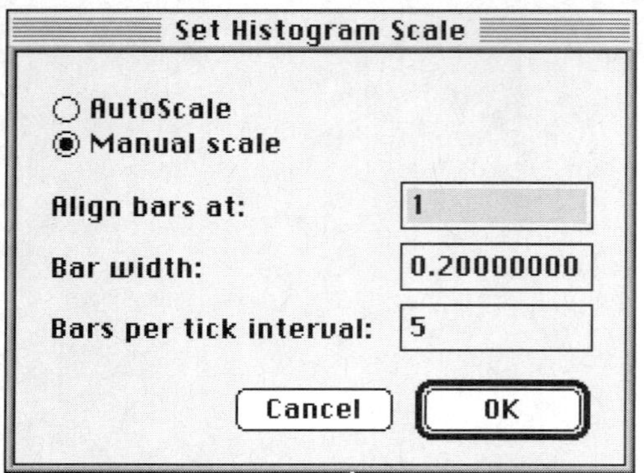

Figure 9-23*. The histogram's scale dialog lets you specify how the histogram in the front window should be drawn.*

Stretching and shrinking a histogram window while holding down the Ctrl key on Windows, or the Option key on Mac, rescales the histogram. For more precise control, choose **Plot Scale...**. from the histogram's global HyperView menu or make the histogram window frontmost and choose {Modify ▶ Scale} **Plot Scale...**. This dialogue gives you control of the bar width and starting point for the first bar (Fig. 9-23).

Data Desk provides a simple way to generate two histograms with the same scale. Select the two variables of interest and choose {Calc} **Histograms**. Drag the icon alias of the histogram whose scale you want replicated into the histogram whose scale you want changed. This process essentially drags the scale and window dimensions from one histogram into the other. Now the histograms are plotted with the same scale and can be more easily compared. Choose {Modify ▶ Scale} **Home** and the histogram returns to its original scale.

SCATTERPLOTS

Any scatterplots (in fact all plots) created in Data Desk are scaled to fit all points in the window. You can customize the scale of plots by choosing **Plot Scale...** from the plot's global HyperView menu or by making the plot frontmost and choosing {Modify ▶Scale} **Plot Scale...**. The options in this dialog allow you to manipulate the plot scale for each axis and change the size of the window.

The scale of each axis is determined by three values: "Lower Bound", "Upper Bound", and "Interval Size". Data Desk initially sets the lower and upper bounds to the minimum and maximum values for the variable plotted on that axis. The initial interval size is set to one-fifth of the variable's range or the next largest "nice" number.

You can change the starting and ending points for either or both axes by entering new values in the boxes for Lower Bound and Upper Bound. You can change the amount of space between each tick mark by entering a new value for Interval Size. If you want the value of the Upper Bound to be the last tick mark on your scale, be sure that the values of the upper bound and lower bound are whole-number multiples of the interval size. For example if you want a scale that goes from 0 to 100, entering a lower bound of 0, an upper bound of 100, and an interval of 20 will produce a plot scale with five tick marks, with the last tick labeled 100 {(100/20) = 5 and (0/20) = 0; both whole numbers}. If you enter an interval size of 30 instead of 20, the axis will have 3 tick marks with the last visible mark labeled 90 {(100)/30 = 3.33, not a whole number}.

Plot scaling works best when the lower and upper bounds are whole-number multiples of the interval size. If you adjust the interval scale without changing the lower or upper bounds, Data Desk will automatically adjust the values for the lower bound and upper bound to values that are whole number multiples of the new interval size. For example, suppose that you have a variable whose minimum value is 100 and maximum value is 200. Your initial scale settings are 100 for the lower bound, 200 for the upper bound, and 20 for the interval size. If you change the interval size to 10, the bound values do not change because both 100 and 200 are whole number multiples of 10. If you change the interval size to 30, the bounds will change to 90 and 120, which are whole-number multiples of the interval size 30.

Precision specifies the number of significant digits in the tick labels. The pop-up menu specifies Scientific notation for tick mark labels.

To bring back the original scale, click the Home button at the top of the plot scale dialog window or select **Restore Automatic Scale** from the plot's HyperView menu.

The **Plot Scale...** dialog also allows you to set the size of the window. Type the values for the horizontal and vertical dimensions in the Plot Dimensions fields. You may specify the dimensions in either inches or centimeters. This option is important for meeting publication requirements and for making it easier to overlay plots in layout windows. We discuss overlaying plots in layout windows in more detail in Chapter 14.

HOW-TO

To assign the scaling parameters of one plot to another, drag the icon alias of the scatterplot whose scale you want replicated into the scatterplot whose scale you want to change.

To manipulate scales so that two plots have the same scaling and size, drag the icon alias of the scatterplot whose scale you want replicated into the scatterplot whose scale you want changed. The scatterplot you dragged into will be scaled and sized exactly like the one you dragged from.

Other Plots

You can change the scale of all the other plots by selecting **Plot Scale...** from the plot's global HyperView menu. The dialogue presented is the same as for scatterplots with each option providing the same functionality. The only difference is that the x-axis cannot be changed for dotplots and boxplots. The global HyperView menu of a slider provides a Plot Scale dialog, which lets you scale only the x-axis because there is no y-axis on a slider. This dialog also lets you specify upper and lower bounds for the x-axis. These bounds act as "bumpers"; the slider cannot slide past them. This constraint is handy, for example, if zero or negative values would produce impossible or illegal results.

9.16 *Visibility*

Several kinds of plots represent each case as a point or symbol on the plot. These include scatterplots, dotplots, rotating plots, lineplots, and normal probability plots. In these plots you can select and work with individual cases by selecting and working with the points that represent them in the plot.

The **Visibility** submenu holds commands that help to focus attention on some of the cases by hiding others. These commands thus relate to the ideas of isolation discussed in Section 9.9. In particular, you can make some points invisible with the **Show Only Selected Points** command. **Show All Points** returns any hidden points to visibility. **Toggle Hidden Points** hides the visible points and makes the hidden points visible. This operation is a particularly effective way to compare two groups. Because it has a keyboard shortcut, **Ctrl-H** on Windows or **⌘-H** on Mac, you can toggle hidden points in a rotating plot while it is rotating.

Ordinarily, the commands in the {Modify ▶ Visibility} menu control only the visibility of points in the frontmost window. However, that can make plots of data appear inconsistent. If you hold down the Ctrl key on Windows, or the Option key on Mac, while selecting any command from the **Visibility** menu, the change in visibility affects all open plots in the relation.

9.17 *Lines*

Another way to indicate grouping in scatterplots and rotating plots is to connect points with lines. This method is best suited to small groups, but works well even if you have many small groups. For example, you can group the before and after values of each case in an experiment by drawing a line between each matched pair of datapoints.

Lines can also show trends and sequences, or even depict simple shapes. Unlike symbols, lines are local to a plot. Connecting two points with a line in one plot doesn't connect them with a line in other plots.

LINES

The Line tool draws lines one by one between pairs of points. To draw a line click on a point and drag the line to another point. To remove a line draw over it again. The Line tool is most useful for adding or deleting a few lines from a plot. By contrast, the {Modify ▶ Lines} **Add** submenu holds commands to add many lines to a scatterplot or rotating plot according to variables that specify the assignment. The **by From/To** command requires that you select two variables; the first holds the case numbers of one end of each line, and the second holds the case numbers for the other end of each line. Thus two variables holding the values:

1 5
3 8
5 3

specify lines from the point representing case 1 to the point representing case 5, from case 3 to case 8, and from case 5 to case 3. Values less than 1 or greater than the number of points in the plot are ignored. The **Record** command records the lines on the frontmost plot as two such variables.

You can also provide a single variable containing the case numbers of points that should be connected with lines and choose the **Add ▶ by Series** command. This method is particularly useful for following a time trend through a plot. For example, you can generate a variable that counts from 1 up to the number of cases with the {Manip} **Generate Patterned Data** command and use it to add lines connecting points in case sequence order.

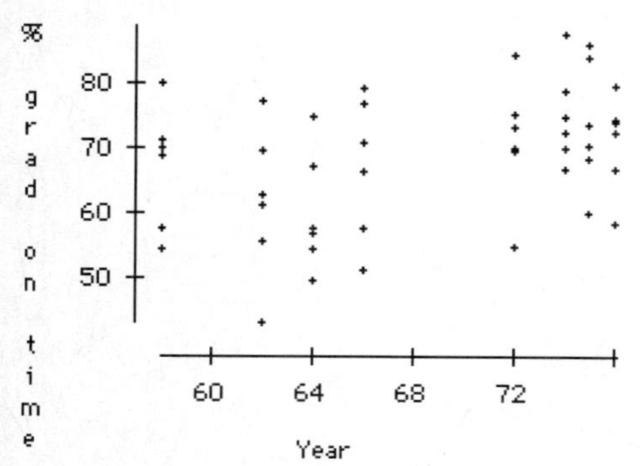

Figure 9-24. Percent of entering class graduating on time by class year.

Finally, you can add separate lines to connect the points in each group. Select a variable containing group identities and choose **Add ▶ by Group** from the **Lines** submenu. Data Desk adds a separate line for each group, connecting the points in case order.

For example, the Graduation dataset reports the percentage of entering freshmen graduating on time from each of several colleges at a major university for each of several years. A plot of *%Grad on Time* versus *Year* shows a general trend of better graduation performance in the 1970s than in the 1960s, but the trends for individual colleges don't show (Fig. 9-24).

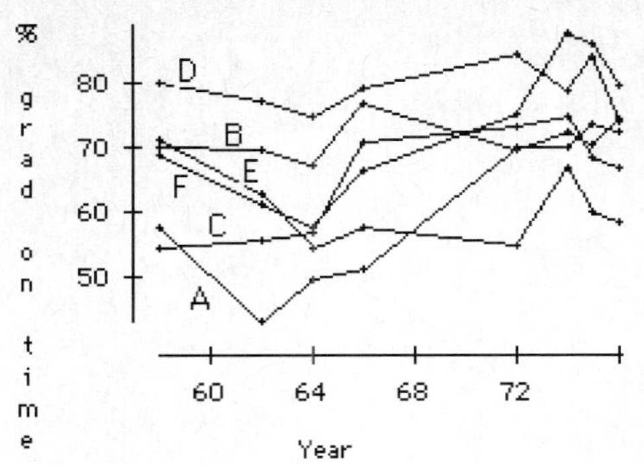

Figure 9-25. Figure 9-24 with lines added with ***by Group*** *for each* School.

However, the *School* variable holds the names of the various colleges in the university. Select *School,* bring the plot to the front, and choose {Modify ▶ Lines ▶ Add Lines} **by Group**. Figure 9-25 shows the result.

Clear Lines removes all lines from the front plot. **Hide Lines** makes lines invisible but remembers them. **Show Lines** replaces **Hide Lines** when lines have been hidden to make all lines visible again.

Drawing a line with the Line tool automatically shows all lines if they have been hidden. You can toggle lines on and off with the **Alt-hyphen** keyboard equivalent command on Windows or **⌘-hyphen** on Mac.

Lineplots plot a sequence variable in order against its case numbers and connect the points in order with lines. Lineplots have the advantage of being generated by the simple {Plot} **Lineplots** command. They have the disadvantage that they generate only an equally spaced *x*-axis. The lines in a lineplot are special and can't be hidden or recorded with the commands of the **Lines** submenu.

The {Plot} **Multiple Lineplots** command plots several variables against a common sequence axis and connects the points in each variable individually. It does so by creating a new relation holding three variables: a variable with copies of the selected variables appended to each other, a variable with a suitable *x*-axis sequence (repeated once for each variable), and a variable holding the names of the original variables as group names. The multiple line plot is a scatterplot with lines and colors added by group. You can work with the variables in the new relation, but because the plot is in its own relation, it doesn't link to the original relation (see Section 8.12).

9.18 *Lines and Color*

When lines are added to a plot drawn in color, the lines are colored as well. Data Desk assigns to each line a color whose index is the average of the color indices of its endpoints. Thus if you add colors by group to a plot and then add lines by group using the same group variable, the lines for each group have a distinct color. Data Desk does this automatically when displaying multiple line plots on a color monitor.

Plots that are colored according to the values in a variable may show overall trends in color. Lines drawn on these plots will conform to the trends.

LAs/LSI Plot
Regression of LAss vs LSI
Correlation of LAss vs LSI
Turn On Automatic Update
Freeze Scale
Show Plot Info
Add Regression Line
Add Color Regression Lines
Smoothing ▶
Make Comments
Selector ▶
Plot Scale...
Text Format...

Figure 9-26. Add Regression Line *command in the HyperView menu adds the "best fit" line to the scatterplot.*

9.19 *Regression Lines*

When looking at data on a scatterplot you will often find it useful to see the "best-fit" line through the data. To add this line to a scatterplot, choose **Add Regression Line** from the plot's HyperView menu (Fig. 9-26). Data Desk displays a line that best fits the data. The line is computed by minimizing the sum of the squared residuals (see Chapter 25). The regression line is often helpful in finding trends and verifying assumptions for linear model–based statistics such as regression and ANOVA.

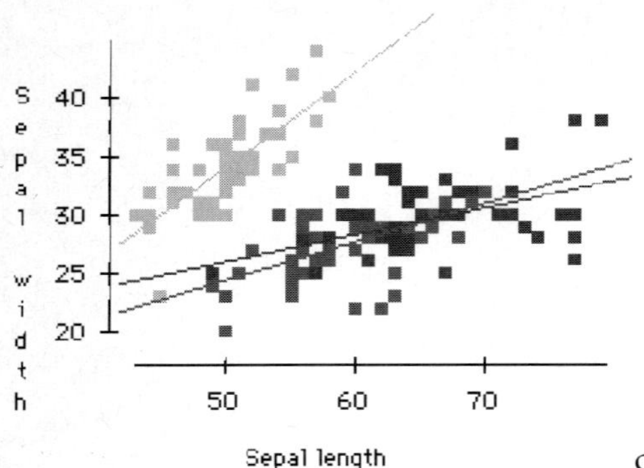

Figure 9-27. Color regression lines added to the scatterplot show that one of the Irises manifests a different trend than the other two.

Another helpful command in a scatterplot's global HyperView menu is **Add Color Regression Lines**. This command is active if you are using a color monitor. This command generates a separate regression line for each set of colored points on the plot (Fig. 9-27). To use this feature, select a variable holding a set of grouping names, and choose {Modify ▶ Colors ▶ Add } **by Group**. Next, choose **Add Color Regression Lines** from the scatterplot's global HyperView menu. When you change a point's color, the lines recalculate immediately. If you change a point's color to white, that point is taken out of the calculation of the lines and the lines redraw to reflect the removal of that point. This technique is especially powerful in observing differences across groups and to explore the effects of outliers.

9.20 *Wrapping Up*

Data Desk offers an extraordinarily rich collection of graphic data analysis tools. It is unlikely that you will ever use all of them. (There are over 1000 combinations of plots, commands, and tools.) Nevertheless, you may well find that each new data analysis leads to a few new methods or plots.

You may also find that there are several ways to accomplish the same goal. For example, you might define an indicator variable by selecting cases in a pie chart or bar chart or by lassoing cases in a scatterplot or rotating plot and saving the selection from the **Modify** menu, by saving the indicator directly with a HyperView menu from a table (see Chapter 16), or by defining a derived variable (see Chapter 11).

Although you can almost certainly *read* Data Desk plots with no practice, you will find that practice improves your facility for *working with* them. Only by doing so will you become more comfortable with basic operations, more adept at wielding plot tools, and more knowledgeable about advanced techniques. Nevertheless, statistical graphics rely heavily on intuition and understanding of the data rather than on mathematics. Many people who might be reluctant to learn about multivariate statistics in depth find sophisticated statistical graphics natural and easy to learn.

APPENDIX 9A *Plot Tool Shortcuts*

For any display, four tools are at your fingertips regardless of the current plot tool selected from the palette. Holding down the Ctrl key overrides the plot tool selection. Ctrl-right mouse button (RM), Ctrl-Shift, and Ctrl-Shift-right mouse button offer three more useful tools.

The spring-loaded tools that are available depend upon the kind of display you are manipulating.

Display	**Ctrl**	**Ctrl-RM**	**Ctrl-Shift**	**Ctrl-Shift-RM**
All plots			?	
EXCEPT:				
Histogram				
Rotating Plots			?	
Bar Chart				
Pie chart				

APPENDIX 9B *Selection Modes*

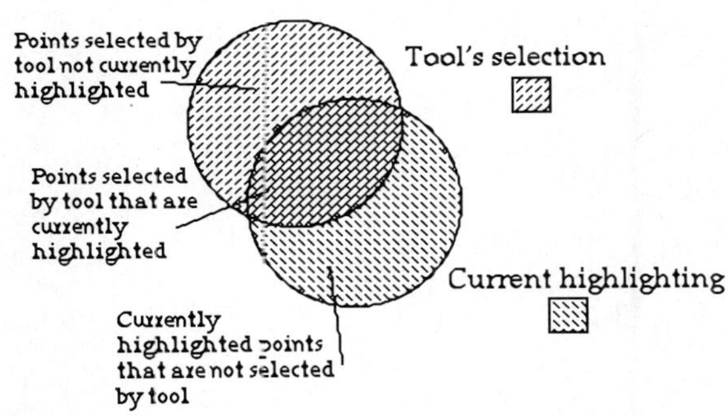

Figure 9-28. *Key to the Selection Modes symbols. Each diagram symbolically shows the points currently highlighted and those selected by the plot tool. The darkest part of the diagram shows which classes of points are left highlighted.*

The Selection Modes palette is in the {Modify ▶ Selection} **Mode** menu. It holds five selection *modes* that temporarily change the way the selection tools work. The highlighting in the Selection Modes palette reverses to indicate which mode is presently selected.

The Selection Modes palette shows five symbols. Each is a symbolic representation of the resulting selection operation known as a Venn diagram. The lower circle on each represents the points or parts of the plot already highlighted. The upper circle represents the points or parts of the plot selected by the selection tool. They can include parts of the plot not previously highlighted and parts already highlighted. The darkest portion of the diagram shows which parts of the plot are left highlighted by this mode of selection. Fig. 9-28 illustrates this representation.

ORDINARY SELECTION

Ordinary Selection is the default selection mode. The points or regions selected by the tool replace any previous highlighting, which is how selection operates in most programs. Whenever you select a new plot tool, the selection mode automatically is set to Ordinary Selection. To use an alternative mode, bring the plot to the front, pick up a plot tool, and click on the alternative mode.

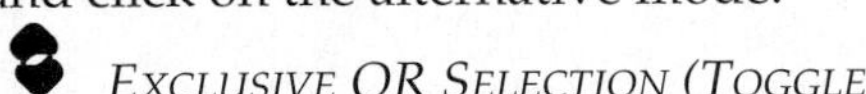

EXCLUSIVE OR SELECTION (TOGGLE)

Points that weren't previously highlighted are highlighted when selected. Points that were previously highlighted are unhighlighted when selected. Thus the highlighting of the selected points is toggled, which is how Ordinary Selection works when the Shift key is depressed.

 *OR Selection (Add)*

Selected points or regions are highlighted. Points that were already highlighted remain highlighted.

 *NOT Selection (Subtract)*

Selected points or regions are unhighlighted. Points that were not highlighted are not changed.

 *AND Selection (Intersect)*

AND Selection leaves highlighted only those points that were *both* previously highlighted *and* selected with the tool. This is an effective way to narrow down highlighted cases that satisfy a combination of criteria. Select cases according to the first criterion. Then set AND selection and select cases according to the second criterion. Only those cases satisfying both criteria will remain selected. You can continue with more criteria. After each AND selection, only cases satisfying all of the criteria will remain selected.

CHAPTER 10

Brushing, Slicing, and Rotating

DYNAMIC PLOTS PROVIDE an extraordinarily effective way to see patterns and structure among several variables. Plots that change over time can reveal significant features of the data. It is usually easier to see changes than to discern patterns in static displays. Change over time thus facilitates recognition of relationships among separate displays. Animation also provides a means of depicting true three-dimensional structure in an intuitive way.

Brushing and slicing provide ways to work with many variables without having to imagine more than three dimensions at once. Rotation provides both a vivid illusion of three-dimensional structure and a convenient way to orient a display to an "interesting" point of view (and, implicitly, an "interesting" projection). As integrated parts of Data Desk, these capabilities provide depth and power that can't be matched by conventional data analysis systems.

10.1 *Brushing and Slicing*

Plot brushing was developed initially by statisticians at AT&T Bell Labs as a way to work with scatterplot matrices and is still offered in that specialized form by some statistics programs. Data Desk generalizes brushing beyond that isolated framework, making the plot brush a tool that works in any appropriate display.

Brushing focuses attention on a selected subset of points while showing them against the background of the rest of the points. A greater variety of plots offers more ways to define the selected subset. Thus, for example, by selecting points in a dotplot you focus on a subrange of the plotted variable to see where those points reside in other displays. By selecting points in a rotating plot, you can orient the rotation to identify a key dimension or to isolate a subgroup.

The wedding of brushing to rotation has also altered the focus of brushing uses. Early applications of brushing included attempts to discern structures in data that are more readily seen by rotation, such as clustering of points into groups. In this chapter we concentrate in part on ways in which brushing and rotation enhance each other.

There are a few basic ways to brush plots:

- Brushing with the standard square or large rectangular brush
- Brushing with a tall and thin or short and wide brush to take "conditional" slices in one plot while observing how they look in other plots
- Brushing with one of the "sticky" selection modes so that brushed points stay selected

It is often worthwhile to select points as you brush horizontally or vertically the x- or y-axis of a plot, leaving them selected as you pass over them. Slicing does so in a convenient way without requiring that you reshape the brush or change selection modes.

10.2 *Principles of Brushing and Slicing*

Brushing and slicing reveal several basic kinds of relationships.

- IDENTITY
  When you brush the upper left corner of a plot, points in the upper left corner of another plot highlight. This pattern continues throughout the plot. Even though the plots don't match point-for-point, they show similar underlying structure. If there is no *a priori* reason for suspecting such an identity, it is worth investigating further.

- EQUIVALENCE
  When you brush the upper left corner of a plot, points in the upper *right* corner of another plot highlight. This pattern continues throughout the plots, with the two plots being nearly identical except for a 90° rotation. The plots show similar underlying structure, provided that the change in orientation isn't meaningful. Most kinds of equivalence among variables concentrate on relationships among variables and are thus not concerned with orientations. Sometimes we may even see plots that are equivalent but for a rotation through an arbitrary angle, or combination of that and a reflection.

- CONDITIONAL DISTRIBUTIONS
  Some relationships change according to values on a third variable. Such change is sometimes thought of as an *interaction* among three variables. One good way to view this interaction is to consider it *conditional* on the value of the third variable. That is, restrict your attention to a small range of the third variable and consider the distribution or relationship of the cases that fall in that region.

  Brush or slice along one variable (for example, on a dot plot) while watching the histograms of others to see conditional distributions. The histograms highlight to show the *conditional distribution* of the selected points. In this way it is easy to answer questions such as "Is the distribution of the stock price of companies with high research and development expenses about the same as that for companies with low R&D expenses?"

  Similarly, brush one variable and watch scatterplots of pairs of other variables. The highlighted points show relationships among the variables that are conditional on the selected region of the brushed variable. By seeing the selected points against the background of the entire dataset you can track changes in the relationship due to the conditioning.

- SIMPLE TRENDS
  Brush along the stripe of a dotplot or along one dimension of a scatterplot and look for trends in other plots. Often slicing up or down the strip is more effective. A trend in this context is not limited to linear patterns or even to ordered patterns. For example, you might find that as you slice along one variable, a scatterplot of two others grows a ball of highlighted points, starting from its center and spreading outward.

  One convenient way to brush or slice along a trend is to make a rotating plot of the same two variables as were in the scatterplot and use the tool to turn the plot until the trend is horizontal.

- *Complex trends*
  Brush along one dimension of a plot or strip of a dotplot and look for changes in the *relationship* of two or more variables in their scatterplot or rotating plot. For example, you can brush along a time variable while watching a scatterplot to answer questions such as "Has the relationship between education and expected earnings changed over time?"

  Alternatively, brush along an axis of a rotating plot that, through rotation, is a complex combination of several variables and look for patterns in still other variables. This analysis is sophisticated, but easily learned.

- *Locating specific points*
  By combining brushing with the *Swap Highlight* selection mode, you can make selected points flash. Shape the brush to a small square, select the *Exclusive OR* selection mode, place the brush over the point to identify it, and hold the mouse button down. The point will flash on and off in all linked windows. A flashing point is easy to find even in the midst of a large cloud of datapoints.

We return to some of these principles later in the chapter.

10.3 *Principles of Plot Rotation*

Data Desk's rotating plots are extraordinarily versatile. Virtually every plot tool and plot modification command operates on rotating plots. If you use multivariate statistics, you will find that rotating plots provide appropriate displays for many of the standard multivariate methods. If you prefer to avoid the complexities of multivariate statistics, rotating plots can provide an intuitive way to learn about relationships among several variables without the need for advanced mathematics.

PRIM-9

The first program for rotating data was the PRIM-9 system developed by Fisherkeller, Friedman, and Tukey in 1972. It required several million dollars worth of computer and display hardware, so it remained a prototype system.

PRIM stood for Projection, Rotation, Isolation, and Masking — the elementary operations that were found to be a basis for using plot rotations in data analysis. As we showed in Chapter 9, Data Desk's plot operations include each of these PRIM operations and enhance them beyond what was possible in the prototype systems.

One good way to start using plot rotations in your data analyses is to understand these elementary operations and how they fit together. This is also a good introduction to the advanced commands in the plot control menus. PRIM is a nice acronym, but the elements are more usefully discussed in "RIMP" order.

- *Rotation* is an excellent general-purpose way to create the illusion of three dimensions. It provides both an immediate three-dimensional view of the point cloud and the ability to orient the point cloud in interesting ways. Early, special-purpose plot rotating programs restricted rotation to motion around one of the three axes, but

Data Desk lets you rotate the points around any axis in the projection plane.

- *ISOLATION* is the identification of subsets of points on the plot and the use of those subsets in further analyses. The original definition of isolation included some functions that Data Desk offers in the **Selection** and **Symbols** submenus of the **Modify** menu. Data Desk's many selection tools, assignment of plotting symbols or colors to subsets of points, and recording of subsets add related features not available in the original PRIM implementations.
- *MASKING* is the ability to hide some part of the plot conditional on some other variable and concentrate on the remaining points. Much of the masking principle is replaced in Data Desk by brushing and slicing. You can, of course, make true conditional displays that hide all but the selected points by using the point hiding commands in the **Visibility** submenu of the **Modify** menu.
- *PROJECTION* is the most subtle of the elementary operations. Rotating plots always show a projection of the point cloud on the screen. This projection establishes a relationship between the original variables (shown by the plotted data axis lines) and the plotting axes that point up–down, right–left, and in–out. Often data originally recorded in several variables can be simplified to a few projected dimensions. Data Desk lets you record these projections either as data values or as algebraic descriptions. The **Equations** commands in the **Modify** menu provide ways to view and work with projections.

10.4 *Making a Rotating Plot*

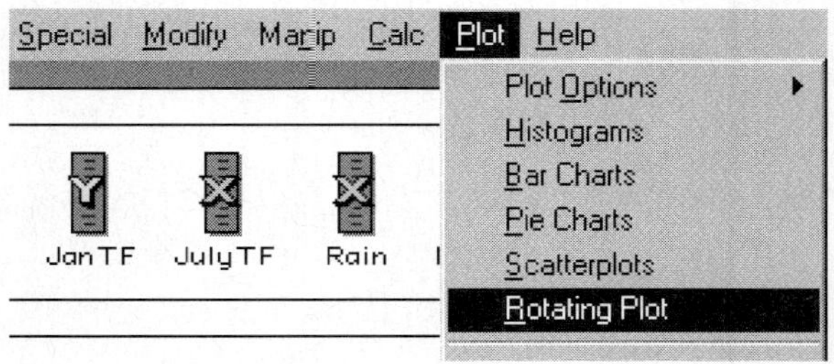

Figure 10-1. *Making a rotating plot of* JanTF *versus* JulyTF *versus* Rain *from the SMSA datafile.*

To make a rotating plot, select three or more variables and choose {Plot} **Rotating Plot** (Fig. 10-1).

The first three variables selected are assigned in order to the *y*- *x*-, and *z*-axes. (Recall that in Data Desk, you ordinarily specify the *y*-axis variable first and the *x*-axis variable second.) When a rotating plot opens, it shows the *y*- and *x*-axes as you would see them in a scatterplot; *y*-axis up and down versus *x*-axis right to left. The *z*-axis is the front-to-back, or in-and-out, direction, but because it runs directly in and out of the screen, you cannot see it until you rotate the plot (Fig. 10-2).

While you can make a rotating plot with almost any number of variables, this chapter starts with three-variable plots.

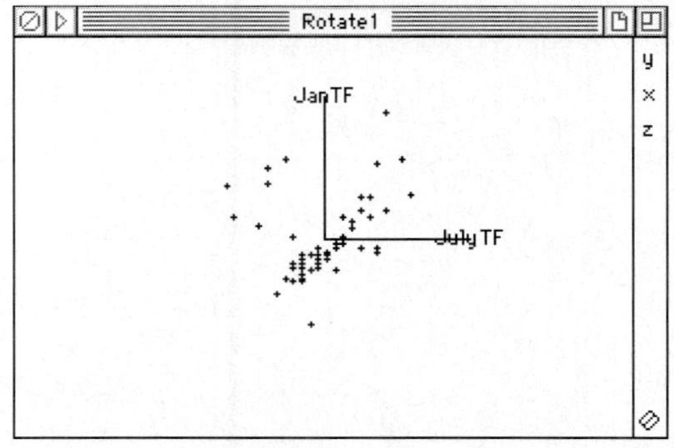

Figure 10-2. *The resulting plot. Rain is on the z-axis running in and out of the screen, so it cannot be seen until the plot is rotated.*

As with any Data Desk window, rotating plot windows can be resized and repositioned on the screen. Unlike some Data Desk plots, rotating plots do not resize when their window changes size. You simply see more or less of the plot. Use the plot rescaling tools (,) to change the size or focus of a rotating plot. You can open as many rotating plot windows as you like, but only one of them can rotate at a time.

10.5 *An Example*

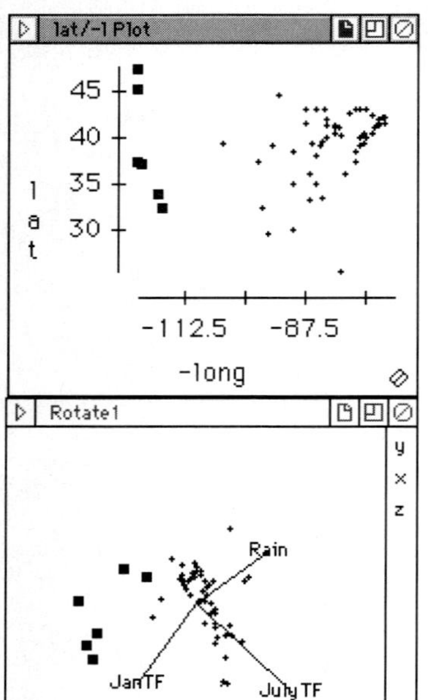

Figure 10-3. *Comparing the "map" with a rotated plot.*

A simple example illustrates the power of combining rotation and brushing. The *SMSA* dataset contains data on 60 U.S. Standard Metropolitan Statistical Areas. Working with that dataset, we make a rotating plot of the three weather variables *JulyTF, JanTF,* and *Rain,* and a scatterplot of the two geographic variables *Lat* and *negLong.* (We must plot negative longitude because longitude increases from east to west, whereas the x-axis of a scatterplot increases from left to right.) A scatterplot of *Lat* versus *negLong* vaguely suggests the map of the United States.

Now brush the "map" and try to orient the rotating plot so that, as points in the map highlight, they highlight in corresponding position in the rotating plot. The orientation shown in Fig. 10-3 is a surprisingly good match, except for the two SMSA's in the Northwest and three in the Northeast.

It is remarkable that we can reproduce the geographic relationships among these cities so closely with only three climate variables. Rotating the plot shows that it has true three dimensional structure. (In particular, the West Coast seems to be in a different plane than the rest of the country.) Note the SMSA's whose climates differ from their geography (for example, Denver, Portland, and Seattle).

10.6 *Seeing Patterns in Rotating Plots*

Some statisticians have proposed that the best way to understand interesting patterns is to consider the *least* interesting pattern possible. For example, the normal distribution, useful though it may be in formal statistics, is fundamentally uninteresting in terms of real data. It is *deviations* from normality that often prove interesting. A rotating plot of random normal numbers is basically uninteresting. The **Generate Random Numbers...** command in the **Manip** menu generates random normal variables that you can then plot.

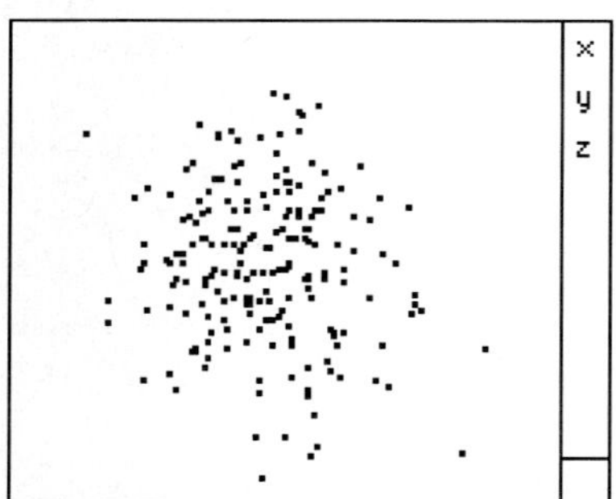

Figure 10-4. *An uninteresting plot of three random normal variables.*

For example, a rotating plot of 200 random Normal cases might look like that shown in Fig. 10-4. Note that the plot shows some datapoints around the edges of the central cloud of points but none that stand out remarkably. Because there is no underlying pattern here, simply being at the edge of the cloud doesn't make a point extraordinary. You might want to make a few plots of random normal variables just to get a feeling for uninteresting displays. Alternatively, plot the variables in the Random Normal datafile.

Fortunately, real data usually are interesting, although interesting patterns may be hidden from view at first. Several kinds of patterns are common and meaningful in data displays.

cluster

> TIP
>
> To select or isolate subgroups:
>
> - Define a 0/1 selector in the {Special} **Assign Selector** command.
> - Use the {Manip} **Split Into Variables By Group** command.
> - In plots, use plot symbols or the{ Modify ▶ Visibility} **Show Only Selected Points** command.

- In some displays, points *cluster* into isolated groups, but only in particular orientations of the display. It is often interesting to know whether the same cases cluster together in other displays of related variables. Assign a different plot symbol or color to each group, highlight clusters, or brush the plots to look for clustering across plots. Single variables with two clusters show up as two-humped, *bimodal* histograms. Slicing across one hump selects those cases so you can consider them in other plots.

  As we noted earlier, recognizing subgroups in data is an important exploratory step. When you find that your data can be split into subgroups, you may first want to find ways to characterize the subgroups. Often the best way to characterize clusters is to use the **?** tool to identify some of the cases in each cluster. For example, you may find that males and females form separate groups in your data (even though gender was not one of the variables displayed), or that region, age, or season define subgroups. If the characterization is one that you did not anticipate, you have discovered what is sometimes called a *lurking variable.*

lurking variable

  Whether you can characterize the subgroups or not, it is often worthwhile to pursue analyses of the subgroups separately. You might use one of the **Record** commands in the **Modify** menus to create an indicator variable (if there are two subgroups) or a group variable (if there are several). For example, you could manually assign a different plot symbol or color to each subgroup and then use the {Modify ▶Symbols} **Record** or the {Modify ▶Colors} **Record** commands. You could then use the Selector or Group buttons (see Chapter 13) to pursue analyses of each subgroup separately or in parallel.

trend

- Some displays show a clear *trend.* Trends that are straight lines can be described with regression analyses or assessed with a correlation coefficient. Trends that are not straight can be assessed with a nonparametric correlation coefficient such as the Spearman or Kendall correlations. Alternatively, they might become both clearer and more useful from transforming one or more of the variables.

surface

- Some rotating plots show a flat *surface.* Flat surfaces can be described statistically with a multiple regression analysis. They tell us that there is a combination of the variables that varies little, suggesting that we don't really need three dimensions to describe the data.

outlier

- One of the most common and most useful patterns is the simple extraordinary point or *outlier.* Points can be extraordinary by being very far from the rest of the data or by failing to conform to a pattern, even though they aren't particularly far from the data. An extraordinary point may be a sign of errors in the data such as a misplaced decimal point or swapped digits. It may be a point that should not be a part of the data (for example, a motorcycle or truck included with cars).

  An extraordinary point may be a perfectly correct and valid point that simply doesn't fit. These are often the most interesting points because we can learn a great deal by discovering *why* the point doesn't fit with the rest. Sometimes it may be better to remove or suppress an extraordinary point during part of the analysis so that it does not dominate the calculations.

complex pattern

- Occasionally a rotating plot reveals a *complex pattern.* Examples of such patterns are planes that twist into a helical shape, parallel or intersecting lines or planes, and patterns with multiple extraordinary points. These represent patterns beyond the reach of any static statistics computation. The only really good way to describe such patterns is with several pictures or with a rotating plot. Unfortunately, rotating plots pasted into text documents and printed no longer rotate so you may find that you must spend the traditional 1000 words to describe the picture.

10.7 Rotating Plot Options

Because rotating plots deal with three or more axes, they have special scaling concerns. The {Plot ▶ Plot Options} **Rotating Plot Options...** command sets the default scaling decisions that affect future rotating plots. The **Rotating Plot Options** dialog can also be accessed from the rotating plot's global HyperView menu (Fig. 10-5). All rotating plots are scaled to fit in their window. The rotating plot options let you control how the axes are centered and scaled relative to one-another *before* being shrunk or inflated to fit in the window.

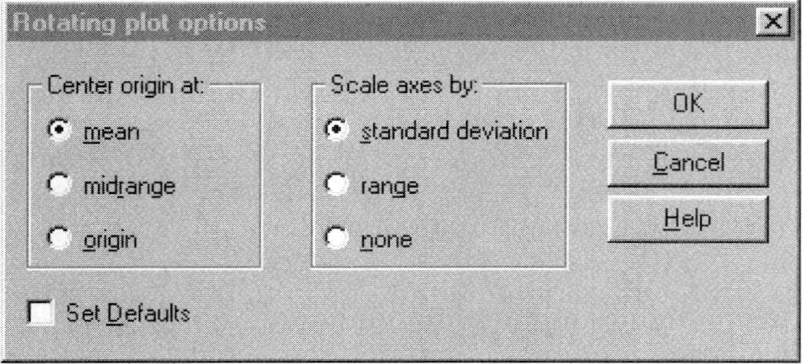

Figure 10-5. *The Rotating Plot Options dialog lets you specify how subsequent rotating plots should be scaled.*

The axes can each be centered at their mean, midrange (the midpoint between the maximum and minimum) or at the value 0, the natural plot origin. The choice is applied to all variables in the plot.

midrange centering

- *Midrange centering* is the most common one for scatterplots because it allows the points to spread as much as possible without losing the extreme points off the edges of the plot window.

mean centering

- *Mean centering* is the default for rotating plots because the multivariate statistics that are often depicted by rotating plots usually start by centering each variable at its mean.

origin centering

- *Centering at the origin* calls for the plot to rotate about the natural origin, (0, 0, 0, …), which may not be near the center of the data.

In addition, each axis can be scaled by dividing by a value determined from the data. This usually improves the chance of seeing a worthwhile pattern in the data because it prevents one variable from dominating the others simply by being measured in larger numbers.

standard deviation scaling

- By default, each variable is divided by its standard deviation. *Standard deviation scaling* corresponds to the scaling most often used in multivariate statistics.

range scaling

- You can choose to divide each axis by its range instead. *Range scaling* lets the point cloud be as big as possible while still fitting inside the plot window.

spatial scaling

- You can choose not to rescale the variables at all. This choice is called *spatial scaling* because it preserves the physical shape of the plot. Spatial scaling is important if x, y, and z are measured in the same units and are directly comparable. For example, x and y might be distances east–west and north–south so that the plotted points, in effect, are on a map. Spatial scaling would preserve the look of the map and the meaning of a 45° line as running northwest, for example. To make sure, the z-axis must either be measured in the same units or be scaled separately (that is by a derived variable).

With spatial scaling a rotating plot can approximate what a three-dimensional computer-aided-design program might do. If you plotted three-dimensional coordinates of a physical object, you could see and rotate it.

For example, if you had longitude, latitude, and depth of the epicenters of earthquakes, you might choose to convert all measures to miles and plot a three-dimensional map showing depth as well as geographic location. Using equal scales would keep the depth axis from being blown up to "fit," and instead would keep it to accurate scale.

CHAPTER 11

Derived Variables

DATA DON'T ALWAYS come ready for analysis. Sometimes we need to compute an entirely new variable as a function of other variables. A transformed version of a variable may be easier to analyze than the original data. New variables defined as transformations or algebraic combinations of other variables are called *derived variables* in Data Desk. The derived variable icon looks like an ordinary variable icon with arithmetic symbols.

You can use a derived variable in plots and calculations just like any other variable. Data Desk automatically computes its values when they are needed, so there is no need to explicitly compute the transformed values.

11.1 The Transform Submenus

The **Transform** submenus in the **Manip** menu provide the easiest way to make simple derived variables. These submenus provide simple functions of one or two variables. Select a y-variable or a y-variable and an x-variable (with y-selection and x-selection, respectively) and choose the appropriate expression from the **Transform** submenus. Data Desk creates a new derived variable containing the requested expression and places it in the same relation as the selected variables. (If you want all derived variables placed in the *Derived* folder in the File cabinet, deselect the "Put Derived With Relation" option in the Preferences dialog.)

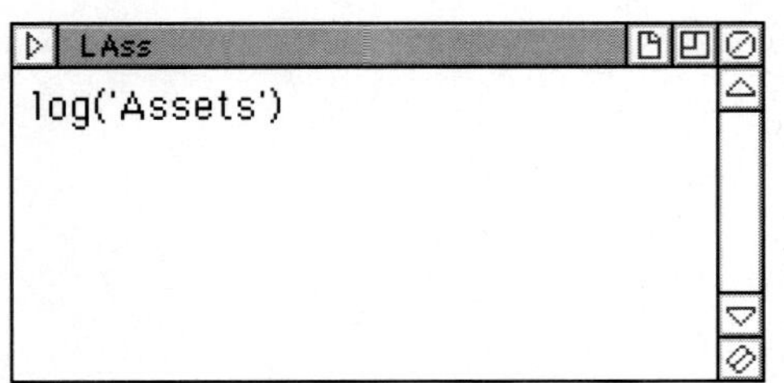

Figure 11-1. *A derived variable editing window.*

For example, if we select *Assets* in the Companies data and choose {Manip ▸ Transform} **Log(y)**, Data Desk creates a variable named *LAss* holding the expression log('*Assets*'), as shown in Fig. 11-1.

Data Desk selects the new derived variable icons, so you can immediately use them in a plot or calculation.

The **Transform** submenus organize functions into related groups. The most common data reexpressions[1] — square root, logarithm, reciprocal root, and reciprocal — appear first. Other less common functions are grouped into a second level of submenus. In Section 11.15 we comment on uses of reexpression in data analysis.

Simple one-variable functions such as the log or square root operate on each selected variable whether it is x-selection or y-selection.

Some functions, such as the Mean(y) or the Max(y) function, summarize the values in a variable. Unlike other derived variable functions, which transform each case in a variable and thus result in a new variable with as many cases as the original, these functions result in a single value. The icons for summarized variables are always placed in the *Derived* folder, which is located inside the *Results* folder.

Many expressions combine two variables. Such expressions compute a value for each case in the variables. For example, the expression $x + y$ specifies a variable in which each case is the sum of that case's values in x and in y. For two variables to be combined case by case in this manner, they must be in the same relation. This restriction is more stringent than

[1]Transformations include any function that alters the data values. We use the term *reexpression* for those transformations that stretch or alter the *shape* of the data's distribution. Transformations such as adding a constant or dividing by a constant simply shift location and scale, but do not change the way a histogram or scatterplot of the data look. By contrast, reexpressions, such as taking logarithms or square roots, treat large numbers differently from smaller numbers and thus alter the shape of the distribution. For example, the logarithms of 1, 10, 100, and 1000 are equally spaced, although the original numbers are not.

requiring both variables to have the same number of cases, but it preserves the sense of what relations mean. Variables in different relations record data about different individuals, even when they have the *same number of cases*. It makes no sense to combine "apples and oranges" in an expression.

Functions of two or more variables treat *x*-selected and *y*-selected variables differently. If you select one *y*- and several *x*-variables (or one *x*- and several *y*-variables), the **Transform** commands generate a transformation for each *x–y* pair. If you select identical numbers of *x* and *y* variables, the **Transform** commands treat them as paired, matching the first *x* with the first *y*, the second *x* with the second *y*, and so on.

> **TIP**
>
> Select two variables and type + to create a derived variable that adds them. This procedure also works for subtraction (-), multiplication (*), division (/) and, for a single variable, log (l).

Several of the popular **Transform** submenu expressions have keyboard equivalents. For example, to quickly create a derived variable that adds two variables (the equivalent to the {Manip ▶Transform ▶Arithmetic} **y + x** command) select the two variables and press the + key. Other shortcuts are '-' for subtraction, '*' for multiplication, '/' for division and 'l' for log.

A Note on Expressions

If you are used to working with a spreadsheet, you will probably find derived variable expressions quite natural. It is common to combine two columns of numbers in a spreadsheet to yield a third column.

If you write computer programs, you have probably worked with arrays of numbers in which a subscript counter directs the calculations to work for each value in turn.

Nevertheless, derived variable expressions are slightly different. In a spreadsheet you would place an expression in each cell (for example, by entering the expression at the top of the column and filling down the column) to complete a row-by-row combination of columns. In a traditional programming language, you might write a loop such as

for i = 1 to n z[i] = x[i] + y[i].

Derived variable expressions operate on all cases in the variables automatically without any need to fill the derived variable with formulas or write a loop to operate on each case in turn. This method is very powerful and effective, but you may want to pause at times to think through how expressions work.

11.2 *Typing Derived Variable Expressions*

Derived variables aren't limited to the simple expressions in the **Transform** submenus. You may type any valid algebraic expression into a derived variable's editing window, either by editing an old expression or starting from scratch. Of course, you edit a derived variable expression in the same way you edit any text in Data Desk. All the common operations in the **Edit** menu are available, so you can copy and paste parts of expressions within a window or from one window to another. On Mac, a double-click selects entire words. On Windows, you need to highlight the selected words with a mouse. Data Desk even provides a full **Undo** function.

When you type or edit a derived variable expression, you may include comments, which will be ignored by Data Desk but will remain part of the expression. Anything enclosed in braces ({ }) or the symbol combinations (* and *) is considered a comment. It is always a good idea to comment on derived variable expressions — especially if they are complex.

To create an empty derived variable, choose {Data ▸New} **Derived Variable**. (The **Derived Variable** command also appears at the top of the **Transform** menu.) Data Desk creates the new derived variable, asks you to name it, appends its icon to the right of the icons in the frontmost data relation, and opens it into an empty editing window.

> **TIP**
>
> To enter variables in a derived variable expression, type the variable names directly or drag variable icons into the derived variable editing window.

You may type any valid expression in the window. For a list of available functions and rules for derived variable expressions see the appendices to this chapter. You enter variables into the expression by either typing their names directly or dragging their icons into the editing window. If you select part of the expression for editing and then drag the icon of a variable into the editing window, the variable's name will replace the selected text.

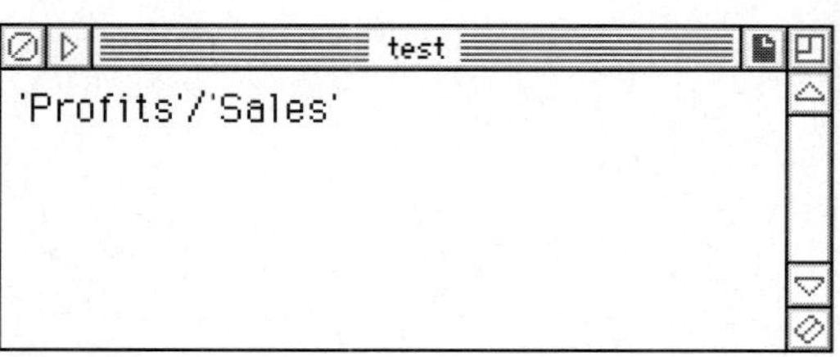

Figure 11-2. *Derived variable editing*

Let's look at an example. In the Companies datafile, the variable *Profits* is skewed to the right, making it difficult to use in analyses. One solution is to divide *Profits* by *Sales*, so that large companies and small companies are measured on a similar scale. Choose {Data ▸New} **Derived Variable** and name the variable *test* (Fig. 11-2). In the derived variable editing window, type the expression

'Profits'/'Sales'

When you close a derived variable window after typing (either to type a new expression or to edit an old one), Data Desk checks the expression to be certain that it recognizes all variable names and function names and that the expression is in proper algebraic form. It complains if it can't understand the expression, and offers to reopen the derived variable for editing (Fig. 11-3).

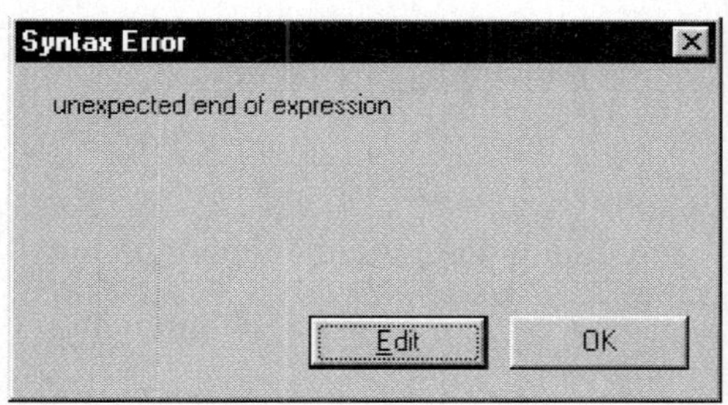

Figure 11-3. *Data Desk notifies you of errors in the expression and offers the chance to edit the expression or close the variable anyway.*

You may leave a bad expression in a derived variable, but you won't be able to use that variable in a plot or calculation until you fix the expression.

Once a derived variable window has closed into its icon, the icon behaves like any other variable, except that when you open it you find not numbers but the algebraic expression you typed. Data Desk evaluates the expression to obtain its values when you use the derived variable, but it doesn't replace the expression with the values.

To see the values of a derived variable, open its icon and choose **Show Numbers** from the derived variable editing window's HyperView menu. This action yields an alternative view of the derived variable; the values can't be edited and will change whenever the derived variable recomputes. You can take a snapshot of a derived variable as a regular variable containing its current values by selecting it and choosing {Data} **Evaluate Derived Variable**.

11.3 *Updating*

Because derived variables are used in other calculations and displays, they always recompute immediately to reflect the current values of their arguments. In this way they differ from plots or tables, which offer to update but do not recompute until you tell them to do so. Any changes made to underlying variables are immediately conveyed to any window that uses the derived variable.

Of course, if the window holds a plot or table, it will offer to update but won't recompute without your permission. When a derived variable uses another derived variable, it recomputes immediately whenever the first derived variable changes, so changes to the base data values may propagate through several levels of derived variables.

Derived variables also update immediately if you edit their expression. The ability to edit a derived variable's expression and have its values recompute (and those changes propagate through all plots, tables, and other derived variables that used the derived variable) offers great power. For example, you can experiment with alternative reexpressions of a variable and immediately see the effect of these changes on a scatterplot.

You can also control parameters in a derived variable with Data Desk's *sliders* (see Section 11.14).

11.4 *Subset Selection in Derived Variable Expressions*

You can restrict the calculation of most collapsing functions (see Appendix 11C) with a "for" clause. Some examples should make this point clearly:

mean ('assets' for 'profits' < 0)

max ('sales' for textof ('sector') = "Energy")

The *for* clause may contain any numeric variable or derived variable, including boolean derived variables (see Section 11.10). Cases with values of 0 or "False" are omitted from the calculation.

11.5 *Expression Types*

Derived variable expressions can be single numbers or entire variables. Variables are simply lists of individual values thought of as successive cases.

Each value in a derived variable expression can be one of three types: numeric, text, or boolean.

A numeric expression is any number. Numeric expressions include integers and decimal fractions, the special value ∞, and the missing value code, •.

A text expression is any collection of characters. Text constants are enclosed in double quotes. Text values may include numerals. Thus "20-

30" is a text string (possibly defining an age category for a table), but *20-30* is a numeric expression evaluating to *–10*.

Data Desk assumes that, when a variable is named in a derived variable expression, its values are numeric. To specify that you want to refer to the text of the variable, use the *TextOf* function. Thus *TextOf('age group')* may consist of text such as "*10-20*", "*20-30*", and so on, but *'age group'* will be evaluated numerically, yielding (for this example) *–10*, *–10*, and so on.

Boolean expressions are expressions that are either true or false. Data Desk provides special functions that work with boolean expressions, so we discuss them at length in Section 11.10.

11.6 *Expression Conventions*

To format a derived variable expression to make it more readable, you can insert any number of spaces within the expression wherever one space could legally occur, except within a variable or function name. For example, extra spaces can go around a + sign or around a variable name. A new line can start wherever a space can appear, so you can split long expressions into several lines to make them more readable.

Derived variables ignore capitalization. You can type variable names and functions with or without capital letters.

single quotes for variable names

Variable names are often enclosed in *single quotation marks*. For example, 'variable name', or log('income'). *You must* use quotation marks if the variable name has a space in it, contains a special symbol or numeral, or is the same as a function name. It is always safest to use the quotation marks; variables dragged into the derived variable editing window, and those included through the **Transform** submenu commands always are enclosed in single quotation marks.

For example, variable names that must be enclosed in single quotation marks include 'two words', '3best' (because it starts with a numeral), '√area', '∑scores' (because they contain function names), and 'assets – liabilities' (because the minus sign is an operator).

double quotes for text constants

Double quotation marks enclose text constants. Braces and the (* and *) combination symbols enclose comments. You may use parentheses freely in derived variable expressions to specify the order of evaluation just as you would in standard algebraic expressions.

In Appendix 11A we discuss the details of evaluating derived variable expressions.

11.7 *Dependencies*

Every derived variable depends on the *underlying variables* used in its definition. Any changes in those underlying variables are immediately reflected in the derived variable and then passed on to the plots, tables, and other derived variables that depend, in turn, on its values.

The chain of dependency can extend through many levels. If derived variable D1 uses derived variable D2, which in turn uses derived vari-

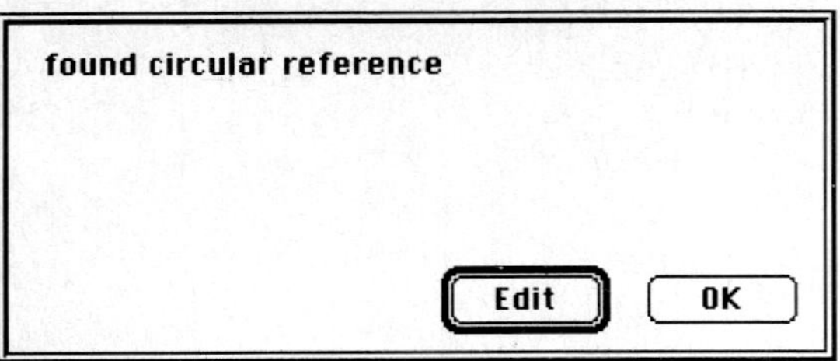

able D3, which uses the ordinary variable *x*, then changing *x* changes the corresponding values in all three derived variables. Any plots or analyses that use any of these derived variables will notice the change and offer to update. The dependency chain cannot be circular. That is, you may not have a chain in which D1 uses D2, which uses D3, which uses D1. Data Desk will notice if you inadvertently define a circular chain and warn you of the problem.

Variables created with the {Data} **Evaluate Derived Variable** command don't change with subsequent changes in the underlying variables. They are frozen snapshots of the derived variable at the time of evaluation. (If you need a variable equal to any other variable that does update, define a derived variable whose expression is simply the name of the variable that you want to copy.)

The {Special ▶ Locate} **Users of** command locates all icons that use any variable (including derived variables that use it) and selects them. Repeating the command (with those icons selected) locates the next level of usage — the icons that use the originally selected icons indirectly.

The {Special ▶ Locate} **Arguments of** command searches in the reverse direction, locating and selecting the icons of the variables that were arguments of the selected icons. If you select a derived variable icon and choose {Special ▶ Locate} **Arguments of**, Data Desk will locate the icons of the variables used in the derived variable expression.

11.8 *Working with Open Derived Variables*

You need not close a derived variable in order to work with it. You can select its (shaded) icon or the icon alias in its title bar and choose a command. If the derived variable is used in a plot or analysis, you can open it and edit its expression and then update or redo the plot or analysis without closing the derived variable. Press the **Enter** key or click on another window to end expression editing and update dependent windows.

The ability to edit derived variable expressions and update values provides a powerful tool for investigating alternative expressions. For example, you can alter an expression and see immediately how the change affects a plot or analysis.

When you work with an open derived variable, Data Desk parses (translates) and evaluates the expression when it is needed. If it encounters an error or ambiguity, it alerts you at once. This alert may be disconcerting if your attention is focused on a plot or analysis. Keep in mind that Data Desk evaluates a derived variable only when it is needed, and it parses derived variable expressions either when the window is closed or when the expression must be evaluated.

11.9 *Calculating in ScratchPads*

Any function or expression available in derived variables can be typed in a ScratchPad window and executed immediately in that window. The

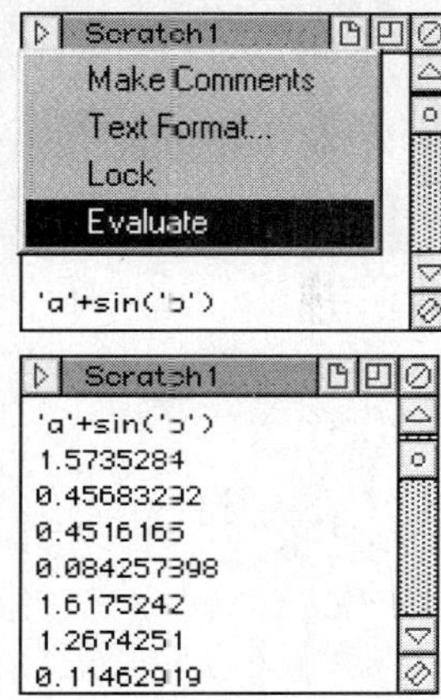

result of the evaluation appears in the Scratchpad window immediately after the expression. This provides a powerful calculator: you can type any expression you might key into a calculator and evaluate it on the spot. Even more usefully, you can evaluate expressions that involve variables in the dataset. To create a ScratchPad, choose {Data ▶ New} **ScratchPad**.

ScratchPads also provide an excellent place to work out complex derived variable expressions. Type the expression into a ScratchPad and evaluate it to see whether it behaves as you intended. If the expression is particularly complex or difficult to figure out, try evaluating each part of the expression and then combining the parts into increasingly complex expressions. (This method is also an excellent way to experiment with derived variable functions, for example to try functions as you read about them here.) When the expression is correct, select it with the mouse and copy and paste it into a derived variable's editing window

To evaluate an expression in a ScratchPad, place the cursor on the line to be evaluated and type ⌘ = on Mac (Alt = on Windows) or choose **Evaluate** from the ScratchPad window's HyperView menu. If the expression covers several lines, select the entire expression before choosing **Evaluate.**

You can, of course, copy a column of results from a ScratchPad and paste it back into an open variable or directly into an icon window with the **Paste Variables** command.

Advanced Topics

Data Desk's derived variable expressions offer many powerful features. In the remaining sections of this chapter we discuss more advanced concepts. You may want to read only selected sections at first. The appendices at the end of the chapter list all the functions that Data Desk recognizes in derived variable expressions.

11.10 *Boolean Expressions*

A *Boolean expression* is any expression that checks a condition that is either TRUE or FALSE. Thus, for example, the expression $y < x$ is a Boolean expression. Like most other derived variable expressions, it has a value for each case. It is TRUE for each case whose y-value is less than its x-value and FALSE for all other cases. A derived variable defined by the Boolean expression $y < x$ (where y and x are variable names), evaluates to a variable holding cases that read 1 for TRUE or 0 for FALSE.

The logical function NOT(y) reverses the truth of any Boolean expression. The Boolean expression NOT($y < x$) is equivalent to $y \geq x$ and evaluates TRUE for each case in which the value of y is not less than the value of x and FALSE otherwise.

You can combine Boolean expressions into more complex expressions with the operators AND, OR, XOR, and DIFF. The expression

<boolean 1> *AND* <boolean 2>

is TRUE only if both expressions <boolean 1> and <boolean 2> are true and FALSE otherwise.

The expression

<boolean 1> *OR* <boolean 2>

is TRUE if either <boolean 1> or <boolean 2> is TRUE or if both are true.

The expression

<boolean 1> *XOR* <boolean 2>

is TRUE if either <boolean1> or <boolean2> is true but not if both are true.

The expression

<boolean 1> *DIFF* <boolean 2>

is TRUE if <boolean 1> is TRUE and <boolean 2> is FALSE have different truth values (is the same as y AND (NOT x)).

Most concepts that are commonly represented in statistics with indicator variables are most easily defined by boolean expressions. For example, we can define membership in a group as

'age' = 18

or

textof('religion') = "Protestant" *OR* textof('religion') = "Catholic".

We can define inclusion in a range as

'income' > 20000 *AND* 'income' < 50000

and inclusion in a cell of a two-way table as

textof('year') = "1990" *AND* textof('month') = "April"

11.11 *IF/THEN/ELSE*

The logical connectives IF, THEN, and ELSE combine simple expressions to make expressions whose value depends on different conditions. They combine into expressions of the form

IF *<Boolean expression>* THEN *<result1>* ELSE *<result2>*

The expressions labeled *<result1>* and *<result2>* can be any valid derived variable expression. IF/THEN/ELSE expressions evaluate to one or the other result expression according to the truth value of the boolean expression. Because the boolean expression typically will have different truth values for each case, IF/THEN/ELSE expressions are a powerful way to select values from each of two variables or select alternative calculations:

IF textof(*'country'*) ≠ *"U.S."* THEN *'km distance'* ELSE *'km distance'* 1.61*{convert from km to miles}.

You must always complete an IF/THEN combination with an ELSE clause.

Text constants (indicated with double quotation marks) can appear as a result expression in an IF/THEN/ELSE expression such as

IF *income* < *50000* THEN *"Middle Class"* ELSE *"Rich"*

However, all results of an IF/THEN/ELSE expression must be of the same type, either text or numeric. You cannot mix types. For example, it is **not legal** to write:

IF *'age'* > *18* THEN *'months since voted'* ELSE *"too young"*

where *'months since voted'* is a variable recording the number of months since the last vote, because months since voted is a variable holding numbers but *"too young"* is a text constant.

REMEMBER

You must always complete an IF/THEN/ELSE combination with an ELSE clause.

IF/THEN/ELSE expressions are themselves legal derived variable expressions, so they can appear within other IF/THEN/ELSE expressions. For example, you can recode ranges of a numeric variable into named categories with an expression such as

IF *'grade'* > *90* THEN *"A"*
ELSE IF *'grade'* > *80* THEN *"B"*
ELSE IF *'grade'* > *70* THEN *"C"*
ELSE IF *'grade'* > *60* THEN *"D"*
ELSE *"F"*

Such nested IF/THEN/ELSE expressions often require careful thought to be sure that you have said exactly what you mean.

The result of the entire IF/THEN/ELSE expression can be a number, so you may write expressions such as

StdBonus + (IF *Sales* > *5000* THEN *250* ELSE *100*)

11.12 *Subscripting*

To refer to individual cases within a variable or derived variable expression that evaluates to a variable, specify the case numbers within square brackets. For example;

age[3]

is the age value recorded for case number 3. The subscript may be an expression that evaluates to a number. Thus

age[(numnumeric('age') + 1) / 2]

selects the middle case out of age, which will be the median age if *age* is sorted. If the subscript value is not an integer Data Desk truncates the value to its integer part.

More generally, the subscript can be a variable holding integers. When the subscript is a variable, each case in the index variable is used in turn as a subscript, so the resulting subscripted expression evaluates to a variable. For example, consider variables with the following values.

Case Number	Data	Index
1	1.1	5
2	2.2	3
3	3.3	3

4	4.4	2
5	5.5	
6	6.6	

The expression *data[index]* evaluates to:

5.5
3.3
3.3
2.2

The first element is *data[5]*, or the fifth case in the variable *data*. In this example it has the value 5.5. The second element is *data[3]*, which is 3.3.

Unlike the variables in most derived variable expressions, the index variable need not be (and, in fact, usually won't be) in the same relation as the data variable. The expression has a case for each case in the index variable and is placed in the relation of the index variable.

If a value of the index variable is not an integer, it is truncated to the next smallest integer. If a value of the index variable is missing, negative, or greater than the number of cases in the data variable, the expression evaluates to "•" (missing) for that case.

The index variable must be numeric (or the result will be missing), but the data variable may be a category variable holding text.

The index variable may also be an expression that evaluates to a variable. Thus, if the variable *letter grade* holds the text values "A", "B", "C", "D", "F", "F", "F", "F", "F", "F", "F", and the variable *test grade* is a score between 10 and 100, the expression

'letter grade' [11 - ('test grade'/10)]

assigns a letter grade to each test grade in the same way as the IF/THEN/ELSE statement in the preceding section. For example, a grade of 95 produces an index of 11 – 95/10 = 11 – 9.5 = 1.5, which is truncated to 1. The expression thus returns *'letter grade'*[1], which is "A".

Finally, the variable whose cases are being extracted may itself be an expression that evaluates into a variable, and subscripted expressions may be part of other expressions. Thus

*('weekly salary' * 52 + 'benefits'['job category']) [3]*

is a legal expression, provided that *job category* and *weekly salary* are in the same relation. It finds the appropriate benefit amount with the first subscript and then returns the sum for the third case. Be sure to enclose any expression in parentheses before subscripting it lest you subscript only the last term in the expression rather than the entire expression.

11.13 *Identifying Variables by Name*

Derived variable expressions refer to variables by name. Data Desk thinks variable names are just labels. Two or more variables can have the same name. Ordinarily, this poses no problem; you simply point and click to select the particular variable you want. However, derived variables can get confused when two variables have the same name.

When you generate a derived variable with the **Transform** menu or if you drag the icon of a variable into the derived variable's editing window, there is no difficulty. Data Desk uses the selected variable icons even if others have the same name. However, if you type a derived variable expression, you may need to tell Data Desk which one of several variables with the same name you want to use. Data Desk checks typed (or edited) derived variable expressions when you close the derived variable window or when you use the derived variable in a display or calculation.

To identify a particular variable as the one that Data Desk should use, select its icon before closing the derived variable window. Data Desk checks the names of selected icons first when searching for variables to match the names in derived variable expressions. In this way you can specify which variable to use in an expression even if its name isn't unique.

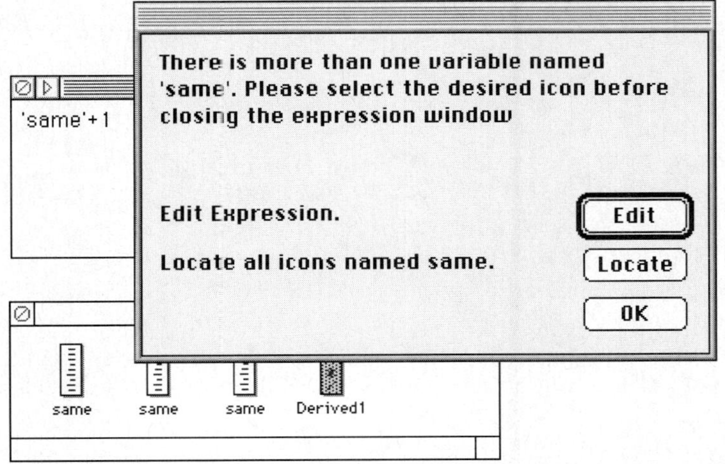

Figure 11-4. *Data Desk asks for help when variable names are ambiguous. The **Locate** button makes all icons with the name in question visible on the desktop and selects them.*

Data Desk searches for the variable associated with a particular name in the following order:

- First, any variable whose icon is selected
- Second (for expressions that have been edited), any variable used in this expression when it was last evaluated
- Third, variables in the same folder as the derived variable's icon.
- Finally, any other variable in the datafile

If two or more variables in the datafile have the same name (and no variables selected or already in use by the expression), Data Desk asks you to identify the icon of the variable you intend to use, or to rename it to avoid the conflict (Fig. 11-4).

11.14 *Dynamic Parameters*

A derived variable expression consists of functions, arguments (usually variable names), and parameters. Usually the parameters are simply numbers. But, as with rotating plots, brushing, and slicing, dynamic control often reveals more than static displays and analyses. *Sliders* are graphical controls that offer dynamic control of parameter values in derived variable expressions. Thus you can use them to create your own dynamic graphics or analyses.

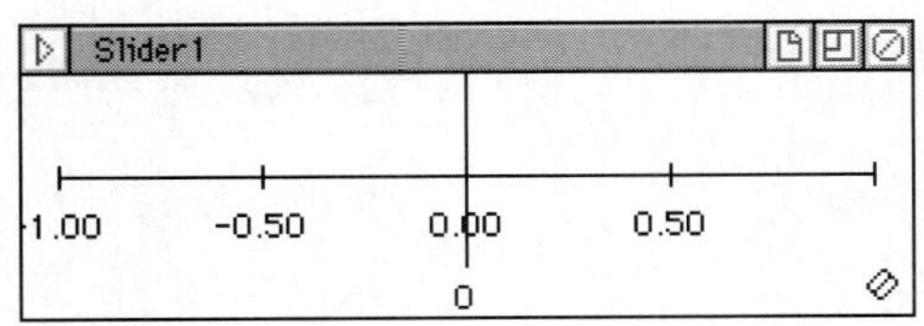

Figure 11-5. *The value of a slider is the number where the hairline crosses the axis.*

The {Data ▶ New} **Slider** command creates a slider. Each slider window shows a single-axis plot with a hairline (Fig. 11-5). You can slide the axis side to side with the tool and rescale it using the **Plot Scale...** command in the slider's global HyperView menu. The Plot Scale dialog also allows bounds to be defined. These bounds act as "bumpers," and prevent the slider from being moved passed a certain value. For example, the dynamic **Mix X and Y** command creates a slider that is bounded by 0 and 1 because the mixture can never contain more than 100% or less than 0% of a variable.

A slider always has a value; specifically the value where the hairline intersects the axis. That value is shown below the hairline and is avail-

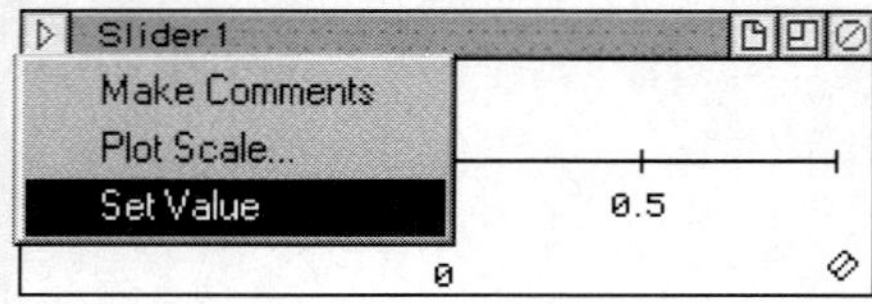

Figure 11-6. The ***Set Value*** *command lets you set the starting point for the slider or move a slider to a specific value.*

able to any derived variable expression that uses the name of the slider as a parameter. Moving the slider's axis side to side changes its value and (as with any change you make to a part of a derived variable expression) changes the value of the derived variable. Derived variables always recompute immediately and notify you of their change. The **Set Value** command in the slider's global HyperView menu provides the opportunity to define a starting point or move a slider to a specific value (Fig. 11-6). Sliders can also have values assigned to them with Action programs. Sliders can be assigned any value in an action program, including the values missing and infinity. Missing and infinity are passed through to any derived variables that use the slider.

If you hold the Shift key and push the axis, the axis continues to slide in the direction of the push. Grab it again or press the Space bar to stop the slide.

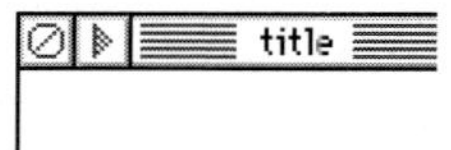

Data Desk plot and table windows typically respond to changes in their underlying variables by offering to update, posting the ! symbol in their global HyperView menu. However, you can set any plot or table to update immediately as soon as it is aware of an underlying change. The global HyperView menu of every plot and table offers a **Turn On Automatic Update** command. When **Automatic Update** is selected, the window updates immediately whenever any underlying variable changes. The triangle marking the global HyperView menu turns gray to indicate **Automatic Update**. (Select **Turn Off Automatic Update** from the global HyperView menu to return to ordinary update-with-approval behavior.)

When a display is set for automatic update and a slider specifies parameters in a derived variable whose values are displayed, sliding the slider will change the display dynamically. Sliders thus provide a way to build your own dynamic displays.

To illustrate sliders, let's use a simple function. Use the {Manip} **Generate Patterned Data...** command to create values from 0 to 1 in steps of 0.01. Rename the generated variable *x*. Create a new slider named *c* and a derived variable named *sinuous* whose expression is

*sin(π *c*x).*

(On Mac, Option–p types π, which Data Desk reads as pi. On Windows type "pi".) Now make a scatterplot of *sinuous* versus *x*. Using the plot's HyperView menu, choose **Turn On Automatic Update** and **Freeze Scale**. The first command tells the plot to update whenever the slider is moved. The second command fixes the plot scale so that it won't change (and speeds response by avoiding plot scaling calculations).

Grab the slider with the ☝ tool and move it side to side. The slider controls the frequency of the sine wave (Fig. 11-7). For added interest, slide the slider to about 4.0, select (with the selection rectangle) the points where the sine crosses 0, and choose a different plot symbol (and color, if you want) for them. Now continue sliding and note the patterns of the selected points. Hold the Shift key, give the slider a push, sit back, and watch the show.

Expressions can use more than one slider. For example, define a second slider named *d* and edit the expression in sinuous to read

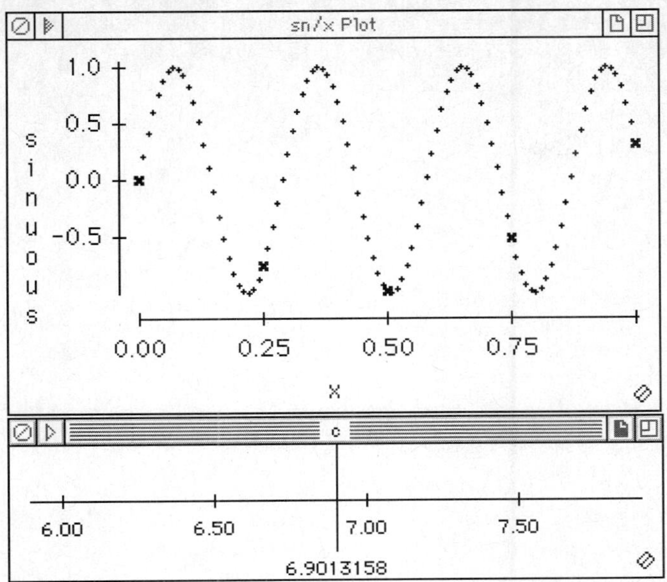

Figure 11-7. *A slider controlling the frequency of a sinusoid.*

> **TIP**
>
> To help sliders work faster, hold down the Ctrl key on Windows, or the Option key on Mac, while sliding the slider. Expressions and displays will recompute only when the hairline crosses a tick mark.

*sin(π*c*x)+sin(π*d*x)*

Now sliding *d* and *c* shows a sum of sinusoids. (You may need to choose **Restore Automatic Scale** to expand the scale if you chose **Freeze Scale** earlier.)

Another use of sliders is to determine a parameter value experimentally. Section 11.16 contains an example.

Sliders make it easy to request far more computing power than your computer can deliver. Of course, the more powerful your computer, the more you will be able to do with sliders.

If a slider seems to stick, the computations requested by each change in its value are taxing the computing power you have. It is always a good idea to plan derived variable expressions for efficient computing, but this step is especially important for expressions that use sliders to create dynamic displays.

You can reduce the computing load by having the slider change only when the hairline crosses an axis tick mark. Hold down the Ctrl key if you're using Data Desk on Windows, or the Option key on Mac, while sliding the slider to place it in this "ratchet" mode. The **Plot Scale...** command in the slider's global HyperView menu provides control over the location and density of tick marks and the values of the upper and lower bounds.

11.15 *Reexpressing Data to Improve Analyses*

The broad value of flexible re-expression is one of the most effective and enduring lessons of exploratory data analysis.

As Mosteller and Tukey (1977) point out

> Numbers are primarily recorded or reported in a form that reflects habit or convenience rather than suitability for analysis. As a result, we often need to re-express data before analyzing it. (p. 89)

There are many examples in everyday experience — such as the Richter scale for earthquakes, the decibel scale for intensity of sounds, average speed in auto races, and gauges of shotguns — in which the data are already in a transformed scale by the time we hear about them. Hoaglin (1988) discusses these and other examples.

We often reexpress variables to find a transformation that simplifies the analysis of the data. Reexpressing variables to a scale such as the logarithm, square root, or reciprocal can simplify patterns and relationships in several important ways. Most often we choose transformations to:

- Improve additivity of a response in relation to two or more factors. Additive relationships are appropriate for analysis of variance (ANOVA) and related analyses.

- Straighten nonlinear relationships. Scatterplots reveal nonlinear relationships. Regression and correlation analyses describe linear relationships formally.
- Promote constant variability across groups or constant variance of measurement across the level of another variable (or over time). Dotplots and boxplots display variability across groups. Scatterplots reveal variability that changes across levels of the x-variable.
- Make univariate distributions more nearly symmetric. Histograms show symmetry well. Probability plots and dotplots are also useful.

Fortunately, these benefits tend to occur together; a reexpression chosen for one reason often helps to improve the data with respect to the other reasons. When we must choose, we usually favor the earlier items on the list over the later ones, but sometimes we can only achieve the latter purposes.

After careful reexpression, analyses and displays are often simpler and more likely to reveal both patterns and unexpected deviations from these patterns. Analyses that were complex and confusing may become simple and straightforward when the data are reexpressed appropriately.

The most common reexpressions are ordered in the sense that the effect of each is slightly more or less than that of its neighbors. Thus you can try a re-expression and, depending on whether it did too little or too much, readjust it easily.

The most common data reexpressions are the powers and the logarithm. They are naturally ordered according to the exponent of the power, with the logarithm occupying the "0" position. Thus we can array the most common reexpressions in the following order.

"ladder of powers"

Exponent	Function	
2	y^2	Square
1	y	Raw data
1/2	$\sqrt{y}$	Square root
"0"	Log(y)	Logarithm
–1/2	$-1/\sqrt{y}$	Reciprocal root (the minus sign preserves order)
–1	–1/y	Reciprocal or inverse (the minus sign preserves order)

Other powers and roots fit into the order naturally. Thus, for example, a cube root (1/3 power) alters raw data less than a logarithm but more than a square root.

The most common reexpressions are at the top of the **Transform** submenu. Other re-expressions are available in the **Transform** submenus or by typing the expression. In Appendix 3A we discuss reexpressions most likely to be useful for various kinds of data.

Because these reexpressions are ordered, we can search effectively for an appropriate reexpression. Data Desk makes this search particularly easy by automatically building an appropriate derived variable controlled by a slider. The slider controls the exponent of the reexpression, so it is easy to slide up and down the list of powers in search of an appropriate one.

To search for a reexpression in this way, select the variable you want to reexpress and choose {Manip ▶ Transform ▶ Dynamic} **Box – Cox Transformation**. Data Desk creates a new folder containing a slider named with an abbreviation of *varname^p* , where *varname* is the name of the variable being reexpressed, and a derived variable containing the expression

IF *'slider'≠ 0* THEN *(exp(ln('variable')*'slider')–1)/'slider')'* ELSE *ln('variable')*

When the slider value is not 0, the expression is equivalent to:

$(variable^{'slider'} - 1) / 'slider'$

a form of re-expression discussed by Box and Cox (1964). Data Desk uses the equation form with logarithms and exponentiation because it is more efficient to compute, especially on machines with floating point units. The expression reverts to *ln(variable)* when the slider value is 0. This prevents dividing the entire expression by 0.

To select a power, make an appropriate display of the derived variable (depending on the purpose of the reexpression), set the display to automatic update (with the command in the display's global HyperView menu), and slide the slider until the display looks right. Normal probability plots and dotplots work well for individual variables. If you are looking at the relationship between two variables, use a scatterplot. For computing efficiency, you may want to hold down the Ctrl key on Windows, or the Option key on Mac, so that the display recomputes only as the slider crosses tick marks. Integer or half-integer powers are usually preferred for simplicity.

Once you find a suitable power, you can move the derived variable to the window holding other variables for analysis and use it in subsequent analyses. Later in your analysis you may want to return to the slider and investigate how sensitive your analysis is to the choice of power. For example, you may compute residuals, display them, and set that plot to automatic update. Now, sliding the slider initiates recomputation of the analysis and residuals. The resulting animated display of residuals will give you a good feel for the stability of the analysis at nearby powers and thus a feel for the sensitivity of your conclusions to the choice of power.

11.16 *An Example*

To illustrate both how reexpressing data can improve your ability to work with it and how Data Desk makes it easy for you to find suitable reexpressions, lets consider data from the Companies dataset. This method incorporates sliders; but reexpressions can also be accomplished by manually editing derived variables expressions.

Select the variables *Assets* and *Sales* and choose {Manip ▶ Transform ▶ Dynamic} **Box – Cox Transformation**. Data Desk creates a folder for each variable containing a slider and a derived variable. The derived variables hold expressions of the form

IF *'Assp'≠ 0* THEN (*exp(ln('Assets')*'Assp')– 1) / 'Assp'*
ELSE *ln('Assets')*

This expression is an efficient way to compute the powers discussed in the preceding section. The expression

exp(ln('Assets')'Assp')*

raises the variable *Assets* to the power *'Assp'*. The natural logarithm (ln) and exponentiation functions compute faster than the "^" operator, especially on machines with a floating point unit. Dividing the result by the power reduces somewhat the tendency of the reexpressed values to change magnitude drastically. It has the additional effect of changing the sign of the expression when the power is negative, thus preserving the order of the data values. The IF/THEN/ELSE structure checks for a 0 exponent. Because the logarithm holds the position of the 0 power in the ladder of powers (see Section 11.15.), the expression checks for a 0 exponent and substitutes the logarithm.

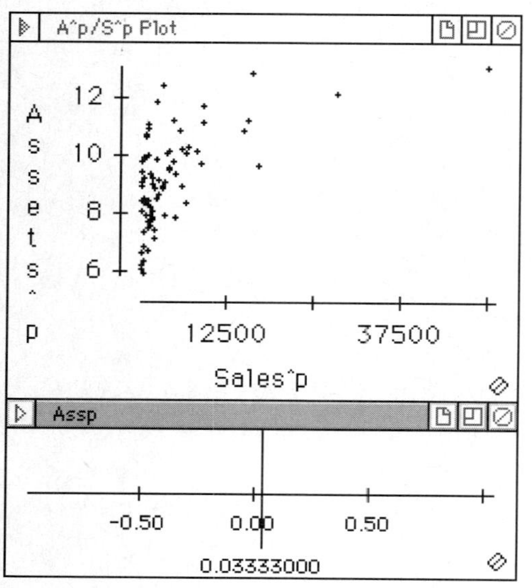

Figure 11-8. *Reexpressing* Assets *to a power near 0 makes the plot look like this.*

Make a scatterplot of *Assets^p* versus *Sales^p*. Set the scatterplot for automatic update by using its global HyperView menu. If you have set the sliders at or near 1.0, the plot should show a wedge shape with most points clustered together at the lower left. Such a pattern often indicates that transforming the data might improve the display.

Try sliding one of them side to side. You can see the plot changing smoothly. If your computer has a hard time keeping the animation smooth, try holding down the Option key (Ctrl key on Windows) as you move the slider. This will limit recomputing to the points where the slider's hairline crosses an axis tick mark.

As the slider approaches 0, the plot will begin to look like that shown in Fig. 11-8. You can go past 0, and the plot will continue to distort in the same way. Leave the slider at or near 0, representing a reexpression close to the logarithm.

Now slide the other slider. As its value gets near 0, the plot begins to look quite reasonable, showing a consistent trend from lower left to upper right (Fig 11-9).

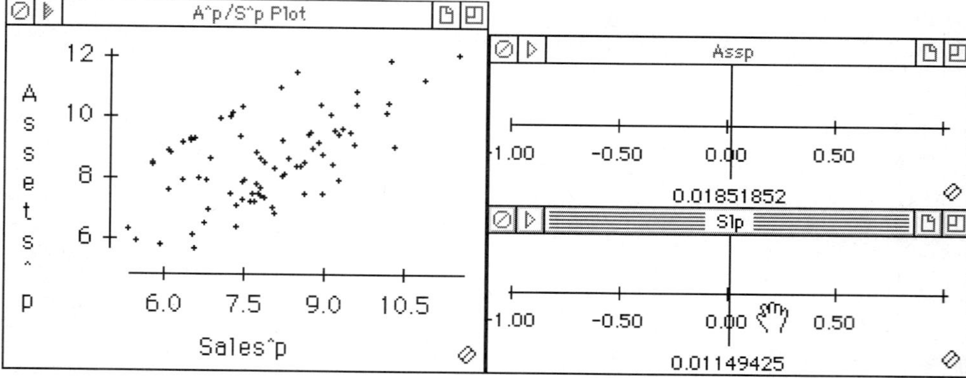

Figure 11-9. *When both reexpressions are near the 0 power (log) the plot looks much better.*

This example shows vividly how the choice of expression can alter a plot. The scatterplot of *log(Assets)* versus *log(Sales)* shows much simpler structure and suggests a relationship that might be suitable for further analysis. The placement of the logarithm at the 0 position in the ladder of powers is clear also; the shape of the plot for powers very near to 0 is virtually the same as the shape for the logarithm.

In general, there is no single correct reexpression for data. Common sense, practice, and practicality all help to determine the choice of a reexpression. Some reexpressions are standard practice. For example, economists often work with logarithms of values for income, assets, and sales. Some reexpressions are convenient because the measurement units are simple. For example the reciprocal of miles per gallon is gallons per mile. Rates such as miles per hour or minutes per task often do well in their reciprocal form (hours per mile, or tasks per minute).

Data reexpression is a rewarding aspect of data analysis that is dealt with in very few accessible books. We recommend Mosteller and Tukey (1977) for an excellent and practical discussion.

11.17 *Rules for Reexpression*

Mosteller and Tukey offer general advice on reexpressing data to simplify and improve analyses. They note that the choice of a reexpression function depends upon the nature of the data. They define seven types of data for this purpose which we discuss in Appendix 3A .

Mosteller and Tukey suggest that it is more often appropriate to reexpress data than to leave values in their original form. They suggest the following reexpressions as a good start, based upon the type of data.

Names: No reexpression can be suitable

Grades: Reexpression is complex and not common.

Ranks: (Discussed in Section 11.19.)

Counts: May benefit from a square root reexpression.

Counted Fractions: Likely to benefit from the family of "folded" powers (discussed in Section 11.18).

Amounts: Cannot be negative. Histograms of amounts often trail off to the high end. Such skewed distributions often benefit from logarithms.

Balances: Often differences of two amounts. It may help to transform each of the amounts and then take their difference or ratio.

Bounds

If data values are bounded at one end, we recommend shifting the data so that the bound is at 0, and treating the result as an amount. Thus for $y \geq A$, treat $y - A$ as an amount. For $y \leq A$, work with $A - y$.

Data that are bounded at two ends can be rescaled and treated as a counted fraction. Thus for $A \leq y \leq B$, treat

$$(y - A)/(B - A)$$

as a counted fraction.

11.18 *Reexpressing Counted Fractions*

Counted fractions are ratios with a fixed base; and most are ratios of counts. The most common counted fractions are percents, which are counted fractions with a base of 100. Counted fractions always lie between 0 and 1.0. Variables holding percents expressed in the range of 0 to 100 must be divided by 100 before you can apply the techniques of this section.

Counted fractions pose a special challenge for reexpression because they are bounded at both ends and are symmetric about 50%. Reexpressions of counted fractions typically "fold" at the 50% point. The simplest folded reexpression is the *plurality:*

$$p - (1 - p)$$

where p is a counted fraction (and thus between 0 and 1). Another common folded reexpression is the *logit:*

$$\log(p) - \log(1 - p) = \log(\, p \;/\; (1 - p)\,).$$

Another common alternative is to think of the counted fraction as a relative frequency and thus much like a probability. You can transform it according to the inverse cumulative distribution function of some distribution, mapping probabilities into standardized scores. In this respect, the *logit* reexpression is the inverse cumulative distribution function of the *logistic* distribution. Another common reexpression is the *normit, probit,* or inverse Gaussian:

$$\mathrm{Gau}^{-1}(p)$$

Finally, in some applications, the *anglit* or *arc sine* reexpression is appropriate. This takes the form

$$2 \sin^{-1} \sqrt{p} - \pi/2.$$

Generally, counted fraction data benefits from reexpressions that stretch their tails. Such stretching usually reflects the increasing difficulty of making a counted fraction more extreme as its value approaches either edge of the range. For example, the approval rating of the President may shift readily between 55% and 60% but is highly unlikely to move from 90% to 95%.

A single family of reexpressions suitable for counted fractions, known as Tukey's lambda family, can approximate all the common reexpressions for counted fractions. Tukey's lambda takes the form:

$$\frac{p^{\lambda} \pm (1 \pm p)^{\lambda}}{\lambda} \frac{1}{2^{\lambda}}$$

To rexpress a counted fraction variable with Tukey's lambda, select the variable's icon and choose {Manip ▶ Transform ▶ Dynamic} **Tukey's Lambda Transformation**. As with the Box–Cox family of reexpressions, Data Desk creates a slider (named "lambda") and a derived variable holding the expression

```
('variable'**'lambda'-(1-'variable')**'lambda')/
   'lambda'*0.500**'lambda'
```

Slide the value of lambda between 1 and 0 (the valid range of lambda) to find a suitable reexpression. Several values of lambda approximate standard reexpressions:

$\lambda = 1$ plurality

$\lambda = 0.5$ folded square root

$\lambda = 0.41$ anglit or arc sine

$\lambda = 0.14$ probit or inverse Gaussian

$\lambda = 0$ logit

Of these, the plurality, folded square root, and logit are exact. The others are remarkably close approximations.

11.19 *Reexpressing Ranks*

When data come as ranks they are constrained to be equally spaced integer values. We can imagine the underlying data that generated the ranks, but we usually cannot see them. Reexpressions that stretch the extreme ranks a bit farther from the center move the ranks toward the underlying values that are likely to have generated the ranks (or at least toward a version of them after a reexpression that introduces symmetry).

The easiest way to do so is to convert ranks to counted fractions and to use the Tukey lambda family.

For ranks that are the *i*th out of *n*, first compute:

$$p = \frac{i - \frac{1}{3}}{n + \frac{1}{3}}$$

where the *i* values are the ranks and *n* is the highest rank. The corresponding derived variable expression is

(ranks – 1/3) / *(NumNumeric(ranks)* + 1/3)

Then reexpress these fractions with Tukey's lambda family.

A discussion of the reasons behind the choice of 1/3 in these expressions is beyond the scope of this book. Mosteller and Tukey (1977) present some of the background.

11.20 *Efficiency*

Derived variables generally compute very quickly. Nevertheless, it is wise to think about computing effort when writing a derived variable expression. For example, isolate any repeated computation that can be made separately. The expression

*sin(2*π*c*x/NumNumeric(x))*

for example, multiplies each value by the constants 2 and π and divides by NumNumeric. It would be more efficient to define a new derived variable, *2πx/n,* consisting of the expression

*2*π*x/NumNumeric(x)*

and then write the above expression as

sin(c '2πx/n')*

reducing the repeated calculations to a single multiply and sine evaluation.

Some efficiencies come from restructuring functions. In generating derived variables to explore data reexpressions (as in Section 11.16), Data Desk avoids the exponentiation (^) operation because it isn't available on the computers with a floating point unit (fpu). When an fpu is present, it is more efficient to use the property of logarithms that

$x^p = e(p*ln(x))$

11.21 *Indicator Variables and Logical Expressions*

Many statistical analyses can be made easier — or possible — by the use of specially constructed indicator variables. Indicator variables typically take on only the values 0 and 1, or the values –1, 0, and 1. Indicator variables are specially constructed to isolate a subgroup or an individual in the data, typically by assigning a 1 to all cases in the subgroup and a 0 to all others.

Derived variables offer a simple and intuitive way to generate indicator variables. When a derived variable containing a logical expression is used as a numeric variable, it generates a 1 for all cases for which the expression is true and a 0 for all cases for which the expression is false. Thus, for example, the derived variable expression

TextOf ('season') = "spring"

defines an indicator variable that isolates two subgroups. It evaluates TRUE (1) for all cases for which the variable season is the word "spring" and FALSE (0) for all others.

Indicator variables constructed to select ranges can be specified in much the same way. For example, the expression

25000 < income AND *income< 40000*

evaluates as TRUE for those individuals whose incomes fall in the specified range and FALSE otherwise, isolating this range of incomes.

11.22 *Working with Several Relations*

Ordinarily all the variables in a derived variable expression must be in the same relation. However, some derived variable functions can work across relations. Several functions provide the kind of capability commonly found in relational database programs. With these functions you can construct complex datasets to reflect the true structure of your data.

The *Lookup* and *GetCase* functions accept arguments from two different relations. The *Lookup* functions (*Lookup, LookupFirst,* and so on) have the form *Lookup(<var>, <value>),* where *<var>* is any expression evaluating to an array of values that could be a variable and *<value>* is any expression evaluating to an array of values to be found in the variable. The *Lookup* functions return an array of indices of the cases in *<var>* that match the values in *<value>* (or the values just below or just above the values if LookupFirst or LookupLast function is used). The result is a variable in the relation of the *<value>* array.

GetCase takes the form *GetCase(<var>, <indices>)* where *<var>* is as in *Lookup* and *<indices>* is an expression evaluating to an array of indices. *GetCase* extracts the values in *<var>* whose case numbers are the values in *<indices>*. It is a variable in the same relation as *<indices>*. If an index is not an integer, it is truncated. If its value is 0 or less or is beyond the last case in *<var>*, *GetCase* returns the missing code, "•".

An alternative form that may be more convenient than *GetCase* is the subscript form using brackets: *<var>*[*<indices>*].

We present details and an example using the relational functions in Appendix 11B.

11.23 Subtle Points

Ordinarily, derived variables behave just as you expect. However, some subtleties of design may be worth a brief explanation. You can skip this section and miss nothing of great importance, but reading it may help you to understand derived variables (and Data Desk) better.

The relation of a derived variable is an ephemeral thing. Surely, an expression transforming one variable or combining two variables that are both in the same relation belongs in that relation. But it is easy to write derived variable expressions that change relations. For example, all collapsing functions yield a single number. Subscripted expressions (Section 11.12) are in the relation of the index variable. You can change the relation of a derived variable by editing its expression or by editing one of its arguments.

When you create a derived variable by selecting a command from the **Transform** submenus, Data Desk tries to place the new icon in the window of the relation to which it most likely belongs. Thus, if you select a variable and choose log(y) from the **Transform** submenus, the resulting derived variable is placed in the same window as the icon of the underlying variable. However, if you create a *New* derived variable, Data Desk has no idea what expression you will type, and thus no idea of the relation of the variable. The new icon is placed in the *Derived* folder, but the relation of the variable is determined by the expression. The Preferences dialog offers an option to place all derived variables with a relation.

If you change the relation of a derived variable after using it, plots and tables that use it may complain of mismatched relations and refuse to recompute.

Although derived variables always update immediately, you may still see the ❢ alert in derived variable HyperView menus. The Show

Numbers view of a derived variable displays a snapshot of the values at the time they were computed. If the expression or arguments of a derived variable change, the numbers view will post the ! in its global HyperView menu rather than update instantly. This action is appropriate because it just provides a view of the variable.

Although derived variables refer to variables by name, once a derived variable expression has been parsed, Data Desk knows the identities of the variables in the expression. If you then rename one of the argument variables, Data Desk won't forget which variables were used in the expression. Indeed, the expression window of the derived variable will post a ! and offer to update, substituting the new variable name for the old one in the expression wherever it occurs.

However, the name of the derived variable icon won't change automatically, even if that name was generated to reflect the derived variable function. Thus, if you select the variable *Sales* and choose {Manip ▸ Transform} **Log(y)**, Data Desk will create a derived variable named *LSales* containing the expression *log('Sales')*, and place it in the same icon window (and relation) as *Sales*. If you now rename *Sales* to *Proceeds* and open the icon *LSales*, the expression will read *log('Proceeds')*. If you had already opened the derived variable, the expression editing window posts a ! when the window is again frontmost, and offers to update. However, the derived variable's name will still be *LSales*. The reason is that you might have renamed the derived variable's icon yourself. Data Desk has no way of knowing whether you want the variable renamed, so it leaves control over variable names to you.

11.24 *Common Errors and How to Avoid Them*

Derived variables are very powerful. However, some subtle errors can be difficult to find. In this section we give some hints for ferreting out such bugs.

- Always complete an IF/THEN/ELSE combination. A common error is to omit the ELSE clause. It is **not legal** to write a statement such as

  IF *income > 0* THEN *profits*

  because Data Desk doesn't know what to do when the condition isn't true.

- **Do not** type an "invisible" character in the expression. Some keys (for example, the Enter key) don't print on the screen. Data Desk complains that you typed an illegal character. Try backspacing from the end of the expression until the rightmost character is deleted. If you can't find the invisible character, try deleting everything in the window and retyping the expression.

- Avoid typing an extra space in a variable name. Spaces may be inserted freely in derived variable expressions between functions and around variable names, but variable names must be typed literally. An extra space between two words of a variable name is hard to see, but the name won't match the icon name. Try retyping the variable name. To be certain to get a variable's name right, drag its icon into the derived variable editing window.

- Remember the *TextOf* function when working with the text version of a variable. Derived variables work with the numeric version of variables by default. This error is often confusing because the expression seems to say what you meant.
- **Do not** mix two different types of outcomes in an IF/ THEN/ELSE expression. For example, the following expression is **incorrect**:

  IF *contribution* > *1000* THEN *'bigGiver'*

  ELSE IF *contribution* > *100* THEN 2

  ELSE *"form letter"*

because in the first two cases it evaluates to a number (if the variable 'bigGiver' is numeric) and the other to a text string.

APPENDIX 11A Derived Variable Expressions

The following components may be used to construct the expression for a derived variable.

NUMBERS

Any number that could appear as a data value may be part of a derived variable expression. Numbers may have a leading + or –, followed immediately by the digits of the number. Numbers may be in *scientific notation* in which the number is written as some value times a power of 10. The power of 10 is separated from the rest of the number by an "E" (for exponent). Thus the number 1000 can be written as 1.0E3 (that is, 1.0 times 10^3). There must be no blanks between the E and the numbers on either side of it.

Both the symbol ∞ (typed as Alt-5 on Windows and as Option-5 on Mac) and the "word" *INF* represent infinity, and may be preceded by a minus sign to indicate negative infinity. The "words" *PI* or pi are recognized as the value pi (= 3.1415926...) (on the Mac the π symbol can be typed as Option-p). Note that you must type 2 * π rather than 2π to mean "two times pi." The symbol • (typed as Alt-8 on Windows and Option-8 on Mac) represents a missing value.

TEXT

Text must be enclosed in double quotes, " ".

NAMES OF VARIABLES

Data Desk ignores capitalization, so 'fun', 'Fun', and 'FUN', all refer to the same variable.

All variables in a derived variable expression must be in the same relation except for the arguments of the relational functions *Lookup* and *GetCase* and subscripted references of the form *variable*[*index*]. Derived variables may use other derived variables (provided they are in the same relation).

Variable names can be typed without any extra punctuation unless they are potentially ambiguous. A variable name is ambiguous if it contains a space or punctuation mark, if it contains another variable name or a function name, or if it is or contains a number (such as '1968'). Ambiguous variable names must be enclosed in single quotation marks ('). It is generally a good idea to enclose variable names in single quotation marks to reduce confusion.

Data Desk searches for variables to match the variable names in expressions starting with the icon window containing the derived variable icon. If it cannot find a match, it searches all icon windows that share the same parent with the home window (in effect, all the "first cousins" of the derived variable's icon). The search widens until it includes all variables in the datafile. If, at any level, Data Desk finds two variables with the same name, it asks you to declare which one you intend to use. Click on the correct variable and try again.

ARITHMETIC OPERATORS

The operators +, –, *, / (or ÷), and ** (or ^) indicate respectively, addition, subtraction, multiplication, division, and exponentiation (raising to a power). When no parentheses are used, operations are performed in the following order:

1) unary negation (minus sign), parentheses, NOT, IF, other unary operations
2) ^, ** (exponentiation (raising to a power))
3) * (multiplication), / or ÷ (division), MOD, DIV, Lesser, Greater
4) + (addition), – (subtraction)
5) <, ≤, =, ≠, >, ≥ (comparisons)
6) AND, XOR (exclusive OR), DIFF
7) OR
8) &, && (concatenate, delimited concatenate)

Multiple operations at the same level are performed from left to right. Thus 12 – 3 – 2 equals (12 – 3) –2, or 7 rather than 12 – (3 – 2), which would be 11, and 12/3/2 equals (12/3)/2, or 2, not 12/(3/2), which would be 8. Similarly, 2**3**4 is (2**3)**4, which is $(2^3)^4$.

PARENTHESES AND BRACKETS

Use parentheses ( ) freely to indicate the order in which the expression should be evaluated. Parentheses must be balanced. That is, every left parenthesis must be closed with a corresponding right parenthesis. Brackets, [ ], denote selected cases in the variable expression they follow. Thus *myvar[3]* is the value of the third case of *myvar*.

COMMENTS

Enclose comments in {braces} or in (* comment parentheses *). Comments may be nested to any depth and may appear any place a space can appear.

CASEWISE FUNCTIONS

Casewise functions produce one value for each case in the variables they use. The arguments of a casewise function are variables specified within the function's parentheses. Arguments can be variables or expressions that evaluate to variables. If a case has a nonnumeric value or is missing, casewise functions produce a missing value called a NaN (for Not a Number) for that case. Capitalization doesn't matter in function names. Some functions have two or three synonyms. Casewise functions are listed in Appendix 11B.

STRING FUNCTIONS

String functions are tools that allow strings to be copied from one variable and placed in a new variable. These commands are based on character position and are similar to those found in spreadsheets and database managers. These functions are listed and described in Appendix 11B.

Collapsing Functions

Collapsing functions use a variable as an argument but produce a single number, which can then be used for further calculation or reported by itself. Nonnumeric values in the argument variable are treated as missing and are ignored both in arithmetic and in counting numeric cases. Infinities are treated as missing values. Collapsing functions are listed in Appendix 11C.

Relational Functions

Relational functions refer to variables in different relations and perform basic relational operations.

HotResult Variables

Data Desk uses a number of internal derived variable functions to provide *HotResult variables* that update automatically when the analysis on which they are based updates. For example, the residuals, predicted values, and diagnostic statistics from a regression analysis (see Chapter 22) are HotResult variables that refer to that analysis. Any change in the analysis causes the HotResult variable to update.

HotResult variables are not editable, although you can open them and see the function name. They are not available for you to type as part of an expression. To build a derived variable expression using, for example, the predicted values of a regression, refer to the HotResult variable holding the predicted values rather than to the *predicted values* function itself.

Appendix 11B Casewise Functions

The following casewise functions are available either from the **Transform** submenus or by typing them as part of a derived variable expression. Capitalization is optional.

Common Reexpressions

The reexpressions on the ladder of powers (see Section 11.15) are commonly used to make patterns and relationships clearer and easier to describe.

√, Sqrt(y)	Square root.
Log(y)	Base 10 logarithm.
inv(y), $1/y$	Reciprocal.
$1/\sqrt{y}$, 1/Sqrt(y)	Reciprocal square root.

Arithmetic Functions

$y + x$	Addition.
$y - x$	Subtraction.
$y * x$	Multiplication.

y / x, $y \div x$	Division (type ÷ as Option –/ on Mac).
neg(y)	Negation. neg(y) = $-y$.
-1/y	Negative inverse.
y DIV x	Integer divide; truncates result to an integer.
y MOD x	Remainder of y/x.
Lesser(y, x)	Pairwise minimum.
Greater(y, x)	Pairwise maximum.

Exponential Functions

Sqr(y)	Square, y^2.
ln(y)	Natural log.
exp(y)	e^y, $e = 2.7182818\ldots$, the base of the natural logarithm.
y^x, y**x	General exponentiation (raising to a power).
10^y	10 to the power of y.
ln1(y)	ln(y+1).
exp1(y)	exp(y)-1.

Logical Functions

Data Desk maintains logical values internally as Boolean (that is, TRUE or FALSE) values. Data Desk translates Boolean values to numbers according to the rule FALSE = 0, TRUE = 1, producing indicator variables suitable for use as selectors.

$y < x$	Returns TRUE (1) for cases in which $y < x$.
y <= x	Returns TRUE (1) for cases in which $y \le x$. Alternatively on Mac, use "≤", typed as Option– ,.
$y = x$	Returns TRUE (1) for cases in which $y = x$.
y >= x	Returns TRUE (1) for cases in which $y \ge x$. Alternatively on Mac, use "≥", typed as Option–..
$y > x$	Returns TRUE (1) for cases in which $y > x$.
y <> x	Returns TRUE (1) for cases in which $y \ne x$. Alternatively on Mac, use "≠", typed as Option– =.
NOT y	Negates the truth value of its argument. When applied to variables rather than expressions, it first converts the variable to a logical expression by using the rule that 0 means FALSE and anything else means TRUE. In this form NOT is equivalent to *(1 - ABS(SGN(y)))*. Alternatively on Mac, use the unary negation sign, ¬ typed as Option–l.
y AND x	Logical AND of two Boolean arguments. When applied to variables rather than expressions, it first converts the variables to logical expressions using the rule that 0 means FALSE and anything else means TRUE. In this form AND is equivalent to *(ABS(SGN(y * x)))*.

y OR *x*	Logical OR of two Boolean arguments. When applied to variables rather than expressions, it first converts the variables to logical expressions using the rule that 0 means FALSE and anything else means TRUE. In this form OR is equivalent to *(ABS(SGN(y + x)))*.
y XOR *x*	Logical exclusive OR of two Boolean arguments. When applied to variables rather than expressions, it first converts the variables to logical expressions using the rule that 0 means FALSE and anything else means TRUE. In this form XOR is equivalent to *(ABS(SGN(y)) ≠ ABS(SGN(x)))*.
y DIFF *x*	Logical difference of two Boolean arguments; *y* DIFF *x* is the same as *y* AND (NOT *x*).

Rounding Functions

ABS(*y*)	Absolute value; |*y*|.
INT(*y*)	Integer part, sometimes denoted [*y*]. The whole number nearer to 0 or equal to the argument value. Int(–2.5) = –2.0. Int(2.5) = 2.
FLOOR(*y*)	The whole number less than or equal to the argument value. Floor(–2.5) = –3.0.
CEILING(*y*)	The whole number greater than or equal to the argument value. Ceiling(–2.5) = –2.0.
SIGN(*y*) SGN(*y*)	The sign of its argument. Returns –1, 0, or 1 according to whether its argument is negative, zero, or positive, respectively.
RoundEven(*y*)	The value rounded to the nearest even whole number. The fraction .5 rounds to the nearest *even* whole number: RoundEven(2.5) = 2.0. RoundEven(–2.5) = –2.0.
RoundUp(*y*)	The value rounded up to the nearest whole number. The fraction .5 rounds up to the *next largest* whole number: RoundUp(2.5) = 3.0. RoundUp(–2.5) = –2.0.
RoundDown(*y*)	The value rounded down to the nearest whole number. The fraction .5 rounds down to the *next smallest* whole number: RoundDown (2.5) = 2.0. RoundDown(–2.5) = –3.0.

Trigonometric Functions

All trigonometric functions work in radians.

sin(*y*)	sine (argument in radians)
cos(*y*)	cosine
tan(*y*)	tangent
arcsin(*y*), asin(*y*)	arcsine
arccos(*y*), acos(*y*)	arccosine
arctan(*y*), atan(*y*)	arctangent

sinh(y)	hyperbolic sine
cosh(y)	hyperbolic cosine
tanh(y)	hyperbolic tangent
arcsinh(y), asinh(y)	archyperbolic sine
arccosh(y), acosh(y)	archyperbolic cosine
arctanh(y), atanh(y)	archyperbolic tangent

PROBABILITY

All probability functions work consistently. *Distr* commands expect the statistic and any required degrees of freedom, and they return the value on the distribution curve. *Cum Distr* commands expect the statistic and any required degrees of freedom, and they return the area under the distribution curve (the prob value). *InvCum Distr* commands expect the probability value and any required degrees of freedom and they return the statistic.

ZDistr(y)
: Returns the value on the distribution curve for the z-statistic specified as y.

CumZDistr(y)
: Returns the probability under the distribution curve, from $-\infty$ to y for the z-statistic specified as y.

InvCumZDistr(y)
: Returns the z-statistic for the probability value specified as y.

CumTDistr(y, df)
: Returns the probability under the students t distribution curve, from $-\infty$ to y for the specified t-statistic and degrees of freedom.

InvCumTDistr(y, df)
: Returns the t-statistic for the specified probability value and degrees of freedom.

CumChiDistr(y, df)
: Returns the probability under the chi-square distribution curve, from $-\infty$ to y for the specified chi-square statistic and degrees of freedom.

InvCumChiDistr(y, df)
: Returns the chi-square statistic for the specified probability value and degrees of freedom.

CumFDistr(y, df1, df2)
: Returns the probability under the F-distribution curve, from $-\infty$ to y for the specified F-statistic and degrees of freedom.

InvCumFDistr(*y*, df1, df2)

Returns the *F*-statistic for the specified probability value and degrees of freedom.

BinomDistr(*y*, *n*, *p*)

Returns the binomial probability for the number of successes specified as *y*, the number of trials specified as *n* and the probability of success specified as *p*.

CumBinomDistr(*y*, *n*, *p*)

Returns the sum of the binomial probabilities, from *y*=0 to *n*, for the number of successes specified as *y*, the number of trials specified as *n*, and the probability of success specified as *p*.

PoisDistr(*y*, lambda)

Returns the Poisson probability for the number of occurrences specified as *y* and the average number of occurrences specified as lambda.

CumPoisDistr(*y*, lambda)

Returns the sum of the Poisson probabilities for y = 0 to *y*, for the number of occurrences specified as *y* and the average number of occurrences specified as lambda.

MISCELLANEOUS

Rank(*y*)

The rank of each case. Lowest number or earliest alphabetic gets rank 1. Ranks are determined either numerically or alphabetically according to the type of its argument.

NScores(*y*)

The *i*th NScore is the median of the sampling distribution of the *i*th order statistic based on a sample of size *n* drawn from a standard normal distribution. See Appendix 8B for details of how NScores are computed.

Nest(*y*)

Returns the cumulative count of the occurrence of each category in *y*, where *y* is a categorical variable.

ZScores(*y*)

The standardized values based on the equation *(x-mean(x))/StDev(x)*.

&, &&

Concatenate. <var1>&<var2> concatenates variables side by side (p.175).

Cross

The **Cross** command creates a HotResult variable, *Cross*, holding structural information about all combinations of categories of the selected variables. The selected variables are treated as category variables and interpreted according to their text rather than numeric values. Each combination of categories from two or more variables is commonly called a "cell." The information held in the *Cross* variable is the "cross" part of concepts such as "cross-tabulation." That is, it holds a case for each possible combination of categories from the selected variables *whether or not any observation falls in each cell.*

This distinction is important. Just like the cross-tabulation command, which can show a cell with a zero count when no observations fit in a particular combination of categories, the *Cross* HotResult variable lists all *possible* combinations of categories, and establishes a case for each combination in its Relation.

Cross HotResult variables are linked across Relations to the original data Relation. Selecting a case in the *Cross* relation selects a cell in the crossing of the specified variables. For example, select *Cross* and choose {Calc} **Frequency Breakdown**. The **Select** HyperView menu command on each cell selects the cases in the original relation. Opening *Cross* displays a view of the crossed variable mapped, with the correct category for each case, to the original relation.

The *Cross* HotResult variable can also be used as the grouping argument for summary reports by groups. Select variables to summarize as *y*, select *Cross* as *x* and choose {Calc ▶ Summaries} **Reports by Groups**. Data Desk provides the information that would be found in a (possibly multiway) table holding the summary values computed for each cell. Such tables (of means and standard deviations) are useful adjuncts to analyses of variance, for example.

gamma(*y*) computes the value of the gamma function for the selected argument. The argument can be a single value or a variable.

lngamma(*y*) computes the value of the natural log of the gamma function for the selected argument. The argument can be a single value or a variable.

Numeric(*y*) Returns 1 for all values that are numeric and 0 for all others. Helpful for creating selector variables that identify missing values. The argument can also be a scalar. For example: Numeric(3) returns 1 but Numeric (0/0) returns 0.

CaseNum(*y*) Returns the case number for each case. If the argument is a scalar, for example, CaseNum(500), it returns a variable holding 1,2,3,...500.

NameOf(*y*) Returns the name of the selected variable. If the argument is a variable socket, it returns the name of the variable currently plugged into the socket.

CoerceToRelation(*y*, *x*)
If *y* and *x* are in two different relations but have the same number of cases, it returns the values of *y*. The derived variable resides in *x*'s relation. If *y* is a scalar and *x* is a vector, it returns a vector in *x*'s relation with each case equal to the value of *y*.

NumCats(*y*) Returns the number categories in the selected variable. The argument must be a variable and not an expression.

Dynamic Functions

Box–Cox Transformation
: Creates a slider and derived variable for exploring reexpressions for the selected variable(s). See Sections 11.15 and 11.16 for details and an example.

Mix X and Y
: Blends two variables with mixing proportions controlled by a slider. The variables are standardized by subtracting their means and dividing by their standard deviations before mixing.

The command creates a slider and derived variable. The blend ranges from 100% of variable x and 0% of variable y through 50% of each to 0% of variable x and 100% of variable y.

Tukey's lambda
: Creates a slider and derived variable for exploring reexpressions of counted fractions and percentages. The counted fractions must be expressed as values between 0.0 and 1.0. The value of lambda is bounded between 0 and 1 as well. The Lambda family includes reexpressions close to the logit, probit, and arcsine. Section 11.18 provides more details.

Lag
: Creates a slider and a derived variable. The lagged variable is shifted up or down by a number of cases specified by the lag parameter. Negative lags shift up, positive lags shift down. The dynamically transformed variable is lagged by the amount specified by the slider. Lags are always integer amounts, so the lagged variable changes only when the lag slider crosses an integer.

Control Functions

TextOf(y)
: The text of the named variable. Ordinarily derived variable functions operate on the numeric values of variables. The TextOf function returns the text values. It is most often used to identify specific cases within a category variable.

IF/ THEN/ ELSE

IF<*logical expression*> THEN <*expression1*> ELSE <*expression2*> evaluates as *expression1* if the logical expression evaluates to TRUE and as *expression2* if the logical expression evaluates to FALSE. For nested expressions, the ELSE works with the closest IF. Either result expression can be a number. Hence IF/THEN/ELSE can be used to recode variables:

```
IF 0 < PAY AND PAY < 10000 THEN 0
        ELSE IF 10000 <= PAY AND PAY < 25000
                THEN 1
                        ELSE IF (etc.)
```

Alternatively, the expressions can be text, so the preceding recoding could take the form:

IF 0 < PAY AND PAY < 7000
THEN "Poor"
ELSE IF 7000 < PAY AND PAY < 25000
THEN "Middle"
ELSE IF (etc.)

The logical expressions themselves can use the *TextOf* function to select groups from a categorical variable:

IF (TextOf('gender') = "female") THEN 0.57
ELSE 1.00

Similarly, the result expressions can simply name other variables:

IF TextOf('Country') = "US" THEN HtInch
ELSE HtCm

The result of the entire IF/THEN/ELSE expression can be a number, so you may write expressions such as

StdBonus + (IF Sales > 5000 THEN 250
ELSE 100)

Manipulation Functions

Lag(y, k) Shifts the cases in variable y down k cases, inserting missing cases as the first k cases and dropping excess cases off the end to preserve the length of the variable. If k is negative, Lag shifts the variable up k cases and inserts missing cases at the end.

Relational Functions

Data Desk's relational functions provide facilities for looking up values across relations. They thus provide the basic operations on which to build a Relational Data Analysis.

GetCase(y, x)

Each value of x is taken to specify a case number in y. The corresponding case value of y is returned. A constant or an expression evaluating to a constant may take the place of x.

Thus *GetCase('income', 5)* returns the income value in the fifth case. Nonintegral case numbers are truncated. Case numbers of 0 or less or case numbers greater than the number of cases in y return the missing value code, •.

To obtain the text value of y at case number x, specify *TextOf*:

GetCase(TextOf('y'), x)

The two arguments need not be in the same relation. The result is in the same relation as x.

An alternative form of *GetCase* is to use the bracket notation. Case numbers enclosed in brackets following a variable name or expression select the cases with those case numbers. Thus *y[3]* is the third case of y. However, the argument in the brackets may itself be a variable holding case numbers. Thus *GetCase(y, x)* is equivalent to *y[x]*.

LookUp(y, x)

If k is a constant and y is a variable, *LookUp(y, k)* is the case number of a case of y for which $y = k$.

If *"text"* is a quoted string, *LookUp(y,"text")* is the case number of a case of y for which *TextOf(y) = "text"*.

If no match is found, *LookUp* returns missing.

If x is a variable, *LookUp(y, x)* returns for each element of x, the case number of a case of y for which y equals the corresponding value in x.

The two arguments need not be in the same relation. The result is in the relation of x because a lookup is performed for each element of x.

LookUpLast(y, x)

If k is a constant and y is a variable, *LookUpLast(y, k)* is the case number of the last case of y for which $y \leq k$.

If x is a variable, *LookUpLast(y, x)* returns a value for each element of x.

If y is not sorted in ascending order, *LookUpLast* first sorts the variable and then finds a case satisfying the condition.

The two arguments need not be in the same relation. The result is in the relation of x because a lookup is performed for each element of x.

LookUpFirst(y, x)

If k is a constant, and y is a variable, *LookUpFirst(y, k)* is the case number of the first case of y for which $y \geq k$.

If x is a variable, *LookUpFirst(y, x)* returns a value for each element of x.

If y is not sorted in ascending order, *LookUpFirst* first sorts the variable and then finds a case satisfying the condition.

The two arguments need not be in the same relation. The result is in the relation of x because a lookup is performed for each element of x.

LookUpCellNumeric(y, x)

If k is a constant and y is a variable, *LookUpCellNumeric(y, k)* is the case number of the case *before* the last case of y for which $y \leq k$.

If x is a variable, *LookUpCellNumeric(y, x)* returns a value for each element of x.

If y is not sorted in ascending order, *LookUpCellNumeric* first sorts the variable and then finds a case satisfying the condition, but it may not be the last one.

The two arguments need not be in the same relation. The result is in the relation of x because a lookup is performed for each element of x.

The *LookUp* functions can be used to group numeric variables into categories. For example, we can define the following variables:

If *letterGrade* contains the text values "F", "D", "C", "B", "A",

gradeBounds contains the "cut" values 0, 60,70, 80, 90, and

numberGrade contains students' numeric averages,

then *GetCase(TextOf('letterGrade'), LookupLast ('gradeBounds', 'numberGrade'))* assigns the appropriate letter grade to each student.

TEXT MANIPULATION FUNCTIONS

& Concatenate. The & operator is a binary operator that concatenates the text of its two arguments adjacently. Thus "Data"&"Desk" yields "DataDesk". The expressions on either side of the & are coerced to text automatically, so numeric expressions become numerals. The & is especially useful for concatenating variables. Thus 'first name'&'last name' yields a single variable combining the two names. "$" & 'salary' puts a "$" in front of the text of salary. When 'var1' and 'var2' name categories, 'var1' & 'var2' names the categories of the two-way table of 'var1' by 'var2'.

&"."& Delimited concatenate. Works like & but inserts the character inside the double quotes between the strings. For example, the expression 'last name'&","&'first name' results in Smith,Mary.

DATE AND TIME FUNCTIONS

Year(date)	Converts dates to decimal year. Decimal year is the fraction of the year and thus offers a continuous scale suitable for statistical analysis.
Quarters(date)	Converts dates to quarters from Jan 1, 1904.
Months(date)	Converts dates to months from Jan 1, 1904.
Days(date)	Converts dates to days from Jan 1, 1904. For example, 1/1/93 becomes 32509. Years after 2010 must include the century digit (2011 as opposed to 11).
Seconds(time)	Converts times to seconds since midnight.

The format for dates and times are extracted from the settings in the "Date & Time" control panel.

STRING FUNCTIONS

String functions are helpful for separating strings from a variable and placing the string in a variable. For example, you might want to create a variable that holds only the values to the right of the decimal point. Or you might want to separate the first three characters of a long category code.

Data Desk's string functions are of two types. The first two commands return, for each case in the variable, a single number. The last three commands return, for each case in the variable, the extracted string.

Len (*y*) returns the length, in characters, of the variable *y*.

Example: If the variable *Name* contains the string John, Len ('Name') returns 4.

Pos (*y, search string, start position*)
searches the variable *y* starting at the character position defined by the third argument, *start position*, for the first occurance of the string defined by the second argument, *search string*, and returns the position of the first character of that string. The search string needs to be either a variable or a string contained in double quotes. This command returns 0 if the string is not found. The first character in the string is position 1, so if you want to search from the beginning of the string, the starting position should be 1.

Example: If the variable *Name* contains the string John, Pos(*'Name'*, "oh", 1) returns 2.

Left (*y, k*) returns the *k* leftmost characters from the variable *y*.

Example: If the variable *Name* contains the string John, Left (*'Name'*, 2) returns "Jo".

Right (*y, k*) returns the *k* rightmost characters from the variable *y*.

Example: If the variable *Name* contains the string John, Right (*'Name'*, 2) returns "hn".

Mid (*y, start position, k*)
searches the variable *y* starting at the character position defined by the second argument, *start position*, and returns the *k* characters from that starting position.

Example: if the variable *Name* contains the string John, Mid (*'Name'*, 2, 2) returns "oh".

APPENDIX 11C Collapsing Functions

Collapsing functions take a variable as an argument but produce a single number. Nonnumeric values in the argument variable are treated as missing and are ignored both in arithmetic and in counting numeric cases. Infinities are treated as missing values except where noted.

Min(*y*) The minimum value of the argument. Min(*y*) returns -*INF* if *y* contains a negative infinity. Min(*y*) returns *NaN* if *y* contains no numeric cases.

Max(*y*) The maximum value of the argument. Max(*y*) returns *INF* if *y* contains an infinity. Max(*y*) returns *NaN* if *y* contains no numeric cases.

∑(*y*), Sum(*y*) Sum of cases in the variable. (Type ∑ as Option–w on Mac.)

SSQ(*y*)	Sum of squares of cases in the variable.
DotProduct(*y*, *x*)	Sum of the product of two variables.
CumSum(*y*)	Cumulative sum. The first case is the same as the first case of the argument variable. The second case is the sum of the first and second cases. The third case is the sum of the first three, and so on.
Mean(*y*)	Sample average or mean of the variable.
Median(*y*)	Median of the variable.
StDev(*y*), SDev(*y*)	Standard deviation.
Variance(*y*)	Variance of the variable.
StdError(*y*)	Standard error of the variable. Equivalent to *StDev(y)/sqrt(numnumeric(y))*NumNumeric(*y*),
NumNum(*y*)	The number of numeric values in the argument. This is the denominator for the mean.
NumNonNumeric(*y*), NumNonNum(*y*)	The number of nonnumeric values.
NumCases(*y*)	The total number of cases. Note that NumCases = NumNumeric + NumNonNumeric.
Corr(*y*, *x*)	The Pearson product correlation for the two selected variables.

EXERCISES

1. Which of the following expressions are legal derived variable expressions? For those that are not legal, state why. Assume that the following variables have already been defined: *Wages, tips, tax rate,* and *bonus.*

(a) 'Wages' + 'tips'

(b) 'Income' = 'Wages' + 'tips' +' bonus'

(c) Log('Wages' + 'tips'))

(d) ('Wages' + 'tips') * 'tax rate'

(e) 'Wages' + 'tips' – ('Wages' + 'tips') * 'tax rate'

(f) Sqrt(SSQ('Wages' – mean('Wages'))/(numNumeric('Wages') – 1))

(g) 'tax rate' ** –1.5

(h) 'tips' * 'tax rate' + 'bonus'

(i) (((3)))

(j) Sin('Wages'/2π)

2. Several of the functions computed by Data Desk can be found in terms of other functions. For each of the following functions, write an equivalent derived variable expression using other functions. Try them out to confirm your answers. Recall that you can type expressions into a ScratchPad and evaluate them there. (Assume that the variable *y* has been defined.)

(a) Mean(y)

(b) Variance(y)

(c) StDev(y)

(d) NumNonNumeric(y)

(e) Abs(y)   (*Hint:* Use Sign( ).)

(f) SSQ(y)

3. In August 1951, the applications of 413 marriage licenses in the city of Seattle with both bride and groom being residents of Seattle were classified by the distance between the groom's residence and the bride's residence. The distribution of the distance between residences was as follows.

Distance (miles)	Midpoint	Number of Licenses	Fraction of Licenses
0.00 – 0.99	0.5	115	.278
1.00 – 1.99	1.5	62	.150
2.00 – 2.99	2.5	48	.116
3.00 – 3.99	3.5	42	.102
4.00 – 4.99	4.5	30	.073
5.00 – 9.99	7.5	76	.184
10.00 – 19.99	15.0	40	.097

Source: Catton, Smircich, and Smircich (1964).

(a) Construct a derived variable to compute the mean of this sample. *(Hint:* The formula for the group mean is *∑(freq * value)/∑(freq).)* Write your derived variable expression, evaluate the derived variable, and report its mean.

(b) Construct a derived variable to compute the standard deviation of this sample. *(Hint:* The formula for the grouped standard deviation is

$$\textit{Std. Dev.} = \sqrt{\frac{\sum_{i=1}^{k} N_i (x_i - \bar{x})^2}{N - 1}}$$

where N_i is the *i*th group frequency.)

Write your derived variable expression, evaluate the derived variable, and report the standard deviation.

4. Create a variable, *x*, that contains the integers from 1 to 30. (Type in the numbers or use {Manip} **Generate Patterned Data...** .) Create a derived variable, *f*(*x*), type the expression in (a), and make a scatterplot of *f(x)* versus *x*. (Use the derived variable icon, but do not evaluate it first.) Make a sketch of the scatterplot showing its general shape.

(a) 3 + (4 * 'x')

Now, for each of the following expressions, edit the expression in *f(x)* to correspond to the expression in the exercise and update the scatterplot by using the HyperView pop-up menu found by clicking on the ! in the upper left corner of the plot. (The ! will appear only after you edit the derived variable and will clear after the plot is redrawn.) You can leave the derived variable window open during this work. Sketch the resulting scatterplots to show their general shape.

(b) 3 – (4 * x)

(c) (x– 15) ** 2

(d) x**2

(e) abs(x - mean(x))

(f) 2 * (x– mean(x))

5. Repeat Exercise 4 for the following functions.

(a) 'x'**2

(b) 'x'

(c) Sqrt('x')

(d) Log('x')

(e) –1/Sqrt('x')

(f) –1/'x'

These transformation functions are in order according to the power to which x has been raised (with the logarithm falling at the 0 power). What ordering can you detect in the shapes of the plots?

6. Use the **Generate Random Numbers** command in the **Manip** menu to simulate 1 sample of 50 numbers from a normal distribution with $\mu = 10$ and $s = 3$. (See Chapter 17 for more on simulation.) The sample will be placed in a variable *Norm:1*. Rename the variable x. Create a derived variable, $f(x)$, type the expression x, and make a histogram of $f(x)$. Use the derived variable icon, but do not evaluate it first. Make a sketch of the histogram showing its general shape.

Edit the expression in $f(x)$ to correspond to each of the following expressions and update the histogram with the HyperView pop-up menu under the ! in the upper left corner of the plot. You can leave the derived variable window open and generate each new plot from the original with the **Redo in New Window** command. Sketch the resulting scatterplots to show their general shape.

(a) 'x'**2

(b) Sqrt('x')

(c) Log('x')

(d) –1/Sqrt('x')

(e) –1/'x'

What patterns do you see in the relative shapes of the histograms?

7. To help assess the extent to which a distribution approximates a normal population, you would examine a ________________________ plot. To construct it, you would plot the sample values (y-axis) against the ______________________ function of these values.

8. The *NScore* of the smallest value in a sample of 20 is the smallest value you could expect to observe if you were to draw a sample of _______ values from a _______________ distribution.

9. Use the **Generate Random Numbers** command in the **Manip** menu to simulate 100 observations from a normal distribution with $\mu = 0$ and $\sigma = 3$. (Refer to Chapter 17 for simulation.)

(a) Make a normal probability plot for this variable. Observe the extent to which the plot is straight. Sketch it.

(b) Repeat this experiment four times. Sketch each trial.

(c) Select one of the simulated samples that appears to be very nearly normal and transform it by squaring its values. Make another normal probability plot. How does it compare to the plot associated with the untransformed sample values? Make the histograms corresponding to each plot for additional information.

10. Construct a normal probability plot for the *Displacement* variable in the Cars dataset and sketch it. Do you think *Displacement* is normally distributed? If not, in which ways does it fail to be normal? (You may want to make a histogram of *Displacement* to compare with the normal probability plot.)

11. Simulate 100 observations from a uniform distribution.

(a) Make a normal probability plot for this sample. Sketch it.

(b) Transform *Unif1* with the derived variable expression √(*Unif1* + 0.5) and make another normal probability plot. Sketch it.

Discuss what you find.

CHAPTER 12

Manipulating Variables

THIS CHAPTER COVERS data manipulations that are different from data editing or transformation. These manipulations act on all the cases of one or more variables to create an entirely new variable.

The commands discussed in the first part of this chapter are in the **Manip** menu. The remaining **Manip** commands are **Transform** (discussed in Chapter 11) and **Generate Random Numbers...**(discussed in Chapter 17). Manipulations found in other menus are discussed in the final sections of this chapter.

12.1 *Sorting*

The **Sort on Y, Carry X's** command in the **Manip** menu reorders the cases in a variable. To sort a variable, select its icon and choose {Manip} **Sort on Y, carry X's**. Data Desk creates a new variable holding the same data values reordered with the lowest (most negative or smallest positive) value in the first case and the highest (most positive or least negative) value in the last case and places it's icon in a new relation.

The new relation also holds a variable of *Unsort Indices*. These record the case number of each case before sorting.

sort key

If you select a *y*-variable and one or more *x*-variables, Data Desk makes copies of all of the variables, reordering them in the same order as the corresponding cases of *y*. The original variables are not changed. When you sort several variables, the *y*-variable is called the *sort key* because it determines the new order of the cases in all of the sorted variables.

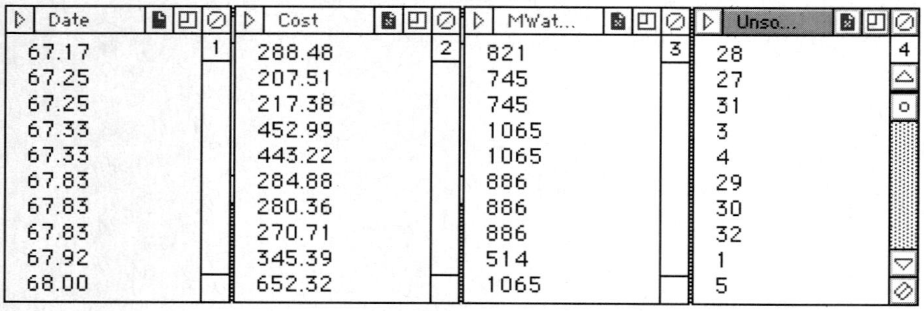

Date (1)	Cost (2)	MWat... (3)	Unso... (4)
67.17	288.48	821	28
67.25	207.51	745	27
67.25	217.38	745	31
67.33	452.99	1065	3
67.33	443.22	1065	4
67.83	284.88	886	29
67.83	280.36	886	30
67.83	270.71	886	32
67.92	345.39	514	1
68.00	652.32	1065	5

Figure 12-1. *Nuclear Plants data sorted according to Date. Note that cases are re-ordered consistently across all three variables.*

For example, the Nuclear Plants dataset contains 32 cases that are not ordered on any of the three variables. Although it might be interesting to sort the data on any of the variables, we will sort the cases chronologically. Select *Date* as *y* and *Cost* and *MWatts* as *x*, and choose {Manip} **Sort on Y, Carry X's**. The sorted variables are shown in Fig. 12-1.

stable sorting

When cases are equal, Data Desk preserves their original order. For example, in the Nuclear Plants data, we can see by checking the unsort indices that whenever two cases have the same Date, the one originally first in the data is still first. Sorting methods with this property are said to be *stable. Stable sorting* allows you to sort on several sort keys one after the other, last key first. Thus, to sort on year and on month within year, sort first on month and then sort the resulting values on year.

If the sort key has any infinities, they are sorted to the ends of the variable (according to whether they are +∞ or −∞). If the variable has any missing values, they sink to the bottom. Alternatively, missing cases can be omitted entirely from the sorted variables.

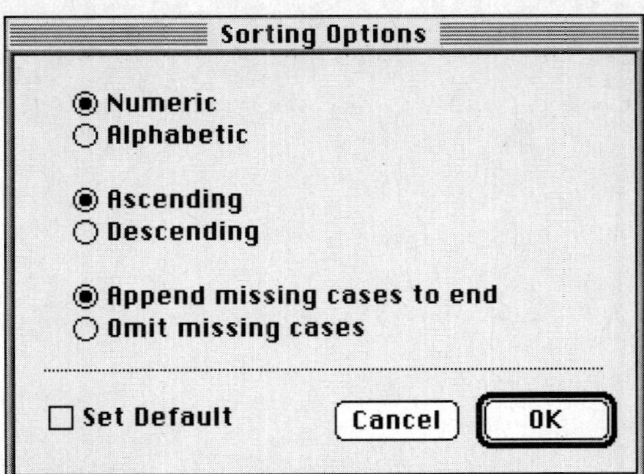

Figure 12-2. The Sorting Options Dialog.

The Sorting Options dialog offers three options to control sorting. It is shown in Fig. 12-2 with the default choices selected. Choose **Sorting Options...** from the **Manipulation Options** submenu to show the dialog. Changed settings affect all future **Sort** commands.

Choose Alphabetic sorting to order cases according to the alphabetic ordering of the text of the sort key variable. You can control the alphabetizing conventions and determine such things as the correct ordering of non-English characters and accents. Consult your operating system documentation for details.

Sorting a numeric variable alphabetically reorders the numbers in proper numeric order. Even if the numbers are imbedded in text, numbers are sorted as numbers, not numerals. So, for example, the values

aa2zz, aa1zz, aa01zz, aa02zz, aa11zz

are sorted correctly as

aa1zz, aa01zz, aa2zz, aa02zz, aa11zz.

Choose descending ordering to place the highest (largest, most positive) values of the sort key first rather than last. Descending alphabetic ordering places "z" before "y", and "b" before "a".

Although the sorted versions of variables deal with the same individuals and have the same number of cases, those cases are in a different order. The sorted variables are thus not in the same relation as the original variables. Data Desk creates a new relation for the sorted data. Although you can drag the variables back to the original relation (Data Desk would check only that they have the same number of cases), doing so would create an anomalous relationship in which cases were linked incorrectly. You should place sorted and unsorted versions of your data in the same relation only if you are very careful about the operations you then perform.

Multiple Key Sort

The **Sort on Y, carry X's** command normally accepts only one *y*, or key. With some basic data manipulation, however, Data Desk can use multiple keys to sort data.

The first step is to concatenate all the sort key variables into one variable using a concatenated derived variable expression (see Appendix 11B). The order of concatenation is important because it determines the nested level of the sort. The leftmost variable in the expression is the outer nest of the key. This pattern of left to right corresponding from outer to inner nesting holds for the entire expression.

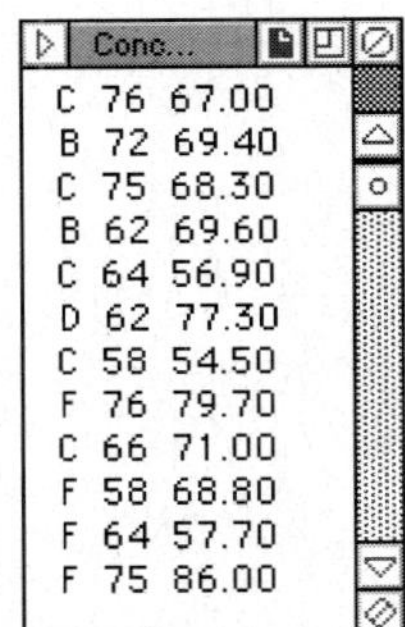

Figure 12-3. Concatenated variable.

Let's use the Graduation dataset as an example. Suppose that you want to sort the three variables, *School, Year,* and *% grad on time* so that the cases are sorted by *School* first, sorted by *Year* inside of *School,* and sorted by *% grad on time* inside of *Year*. Choose {Data ▶ New} **Derived Variable**, name the variable *Sort Key,* and type the expression

'School'&&'Year'&&'% grad on time'

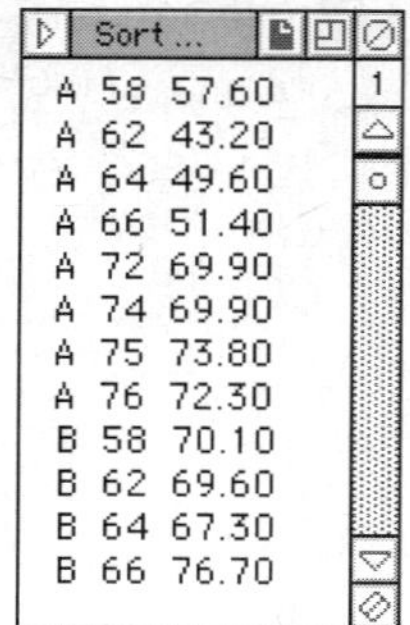

Figure 12-4. *Sorted variable.*

Choose **Show Numbers** from the derived variable's HyperView menu to open a window displaying the concatenated variable (Fig. 12-3).

Choose {Manip ▸ Manipulation Options} **Sorting Options...** and select *Alphabetic Sort*. Select *Sort Key* as *y* and *School, Year,* and *% grad on time* as *x*, and choose {Manip} **Sort on Y, carry X's**. A new relation is created holding the sorted variables. Open the new variables and compare your results with Fig. 12-4.

12.2 *Ranking*

Many statistics methods (especially nonparametric methods) work with the *ranks* of the cases in a variable rather than with their numeric values. The rank of a case is the case number of its position in a sorted version of the variable. The lowest valued case has rank 1, the next largest has rank 2, and so on.

HOW-TO

To compute the ranks of variables:

- Select one or more variables.
- Choose **Rank** from the **Manip** menu.

Each selected variable generates a variable of ranks.

To find the ranks of some variables, select them and choose {Manip} **Rank**. A new variable is created for each variable selected and is named *Rank:<varname>*.

When two or more values are identical, they are usually given the same rank. The rank assigned is the average rank of all cases with that value. For example, the ranks of 1, 2, 2, and 3 are 1, 2.5, 2.5, and 4, respectively. Except for the fractions that can result from this averaging, rank variables contain integers.

One advantage of working with ranks is that the most common data transformations preserve order and thus do not change the ranks. Transformations that preserve order include the logarithm, square root, and negative reciprocal. Statistics procedures based on ranks therefore yield the same results when such transformations are applied to the data. Rank assigns a missing value to any cases that are missing in the variable being ranked.

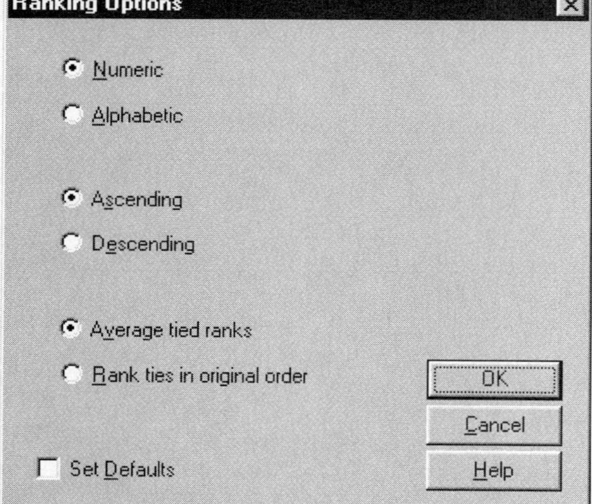

Figure 12-5. *The Ranking Options dialog.*

The {Manip ▸ Manipulation Options} **Ranking Options...** command, whose dialog is shown in Fig. 12-5, lets you specify how ranking should be performed. Ordinarily, tied values are assigned the average of their ranks, but one option allows them to be ranked in their original order. You can also specify that cases are to be ranked alphabetically rather than numerically.

12.3 *Generating Patterned Variables*

Variables whose case values follow a pattern are useful in many ways. For example, the numbers from 1 to 100 might be useful as the *x*-axis of a 100-point scatterplot where case order is of interest. Patterned variables often can label categories for an Analysis of Variance. {Manip} **Generate Patterned Data...** generates new variables *Pattern1, Pattern2,* and so on.

The **Generate Patterned Data...** command presents a dialog to specify a sequence of numbers from any number to any number, in steps of a

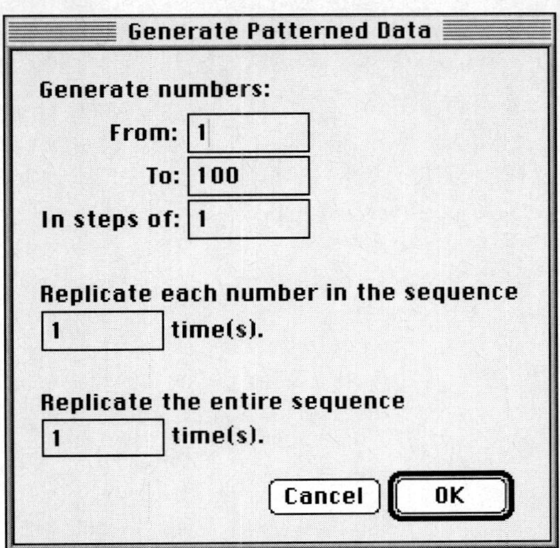

Figure 12-6. *The Generate Patterned Data dialog.*

specified size (Fig. 12-6). For example, a sequence from –3 to 9 in steps of 3 is –3, 0, 3, 6, 9. By default it offers the sequence that counts from one up to the number of cases in the frontmost relation, in steps of 1.

The dialog also offers to repeat each value any number of times and to replicate the sequence any number of times. For our example, repeating each value in the original sequence 3 times generates –3, –3, –3, 0, 0, 0, 3, 3, 3, 6, 6, 6, 9, 9, 9. Repeating the example sequence twice generates –3, 0, 3, 6, 9, –3, 0, 3, 6, 9. Both kinds of replications can be used in the same data generation. (It doesn't matter which kind of replication is performed first; the resulting sequence is the same.)

Data Desk places newly generated patterned variables in the frontmost relation that has the same number of cases. If it can find no appropriate relation it creates a new one, places its icon in the *Data* folder, and opens it to show the new variables. If you generate patterned data to use with existing data, but the patterned variable won't go into the data's relation, check that you are generating data with the correct number of cases.

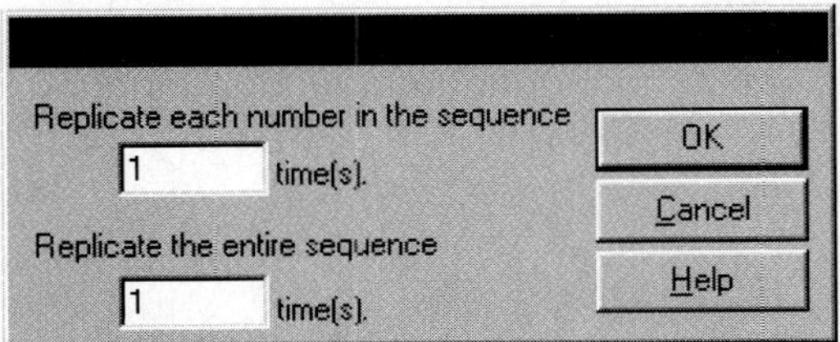

Figure 12-7 *The Repeat Variables... dialog.*

The **Repeat Variables...** command generates a patterned variable by replicating the cases of an existing variable. This capability might be valuable, for example, to create a factor variable for an experimental design model. Select one or more variables you want to repeat and choose {Manip} **Repeat variables....** Specify how you want the new variable to be constructed in the dialog (Fig. 12-7).

You can replicate each case, the entire variable, or both any number of times. The selected variable may hold numeric values, text values, or both. For example, if the original variable sequence is Hi, Lo, replicating each number in a sequence twice and replicating the entire sequence three times generates a variable holding Hi Hi Lo Lo Hi Hi Lo Lo Hi Hi Lo Lo. Data Desk names the generated variable with the same name as the original variable and places it in a relation that has the appropriate number of cases. If Data Desk can't find a relation with the same number of cases, it creates a new one and names it *Data.* Repeated variables are often useful along with variables constructed by appending different variables together, as discussed in the following section.

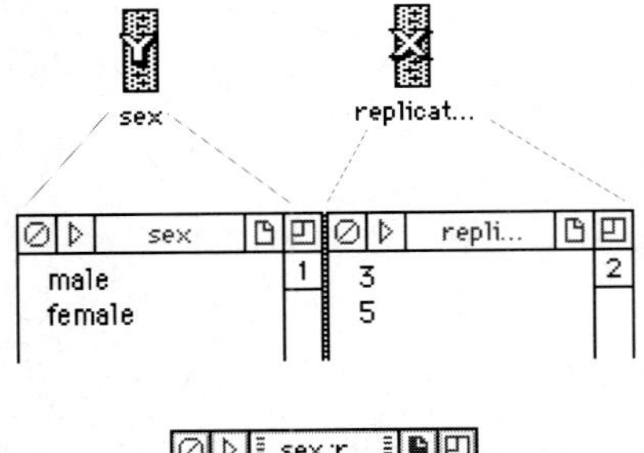

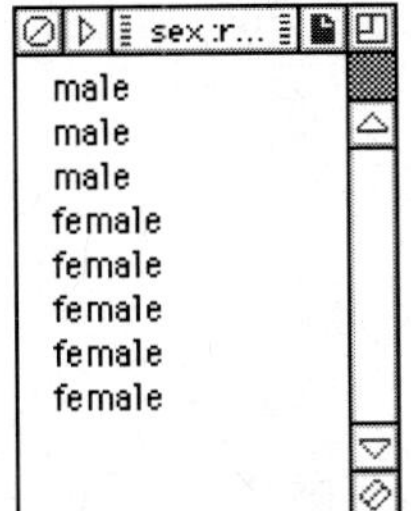

Figure 12-8. *The* ***Replicate Y by X*** *command creates a new variable which repeats categories in y the number of times listed in x.*

The **Replicate Y by X** command is helpful for data that come as summary counts by group. It expands the summary counts into a variable that has one case for each individual, to do so, it creates a new variable holding the text string for each case in the *y*-variable repeated by the value specified in the *x*-variable. For example, suppose that you had two variables, each with two cases — one called *sex* and one called *replicates*. The variable *sex* contains the text string 'male' in the first case and the text string 'female' in the second case. The *replicates* variable holds the value 3 in the first case and 5 in the second case indicating 3 males and 5 females. If you select *sex* as *y* and *replicates* as *x* and choose {Manip} **Replicate Y by X**, Data Desk creates a new variable called *sex:replicates*, holding 8 cases; 3 cases of 'male' followed by 5 cases of 'female' (Fig. 12-8).

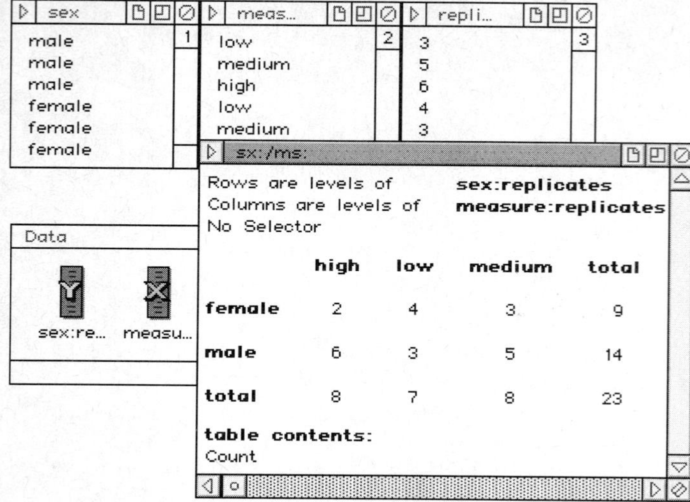

Figure 12-9. *The* ***Replicate Y by X*** *command can be used to create two category variables that can then be used in a contingency table.*

Replicating summarized data makes variables that can be used to create bar charts, frequency tables and as factors in linear models.

Summarized data might describe a two-dimensional data table, recording a row category, a column category, and a count of individuals in both categories (and thus in the corresponding "cell" of a two-way table). The summarized data should look like that shown in Fig. 12-9. Select the two category variables as *y*, the variable holding the counts as *x* and choose {Manip} **Replicate Y by X**. Data Desk creates two new variables that can be used as arguments for a contingency table.

12.4 *Appending and Splitting Variables*

Data in which each case belongs to one of several groups can be represented in two different ways. Data for the groups can reside in separate variables in separate relations. Alternatively, all the data can reside in a single variable, with a second variable supplying a category name for each case.

Part	Hei...
Soprano	64
Soprano	62
Soprano	66
Soprano	65
Soprano	60
Soprano	61
Soprano	65
Soprano	66
Soprano	65
Soprano	63

Figure 12-10. Part *and* Heights *of singers as two variables.*

The Singers dataset has data arranged both ways. There are four relations; sopranos, altos, tenors, and basses. The variables in these relations are appropriate for producing histograms to compare the distributions of heights according to vocal part. The dataset also has a variable, *Heights,* that holds the heights for *all* the singers. These are the same heights as in the individual variables but are stacked one after the other. Another variable, *Part,* holds the vocal part associated with each case in the *Heights* variable. Thus the first height is recorded for a soprano, and the group variable *Part* says "Soprano" for the first case (Fig. 12-10).

The **Manip** menu provides two commands for moving between these two forms. The **Append & Make Group Variable** command works when two or more variables are selected. It appends the case values of the second selected variable to the end of the first. It then appends the third variable's cases to that, and so on. The result is a single variable containing all the data values of the selected variables, *Data*. In addition, the command creates a group variable containing, for each case, the name of the variable from which it originally came and names the variable *Group*. It then creates a new relation to hold these variables and opens it to show them.

Parallel Append

If you select two or more *y*-variables and an *equal* number of *x*-variables, the command changes to **Parallel Append** (Fig. 12-11). **Parallel Append** appends the first *x*-variable selected to the end of the first *y*-variable selected, the second *x*-variable to the end of the second *y*-variable, and so on. It creates a *Group* variable with the group names *y* and *x*.

Parallel Append is an ideal tool for appending new data to an existing set of variables. You may have a dataset that has been split into two files or that has come to you as separate files. If the files have different cases but report the same variables, parallel append makes it easy to append the cases from one file onto the end of the cases in the other file.

Parallel Append

One file may already be a Data Desk datafile. If both files are text files or in some other form (a spreadsheet or database, for example), import or paste the data from one file into Data Desk. (See Chapter 6 for a discussion of importing data.) Now import or paste the data from the second file. Data Desk will place the new data in its own relation.

Select as *y* each of the icons in the first relation's window from left to right. (On a Mac, Option–⌘–**A** selects all icons in the frontmost window as *y*. Alternatively if the first and second relations have the same variables in the same order, just select the first relation's icon as *y*.) Select as *x* all the icons in the second relation's window in the same order as their corresponding variables in the first relation. (On a Mac, Shift–⌘–**A** selects all icons in the frontmost window as *x*. Alternatively, if the first and second relations have the same variables in the same order, just select the second relation's icon as *x*.) If an equal number of icons have been selected as *y* and *x*, the **Append & Make Group Variable** command changes to **Parallel Append**.

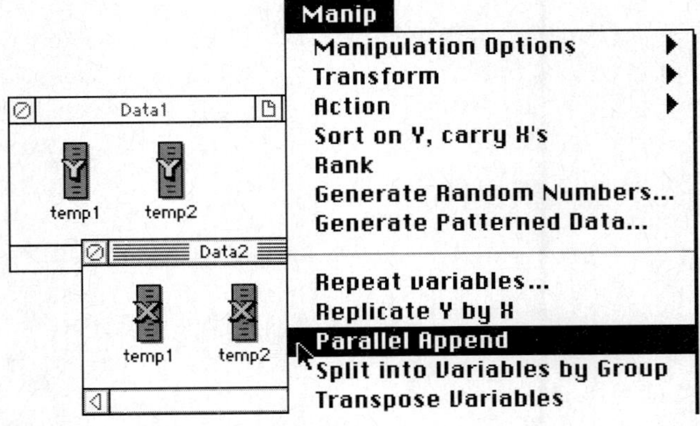

Figure 12-11. *When you select an equal number of* x- *and* y-*variables the* ***Append & Make Group Variable*** *command changes to* ***Parallel Append.***

Parallel Append creates a new relation, *Parallel Append,* and places in it variables named to correspond to the *y*-selected variables. Each holds the cases from the first relation followed by the cases from the second relation. Each variable in the second relation is appended to the end of the corresponding variable in the first relation. **Parallel Append** also creates a *Groups* variable, as did the **Append & Make Group Variable** command.

Split into Variables by Group is the reverse of **Append and Make Group Variable.** When a variable holding data values is selected as *y* and a grouping variable is selected as *x*, this command creates a separate variable for the data associated with each category in the grouping variable. For example, open the Singers datafile, select *Heights* as *y*, *Part* as *x*, and choose {Manip} **Split into Variables by Group**. Data Desk creates four new variables — *Alto:Heights, Bass:Heights, Soprano:Heights,* and *Tenor:Heights.* Because each variable holds values for unique subjects, each variable is placed in its own relation.

The **Split into Variables by Groups** command is helpful for creating variables that can be used with the commands in the **Test...** and **Estimate...** menus. These commands analyze and compare data that are in separate variables. If your data are entered in one variable with a second variable holding the category, use the **Split into Variables by Groups** command to create the required variables.

12.5 *Transpose*

The **Transpose** command exchanges rows and columns for all selected variables. The cases that were in each selected variable become a row (and thus a case) in these newly created variables. There is one new variable for each case in the selected variables. The effect is the same as transposing a matrix.

To transpose, select one or more variables as x-variables (hold down the Shift key while selecting them) and choose {Manip} **Transpose Variables**. Data Desk creates new variables, one for each case in the selected variables: *case1, case2,* and so on. Data Desk also creates a variable named *Variables* that holds the names of the original variables corresponding to each row of the new transposed variables.

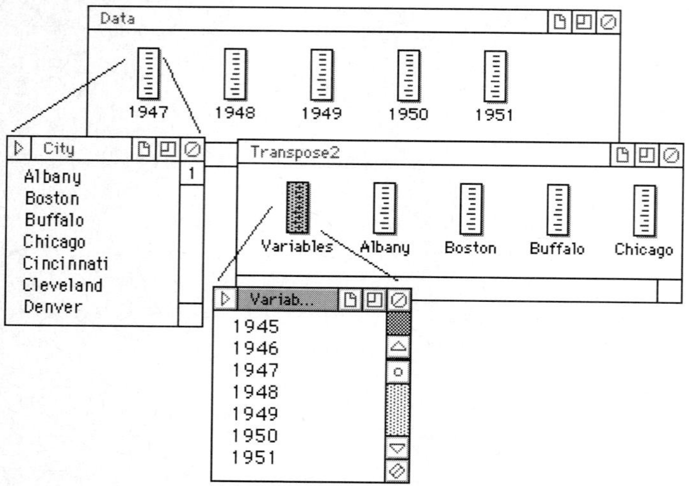

Figure 12-12. *Transposing variables creates a new relation holding variables one for each case in the variable* City *and each holding population values for 30 years in order.*

If you have a variable that names cases, you can select that identifying variable as the y-variable and the other variables as x-variables. {Manip} **Transpose Variables** names the newly created variables with the case identifiers found in the y-variable.

Thus, for example, data reporting the population of each of 40 cities for each of 30 years might be recorded in 30 variables (one for each year), each holding 40 cases (one for each city), along with a variable that named the cities. Selecting the city name variable as y, and the other variables as x, and choosing {Manip} **Transpose Variables** creates 40 variables, each named with a city name and each holding 30 population values in order. An additional variable will hold the names of the original variables, in this case *Year* (Fig. 12-12).

Transpose may stretch the memory constraints of your computer. If you are using Mac, you may want to allocate more memory to Data Desk if the variable to be transposed holds more than 100 cases.

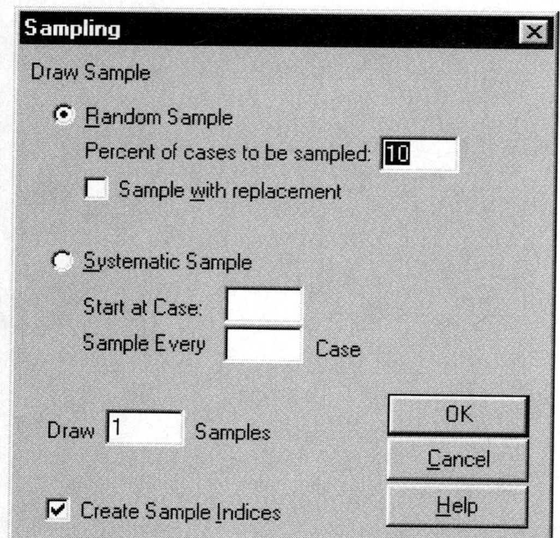

Figure 12-13. *The Sampling dialog offers several ways to extract cases from the selected variables.*

12.6 *Samples*

The **Sample...** command extracts subsets of cases from the selected variables and places them in a new relation. Random samples are representative subsets of the full dataset. A random sample is likely to be more manageable than a large dataset for initial exploration. Datasets larger than 10,000 cases often benefit from a quick exploration of a representative sample.

Select the variables from which to sample and choose {Manip} **Sample...**. The Sample dialog offers several ways to draw samples and allows you to specify the number of samples to draw (Fig. 12-13). Random samples give each case an equal and independent chance of selection. Thus they draw what is formally called a *Simple Random Sample.* (See Section 17.2 for a discussion of sampling in Data Desk.)

12.7 *Duplicating Icons*

The {Data} **Duplicate** command duplicates each selected icon. The copies have the same name as the original icons.

Duplicate is an extraordinarily powerful command because it performs a *smart duplication.* Any result icon, such as a derived variable, plot, or

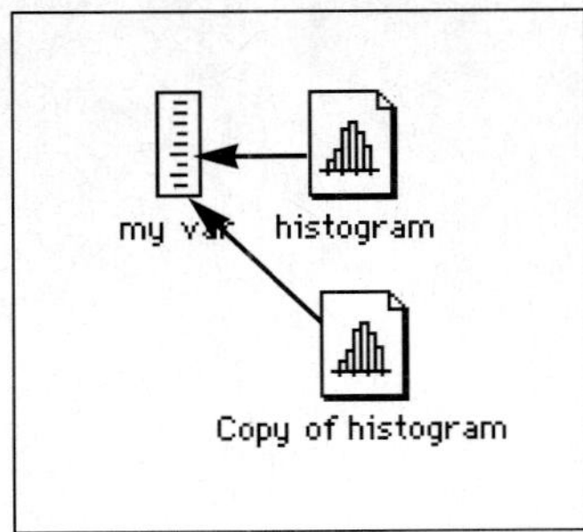

Figure 12-14. *Duplicating an icon by itself makes a copy that uses the same variables as the original.*

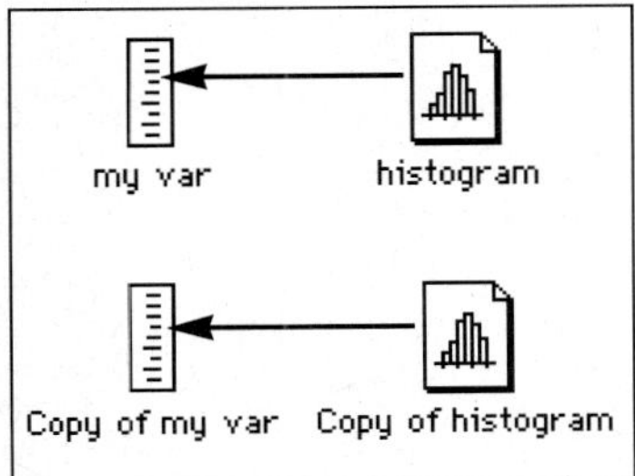

Figure 12-15. *Duplicating both the "user" and "used" icons simultaneously copies the entire structure. Here the duplicate histogram uses the duplicate variable.*

table, may use other icons. When an icon that uses others is duplicated, its duplicate uses the same icons as the original did. However, if an icon and the icons it uses are duplicated together, the entire structure is duplicated so that the duplicated result icon uses the corresponding duplicated variable icons.

For example, the histogram icon shown in Fig. 12-14 uses the variable *my var*. Duplicating *histogram* produces a copy also named *histogram* that uses the original variable *my var*. Duplicating both *my var* and *histogram* (Fig. 12-15) produces a copy of *histogram* that uses the variable *Copy of my var*.

Smart duplication makes it possible to reproduce entire data structures. For example, reproducing a folder that contains both a relation and any combination of derived variables, plots, and results icons that use the variables in the relation, makes a full copy of both the icons and their interrelationships. In doing so, it preserves all relation structure and the dependencies of icons upon each other. You can then experiment with the copy. Changes you make to the copy don't affect the original plots and analyses.

12.8 Variable Tables

The Data Desk **Manip** menu provides two commands for making tables from variables and sliders. The **Make Variable Table** command displays the contents of variables side by side in a spreadsheet-like table. They are a convenient way to view the contents of variables, especially when you want to read across several columns. The selector and group variables restrict a variable table to a subset of cases. Using a HotSet selector with a variable table is a powerful way of creating a table that displays information only for those cases that have been highlighted in a plot or selected in another table. As you change your selection set, the table updates to reflect the new cases. (See Chapter 13 for more information on selector and group buttons.).

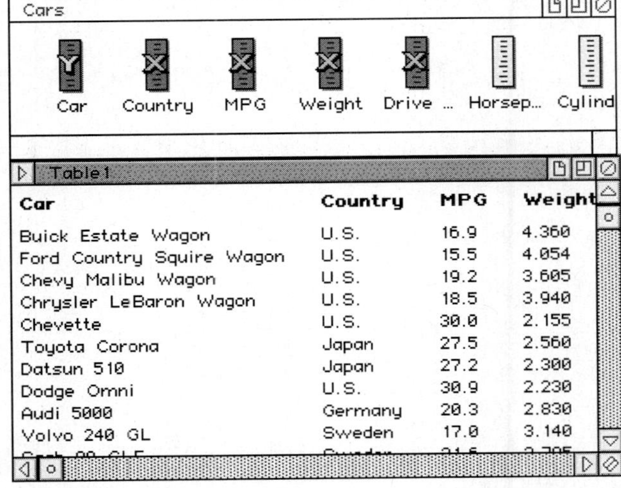

Car	Country	MPG	Weight
Buick Estate Wagon	U.S.	16.9	4.360
Ford Country Squire Wagon	U.S.	15.5	4.054
Chevy Malibu Wagon	U.S.	19.2	3.605
Chrysler LeBaron Wagon	U.S.	18.5	3.940
Chevette	U.S.	30.0	2.155
Toyota Corona	Japan	27.5	2.560
Datsun 510	Japan	27.2	2.300
Dodge Omni	U.S.	30.9	2.230
Audi 5000	Germany	20.3	2.830
Volvo 240 GL	Sweden	17.0	3.140

Figure 12-16. *A variable table displays the contents of the selected variables.*

To make a variable table, select the variables you want to put in the table and choose {Manip} **Make Variable Table**. The resulting table shows the variables in left-to-right order in selection order. Drag the icons of additional variables into a table to add their contents to the table (Fig. 12-16).

The **Use Colors** command in the table's global HyperView menu displays each case in the table in the color with which it is plotted. You can view the colors assigned to each case, but you can't add or change the color of the cases from a table.

The variable names at the top of the table don't scroll with the table, so they are always available to label the data. HyperView menus attached to the variable names offer to locate, select, or remove the named variable. As with other selection commands in HyperView menus, you can hold the Shift and Alt keys on Windows, or the Shift and Option keys on Mac, to select as *x* or *y*, respectively. If you want, you can use this feature to establish an interface similar to spreadsheet-oriented programs, displaying your data in a variable table, making selections by clicking on the column names, and choosing commands from the menus.

The **Make Scalar Table** command displays the contents of sliders and single-value variables in a two-column table. The left column lists the names of the sliders and variables, and the right column lists their values. To create a scalar table, select the sliders and variables you want to display in the table, in the order in which you want them to be listed, and choose {Manip} **Make Scalar Table**.

Like variable tables, scalar tables can have selector variables and group buttons assigned to them. And, because the table can be placed in automatic update mode, any changes made to the slider and variables are reflected immediately in the table.

CHAPTER 13

Integrated Analyses

TRADITIONAL DATA ANALYSES are based upon the assumption that the data are homogeneous; that the patterns that describe the data describe all parts of the data equally well. However, in real data this assumption often is invalid. Data exploration, graphing, linking (to examine data from alternative points of view simultaneously), and diagnostic statistics often reveal interesting clusters of data. These clusters are valuable. First, they often show interesting patterns and relationships that can help you understand the data better. For example, learning that men and women exhibit a different relationship between two variables (especially if you didn't suspect that gender mattered) can help you understand how that relationship operates. Second, they can make traditional analyses both more appropriate and more effective. When you discover subsets of the data that behave differently, it is almost always best to analyze each subset separately. The resulting analyses are more appropriate because the subsets are more homogeneous (and thus satisfy the standard assumption). They are more effective because differences among subsets in the data introduce spurious variation and thereby inflate confidence intervals and reduce the power of tests.

Data Desk provides tools for exploring specific subsets individually or several subsets in parallel, without any time-consuming data manipulation or recoding. Subset analysis is performed with user-defined indicator variables called selector variables. Parallel analyses use group variables. Each can be defined as a button on the desktop and applied to any analyses and plots. In addition, many analyses accept selector variables directly.

13.1 *Selector Variables*

Selector variables are indicator (sometimes called "dummy") variables used to restrict analyses to a subset of cases. The standard coding of a selector variable is 1 for any case to be included in the analysis and 0 for any case to be excluded. This coding is the usual definition of an indicator variable. However, in Data Desk, selector variables can be more general. In fact, any case coded either 0 or nonnumeric will be excluded, and any case coded with a nonzero numeric value will be included. In addition, logical (Boolean) variables holding the values TRUE and FALSE can serve as selectors, with FALSE indicating the cases to exclude and TRUE indicating those to include.

You can always type in values for a selector variable, but the easiest way to create one is with a derived variable expression that specifies a condition for inclusion. Alternatively, you can select cases in a plot or table and record the selection with the **Record** commands in the {Modify} **Selection** submenu.

For example, to select a subset of shorter singers (using the Singers dataset), we might define a derived variable named *Ht < 5′6″* with the expression 'Heights' < 66. This logical expression is either true or false for each individual and thus evaluates to the values TRUE and FALSE. Those cases that are TRUE for this selector (that is, individuals whose

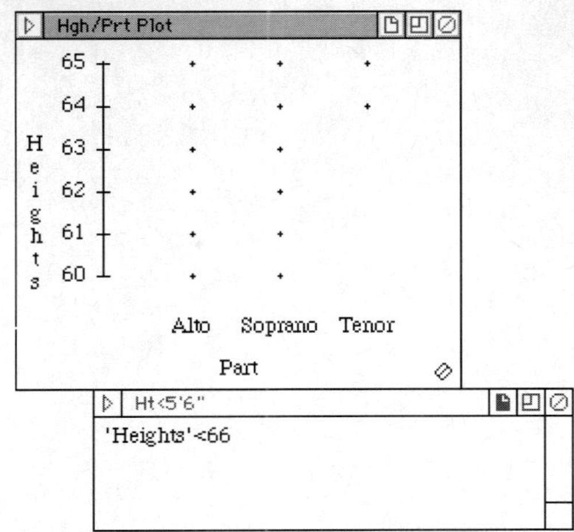

Figure 13-1. The dotplot shows only the data for singers whose heights are less than 5'6".

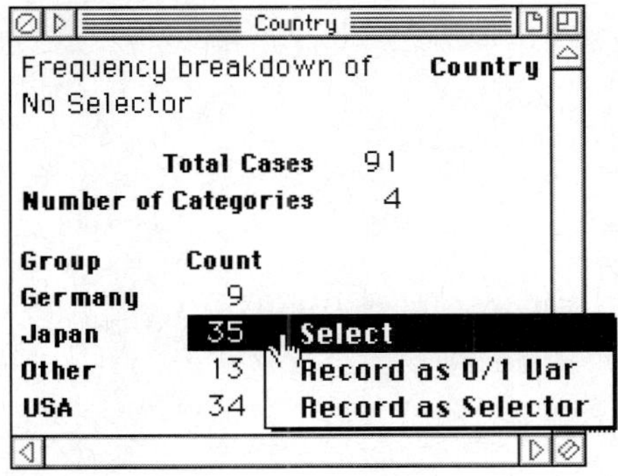

Figure 13-2. HyperView menus attached to the cells of tables offer to select cases.

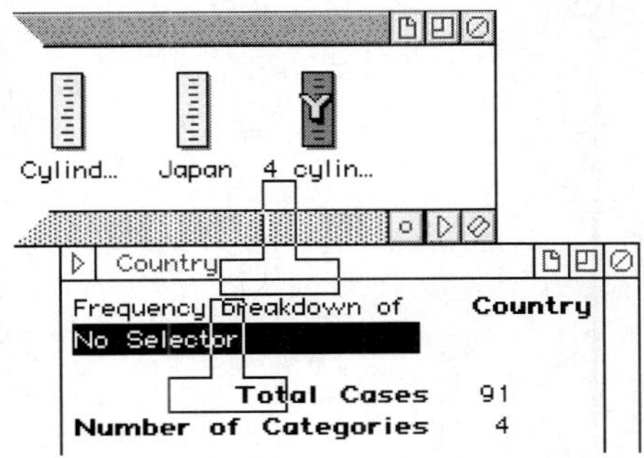

Figure 13-3. Dragging the selector variable over the "No Selector" line in the table will cause the table to recompute for the selected cases.

heights are less than 66 inches) will be selected for analysis and display. Those that are FALSE (that is, individuals whose heights are 66 inches or more) will be excluded. Fig. 13-1 shows a dotplot of *Heights* by *Part,* with *Ht < 5'6"* set as the selector. The effect of the selection is clear in the plot (Fig 13-1).

Derived variables offer a direct and precise method for defining selector variables. You could use a logical expression to select all the men in a sample with the expression *TextOf(gender)* = "male", or the richest members of the sample with the expression 'income' > 100000. You can make your expressions as complicated as you need them to be. For example, the expression, If *age* > 60 and *Weight* > 200 then 1 else 0, combines a selection criteria from two variables, although the somewhat simpler expression, *age* > 60 and *Weight* > 200 (which evaluates to TRUE and FALSE instead) would do as well.

Often it is convenient to create a selector variable from a plot or table. A scatterplot might reveal a cluster of points that differ from the others. To make a selector variable for these points, select the points by using any of the plot selection tools, such as the Lasso or Rectangle, and choose {Modify ▶ Selection} **Record**. Data Desk creates a variable whose value is 1 for each selected case and 0 for all the others, asks you to name the new variable, and then places the variable's icon at the right end of the data relation. To select cases from frequency and contingency tables, click on a cell or on the label of a row or column and choose the **Record as 0/1 Var** command from the HyperView menu that pops up (Fig. 13-2).

Of course, your data may already include appropriate indicator variables. There is no need to create special selector variables if suitable variables already exist. Using a variable as a selector in no way changes its availability for other uses.

13.2 *Assigning Selector Variables*

Data Desk provides three alternative methods for applying a selector variable to analyses and displays. The most direct method of applying a selector variable is to drag the variable into the analysis you want to restrict. All Data Desk analysis tables and some plots allow selector variables to be dragged into them. Analysis tables include a line that either names the selector variable currently applied or simply states "No Selector." (In some analysis tables such as, for example, linear model tables, you may need to open the "Modifications" panel of the table to see the selector line.) To assign a selector variable to the analysis, simply drag the variable's icon over the selector line. The line will highlight to acknowledge the drag. Drop the icon there to modify the analysis (Fig. 13-3). The selector line changes to read "cases selected according to 'selector variable'", and Data Desk recomputes the results for the selected subset of cases. When a selector is active for an analysis table, the selector line holds a HyperView menu that includes a **Remove Selector** command. Choose this command to remove the selector and recalculate the analysis for the full set of cases.

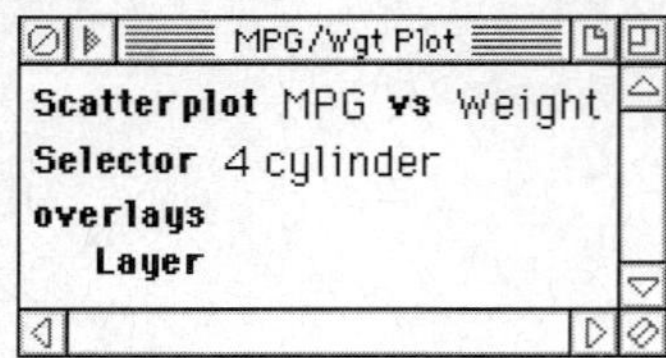

Figure 13-4. The Plot Info window displays selector status for the plot.

Scatterplots, dotplots Y by X, boxplots Y by X, and lineplots can also accept dragged selectors. Open the plot key with the **Show Plot Info** command in the plot's HyperView menu. The Plot Info window specifies details of the plot and includes a selector line, which works in just the same way as in analysis tables. You need not keep Plot Info open to use the plot (Fig. 13-4).

Another way to apply a selector variable to a display or table is to select the icon of the selector variable and choose {Selector} **Assign Selector** from a HyperView menu. In displays, the **Selector** commands are found in the global HyperView menu. In tables, they are found in the HyperView menu attached to the selector line. When you assign a selector, take care that only the selector variable's icon is selected. Choose {Selector} **Remove Selector** from the HyperView menu to return to the full set of cases.

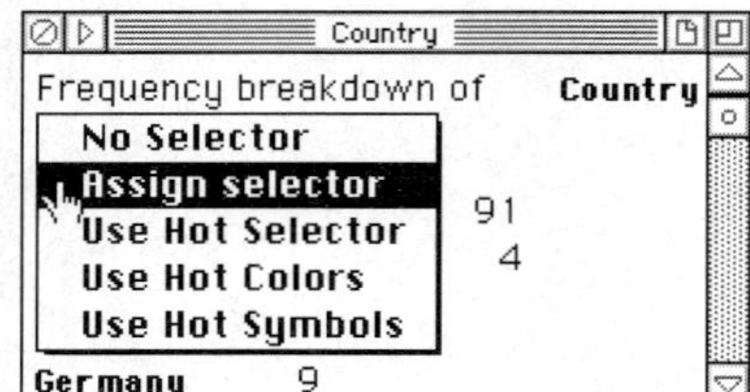

Selector variables can be assigned using the **Selector** button. Select the selector variable's icon and choose {Special ▶ Selector} **Assign**. Data Desk creates a **Selector** button, which appears in the lower left corner of the Data Desk desktop. Initially it is turned on (highlighted).

Click the **Selector** button to toggle it off and on. When the **Selector** button is highlighted (on), all Data Desk commands operate only on the selected cases. After a command is executed, the button turns off. Press the button again to highlight it and invoke selection for the next command.

To change the selector variable in the **Selector** button, select the new selector variable and choose {Special ▶ Selector} **Assign**. To clear the selector and to remove the button from the desktop, choose {Special ▶ Selector} **Clear**. Discarding the selector variable and emptying the Trash also clears the selector if that selector variable isn't used by any remaining object. (If it is in use, it can't be discarded.) The {Special ▶ Selector} **Locate** command locates the selector variable so that you can examine or edit it. The {Special ▶ Selector} **Button On** command makes the selector button active and turns the button black. Choosing this command again deactivates the selector button.

The {Modify ▶ Selection} **Assign Selector** command is similar to the {Modify ▶ Selection} **Record** command but, in addition to creating a selector variable, it immediately assigns the selector variable to the **Selector** button. Select the cases to analyze separately and choose {Modify ▶ Selection} **Assign Selector**. Data Desk creates a selector variable, asks you to name it, places its icon in the data relation, assigns it to the **Selector** button and makes the button active. You can then immediately perform an analysis or make a display for the selected cases. This path is designed to make it easy to pursue inquiries such as "I wonder if this cluster of cases is really different when it comes to xxx" or "I wonder what makes these cases different from the others" without losing the original analysis path.

13.3 *Dependencies*

A plot or analysis made with a selector variable is a user of that selector variable and is dependent upon its values. As with all Data Desk dependencies, if you change the underlying values of the selector variable, or (if the selection is defined in a derived variable) change the defining expression, all dependent displays and analyses offer to update to reflect the change.

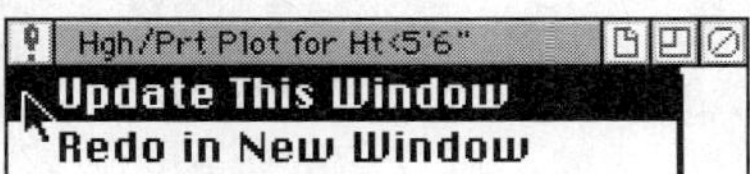

Figure 13-5. The dotplot offers to update because the selector variable has changed.

For example, the derived variable *Ht < 5'6"* is used by the dotplot created in Fig. 13-1. You can edit the expression by opening the derived variable and changing the 66 to, say, 70. Because it depends upon the selector, the dotplot immediately offers to update. Choose **Update This Window** from the HyperView menu under the ! symbol (Fig. 13-5). The updated plot is shown in Fig. 13-6, with three basses now represented.

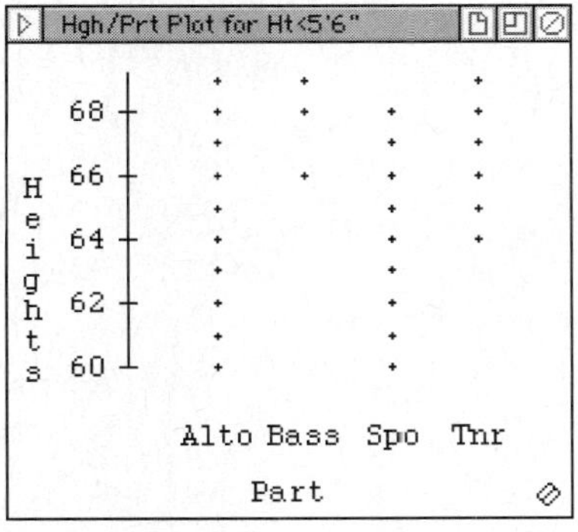

Figure 13-6. The updated plot shows three basses are now represented.

A selector variable must be in the same relation as the variables in the analysis or display that it modifies. It would make no sense to select cases in one relation but apply the selection to another relation. Data Desk alerts you of mismatches between selectors and variables.

Selection is a fundamental property of all Data Desk results. If you are investigating a subset, you may want to examine several displays and perform several analyses. If you use the HyperView menus of a table or display to generate a new table or display (for example, selecting the **Histogram** command from the HyperView attached to a scatterplot axis name, or requesting a probability plot of residuals from a regression analysis), the new display or analysis automatically inherits the selection of the parent window. This action guarantees that the new display or analysis will be for the same cases as (and thus be comparable to) the parent window. It also guarantees that, if you modify the selector, all the results will update appropriately. (If you select variables from the desktop instead, Data Desk will not restrict the resulting analyses and displays unless you specify the selector for the new results.)

The ability to pass subset selection to related analyses and displays is fundamentally important to maintain consistency and coherence when you examine subsets. It is a powerful, yet subtle feature of Data Desk. It also is an important reason to pursue an analysis path through HyperView menu selections rather than by returning to the desktop to select the original icons. Only when you work through HyperView menus can Data Desk know the correct subset of cases to select. (In Chapter 4 we discuss HyperView menus and their use for generating new analyses and displays.)

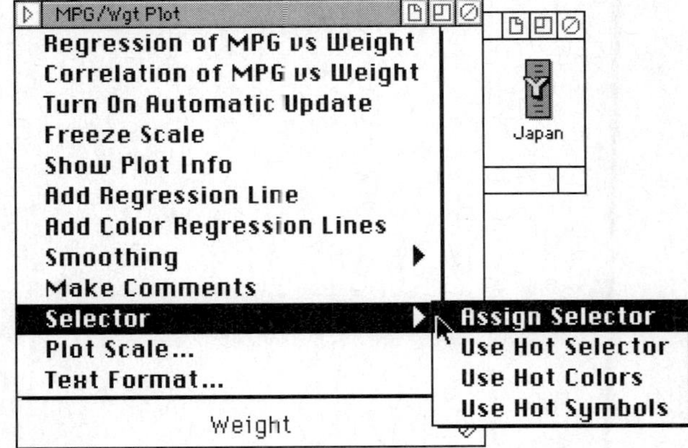

Figure 13-7. Select the variable Japan *and choose {Selector}* **Assign Selector** *from the scatterplot's HyperView menu.*

13.4 *An Example*

When the points you want to eliminate from, or isolate, on a plot are clearly defined, it is usually easiest to create a selector variable graphically. Let's look at a simple example using the Cars91 datafile. Open the file, select the variables *MPG* and *Weight* and choose {Plots} **Scatterplots**. Here we are interested in isolating the analysis to cars manufactured in Japan.

Select the *Country* variable and choose {Plot} **Bar Charts**. Select the bar labeled *Japan* in the bar chart by using either the ↘ or ☞ tool. Next, choose {Modify ▶ Selection} **Record**. Data Desk creates a new variable, places its icon at the end of the relation and asks you to name it. Type in

"Japan" and press Enter. Select the new variable *Japan* and choose {Selector} **Assign Selector** from the scatterplot's HyperView menu (Fig. 13-7). The plot updates to show only the cars manufactured in Japan.

Dependent variable is:	MPG
cases selected according to	Japan

91 total cases of which 70 are missing
R squared = 76.7%   R squared (adjusted) = 75.5%
s = 2.466 with 21 - 2 = 19 degrees of freedom

Source	Sum of Squares	df	Mean Square	F-ratio
Regression	380.300	1	380.300	62.6
Residual	115.510	19	6.07945	

Variable	Coefficient	s.e. of Coeff	t-ratio	prob
Constant	48.0110	2.805	17.1	≤ 0.0001
Weight	-7.84609e-3	0.0010	-7.91	≤ 0.0001

Figure 13-8 *Choose* ***Regression*** *from the scatterplot's HyperView menu. The results are calculated only for the cars manufactured in Japan.*

When a display has a selector variable assigned to it, any plot or table generated from the restricted display also has the selector variable assigned to it. The restricted scatterplot of *MPG* versus *Weight* provides a good example. Choose **Regression of MPG vs. Weight** from the scatterplot's HyperView menu. The resulting regression table is calculated using only the Japanese cars, and names the selector variable in the appropriate row of the table (Fig. 13-8).

13.5 *Performing Analyses by Group*

In Data Desk, data in which each case belongs to one of two or more groups can be represented in two different ways. Data for each group can reside in a separate relation with the variables repeated in each relation, or all data can reside in a single relation, with a special variable supplying a category name for each case. The latter arrangement is almost always more convenient. If you want to perform analyses or make plots for each of the groups side by side when the groups are in separate relations, you must select variables and perform the analysis repeatedly in each of the relations. If the groups are specified with a single grouping variable, Data Desk offers a more convenient alternative.

Group Variable: Cylinders

Select the variable that holds the group names and choose {Special ▸ Group} **Assign**. A **Group** button similar to the **Selector** button is placed on the lower left of the desktop and highlighted. Whenever the **Group** button is highlighted, any command in the **Calc** or **Plot** menus generates an entire folder of results, creating a table or plot for each group named by the grouping variable.

Let's use the Cars91 dataset as an example. We can examine the relationship between horsepower and drive ratio for cars with different numbers of cylinders. The *Cylinders* variable holds five different categories: 4, 5, 6, and 8 cylinder cars, so setting it as the **Group** button makes five different plots or tables for any display or analysis.

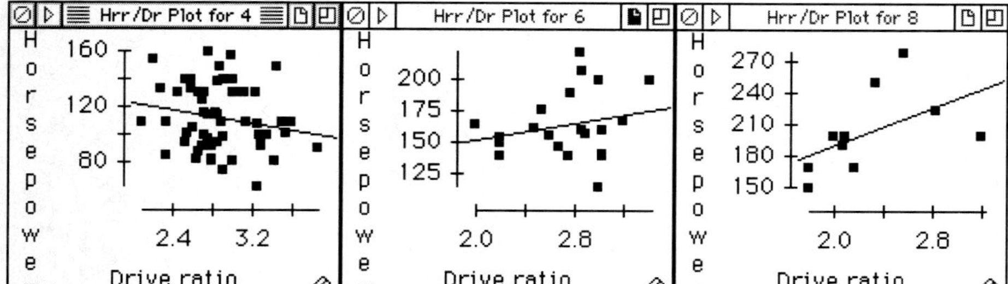

Figure 13-9. *Scatterplots of* Horsepower *versus* Drive Ratio. *Plot scales have been matched and regression lines added to show differences in the slope by group.*

Select *Cylinders* and choose {Special ▸ Group} **Assign**. A button labeled Group Variable: Cylinders appears on the bottom of the Data Desk desktop and is highlighted. Select *Horsepower* as *y* and shift-click to select *Drive Ratio* as *x*. Next, choose {Plot} **Scatterplots**. Data

Desk opens five scatterplots, one each for 4-cylinder cars, 6-cylinder cars, and so on. It might be helpful to add a regression line to the plots. Choose **Add Regression Line** from the HyperView menu of each scatterplot (Fig. 13-9).

	X Axis	Y Axis
Lower Bound	1.5000000	50
Upper Bound	4.5000000	275
Interval Size	0.75000000	50

Figure 13-10. *Set the plot scale.*

To compare these plots let's set them to the same scale. Choose **Plot Scale...** from one of the plot's HyperView menus, and set the scale as shown in Fig. 13-10. Then drag the icon alias of the rescaled plot into the other plots to match the scales (see Section 9.15). We can now see how the slope of the relationship between horsepower and drive ratio varies with the number of cylinders. Figure 13-9 shows three of them (excluding the plots for the 3- and 5-cylinder cars, which show single points).

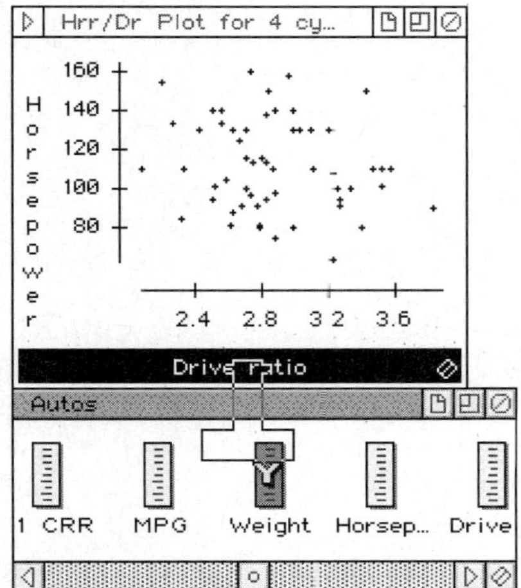

Each of the displays and tables generated in this way for a group selects only the cases in the specified group. As when selection is in effect, analyses specified from HyperView menus in any of these windows inherit the group selection from their parent window. This capability makes it easy to pursue your understanding of a group without having to respecify the group at each step. For example, the lines added to the plots in Fig. 13-9 were computed only for the points represented in each plot. You can even drag the icon of another variable onto an axis label of one of these plots; the plot continues to focus only on the points in its group.

Although the windows holding the results for each group are in the same relation, it makes no sense to brush or slice to relate windows. The reason is that any one case can be in only one group and thus can appear in only one window. Data Desk places the icons of the plots for each group in the same folder, the *Results* folder. Thus you can close all of them by choosing {Data ▶ Close All} **Siblings** when any one of the plots is the frontmost window.

If the **Group** and **Selector** buttons are active simultaneously, Data Desk produces a window for each group. However, only those cases indicated by the selector are available.

13.6 *HotSet Variables*

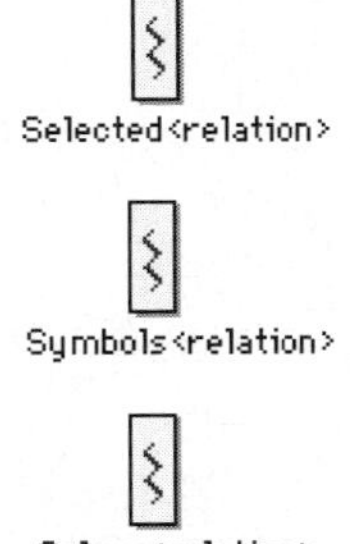

HotSet variables are HotResult variables (see Section 4.7) that reflect the current selection, color, or symbol for each case in a relation with a numeric code. For example, HotSet variables for selection are 1 for each selected case and 0 for each unselected case; HotSet variables for color hold the number of the color (0 = white, 1 = the color in the upper left box of the colors palette, …, 63 = the color in the lower right box of the colors palette) for each case. HotSet variables for symbol hold a code number for the symbol (0 = dot, 1 = o, 2 = +, …, 7 = /). The numeric codes change immediately whenever the specified attribute of a case changes.

Selection, color, and symbol are properties of each case in a relation; every display in a relation shows the same cases highlighted and displays each case with its own color and symbol. Therefore each relation can have only one HotSet variable corresponding to each attribute. HotSet variables' names specify both their relation and the attribute code.

One of the most effective ways to explore complex patterns in data is with movement and change. Rotating plots, plot matrices, and sliders all provide ways to alter your view of the data in a smooth and systematic manner to help you understand changes in relationships. Unlike these methods that control change, HotSet variables offer control of discrete changes rather than continuous changes. The attributes that HotSet variables represent change abruptly from one state (selected, blue, x) to another (unselected, red, o). HotSet variables are thus especially effective for comparing groups, for understanding the consequences of omitting outliers, and for identifying and focusing on important subgroups in data.

13.7 *Creating HotSet Variables*

Because HotSet variables depend upon attributes of cases seen in displays, you usually create them from a display in which cases show individual selection, color, and symbol such as a scatterplot, dotplot, rotating plot, or normal probability plot. The commands to create HotSet variables are in the **Modify** menu within the submenus dedicated to each display attribute that they can code: **Selection**, **Color**, and **Symbol**.

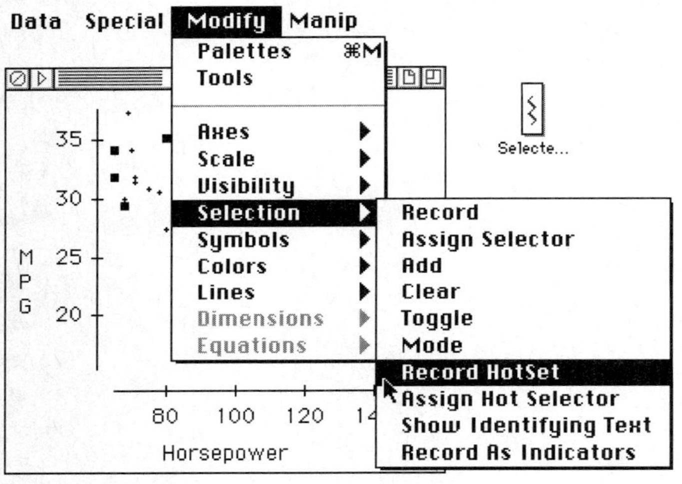

Figure 13-11. *Choose {Modify ▸Selection}* ***Record HotSet*** *to create a HotSet variable that creates a variable that always holds the current selection state.*

For example, the {Modify ▸ Selection} menu holds two Hotset commands: **Record HotSet** and **Assign HotSet Selector**. These commands are active whenever a suitable display (that is, one in which individual case selection is evident) is frontmost. **Record HotSet** creates a HotSet variable named "Selected(<relation name>)" and places it in the frontmost variable window of the relation (Fig. 13-11). Choosing **Assign Hot Selector** records the HotSet variable, sets it as the selector variable, and highlights the **Selector** button. (You may want to review the **Selector** button discussion in Section 13.3.)

You can create HotSet variables for color and symbol in the {Modify ▸Colors} and {Modify ▸Symbols} submenus. These commands create HotResult variables named "Colors(<relation>)" and "Symbols(<relation>)", respectively. The resulting HotSet variables hold integer values that reflect the current color and symbol assignments for each case in the relation. Because they typically name more than two categories, commands in the **Colors** and **Symbols** menus offer to set them in the **Group** button rather than in the **Selector** button. With a HotSet variable as the group variable, **Calc** and **Plot** menu commands create a window for each level of the HotSet variable. Changes in color or symbol immediately notify displays and tables of the need to update; if they are set to automatic update, they will change immediately.

Another way to create HotSet variables is offered in a HyperView menu found at the top of every output table. Tables display "No selector" when no selector variable has been specified. Selecting this line drops a HyperView menu that offers to create and then use a HotSet variable as a selector, based upon selection, color, or symbol.

13.8 HotSet Selector Variables

HotSet selector variables are dynamic 0/1 indicator variables that reflect the current selection state of cases in a relation. Indicator variables can be used in many statistics calculations; HotSet selectors automatically make such calculations dynamic. The most common use of HotSet Selectors is as selector variables. When used as a selector, they restrict a calculation or display to only the cases that have been selected. If you set analyses and displays to automatic update (with the **Turn On Automatic Update** command in the windows' HyperView menus), they immediately update to reflect the selection. For example, you can select each bar of a bar chart in turn and observe the changes in a set of analysis windows from group to group. (This way of viewing the same aspect, analysis, or display of data for groups, successively in the same window has been called "alternagraphic" viewing by John Tukey, the founder of exploratory data analysis.)

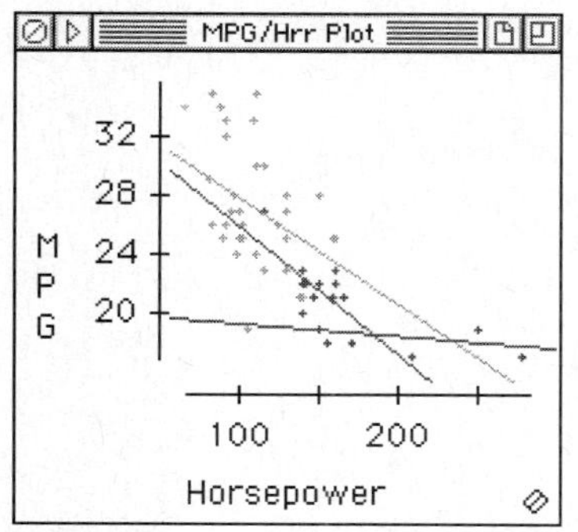

Figure 13-12. Scatterplot of MPG *versus* Horsepower *with color regression lines added before the HotSet selector has been assigned.*

In the Cars91 data, we can learn much by looking at different types of cars. Open the Cars91 datafile, select *MPG* as *y* and *Horsepower* as *x*, and choose {Plot} **Scatterplots**. Select *Cylinders* and choose {Modify ▶ Colors ▶ Add} **By Group** and then choose **Add Color Regression Lines** from the scatterplot's HyperView menu. Data Desk displays a plot showing the relationship between MPG and horsepower and the differences in that relationship for the different types of cars (Fig. 13-12).

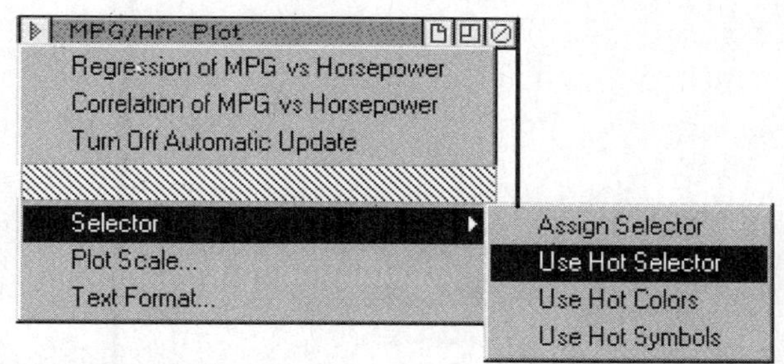

Now, select *Country* and choose {Plot} **Bar Charts**. Position the windows so that both plots are visible and choose **Turn on Automatic Update** and {Selector} **Use Hot Selector** from the scatterplot's global HyperView menu. Pick up the tool and select the bar labeled Japan in the bar chart. The scatterplot updates immediately, showing only cars manufactured in Japan. Now select the bar labeled USA. Note how the plot changes. Select each bar in turn to understand how the relationship between MPG and horsepower changes for cars from each country (Fig. 13-13). You might have a scatterplot with no points displayed — don't worry. It simply means that no cases have yet been selected.

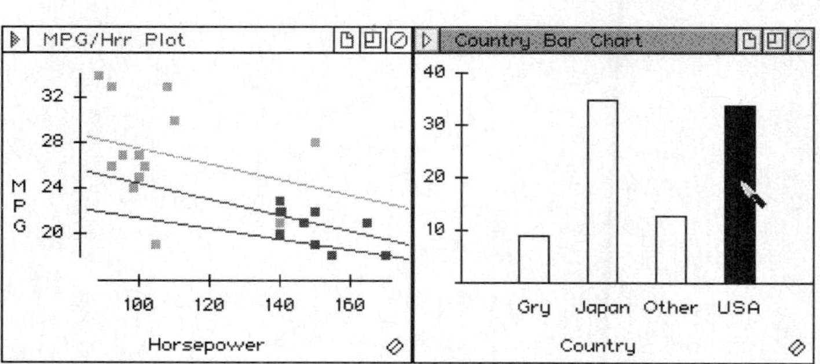

Figure 13-13. Select the bars in the barchart to change the subset of points displayed in the scatterplot.

The selection HotSet variable updates to reflect the current state when the mouse button is released; it doesn't change during brushing or slicing. It does change, however, as soon as the mouse is released after brushing or slicing.

13.9 *Homogeneity*

Data often aren't homogeneous. Some cases may behave differently than others. At times, there is an obvious distinction between groups that behave differently (for example, men may respond to a medical treatment differently than women; banks in the Companies data are distinct from other companies). At other times, we can only note the difference and hope to explain it later.

Traditional statistics methods are based upon the assumption that data are homogeneous. (Indeed, they often are based upon the stronger assumption that the true values all follow the same model and that the errors all follow the same distribution.) If you have nonhomogeneous data, no traditional statistics method is likely to work (or to be valid).

One excellent way to explore possible subgroups in your data to see if they appear to be homogeneous is to assign each a separate color or symbol and then use the corresponding HotSet variables to analyze them side by side. You can easily alter the assignment of individual cases to groups by changing their symbol or color; the analyses dependent upon the HotSet variables will update automatically.

For more on this and related subjects, see Draper, Hodges, Mallows, and Pregibon (1993).

13.10 Color HotSets

Color HotSet variables offer special power for dealing with groups. A color HotSet variable records the color of each case in its relation as an integer between 0 and 63; 0 is always white; and 1 records the color in the upper left square of the Colors palette (see Section 9.13 for more on Color).

If a Colors HotSet variable is placed in the **Group** button, any analysis or plot is computed for the cases having each color. Changing the color of any case reassigns it to a different group and the corresponding windows offer to update. For this purpose, white isn't considered a color. Making a point white (for example, by selecting it and clicking the white cell in the Colors palette) effectively removes it from all group calculations. You can study dynamically the influence of a point by changing its color and watching plots and analyses update.

HotSet variables can also serve as variables in plots and tables. For example, a colors HotSet variable can be a factor in a linear model. You can then reassign group membership or define new groups simply by changing the colors of points in a scatterplot. Explorations of this kind are not discussed in most statistics texts. They can be extraordinarily powerful for understanding the effects of individual cases and subsets of cases, or for studying the design of an experiment as well as its apparent results.

CHAPTER 14

Layouts

LAYOUT WINDOWS IN Data Desk are an effective place to record the progress of your analysis, to create presentations of your data, and to design figures that combine plots, tables, and text for use in other programs. You can drag in the icons of open windows to place a picture of a display or table in the layout, or drag in a closed icon to place a button in the layout that can locate the original window. You can add annotations and comments by using editable text boxes to produce interactive demonstrations for customers or colleagues.

14.1 *Layout Windows as Notebooks*

Data analyses rarely follow exactly the path that we expect when we begin. Sometimes we begin free of any expectations. It is wise to record in a notebook what you do and your thoughts and ideas during the analysis. Because Layout windows record both your thoughts and your results they provide a convenient place to record a complete analysis process. The objects in the Layout window provide links to the analyses themselves, so they comprise a powerful record that equips you to continue your analysis in any direction. And, of course, you can always print a layout window or copy it and paste it into a word processor or graphics program.

14.2 *Working with Layout Windows*

To make a new Layout window select {Data ▶ New} **Layout**. Data Desk creates a new Layout window and opens it. To place pictures of plots or tables in the Layout window drag the icon (or icon alias) of the plot or table window into the Layout window. You can also use the {Edit} **Copy Window** command to copy a picture of the window, click on the layout window, and choose {Edit} **Paste**. If you drag the icon of an unopened window into a layout window, Data Desk creates a button that links to that window — when you press the button the window opens. To reposition a picture in the layout window, click on it and drag it to where you want it. Plots in Layout windows are transparent, so you can overlay several plots.

When you add a picture to a Layout window, the date and time are automatically recorded as part of the title. Such documentation helps you to track the history of your analysis and provides a type of audit trail.

Layout windows can extend to more than one page. Specify the size of the page with the **Page Setup** command in the **File** menu. Gray lines indicate the page boundaries so you can position items within each page rather than across pages. Layout windows add new pages to the right and bottom as needed and remove blank pages automatically. When you delete the last item on a page that is the rightmost or bottommost page, that page is automatically deleted from the Layout window.

TIP

If you can't select text or pictures in a Layout window by clicking on them, the Layout window may be locked.

Choose **Unlock** from the window's global HyperView menu.

To control objects in a Layout window, simply click any object to select it. The object is surrounded by a box to indicate that it is selected. You can extend the selection in the usual manner, holding the Shift key and clicking additional objects. Dragging any selected object drags all the selected objects, preserving their relative positions. If you drag beyond the current page, Data Desk adds the necessary pages. Press the Delete key (or choose {Edit} **Clear**) to delete all selected objects.

Selected objects respond in the usual way to the cut, copy, and clear commands in the **Edit** menu.

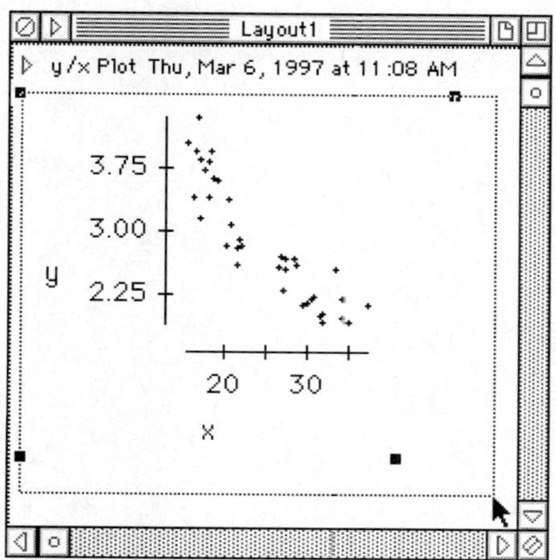

Figure 14-1. *Grab any of the squares and drag to resize the picture in the Layout window.*

You can resize and rescale pictures in a Layout window in much the same way as in common graphics programs. When selected, graphic objects show small squares at each corner of their enclosing rectangle. Grab any of these squares and drag it to resize the picture. Hold the Shift key down when you drag to restrict movement to either horizontal or vertical (whichever direction is used first). Hold down the Ctrl key, or an Option key on Mac, when you drag to preserve the relative vertical and horizontal scales. Ctrl-drags or Option-drags on Mac, are usually the correct rescalings for plots because. By preserving the relative scales of x and y, they don't distort the picture. Double-click on any of the four squares to rescale the picture to its original aspect ratio (relative size of vertical and horizontal dimensions).

Data Desk lets you preserve the relative positions of several windows on the desktop in a layout window. Select two or more icons or icon aliases and drag them into a Layout window with the same drag operation. The contents of their windows are added to the Layout window with the same relative positions as they had on the Data Desk desktop (but, of course, without the window frames, titles, close boxes, scroll bars, and other controls). You can drag a folder into a Layout window to add the contents of all open windows of icons in that folder to the layout window, preserving their relative positions.

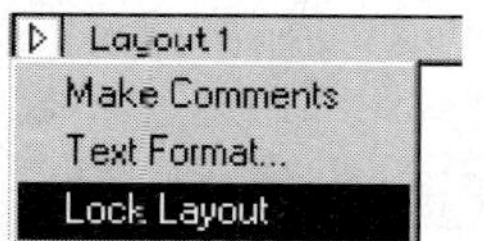

You can lock a Layout window so that its elements can't be accidentally repositioned or deleted. Locked windows are useful for creating demonstration files to be used by others. The **Lock** command is in the window's global HyperView menu. Items in locked Layout windows link to their original windows via single mouse clicks, unlike the double-click sequence for unlocked windows. Data Desk hides the HyperView menu triangle above each object in locked Layout windows. Locked Layout windows don't accept any new pictures or text boxes, and they don't allow objects to be moved or resized.

14.3 *Text in Layouts*

text box

Data Desk lets you type or paste text into Layout windows. When a Layout window is frontmost, pressing any letter, number, or symbol key on the keyboard or pasting text creates a *text box* within the Layout window. These text boxes can be repositioned like any other object in a Layout window. After you finish typing, click anywhere in the Layout window outside the area holding your text, then click back on the text. The text box is outlined by four black squares in its corners and can be dragged to a new position in the Layout window and resized by dragging any of its corners. (Unlike pictures, resized text areas simply reflow the text to fit the rectangle rather than distorting the look of the text. Data Desk won't allow the text rectangle to be made too small to hold the text.) To edit the text again or to modify its font, style, or size, double-click the picture of the text. You edit the text in the window as you would ordinarily edit text. Select the desired text and choose **Text Format...** from the Layout window's global HyperView menu to set font, size, style, and alignment. (Text format is not available on Windows in this version.)

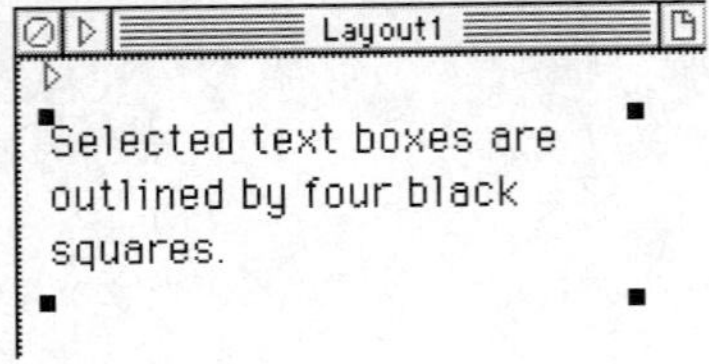

There are two ways to copy typed text from a Layout window, each producing a different result. If you double-click on a text object to edit it, you can then select parts of the text and cut or copy as you would when editing any text in any text editor. The text copied to the clipboard with this method can be copied into and edited in any program that accepts ASCII text. If you simply select the text box (typically with a single-click on it; the box shows the black border with black squares at the corners that marks it as selected), the **Cut** and **Copy** commands place a picture of the text in the clipboard rather than the text itself. When you paste this picture, the resulting object can be resized, but the text will resize as well and can't be edited in most programs. If you can't select the text in either way, the Layout window may be locked.

14.4 *Linked Figures in Layout Windows*

In addition to pasting pictures into Layout windows, you can drag the icon or icon alias of any Data Desk display into a Layout window. The result of the drag is a picture of the display in the Layout window that is linked to the original Data Desk display. A double-click (single-click for locked windows) on the picture opens the original Data Desk display.

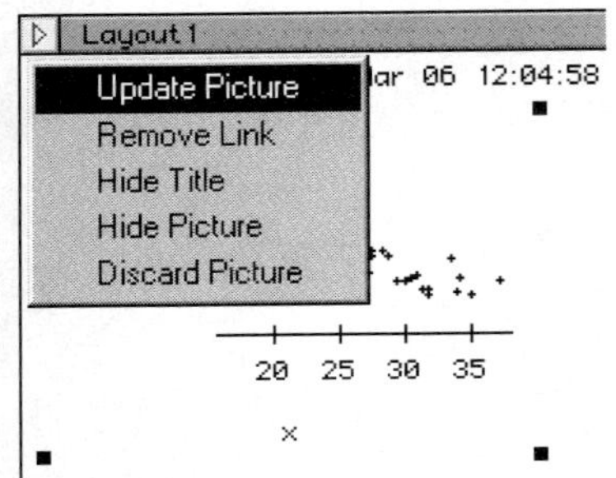

Figure 14-2. Each picture's HyperView menu holds commands specific to that picture. The ***Update*** *command offers to update the picture to reflect any changes in its original window.*

Because the picture of the display in the Layout window isn't an active window, it no longer highlights or changes color or symbol immediately when other displays are modified. However, any picture in a Layout window can recall its source window. The **Update Picture** command in the picture's HyperView menu offers to update the picture to reflect any changes in its original window (Fig. 14-2). Of course, you may not want to update the picture if the Layout window holds details of the history of your analysis. Instead, you might drag the icon of the window into another part of the Layout window to record its current state. If you choose to update the windows picture in the Layout window, the date/time stamp will update as well.

To unlink a picture from its window, select the picture and choose **Remove Link** from its HyperView menu. Alternatively, hold down the Ctrl key (Option key on Mac) when you drag the window's icon into the Layout window. The picture in the Layout window will look the same as before, but it won't be linked to its source and it won't have an automatic title, date, and time. Beware that the **Remove Link** command is *not* reversible. A window that is linked to a Layout window cannot be discarded (unless you discard the Layout window as well or unlink the window's picture in the Layout window from the window itself), so you may want to drag with the Ctrl key pressed (Option key for Mac) if you plan to discard the original icon.

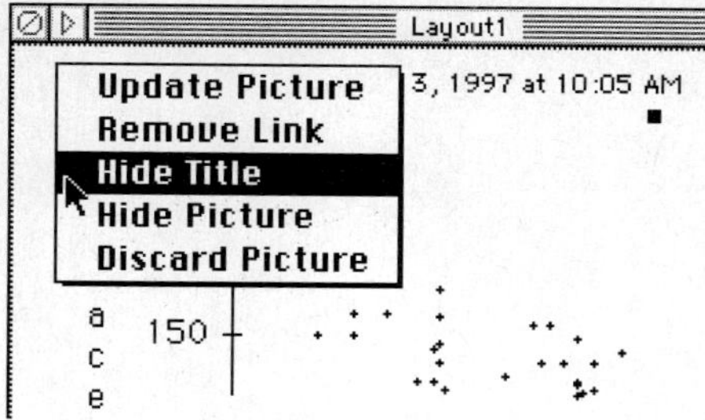

Each picture's HyperView menu contains commands to affect the appearance of the object. **Hide Title** removes the object's title from the Layout window and changes the command to **Show Title.** The **Show Title** command restores the title. **Hide Picture** removes the object from the Layout window and changes the command to **Show Picture**. The **Show Picture** command redisplays the object on the screen.

When you lock a Layout window, each of the pictures behaves like an ordinary button. A simple mouse click on a picture locates the original window. (A simple click can't work that way in unlocked Layout windows because you must be free to drag pictures around to any location and to resize them. Once the Layout window is locked, these features are turned off.) Choose **Discard Picture** from the object's HyperView menu to replace the picture with a standard button containing the name of the window. The picture of the original display is deleted, but the button is still linked to that original display.

Although most objects inside Layout windows have links to original displays, it is also possible to link text objects in a Layout window to other text objects or pictures within the same Layout window. Click on any text box in the Layout window and then Ctrl-click (Option-click on Mac) on another item. The second item will now behave like a button linked to the initially selected text box. Click the button to scroll automatically the Layout window to the second object. To unlink items linked in this way, select the text box and then Ctrl-click (Option-click on Mac) on the same text box (linking it to itself).

CHAPTER 15

Presentations

Data Desk's *Slide Show* facility presents analyses or simply data themselves so that you can guide others through a sequence of views of the data in a simple, orderly way. A Data Desk *Slide* is simply a collection of Data Desk windows that have been positioned on the desktop where you want them to be seen. Each of these windows is a fully functioning Data Desk window; linking, movement, updating, and all HyperView menus continue to work in windows that have been placed in slides. However, these windows no longer have individual icons; they have been merged into the slide's icon. (Thus they have no Close box or Zoom box in their title bars; windows in slides have fixed size and Open and Close as part of the collection of windows in the slide.)

Slides can be designed to combine plots and analyses with notes, pictures, Corkboards, ScratchPads, and layouts that serve to explain what the plots and analyses show, or with buttons that offer alternative views or paths through the analysis. In this way, presentations made with Slide Shows can be interactive with the path determined by the viewer.

15.1 *Slide Basics*

Every datafile can have only a single slide show. The slide show is held in a special *Slide Show* folder, in the File cabinet (ordinarily at the top right of the desktop).

The slide show is controlled by the Slide Show palette. To open the Slide Show palette, choose {Special} **Slide Show…**. The buttons along the top of the slide show palette navigate the viewer through the slide show. The first, |◁, displays the first slide; ▷ moves to the next slide; ◁ moves to the preceding slide; and ▷| shows the final slide. The second panel of the palette indicates the status of the slide show. If no slide show has been created for this dataset, it reads "No Slide Show". If one has already been created, it may read "None of N" (where N is the number of slides already created, or it may read "k of N" if the *k*th slide is currently being displayed.

Each Slide has an icon in the *Slide Show* folder. A slide icon opens into a window that names the windows in that slide.

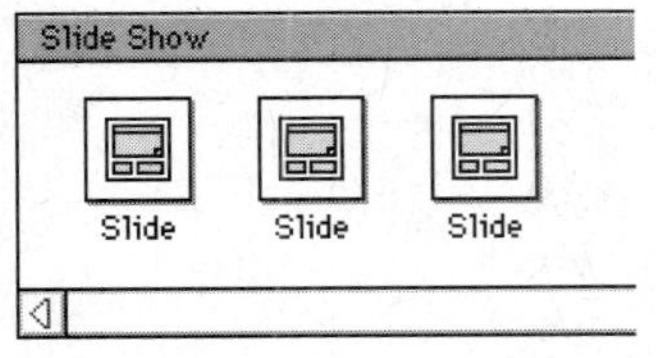

You can add a window to the slide by dragging its icon or icon alias into the slide's window or icon.

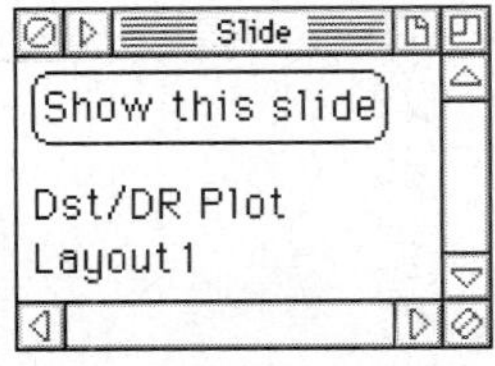

The sequence of slide icons in the *Slide Show* folder determines the order of slides in the slide show. The leftmost slide is the first one; the rightmost slide, the last. To reorder the slides, just drag their icons into the order you want. The active slide's icon is shaded. Dragging a slide's icon out of the *Slide Show* folder removes it from the slide show. You can discard a slide by dragging its icon to the Trash — but remember that the slide's icon holds all the windows in that slide. Discarding the slide also discards all those windows. To remove a window from a slide, open the slide (for example by opening the slide's icon and pressing the **Show this slide button**) and drag the icon alias of the window you want to remove into any icon window or onto the Data Desk desktop. (The window's title bar will change to show a close box and zoom box. If the window still lacks these features, it hasn't been removed from the slide.)

Slide icons are named Slide when they are first made. Feel free to rename them as you would any Data Desk icon.

15.2 *Creating and Editing the Slide Show*

To create or edit the slide show, you must have the Slide Show palette open on the Data Desk desktop. The {Special} **Slide Show...** command opens the palette. Click on the lower panel of the palette and choose **New Slide** from the pop-up menu there (Fig. 15-4). Data Desk will do the following things:

***Figure 15-1.** To create a slide show, choose **New Slide** from the pop-up menu.*

- Place a new slide icon in the *Slide Show* folder to the right of any slides already there
- Close any slide that may be open
- Prepare to accept windows into the new slide

Now open or create the windows that you want to have as part of this slide. Position them on the desktop as you want them to appear in the slide. Note that not all computer displays are the same size. Even if you have a large monitor, it is wise to restrict slides to the 640 by 480 pixel size that is most common if you expect your slides to be viewed by others. When the windows are properly positioned, add each of them to the slide in any of the following ways.

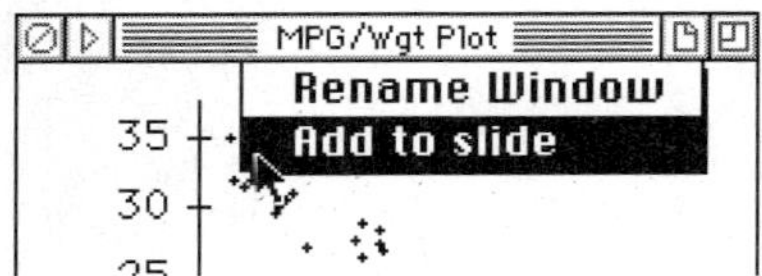

***Figure 15-2.** To add the window to a slide, right mouse click, or command-click on Mac, on the window's title bar and choose **Add to Slide**.*

- Click on the window to make it frontmost and press Ctrl-**U**, ⌘-**U** on Mac.
- Click the right mouse button on the window's title bar (⌘-click on Mac) (Fig. 15-2). If a slide is active, the menu that pops up will include an **Add to Slide** command. (Once the window has been added to the slide, this command changes to **Remove from Slide**.) This method is straightforward but tedious if many windows are involved.
- Open the *Slide Show* folder and drag the icon alias of the window into the slide's icon; drop it there when the icon acknowledges the drag. (The Slide Show palette's pop-up menu has a **Locate Slide Icon** command that conveniently finds and shows the active slide's icon (Fig. 15-3).)
- Open the slide's icon and drag the icon alias of the window into the slide's window. If you are adding many windows at once, it can be more convenient to select all their icon aliases (Shift-click extends the selection) and drag them to the slide's icon or window. If the windows are positioned appropriately, you can click on the Data Desk desktop and drag a selection rectangle around the windows you want to select. However, you must be careful not to touch any window that you do *not* want selected.

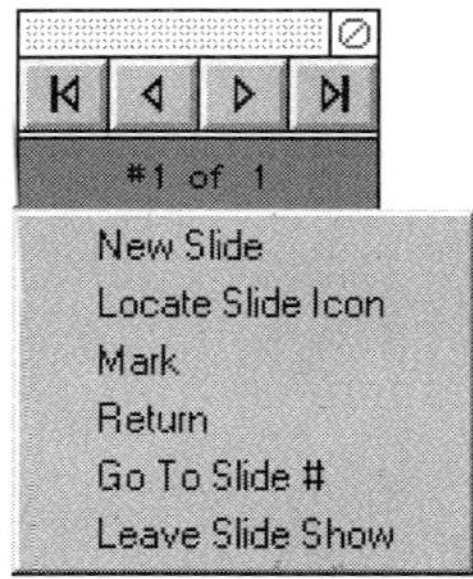

***Figure 15-3.** Slide Show commands.*

Remember that windows added to a slide no longer have their own icons; they are part of the slide and open and close only with the slide. To remove windows from a slide, open the slide, select the icon aliases

TIP

Ctrl 1: Display the first slide.
Ctrl 2: Display previous slide.
Ctrl 3: Display next slide.
Ctrl 4: Display the last slide.

of the windows and drag them anywhere else that accepts icons, such as an icon window, a folder, or the Data Desk desktop. Alternatively, ⌘-click on Mac, or right mouse button click on Windows, and choose **Remove from Slide**.

To add another slide to the slide show, select **New Slide** from the Slide Show palette's pop-up menu. The current slide will close, but any other open windows that aren't part of a slide will remain open.

The other commands in the slide show pop-up menu help you navigate through a slide show. **Mark** (⌘6 on Mac, Ctrl 6 on Windows) places a bookmark at the current slide and indicates it by displaying an *m* next to the slide number in the palette. When a slide is marked, the **Return** (⌘5 on Mac, Ctrl 5 on Windows) command will open that slide immediately. Choosing **Return** again returns to the slide that was open when **Return** was first selected, toggling between the two slides. **Go To Slide #** asks for a slide number and opens it directly. You can assign a similar function to a button (see Section 4.10); simply drag a slide's icon into the button. Press the button to open that slide. Because buttons can themselves be part of a slide, you can easily set up paths that allow the viewer to navigate an individual path through a slide show.

Leave Slide Show closes the current slide. It doesn't close the Slide Show palette; click its close box to do so.

CHAPTER 16

Tables

SOME DATA IDENTIFY groups or categories rather than reporting values. It isn't appropriate to perform arithmetic on category identifiers (even if they are numerals), so group data must be analyzed differently than numeric data. An average family income is a reasonable concept when you know incomes in dollars, but you can't average "lower middle class", "middle class", "upper middle class", and "rich".

16.1 *Frequency Counts and Percentages*

frequency table

The natural thing to do with category data is to count them. A *frequency table* reports how many cases fall into each category. To make a frequency table in Data Desk, select the category variable and choose **Frequency Breakdowns** from the **Calc** menu.

For example, a frequency table of companies by market sector in the Companies data appears in Fig. 16-1.

Frequency breakdown of **sector**
No Selector

Total Cases	79
Number of Categories	9

Group	Count
Communication	2
Energy	15
Finance	17
HiTech	8
Manufacturing	10
Medical	4
Other	7
Retail	10
Transportation	6

Figure 16-1. *Frequency table by sector for the Companies data. The default table displays counts and the number of categories.*

Frequency tables are a good way to see:

- Patterns or trends across categories
- Individual categories that are extraordinarily large or small
- The relative allocation of cases to different categories.

Frequency tables can provide more information than counts and percents. The Frequency Options dialog offers a variety of alternatives. You can open this dialog from either the {Calc} **Calculation Options** submenu or the Frequency Table's global HyperView menu. Changes made to this dialog only cause any active (frontmost) frequency table to update immediately. If a Frequency Table isn't the frontmost window, changes made to this dialog are saved as the global defaults and only affect future frequency tables. If you make changes to a dialog with a Frequency Table active and want the new selections to be the global defaults for future tables, select the **Set Defaults** button at the bottom of the dialog (Fig. 16-2).

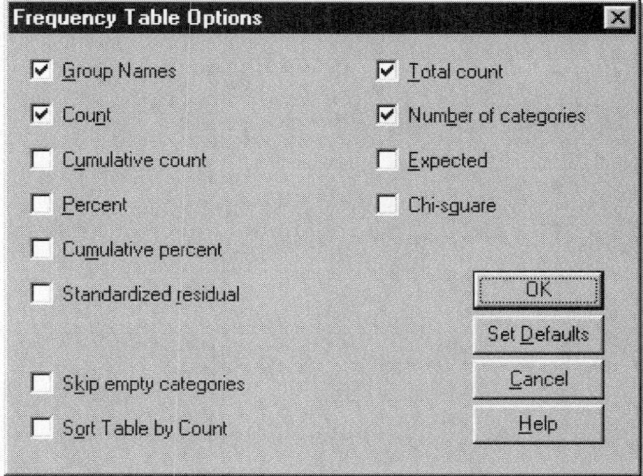

Figure 16-2. *The Frequency Table Options dialog offers a variety of choices for frequency tables.*

To change the output displayed in Frequency Table, select the box next to each desired option. To remove an option, select the box again.

Group Names puts the category names in the first column of the table.

Count reports the number of cases for each category.

Cumulative count reports the number of cases for each category, plus the counts from the categories listed above that category.

Percent reports the percentage of the total sample falling in each category.

Cumulative percent reports the percentage of the total sample falling in each category plus the categories listed above that category.

Standardized residual reports the value describing the difference between the observed count and the expected count for each category (see Appendix 16A).

Total count displays the total number of cases.

Number of categories displays the number of categories.

Expected displays the expected value for each cell.

Chi-square displays the chi-square statistic and its prob value (see Section 16.5).

Skip empty categories omits from the table any categories having no cases. Categories can be empty because cases have been made missing or because a selector variable has omitted them (see Chapter 13).

Sort Table by Count orders the table so that categories with the largest counts appear at the top. (The default order is alphabetical by category name.)

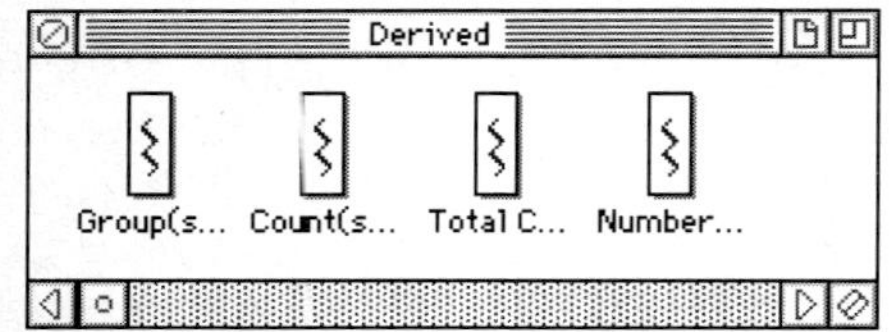

The **Generate Hot Variables** command in the global HyperView menu creates HotResult variables and places them in the *Derived* folder in the File Cabinet. The first variable holds the row labels of the table. The other HotResult variables hold the values for each column in the table. The HyperView menu commands attached to the **Number of Categories, Expected** and **Chi-Square** rows generate HotResult variables that hold the values for each of those headings. Once you have created them, you can use these variables in any plot or table, just like regular variables. HotResult variables update automatically in response to changes in the table. If the data underlying the table change, the values in the HotResult variables update, as do any plots or tables built with these variables.

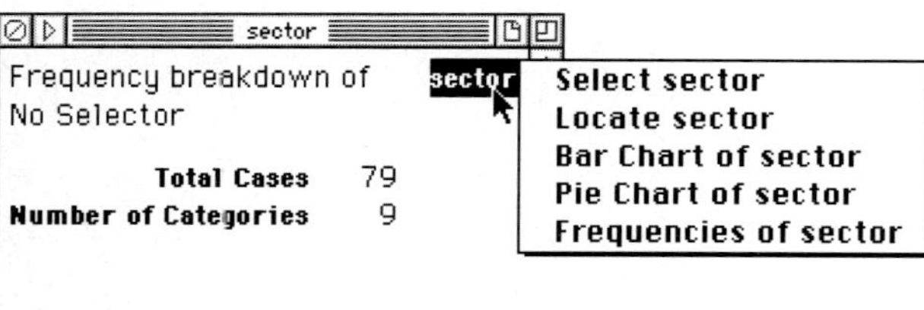

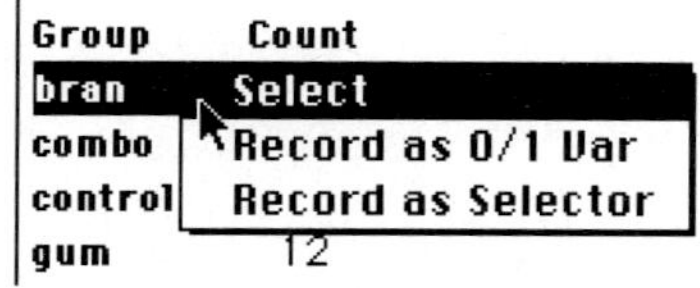

Pie charts and bar charts show graphically much of the same information as frequency tables. You can access these plots from the HyperView menu attached to the variable name at the top of the table. Frequency tables link with other Data Desk results. The HyperView menus connected to the category labels of a row of a frequency table offer to select all the cases falling into that category. You can extend your selection to more than one category by holding down the shift key and choosing **Select** from the HyperView menu of the category you want to add to

> **REMEMBER**
>
> Category variables treat values that are empty or contain the symbol • as missing.

the selection. The HyperView menu attached to the **Total Cases** row allows you to select all of the cases displayed in the table.

Data Desk uses the text of variables to determine categories. Cases whose values are empty or contain the • symbol (typed as Alt–8 on Windows and Option–8 on Mac) are considered to be missing and are not selected.

16.2 *Two Factors*

factors

level

cell

Data that can be categorized in two ways are often arrayed in a two-way table. A typical table has two *factors,* one with categories labeling the rows of the table and another with categories labeling the columns. A category within a factor is called a *level* of the factor. Every combination of a row level and a column level specifies a *cell* of the table (Fig. 16-3).

Rows are levels of **Bloat**
Columns are levels of **Cracker**
No Selector

		bran	**combo**	**control**	**gum**
The factor levels are named at the top and side of the table.	**high**	C	2	0	5
	low	4			2
	med	1			3
	none	7	2	6	2

The intersection of each row and column is a cell in the table.

table contents:
Count

Figure 16-3. *A two-way contingency table shows the counts of cases falling in each combination of levels on each of two factors.*

Tables are particularly good at showing:

- Patterns or trends across rows (where the row level stays the same while the column level changes) and down columns (where the column level stays the same while the row level changes)
- Individual cells that are extraordinarily large or small
- Indications of whether the factors are statistically independent or whether they are related to each other

16.3 *Contingency Tables*

Contingency tables are tables of counts used primarily to investigate the dependence (hence the term "contingency") of two categorical factors on each other. Each case in the data falls in one of the levels on each of the two factors. Each cell of the table represents a combination of a level on the row factor and a level on the column factor, so each case falls in one cell. Contingency tables count the number of cases falling in each cell and report the counts and related statistics.

As in frequency tables, the variables used to construct contingency tables are categorical. Thus, rather than holding measurements or amounts, each case identifies a category. Categories may be numeric but are identified with text labels, so numeric labels are treated as category names made up of numerals. Thus a variable that names an individual's religion is categorical. A variable reporting the number of cylinders in a car engine might also be considered categorical because there are relatively few possible values.

To make a contingency table, select two categorical variables identifying the two factors, and choose {Calc} **Contingency Tables**. You can change the category variables in the table by dragging a new category variable icon on top of the name of the variable you want to replace. These names are displayed at the top of the table and will highlight when touched by the cursor during the drag. To replace both factors, select two new category variables and drag them both into the center of the table. If your data are already tabulated, you need to use the **Replicate Y by X** command from the **Manip** menu (see Section 12.3).

Warn At [50] Categories

Figure 16-4. You can change the trigger point for the warning in the Preferences file.

Data Desk tries to protect you from choosing variables that don't make sense for contingency tables. If you ask for a contingency table (or a frequency table, bar chart, or pie chart), and one or both of the variables holds more than 50 categories, Data Desk will post a warning, giving you the option to proceed or to cancel. The trigger point for this message can be changed in the Preferences file (Fig. 16-4). For example, if you are working with data on each of the 50 states in the United States, you may want to set the trigger point at 51. Choose {Edit} **Preferences...** and type a value in the box labeled "Warn at ___ Categories".

16.4 *Table Contents*

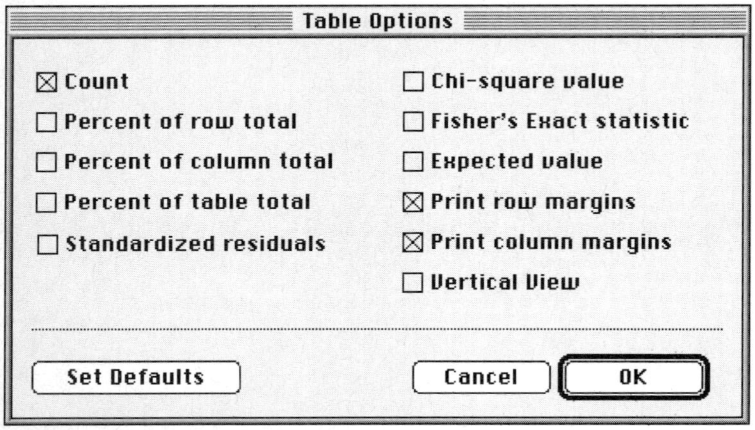

Table Options

- ☒ Count
- ☐ Percent of row total
- ☐ Percent of column total
- ☐ Percent of table total
- ☐ Standardized residuals
- ☐ Chi-square value
- ☐ Fisher's Exact statistic
- ☐ Expected value
- ☒ Print row margins
- ☒ Print column margins
- ☐ Vertical View

[Set Defaults] [Cancel] [OK]

Figure 16-5. Contingency table options.

Data Desk can place a variety of information in each cell of a contingency table. The Table Options dialog, found in the table's global HyperView menu or the {Calc} **Calculation Options** submenu, offers a choice of items (Fig. 16-5). This table works the same as the Frequency Table Options dialog (see Section 16.1).

One way to describe alternatives for filling contingency tables is by example. The Fiber dataset is from a study in which subjects were fed one of four types of cracker before meals. Bran fiber, gum fiber, and a combination of the two, along with a control cracker containing no fiber, were used. One of the observed effects was occasional gastric upset in the form of bloating. The contingency table of *Cracker* versus *Bloat* is one way to examine this effect.

Rows are levels of **Bloat**
Columns are levels of **Cracker**
No Selector

	bran	combo	control	gum	total
high	0	2	0	5	7
low	4	5	4	2	15
med	1	3	2	3	9
none	7	2	6	2	17
total	12	12	12	12	48

table contents:
Count

Figure 16-6. A contingency table of Cracker *versus* Bloat *for the Fiber data.*

The *Count* is the number of cases falling into each cell of the table. Counts sometimes show cells with unusually many or unusually few cases, or patterns and trends. The counts of *Fiber* versus *Bloat* are shown in Fig. 16-6.

The category names appear around the edges of the table in boldface to label the rows and columns. This feature is one good reason for using category identifiers that name the category rather than numeric codes. *Print row margins* and *Print column margins* report row and column totals, on the right and bottom of the table. Note that there are 12 datapoints for each cracker, by design — each of the 12 subjects was fed each of the crackers in the course of the study. Also note the pattern in the counts. For example, neither the control nor the bran crackers seem to have caused high levels of discomfort.

Rows are levels of	Bloat			
Columns are levels of	Cracker			
No Selector				

	bran	combo	control	gum	total
high	0	16.7	0	41.7	14.6
low	33.3	41.7	33.3	16.7	31.2
med	8.33	25	16.7	25	18.8
none	58.3	16.7	50	16.7	35.4
total	100	100	100	100	100

table contents:
Percent of Column Total

Figure 16-7. A column percent contingency table for the Fiber data. The percentages in each column sum to 100%.

The counts can also be converted to percents. *Percent of column total* computes, for each column, the percent of its values in each cell in that column. As a result, the percents sum to 100% down each column. A column percent table for the Fiber data is shown in Fig. 16-7.

Half (50%) the subjects who were fed the control cracker reported no bloating, but almost 42% of the subjects fed gum fiber reported a high level of bloating. The column totals show that about 35% of the time subjects reported no bloating and about 14.5% of the time they reported high levels of bloating.

Percent of row total computes the corresponding percents within each row. Here the percents sum to 100% across each row.

Rows are levels of	Bloat			
Columns are levels of	Cracker			
No Selector				

	bran	combo	control	gum	total
high	0	28.6	0	71.4	100
low	26.7	33.3	26.7	13.3	100
med	11.1	33.3	22.2	33.3	100
none	41.2	11.8	35.3	11.8	100
total	25	25	25	25	100

table contents:
Percent of Row Total

Figure 16-8. A row percent table for the Fiber data. The percentages in each row sum to 100%.

Figure 16-8 shows, for example, that of all the instances of high levels of bloating, 71% occurred when subjects were eating gum crackers. This result was of particular interest to the researchers who were investigating the possible use of the gum fiber as a healthful appetite suppressant but concluded that the bloating would discourage people.

Rows are levels of	Bloat			
Columns are levels of	Cracker			
No Selector				

	bran	combo	control	gum	total
high	0	4.17	0	10.4	14.6
low	8.33	10.4	8.33	4.17	31.2
med	2.08	6.25	4.17	6.25	18.8
none	14.6	4.17	12.5	4.17	35.4
total	25	25	25	25	100

table contents:
Percent of Table Total

Figure 16-9. A table percent contingency table for the Fiber data. The percentages over all cells sum to 100%.

Percent of table total reports, for each cell, the percent of the total count for the table falling in that cell. Now the percents in all the cells of the table (excluding the row and column totals) sum to 100% (Fig. 16-9).

Vertical View places the category labels for both variables in two columns and creates a column for each value requested in the Table Options dialog. It is just a different way to view the same data. The values do not change.

Standardized residuals, the chi-square statistic, Fisher's Exact statistic and *expected values* are used to test independence. We describe them in the next section.

16.5 *Independence: Chi-Square and Fisher's Exact Tests*

It is possible to construct a hypothesis test to investigate whether the two factors in a contingency table are related or independent. In Chapter 18 we discuss hypothesis testing in detail; in this section we introduce the Chi-square and Fisher's Exact tests and in Appendix 16A present the underlying formulas. Use the Table Options dialog to display the statistics discussed in this section.

chi-square test

The null hypothesis associated with the *chi-square* (χ^2) *test* for independence states that the two factors are statistically independent. In other words, the probability that a randomly selected case falls in a specified cell depends only upon the probability that the case falls in the specified column and the probability that it falls in the specified row.

For the Fiber data, we hypothesize that bloating is independent of the type of fiber eaten. That is, if we knew what fiber a subject ate we would have no additional information about the likelihood of bloating. Similarly, if we knew the level of bloating reported by the subject, we would have no additional information about the kind of fiber eaten.

expected values

For each cell in the table, we calculate the number of cases we expect there to be were the null hypothesis true. These are called the *expected values.* If the null hypothesis *is* true, then the observed cell counts will tend to approximate the expected cell counts. If the null hypothesis is false, then the observed cell counts will tend to differ from the expected cell counts in some way.

standardized residual

For each cell, we calculate a *standardized residual* to describe the extent to which the observed count differs from the expected count. Data Desk can display the standardized residuals, but you need not do so to compute χ^2. The χ^2 value is the sum of the squared standardized residuals across all the cells in the table. If the value of χ^2 is relatively large, we reject the null hypothesis of independence. Otherwise, we fail to reject the null hypothesis. The probability value (listed below the χ^2 value) reports the probability that we would observe a χ^2 value at least as large as the one we have observed if the null hypothesis were true.

degrees of freedom

Probability values of χ^2 depend upon the *degrees of freedom.* A χ^2 statistic associated with a contingency table of r rows and c columns has $(r - 1) \times (c - 1)$ degrees of freedom. If the probability value is relatively small, we can reject the null hypothesis.

For example, Fig. 16-10 shows the counts, expected values, and standardized residuals for the Fiber data. By examining the standardized residuals, we can pick out the cells where the violation of the null hypothesis is greatest.

Some authors recommend that the chi-square statistic be computed only for tables in which the expected value of each cell is at least 5. Data Desk, however, does not enforce this restriction.

alternative hypothesis

The *alternative hypothesis* for the chi-square test is that the two factors are *not* independent. There are many ways in which a lack of independence could appear. There might be a trend across rows or down columns, one row or column could be unusual, or even a single cell could make the test significant. It is therefore a good idea to examine the standardized

Rows are levels of **Bloat**
Columns are levels of **Cracker**
No Selector

	bran	**combo**	**control**	**gum**	**total**
high	0	2	0	5	7
	1.75000	1.75000	1.75000	1.75000	7
	-1.32288	0.188982	-1.32288	2.45677	0
low	4	5	4	2	15
	3.75000	3.75000	3.75000	3.75000	15
	0.129099	0.645497	0.129099	-0.903696	0
med	1	3	2	3	9
	2.25000	2.25000	2.25000	2.25000	9
	-0.833333	0.500000	-0.166667	0.500000	0
none	7	2	6	2	17
	4.25000	4.25000	4.25000	4.25000	17
	1.33395	-1.09141	0.848875	-1.09141	0
total	12	12	12	12	48
	12	12	12	12	48
	0	0	0	0	0

table contents:
Count
Expected Values
Standardized Residuals

Chi-square = 16.94 with 9 df
p = 0.0496

Figure 16-10. *Counts and chi-square components for the Fiber data.*

residuals for hints about how the data might violate the null hypothesis — whether a few cells are making the value of χ^2 large, or whether the entire table shows a lack of independence between the factors.

Fisher's exact test

Data Desk offers to computes *Fisher's Exact test* for any 2X2 contingency table. Fisher's exact test considers all possible 2X2 tables with the same marginal frequencies. From among these tables, it classifies tables according to the strength of the association between the categorizations. The exact test computes the probability of obtaining a table of categorizations with the same marginal frequencies for which the association would be as strong or stronger than the association in the observed table. This value lies between 0 and 1, where a value of 1 indicates the virtual absence of association and a value of 0 indicates the strongest possible association.

16.6 *HyperView Menus in Tables*

The HyperView menus connected to each cell of a table offer to select the cases corresponding to that cell. The selection highlights cases in all windows that display data from the same relations. Alternatively, you can record the selection as a 0/1 indicator variable or record it and place it in the **Selector** button immediately. To extend the selection to cases in more than one cell in the contingency table, press the Shift key and choose **Select** from the HyperView menu of the cell to be added (see Figure 16-11).

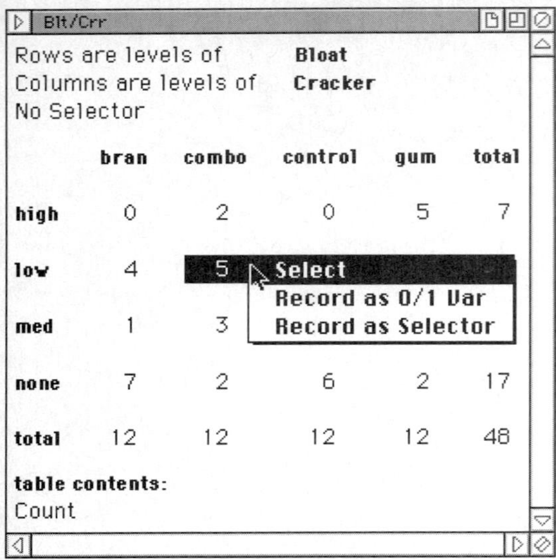

Figure 16-11. *The HyperView menu of a cell of a table offers to select the cases counted in that cell.*

The HyperView menus connected to each row or column title offer to select the cases corresponding to the named levels of their respective factors.

By recording a selection as the selector and then making a new table of other factors, you can generate any of the parts of a three- or four-way contingency table. Multiway contingency tables categorize data on more than two factors. They can be visualized as having a two-way contingency table within each cell of another one- or two-way table. Appendix 16B shows how the **Group** button can be used to make a three-way contingency table.

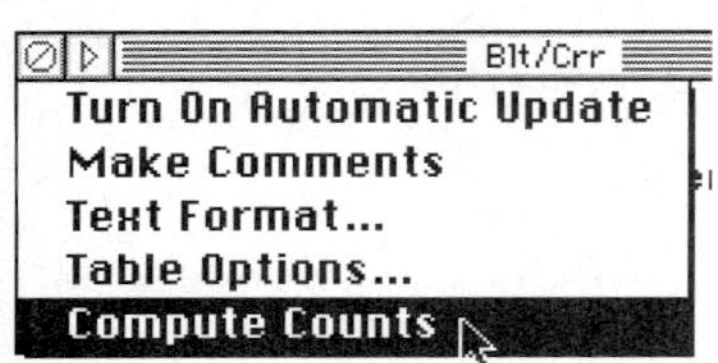

The **Compute Counts** command in the global HyperView menu creates four HotResult variables. It places in the *Results* folder a variable holding the column labels of the table, repeated once for each row, and another variable holding the row labels of the table, repeated once for each column. Together, these two variables name each cell of the table. The third variable placed in the *Results* folder holds the counts for each cell of the table, as named by the first two variables together. Because these are HotResult variables, they update automatically if the table or any of the data underlying the table is changed. The ability to update in this manner makes these HotResults powerful tools for displaying information about the table.

Compute Counts places a fourth HotResult variable in the original data relation. This HotResult variable holds a *Cross* function of the two variables making up the table. (See Appendix 11B for a discussion of the *Cross* function.)

16.7 *Copying and Printing Tables*

The **Copy Window** command, which replaces the **Copy** command in the **Edit** menu when an output window is frontmost, offers a choice of copying the contents of the frontmost window as a picture (as it appears on the screen) or as text (Fig. 16-12).

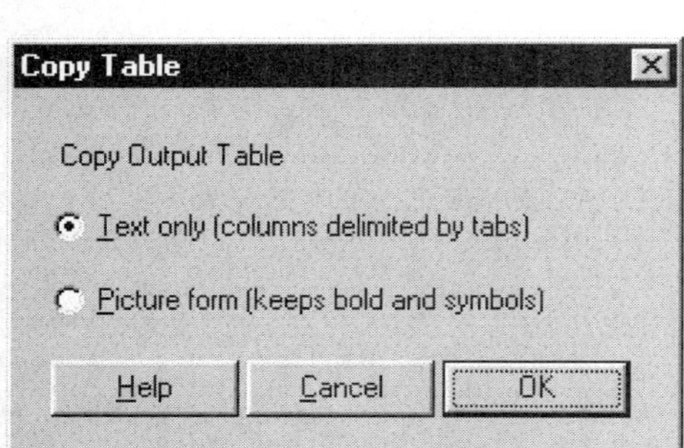

Figure 16-12. *The Copy Table dialog offers a choice of tab-delimited text and picture format.*

If you copy in Picture form, the Clipboard will hold an image of the table. If you copy in Text form, the text of the window is copied. The columns of the table are separated by tab characters, so you need only set tab stops in a word processor to make the table look as you would like.

When a table is the frontmost window, the {File} **Print...** command prints a copy of the table. The table is printed using an intermediate form, so it appears at the full precision of the printer.

APPENDIX 16A *Equations*

If we denote the probability that a randomly selected case is in the *i*th row by π_i, the probability that it is in the *j*th column by π_j and the probability that it is both in the *i*th row and the *j*th column by π_{ij}, the null hypothesis of statistical independence is

$$H0: \pi_{ij} = \pi_i \pi_j$$

This hypothesis is the one usually tested with the chi-square (χ^2) test of independence. The χ^2 statistic is computed as

$$\chi^2 = \sum_{i,j} \frac{(O_{ij} - E_{ij})^2}{E_{ij}}$$

where O_{ij} is the observed count for the cell in the *i*th row and *j*th column, and E_{ij} is the expected count for that cell, found as

$$E_{ij} = \frac{O_i O_j}{n}$$

The *expected values* are the E_{ij} terms in the formula for χ^2. Comparing them with the observed counts gives some idea of the nature of the differences.

The *standardized residuals* are the individual contributions to the χ^2 statistic. The *i, j* cell contains

$$\frac{(O_{ij} - E_{ij})}{\sqrt{E_{ij}}}$$

The sum of the squared standardized residuals across all cells of the table is equal to χ^2, so each standardized residual reports the contribution to that sum due to its cell.

The degrees of freedom is (#*rows* – 1) x (#*cols* – 1), which depends upon the table size rather than on the number of cases. However, the value of χ^2 is likely to increase as the sample size increases if the null hypothesis isn't strictly true. In most situations the null hypothesis, at best, can be only approximately true, so the χ^2 test is likely to reject the null hypothesis for very large samples. It is always a good idea to examine the standardized residuals to get some idea of what is really going on in the data. If you see no consistent patterns or significantly deviant cells and have a large sample size, you should be suspicious of marginally significant χ^2 values.

APPENDIX 16B *Multiway Tables*

The basic Contingency Tables command makes a two-way table, but you can construct tables with three or even more category variables by using the **Group** button. For example, a three-way table is often thought of as simply a collection of two-way tables, one for each level of a third variable.

To make a three-way table, select one of the category variables and choose {Special ▶ Group} **Assign**. Then select the other two variables and choose the **Contingency Tables** command as before. Data Desk will make a separate table for each level of the group variable. The resulting tables together form a three-way table.

If there is no particular reason to favor one variable over the others, you will have a better chance to see more of the results by making the variable with the fewest number of categories the group variable. This will produce fewer windows, so you can see more of them together on the screen.

One advantage of this kind of three-way table is that you can rearrange the component tables in any order to make it easier to look for patterns across tables. A disadvantage is that the χ^2 statistic is computed for each two-way table and isn't adjusted for a three-way table computation.

You can also use HotSet selector variables to create dynamic multiway tables. (See Section 13.6 for more information on HotSet selector variables.) Select one of the categorical variables and choose **Frequency Tables** from the **Calc** menu. Then select the other two categorical variables and choose **Contingency Tables** from the **Calc** menu. Select the No Selector row in the contingency table and choose **HotSet Selector.** From the contingency table's global HyperView menu, choose **Turn On Automatic Update.** Select a category in the frequency table and choose **Select** from the HyperView menu. Data Desk updates the contingency table, displaying only the information for the cases selected in the frequency table.

EXERCISES

1. Contingency tables are tables of _______________ used primarily to investigate the dependence of two categorical factors on each other. Each _______________ of the table represents a combination of a category on the row factor and a category on the column factor, so each case falls in one cell. Contingency tables count the number of _______________ falling in each cell and report the counts and related statistics.

2. The variables used to construct contingency tables must be ______________________. They may be numeric, but they are also often identified with text labels.

3. The margins of a contingency table report row and column _______________.

4. If you are concerned with investigating the dependence between two categorical variables, the natural null hypothesis to test is the hypothesis that they are statistically _____________________. That is, the probability that a specified case falls in a particular cell depends *only* upon _____________________________ and _____________________________________. Mathematically, this can be written:

P(case falls in row i *and* column j) = P (_________) × P (__________)

5. The null hypothesis of independence is tested with the ____________________ statistic. Write the algebraic definition of this statistic, defining your notation. (*Hint:* refer to Appendix 16A.)

6. You reject the null hypothesis of independence when the value of the statistic is relatively _______________. Probability values of the statistic depend upon ______________________________.

7. If a contingency table has r rows and c columns, the associated chi-square statistic has _________________ degrees of freedom. Write the algebraic expression for degrees of freedom.

8. In the calculation of the chi-square statistic, the *observed* counts are compared to the counts you would *expect* if the null hypothesis of independence were true. If the observed counts and expected counts generally differ, the factors are likely dependent. For a cell that falls in row i and column j, write its expected count if the null hypothesis is true. Define your notation.

9. If the null hypothesis of independence is rejected, does the chi-square statistic tell you how the two factors are related? Explain.

10. Although Data Desk doesn't enforce this restriction, it is recommended that the chi-square statistic be computed only when the expected count in each cell is at least ________.

11. Write the algebraic expression for a cell's standardized residual. Define your notation.

12. The standardized residuals are the individual contributions to the chi-square statistic. For a particular table, the ______________________________ of the standardized residuals across all cells of the table is equal to the χ^2 value.

13. We can simulate a contingency table for which the categorical variables are statistically independent in the following way. Use the **Generate Random Numbers...** command to construct two random variables drawn from a binomial distribution. Generate one binomial variable of 100 cases with 3 Trials/Experiment and a success probability of .6. Generate a second binomial variable of 100 cases with 2 Trials/Experiment and a success probability of .5.

(a) Set Table Options for count, expected count, standardized residual, and χ^2 and make a contingency table of the two generated variables. Does the χ^2 test indicate significant lack of independence? Should it? Explain.

(b) Write the calculation of the degrees of freedom. Square each of the standardized residuals and verify that the sum of squares equals the χ^2 value.

CHAPTER 17

Random Numbers and Simulation

THUS FAR WE HAVE considered ways to depict and explore data. In this chapter and those that follow we discuss ways to draw firm conclusions from data. These two approaches are sometimes called *exploratory* and *confirmatory* analyses, but the imaginary line between the two is really quite fuzzy. Many so-called confirmatory techniques are excellent tools for exploring data and many explorations lead to firm conclusions.

17.1 Randomness

The techniques in this book pertain to formal methods for drawing conclusions from data. The chief concern of these methods is that the inferences drawn from the data reflect genuine relationships and not random patterns that might appear structured just by chance.

Human vision is a marvelous tool for finding patterns. It can turn dots of light moving back and forth on the screen into a rotating cloud of points. Unfortunately, sometimes the mind is so good at seeing patterns that it sees them where there are none. The best way to get a feel for what truly unstructured random values look like is to look at some examples. Data Desk provides ways to generate random values from a variety of distributions.

Of course, random values have other important uses. Chief among them is their use in selecting a sample of cases from a larger population. In general, to draw conclusions about data or make inferences about the population from which the data were drawn, we must take into account how the data were collected. In particular, most statistics methods require that the data we work with be sampled *at random* from the population of interest.

Randomness is a concept that everybody has some general feel for. Many card tricks, for example, play upon expectations of what ought to happen when a card is selected "at random" from a shuffled deck. But when it comes to discussing randomness precisely, most people need some help. Computers provide particularly good ways to experiment with randomness to get a better feel for the consequences of random sampling.

simple random sample

A *simple random sample* is one in which each member of the population has an equal and independent chance of being selected. In this context, being independent means that the chance of selecting a particular individual isn't affected by the selection of any other individuals.

Much of statistics theory is based on the assumption that the population of interest is infinitely large. It would seem to be impractical to experiment with simple random samples from infinite populations, but Data Desk can get very close to this ideal model. The secret is that computers can generate numbers that appear to be selected randomly from practically infinite populations. Although the numbers aren't truly random and the populations are only very, very large, the differences between the simulation and the ideal model are negligible.

pseudo-random numbers

To be precise, the random numbers computers generate are called *pseudo-random numbers.* They are designed to be almost indistinguishable from truly random numbers (see Appendix 17A.).

17.2 *Creating Random Subsamples*

There are many situations when you will want to work with random samples datasets. A dataset might be too large to analyze practically. Or you might want to work with several small samples and use the full dataset for confirmatory analyses. In Data Desk there are several ways to create random samples.

In this section we discuss how to create a random sample and place it in its own relation. The methods discussed in Sections 17.5 and 17.8 use 0/1 indicator variables and a **Selector** button to simulate random samples within the existing relation. In Section 17.5 we discuss samples that include a specified percent of the original cases. In Section 17.8 we show how to generate random samples with an exact number of cases.

The major advantage of having a random sample placed in its own separate relation is that less memory is required for processing the sampled data in subsequent analyses. Random samples generated with 0/1 indicator variables hold all the cases in memory for your analyses. Working with smaller relations reduces the time it takes to perform analyses; thus you can work with more samples and to explore more paths through your data.

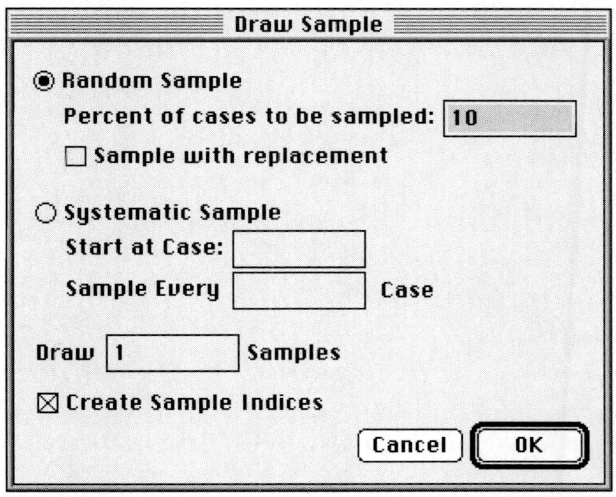

Figure 17-1. *To specify a random sample, type the percentage of cases you want to include in the sample. To specify a systematic sample, type the starting case and the number of cases to skip.*

To draw a random sample, select the variables from which you want to sample and choose {Manip} **Sample...**. The dialog shown in Fig. 17-1 appears. Click on the button labeled **Random Sample**, specify a percentage of cases you want to include in your sample, and click the **OK** button.

For example, to sample 20% of the original cases, type 20 and choose **OK**. Data Desk generates a new relation, called *Random1*, holding 20% of the cases drawn from the selected variables. The relation is placed in the *Data* folder. It includes a new variable, *Indices,* that holds the case number from the original relation for each case.

Data Desk samples without replacement unless you click the Sample with Replacement box. Sampling with replacement gives every case the same probability of being chosen each time a case is drawn.

Data Desk also draws systematic samples; which draw a sample in a specified pattern. Click the **Systematic Samples** button and type the starting case number in the Start at Case box and the number of cases to skip between sampled cases in the Sample Every box; then choose the **OK** button. A new relation labeled *Systematic1* will be placed in the *Data* folder.

17.3 Distributions

Histograms display the distribution of values in a variable. We can consider the distribution of values in a population in a similar way. With an infinite population we must use a mathematical description of the distribution shape rather than counts of observations falling between fixed bounds. Nevertheless, the ideas are the same: A distribution describes the fraction of cases falling within any specified part of the range of possible values.

parameters

statistics

Quantities that characterize a population's distribution, such as its mean and variance, are called *parameters*. Parameters are typically denoted with Greek letters to distinguish them from their sample-based counterparts, called *statistics*.

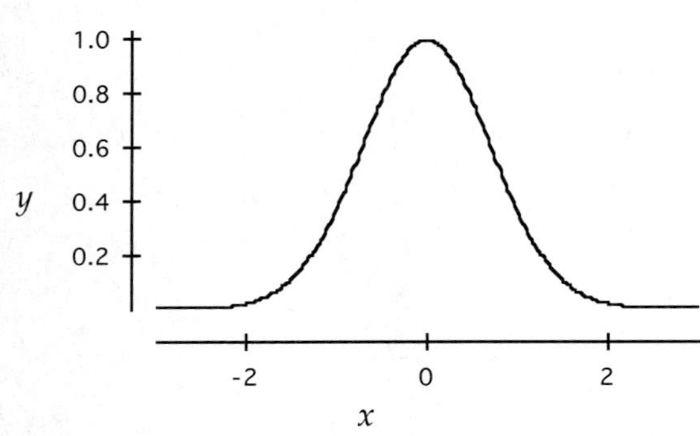

Figure 17-2. *The mathematically described normal distribution is a smooth curve. The parameters of this particular normal distribution are* $\mu = 0$ *and* $\sigma = 1$.

Most useful distributions are completely determined by one or two simple parameters (Fig. 17-2). For example, a normal distribution is completely determined by its mean, μ (mu) and standard deviation, σ (sigma). A Poisson distribution is completely determined by its mean, λ (lambda).

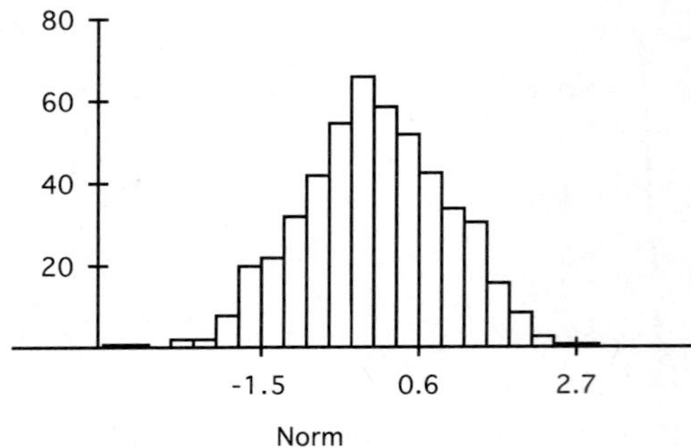

Figure 17-3. *A histogram of a sample of 500 cases from a normal distribution follows the general shape of the mathematical description but shows that samples do not exactly follow the distribution of the population.*

When we use statistics to draw inferences about the sample's underlying population, we usually must assume that the population's parameters are known quantities. Often we are asked to assume that observations or errors made in the observations follow a particular distribution shape or even that they come from a distribution with a particular mean, standard deviation, or some other parameter. Of course, when dealing with real data, we can't be certain of the underlying distribution because we usually can't observe the entire population (Fig. 17-3). However, computers can simulate random samples drawn from specified distributions with specified parameters. The control that this provides is particularly valuable for understanding randomness.

17.4 Generating Random Samples

To generate random numbers from distributions in Data Desk, select the {Manip} **Generate Random Numbers...** command. Data Desk presents a

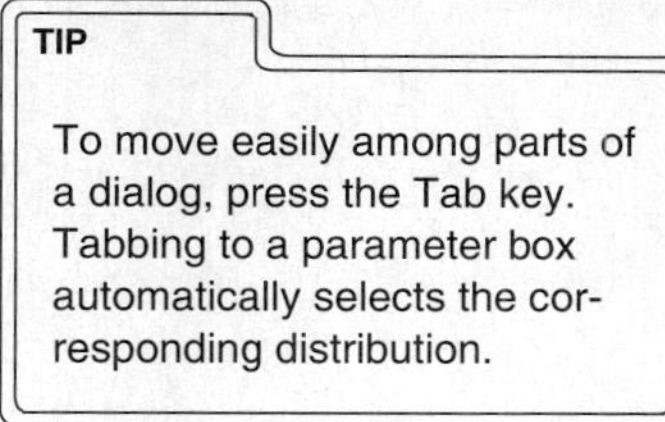

Figure 17-4. Generate Random Numbers… *offers to create any number of randomly generated variables with any number of random values in each one.*

Distribution:
Uniform
Normal: μ = sigma =
Bernoulli trials: Prob(success) =
Binomial experiments:
Bernoulli trials / experiment =
Probability (success) =
Poisson: lambda =
Seed =
Generator Congruential
Cancel
OK

Figure 17-5. *You have a choice of distributions for* ***Generate Random Numbers…****; specify parameters in the corresponding boxes.*

dialog that, in part, looks like that shown in Fig. 17-4. The value in the *cases/variable* box is, by default, the number of cases in the frontmost relation. This value makes it easy to generate samples that will fit into the relation holding the variables that you are currently working with. If there are no relations in the datafile, this value defaults to 100. To change this value, type the sample size in the box. Data Desk places samples that don't fit into the frontmost relation in their own relations.

The second part of the dialog offers a choice of distribution (Fig. 17-5). All distributions but the Uniform require values for the parameters defining the distribution. When you click the **OK** button, Data Desk generates numbers that behave as if they were sampled from the specified distribution and groups them into variables of the requested sample size, one variable for each sample requested.

seed

Random number generation works with an initial number called the *seed.*

17.5 Bernoulli Trials

Bernoulli trials (named for James Bernoulli, 1654–1705) are experiments with two possible outcomes, usually labeled "success" and "failure". The most common Bernoulli trial is flipping a coin. To generate sample Bernoulli trials, specify the probability of a success in the underlying population.

Sometimes we express probabilities in percentage form ("a 56% chance of a success") and sometimes as a fraction between 0 and 1. Data Desk expects probabilities to be between 0 and 1, and will ask you to correct any that aren't in this range. Data Desk performs the requested number of trials and records either a 0 or a 1 for each, where 1 marks a "success". The result is a variable containing zeros and ones randomly.

One special application of the Bernoulli distribution is to draw a simple random sample from your data. To do so in Data Desk, generate a Bernoulli variable with as many cases as there are cases in the variables to be sampled, and with a probability of success of k/n, where k is the number of cases you hope to have in the sample and n is the total number of cases. The Bernoulli variable can now be used as a selector variable to restrict analyses to those cases coded as '1' (see Chapter 13).

Now all analyses for which the selector variable is active will be performed on a random sample of the data; specifically, those cases with a 1 in the Bernoulli variable will be selected. Note that you aren't guaranteed to get exactly k cases in your sample. Instead, you are selecting cases with a probability of k/n, so you can expect to have approximately k cases in the sample. In Section 17.8 we discuss a way to draw a simple random sample that guarantees the sample size.

17.6 *Binomial Distribution*

The binomial distribution counts the number of "successes" in some number of Bernoulli trials. The sum of a Bernoulli variable is a binomial quantity. In the binomial experiments portion of the Generate Random Numbers dialog, specify the number of Bernoulli trials in each binomial experiment, and the probability of a success. A binomial variable consists of integer values between 0 and the number of Bernoulli trials specified.

The number of Bernoulli trials in a binomial variable is a parameter of the distribution and thus is specified in the Generate Random Numbers dialog.

17.7 *Poisson Distribution*

The Poisson distribution, like the Binomial distribution, describes probabilities of discrete events. It is appropriate in situations when the probability of an event is very small but there are many trials so that there is a measurable probability of 0, 1, 2,... events.

For example, the probability of a car accident on any short stretch of road on any one day is very small. But if we consider a long stretch of road (for example, all of Interstate 80), the probabilities that on any particular day there will be 0, 1, 2, ... accidents is moderate. If we know the true average number of accidents in a day on the entire road, we can use a Poisson distribution to describe the distribution of the number of accidents.

The Poisson distribution is described by a single parameter, λ, which is defined to be the number of events that are expected to occur over a period of time. The mean and variance of a Poisson distribution both equal λ. A Poisson variable consists of integer values 0, 1, 2, ..., with values near λ more likely than values far from λ.

17.8 *Uniform Distribution*

The uniform distribution is defined so that every value between 0 and 1 is equally likely. Histograms of samples from the uniform distribution tend to be relatively flat with several small modes. For example, a histogram of 250 numbers drawn from a uniform distribution might look like that shown in Fig. 17-6.

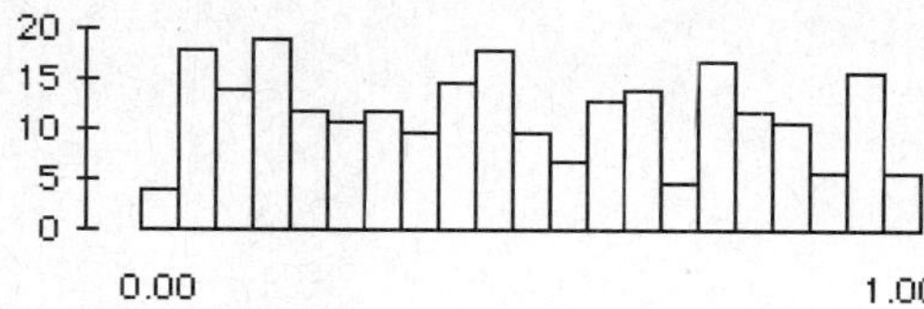

Figure 17-6. *A histogram of 250 random uniform values is relatively flat.*

The uniform distribution is a convenient source of randomly distributed values. To generate a random permutation of cases, generate a variable with the same number of uniform random values as your relation. Choose {Manip} **Generate Random Data...** and specify one uniform variable with as many cases as the target variables. Select the random uniform variable as y and the variables to permutate as x and choose {Manip} **Sort on Y carrying X's**. This sorts the uniform variable and reorders the other variables randomly.

17.9 Normal Distribution

The normal distribution is also called the Gaussian distribution because it was discussed extensively by the famous mathematician, C. F. Gauss (1777–1855). The normal distribution is one of the simplest distributions to deal with mathematically, in part because it is described entirely by its mean, μ, and its standard deviation, σ. Indeed, the most common way to describe the relative locations of values in a normal distribution is as numbers of standard deviation units above or below the mean.

standard normal distribution

Data Desk can simulate samples from a normal population with any mean and standard deviation. A normal distribution with a mean of 0 and a standard deviation of 1 is called a *standard normal distribution* because it is the simplest choice of values. Many statistics books include tables of probabilities for standard normal distributions, but Data Desk has these tables built in.

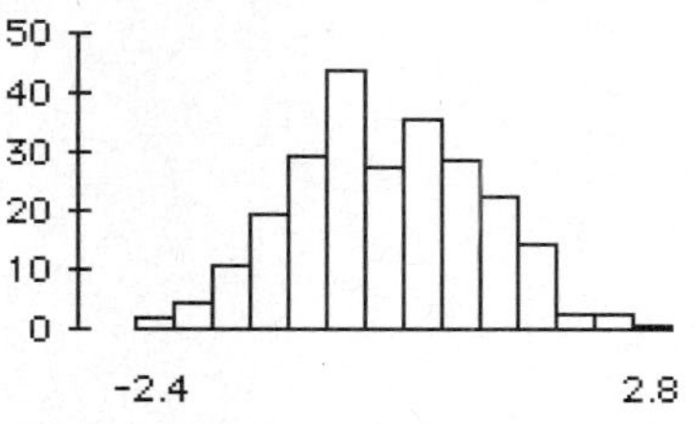

Figure 17-7. *A histogram of 250 random normal values.*

When we draw a random sample from a standard normal population, as in Fig. 17-7, a histogram of the sample isn't a perfect normal distribution shape. If we were to draw another sample of 250 from the standard normal population, or if you perform the experiment yourself, the histogram would look somewhat different, but would still tend to have a central peak and an overall bell shape as shown.

17.10 The Law of Large Numbers

People have an intuitive feeling that "in the long run" things average out about right. A particular flip of a coin or roll of the dice may not be predictable, but in the long run, people are fairly confident that about half of their coin flips will be heads and that all six numbers on each die will come up about an equal number of times.

More generally, people can be confident that as they draw larger and larger samples, the average of the sampled values will approach the true population mean. The law of large numbers verifies formally that this intuition is right. Averages of larger samples tend to be closer to the true population mean.

You can illustrate the law of large numbers with a simple simulation. Generate 1000 numbers from a normal distribution with any mean and standard deviation you want — but remember the mean that you select. Rename the resulting variable y. Then generate patterned data with the default settings: numbers counting from 1 to 1000. Rename that variable n.

Now, make a new derived variable and name it *means*. Type the following expression into the derived variable window:

CumSum(y)/n

The *CumSum* function computes the cumulative sum of y. The first case of the cumulative sum is the first case of y. The second case is the sum of the first and second cases of y: $y[1] + y[2]$. The third case sums the first three cases: $y[1] + y[2] + y[3]$, and so on. The variable n gives the number of values summed (1, 2, 3, ...). Thus the derived variable expression computes first the first case, $y[1]$, then the average of the first two cases, $(y[1] + y[2])/2$, then the average of the first three cases, and so on. As the averages involve more and more cases, the law of large numbers says that they will approach the true mean. (You do recall the mean you specified when you generated the random numbers, don't you?)

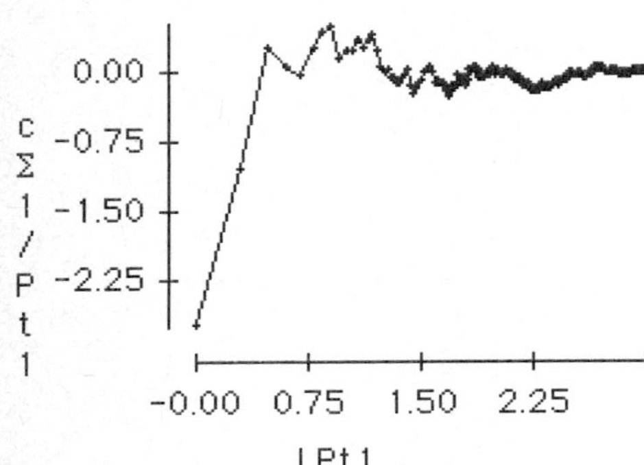

Figure 17-8. The law of large numbers states that, as the sample size increases, the average should approach the population mean. This lineplot shows averages for between 1 and 1000 random numbers drawn from a standard normal distribution. The horizontal axis is a log scale to stretch out the early fluctuations. It is easy to see the convergence toward the true mean of 0.

A lineplot of means shows how these means start out oscillating quite wildly but settle down close to the true mean. For a slightly better plot, reexpress n by taking its logarithm and drag the re-expressed variable onto the x-axis of the lineplot. The log scale stretches out the early means and compresses the later ones, emphasizing the convergence. Fig. 17-8 shows an example.

If you are comfortable with Data Desk, try the following sequence of operations to get the same result. Use the **Generate Random Number...** command, specify normal distribution, and pick a mean and standard deviation. Data Desk leaves the random variable selected, so you can use {Manip ▶ Transform ▶ Summary} **CumSum(y)**. The resulting variable is named *cumΣNr1*. Open the Generate Patterned Data dialog and hit Enter — the defaults are right. Select *cumΣNr1* as y and *Pattern1* as x, and choose {Manip ▶ Transform ▶ Arithmetic} **y/x** to create *cΣ1/Pt1*. Choose {**Plot**} **Lineplots**. Now select *Pattern1*, choose {Manip ▶ Transform} **Log(y)**, and drag the resulting variable onto the y-axis of the lineplot.

17.11 Sampling Distributions

When we draw a sample from a population and compute a statistic, we know that were we to draw another sample of the same size independently from the same population and compute the statistic on the new sample, the second value would probably differ from the first. We want to take this fact into account when interpreting any statistic that we might compute from a specific sample.

sampling distribution

Independent samples drawn from the same population differ from each other in the individual numbers observed and consequently, in the values of statistics computed from them. A statistic's *sampling distribution* describes this sample-to-sample variation in its observed values. If we were to draw a multitude of samples of a fixed size from the same population, compute the value of a statistic, and make a histogram of the collected statistic values, the distribution shown by the histogram approximates the sampling distribution of the statistic.

Usually, we can't afford to sample repeatedly from a real population. Instead, we draw a single sample as large as we can manage and work with that. Fortunately, the sampling distributions of most common sta-

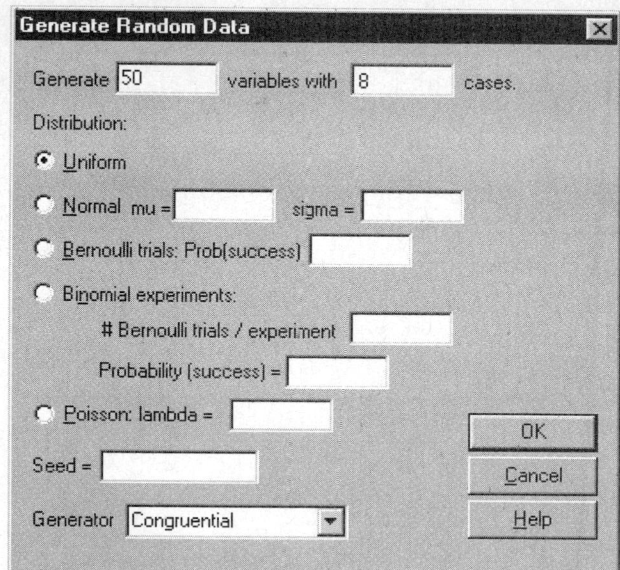

Figure 17-9. Generating random Uniform variables.

tistics are known mathematically and can be looked up in texts. Nevertheless, we can get a much better idea of how sampling distributions behave by performing the experiment on the computer and seeing the distributions for ourselves.

To simulate a sampling distribution, generate many variables from the same population and compute a statistic on each of them. For example, you can generate 50 samples of 8 numbers each from a Uniform distribution (Fig. 17-9.).

Data Desk places the samples together in a new relation, *Ran Data1*, and places this relation in the *Data* folder (Fig. 17-10).

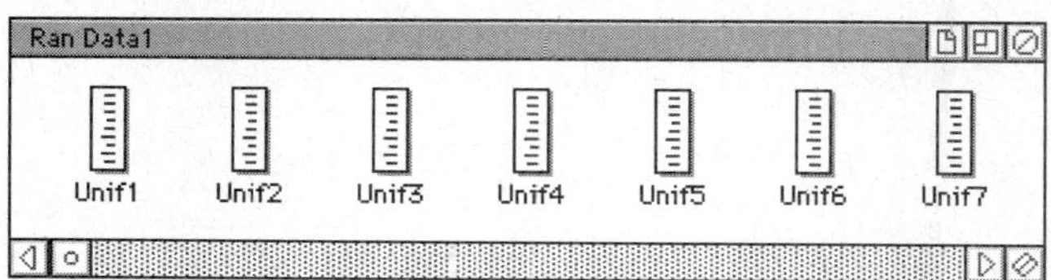

Figure 17-10. *The random Uniform variables are automatically placed in a relation named Ran Data.*

To compute the range for each of the 50 samples, select Range in the dialog presented by the {Calc ▶ Calculation Options} **Select Summary Statistics** command (Fig. 17-11).

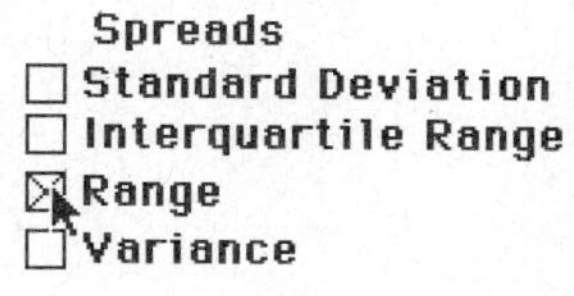

Figure 17-11. *Selecting the range.*

Select the icon of the *Ran Data* relation (whether its window is open or not) and choose {Calc ▶ Summaries} **As Variables**. This command computes the range for each of the samples in that relation (Fig. 17-12).

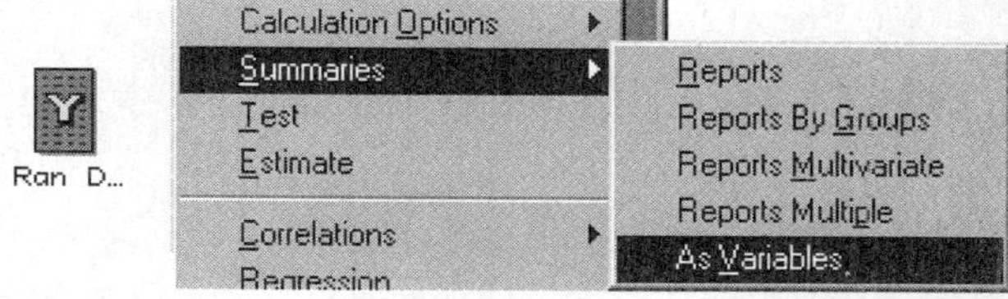

Figure 17-12. *Selecting {Calc ▶ Summaries}* ***As Variables*** *for the entire* Ran Data *relation.*

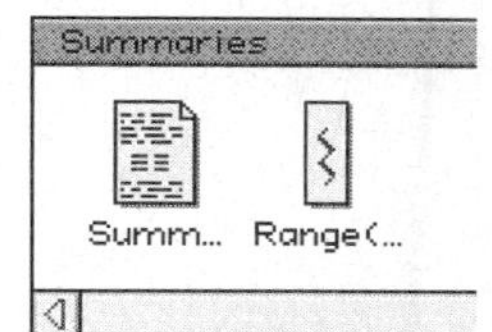

Figure 17-13. *Summary statistics for each simulated variable are collected into a new variable.*

The {Calc ▶ Summaries} **As Variables** command generates a variable named *Range(Summary1)* containing the ranges of the 50 simulated variables (Fig. 17-13).

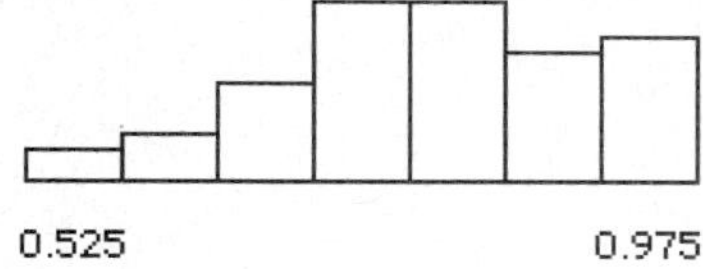

Figure 17-14. *A histogram of the ranges of one instance of random uniform variables. If you repeat the experiment, your histogram may look slightly different but should have the same general shape.*

The histogram of these values approximates the sampling distribution of the range for samples of eight cases drawn from a uniform distribution. Fig. 17-14 shows the histogram for one trial of these experiments.

17.11 Central Limit Theorem

The Central Limit Theorem states:

The theoretical sampling distribution of the mean of independent samples, each of size n, drawn from a population with mean μ and standard deviation σ, is approximately normal with mean μ and standard deviation $\sigma/\sqrt{n}$. The approximation to normality improves as n grows.

Central Limit Theorem

The theorem is fundamental to much of statistical inference, but the proof is beyond most introductory statistics courses. Data Desk can illustrate the Central Limit Theorem by approximating the sampling distribution of the sample mean by simulation (Fig. 17-15).

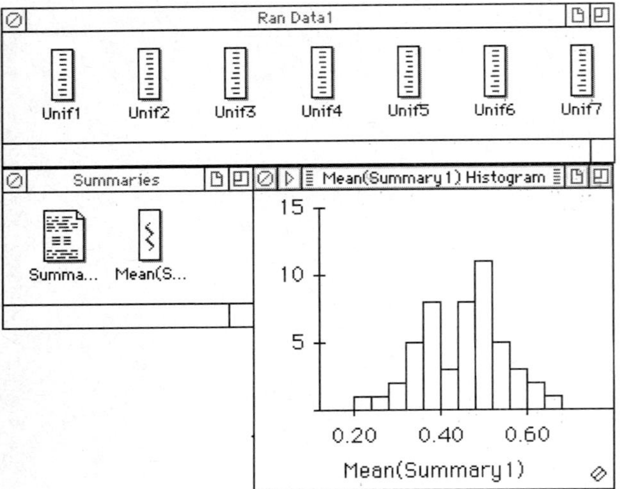

Figure 17-15. *We illustrate the Central Limit theorem by simulating the sampling distribution of the mean of samples from a uniform population.*

For example, by using the same methods as in the previous section, we can generate, say, 50 variables with 9 cases from a uniform distribution. The uniform distribution has a population mean, μ, of 0.5, and a population standard deviation, σ, of 0.289.

Applying the {Calc ▶ Summaries} **As Variables** command to the relation full of random variables generates a variable called *Means* containing the 50 means — 1 computed for each of the 50 uniform variables. A histogram of *Means* shows how the means of these random samples are distributed and thus approximates the true sampling distribution of the sample mean.

As expected from the Central Limit Theorem, the histogram of the means looks like a histogram of values from the normal distribution even though the samples themselves were drawn from a uniform population. A virtue of the Central Limit Theorem is that, regardless of the underlying population from which samples are drawn, the sampling distribution of the sample mean is approximately normal.

We can also check whether the mean and standard deviation of *this* distribution (that is, of the collection of 50 sample means in the variable *Means*) are as the Central Limit Theorem says they should be.

```
Summary statistics
for Means

NumNumeric = 50
Mean = 0.50576
Standard Deviation = 0.08103
```

The mean is near 0.5, the population mean for the uniform distribution. The standard deviation expected from the Central Limit Theorem is $\sigma/\sqrt{n}$, or 0.096 — a bit higher than the value 0.081 observed here, but still reasonably close. In drawing only 50 samples, we can only approximate the true sampling distribution of the sample mean. Theoretically, if we were to draw infinitely many samples, the mean and standard deviation of the corresponding *Means* variable would be 0.5 and 0.96 exactly.

The simulation strategies presented in this chapter help to make many aspects of statistical inference more intuitive. Many statistics perform well "on average" or "in the long run." For all these methods, it can help your intuition to simulate "the long run" by generating independent random samples and applying the statistic of interest to those samples.

APPENDIX 17A *Details and Formulas*

The default pseudo-random numbers used by Data Desk is of a type known as a *multiplicative congruential* random number generator. Specifically, given the ith number, x_i, in the range $0 < x_i < 2{,}147{,}483{,}647$, the next random number is generated as:

$$(x_{i+1} = (x_i * 7^5) \bmod (2^{31} - 1))/2^{31}.$$

The initial random number (known as the "seed") is selected when Data Desk starts up by consulting an internal clock that counts 60^{th}s of a second since the machine was turned on. You can set the seed to be any large integer less than 2,147,483,647 by clicking in the seed window and typing the number you want. *If you start a simulation with the same seed and perform it in the same way, you will always get the same random numbers,* so you can repeat an experiment exactly if you wish. Usually, there is no need to adjust the seed.

Unlike other computations in Data Desk, random numbers are not generated to full 20-digit precision (because the largest number that can be generated by this generator is $2^{31} - 2$, which has only 10 digits).

This particular random number generator has been studied extensively and is known to perform well; sequences of random numbers show very little structure.

The random number generator itself generates random Uniform values. Random Normal values are computed by transforming pairs of random Uniforms using the Box-Muller transformation.

Random Bernoulli trials are generated by testing a random Uniform to see if it falls above or below a particular cut point (determined by the probability of a success). Random binomials are computed from repeated random Bernoulli numbers for large probabilities of success and with a wedge-tail approximation for small probabilities.

Other random number generators are available. Click on the Generator pop-up menu at the bottom of the dialog and choose the desired random number generator.

EXERCISES

1. Define the term *simple random sample.*

2. Suppose that you were to draw a simple random sample from a normal population. If you use the sample's numbers to construct a summary value (mean, variance, range, and so on), this summary value is called a *statistic.* A statistic is a sample value. By contrast, a value that describes some aspect of the underlying population is called a ______________________________ .

3. A normal population is completely described by its ______________________________ and ______________________________ . In a standard normal distribution, these parameters equal ______________ and ______________ , respectively.

4. A normal population has a shape that is (circle all that apply):

(a) Multimodal and skewed
(b) Bimodal and flat
(c) Rectangular
(d) Unimodal and symmetric
(e) Dependent upon the population's mean

5. Suppose that the coin used to decide who should kick off in the football games of your favorite team is biased, landing heads 56% of the time in the long run. You accumulate data for a sequence of 30 coin flips. Using the **Generate Random Numbers...** command from the **Manip** menu, simulate 30 trials from a Bernoulli distribution with P(success) = .56. Repeat the experiment 4 more times. For each experiment, count the number of heads (successes) and write them in the space provided.

How strong is the evidence for a biased coin?

What might you do to strengthen the evidence of bias?

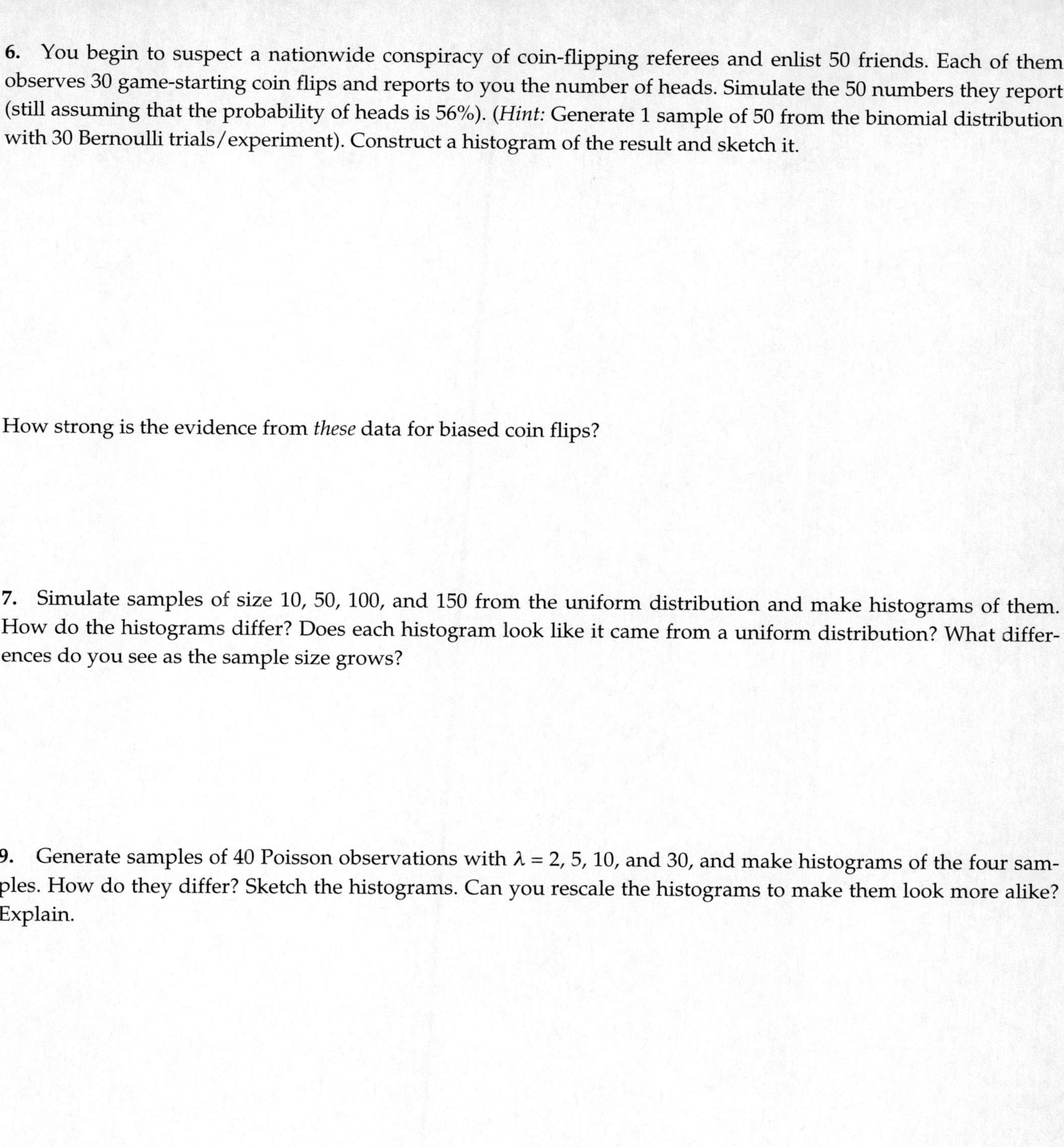

6. You begin to suspect a nationwide conspiracy of coin-flipping referees and enlist 50 friends. Each of them observes 30 game-starting coin flips and reports to you the number of heads. Simulate the 50 numbers they report (still assuming that the probability of heads is 56%). (*Hint:* Generate 1 sample of 50 from the binomial distribution with 30 Bernoulli trials/experiment). Construct a histogram of the result and sketch it.

How strong is the evidence from *these* data for biased coin flips?

7. Simulate samples of size 10, 50, 100, and 150 from the uniform distribution and make histograms of them. How do the histograms differ? Does each histogram look like it came from a uniform distribution? What differences do you see as the sample size grows?

9. Generate samples of 40 Poisson observations with $\lambda = 2, 5, 10$, and 30, and make histograms of the four samples. How do they differ? Sketch the histograms. Can you rescale the histograms to make them look more alike? Explain.

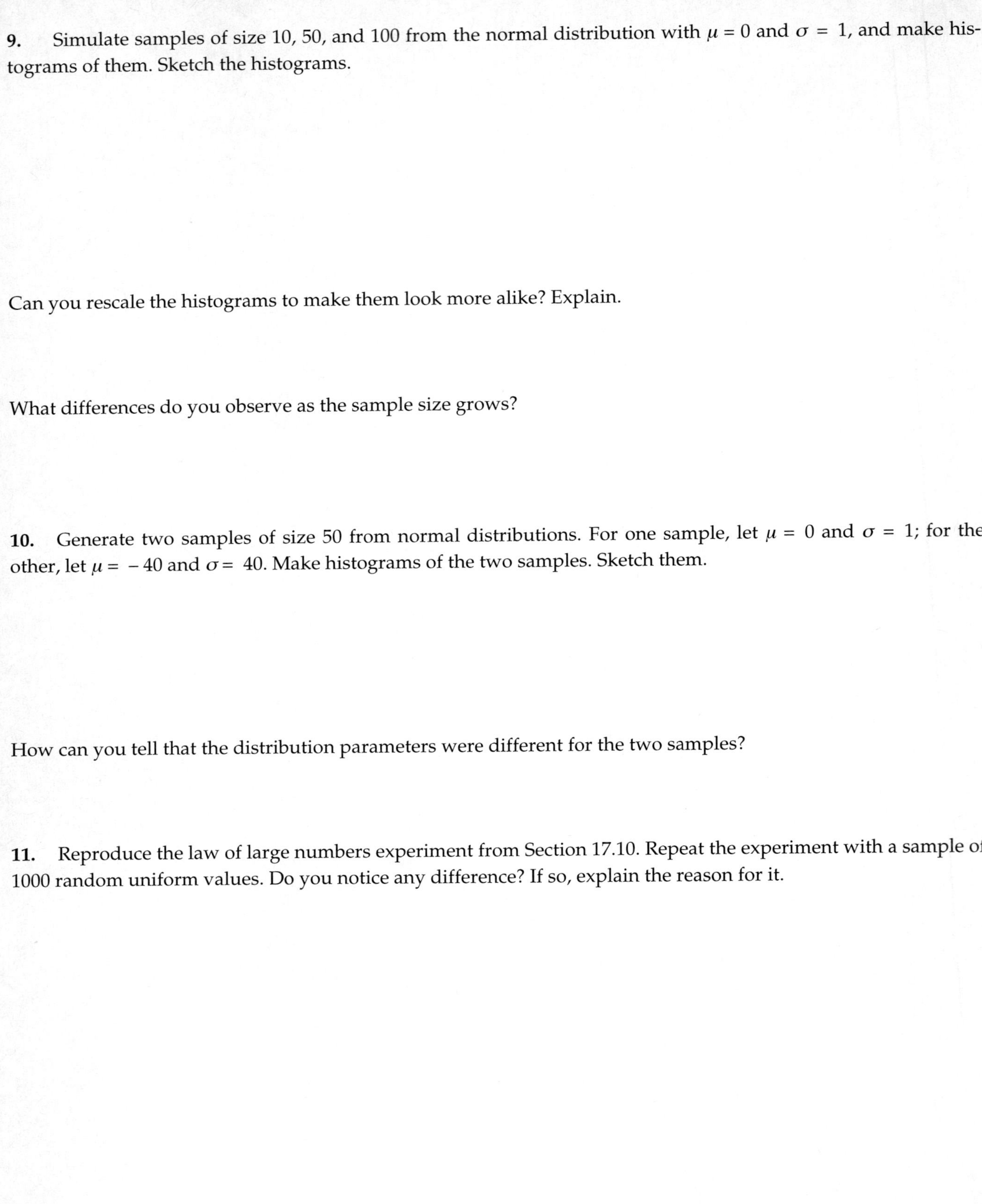

9. Simulate samples of size 10, 50, and 100 from the normal distribution with $\mu = 0$ and $\sigma = 1$, and make histograms of them. Sketch the histograms.

Can you rescale the histograms to make them look more alike? Explain.

What differences do you observe as the sample size grows?

10. Generate two samples of size 50 from normal distributions. For one sample, let $\mu = 0$ and $\sigma = 1$; for the other, let $\mu = -40$ and $\sigma = 40$. Make histograms of the two samples. Sketch them.

How can you tell that the distribution parameters were different for the two samples?

11. Reproduce the law of large numbers experiment from Section 17.10. Repeat the experiment with a sample of 1000 random uniform values. Do you notice any difference? If so, explain the reason for it.

12. If you were to draw infinitely many samples of a fixed size from the same _______________, compute the value of a _______________, and make a histogram of the collected values, the distribution of values shown by the histogram would be called the _______________________________________.

13. Make a histogram to display the sampling distribution of the median for samples of size 10 from the standard normal distribution. Follow the example in the chapter, but generate 25 samples and use **Summary Statistics Options** to select the median to use in the **Summary Statistics as Variables** command. You may want to rescale the histogram to find a scale that best depicts the distribution. Repeat the experiment a second time and compare the two trials. Sketch both histograms. (It is a good idea to discard the random samples generated the first time and empty the Trash before repeating the experiment.)

14. Repeat Exercise 13 for samples of size 5. What differences do you see?

15. The Central Limit Theorem states that the sampling distribution of the sample mean of n independent observations, drawn from a population with mean μ and standard deviation σ, is approximately normal with mean ____________ and standard deviation _______________ and that the approximation improves as n grows. According to the theorem, do the independent observations upon which the sample means are based need to be drawn from a normal distribution? __________ Explain.

16. (a) Simulate the sampling distribution of the mean of 16 independent observations drawn from a normal distribution with $\mu = -4$ and $\sigma = 8$. Generate 20 samples. Compare the mean and standard deviation of the sample means to what you would expect from the Central Limit Theorem.

Observed mean: __________
Observed standard deviation: __________

Theoretical mean: __________
Theoretical standard deviation: __________

(b) How might you reduce the difference between what you observe in your simulation and what is expected theoretically?

(c) Construct a normal probability plot of the empirical sampling distribution and sketch it. Does it appear to be approximately normal? ______________

(d) What might improve the approximation to normality?

17. (a) Simulate the sampling distribution of the mean of 16 independent observations drawn from a uniform distribution. Generate 20 samples. Compare the mean and standard deviation of the sample means to what you would expect from the Central Limit Theorem. (The mean of a uniform distribution is 0.5 and its standard deviation is $1/\sqrt{12}$.)

Observed mean: __________
Observed standard deviation: __________

Theoretical mean: __________
Theoretical standard deviation: __________

(b) How might you reduce the difference between what you observe in your simulation and what is expected theoretically?

(c) Construct a normal probability plot of the empirical sampling distribution and sketch it. Does it appear to be approximately normal?

(d) What might improve the approximation to normality?

(e) How do these results compare to those in the experiment in Exercise 16?

CHAPTER 18

Simple Inference

STATISTICS PROVIDES WAYS to draw inferences about a population by examining a random sample from that population. Although we don't expect to be able to make a precise statement about the entire population, we can use statistics to make a statement that is *likely* to be true and to understand how large an error we have probably made. In this way, we can control the error and draw conclusions from imperfect information.

Statistical inference usually considers the data at hand to be a representative sample from some population. We analyze the sample but make inferences about the population. We usually cannot examine the entire population, so we rarely learn whether the inferences we make are in fact correct. Simulation techniques, such as those described in Chapter 17, allow you to control the characteristics of a special population to try to learn more about how inferential statistics work.

18.1 *Confidence Intervals*

We showed in Chapter 17 that the sample means of many samples drawn from the same population fluctuate around the true mean of the population. When we want to estimate the population mean but have only one sample, we must account for the variability of the sample mean. Hence reporting a range of probable values for the population mean is preferable to reporting the single sample average at hand. Confidence intervals provide a systematic way to construct a reasonable range of probable values.

Confidence intervals confront us with a trade-off between precision and certainty. Ideally, we would like to compute a single, precise, value and be certain that we had found the true population value. For example, it would be nice to know with absolute certainty what the sales volume of a business will be tomorrow based on a sample of recent sales performances.

One alternative would be to acknowledge that we can't predict unknown values with certainty and instead make probability statements about precise values. For example, we might say that the sales volume will *probably* be precisely $2745.12. Unfortunately, because it is so precise, the probability that this statement is true is so small that it makes the statement worthless.

Another alternative would be to sacrifice precision to preserve certainty. For example, we could select a range of possible values but be certain that the true value is in the range. We might say that, even though we can't know the exact sales volume, it will certainly be between $0 and $5000. Unfortunately, such certainty is possible only for ranges that are so large as to be uninteresting.

Ultimately, we are forced to forgo both certainty and precision by estimating both a range and a probability that the range encloses the true value. Thus we might say that, although we don't know the true sales volume, we are 95% certain that it will fall between $2500 and $3000. That is, in the long run, 95% of the intervals that we might construct by similar processes would include the true sales volume (and 5% of them wouldn't).

We still have tension between precision and certainty. The more certain we want to be, the less precise we can be. The more precision we seek (as a narrow interval of values), the less certain we can be that the interval really encloses the true value.

18.2 *Confidence Intervals for μ When σ Is Known*

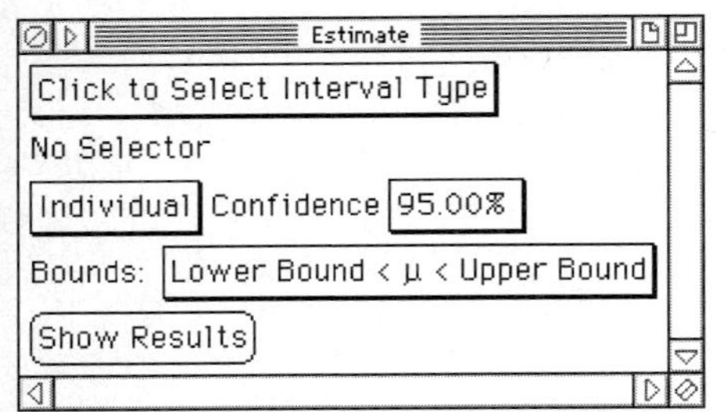

Figure 18-1. *The Estimate Window.*

To find a confidence interval for a population mean, μ, select a variable that contains a sample drawn from the population and choose {Calc} **Estimate**. Data Desk opens an Estimate window (Fig. 18-1). This window presents confidence interval results, expanding and recomputing according to the choices you make.

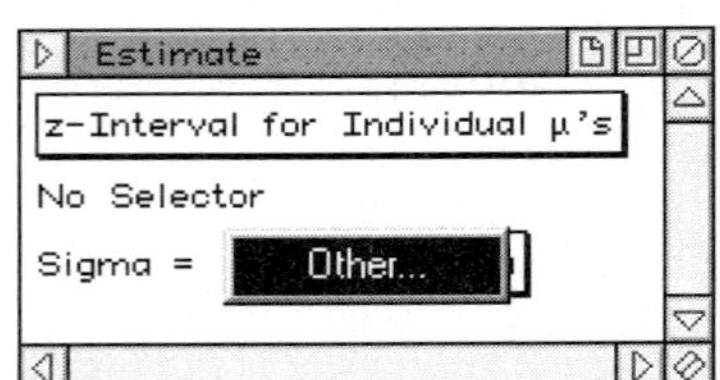

The first pop-up menu offers a choice of interval types. If the population standard deviation, σ, is known (not just estimated), a z-interval is appropriate.

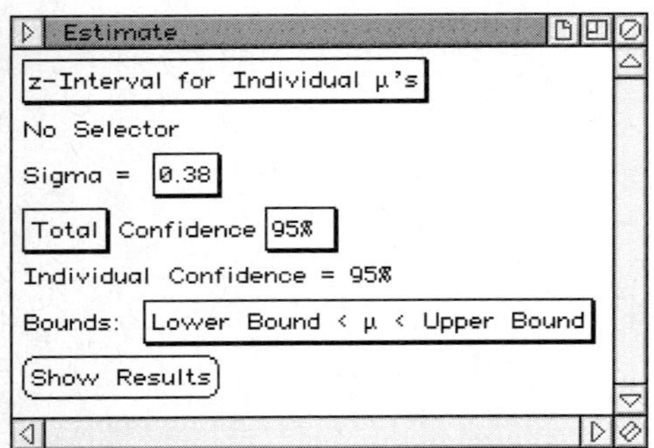

Figure 18-2. *Specifying z-Interval for μ.*

In the topmost pop-up menu which holds the different interval choices, select **z-Interval for individual μ's**. Choose the **Specify Sigma** pop-up menu, then choose **283**and type the population standard deviation value in the window provided. The Estimate window expands to look like that shown in Fig. 18-2.

Data Desk computes z-intervals as

$$\bar{y} \pm z^* \sigma / \sqrt{n}$$

confidence level

where $\bar{y}$ is the sample mean, σ is the population standard deviation, n is the sample size, and z^* is the number of standard deviations required on both sides of the mean in a normal distribution to include the fraction of the distribution specified by the *confidence level*. The z^* values are also called the *percentage points* of a normal distribution.

The confidence level characterizes the choice made in balancing precision and uncertainty. If you imagine repeating many times independently the experiment that generated the data and computing, say, 95% confidence intervals with each sample, you would expect that in the long run, 95% of the computed intervals would in fact contain the true population mean and 5% of them would not.

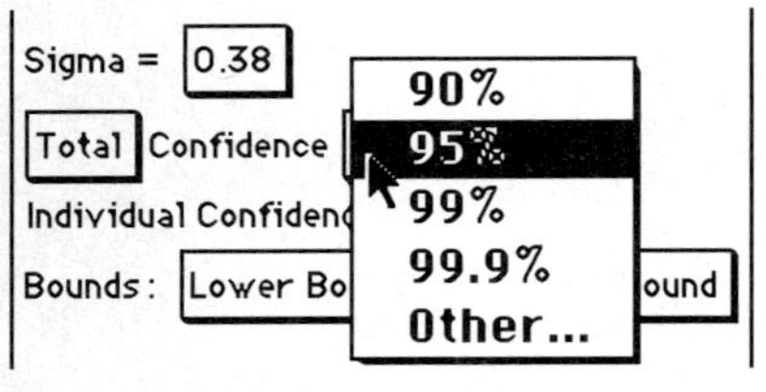

Figure 18-3. *Click the* ***Confidence*** *pop-up menu to specify the level of significance.*

Specify the appropriate confidence level from the **Confidence** pop-up menu (Fig. 18-3). Although 95% is a confidence level commonly used, there is no correct value. If you want a level other than one of those listed, choose Other from the pop-up menu and type a different confidence level in the window provided. The confidence level is specified as a percent, so type 85, rather than 0.85, for 85%.

Most confidence intervals are symmetric. We compute a statistic to estimate a population parameter and construct an interval that extends an equal distance above and below the value of the statistic. Sometimes however, you can be certain that the population parameter can't be on

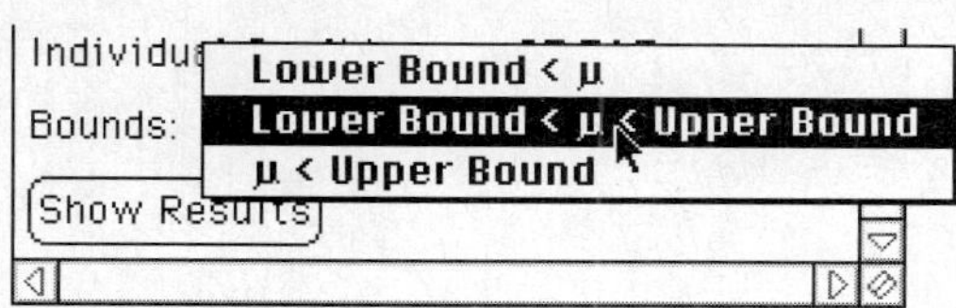

Figure 18-4. *Click the **Bounds** pop-up menu to select the type of confidence interval.*

one side or the other, or you are concerned only with a particular range of possible parameter values. In such cases, you may choose to construct a one-sided confidence interval. One-sided intervals can be either above or below the mean. Use the **Bounds** pop-up menu to choose between a one-sided or two-sided confidence interval (Fig. 18-4).

The pop-up menu to the left of the confidence level holds the options Total and Individual. These options are important when you are computing two or more confidence intervals at once (see Section 18.5).

To compute the interval, click the **Show Results** button.

18.3 Confidence Intervals for μ When σ Is Unknown

t-distribution

degrees of freedom

Usually we do not know the standard deviation of the population and must estimate it from the sample. Confidence intervals based on the *t-distribution* use a sample-based standard deviation estimate. Like the normal distribution, the *t*-distribution is symmetric about its mean. However, the peakedness of the *t*-distribution varies according to the size of the sample on which the standard deviation estimate is based, which determines the *degrees of freedom*. You need not specify degrees of freedom to construct a *t*-interval; Data Desk computes and reports degrees of freedom automatically.

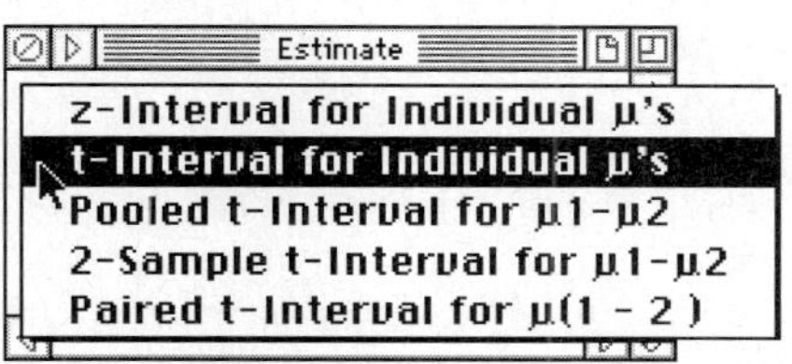

Figure 18-5. *Select **t-Interval of Individual** μ**'s** from the pop-up menu.*

To construct a confidence interval for μ when σ is unknown, select **t-Interval for Individual** μ**'s** in the Estimate window's top pop-up menu (Fig. 18-5). The window expands to show additional choices. Select the appropriate confidence level from the **Confidence** pop-up menu. Choose between a one-sided or two-sided confidence interval with the **Bounds** pop-up menu. The results appear at the bottom of the window when you select the **Show Results** button.

Data Desk computes *t*-intervals as

$$\bar{y} \pm t^*_{(n-1)}\, s/\sqrt{n}$$

where $\bar{y}$ is the sample mean, s is the sample standard deviation, n is the sample size, and $t^*_{(n-1)}$ is the appropriate percentage point of a *t*-distribution with $(n - 1)$ degrees of freedom. Unlike the normal distribution's, the *t*-distribution's shape, and thus its percentage points, depends upon degrees of freedom.

18.4 Where Is the Randomness?

When constructing confidence intervals keep in mind that the confidence interval is the random quantity whereas the population parameter is fixed and unchanging. Interpretations of confidence intervals should reflect this distinction. When we say "With 90% confidence, $63.5 \le \mu \le 65.5$," we do *not* mean that "90% of the time μ will fall between 63.5 and 65.5," but rather that in the long run, 90% of the intervals we compute from independently drawn samples will include the true mean.

Of course, in practice we construct a single confidence interval from the sample at hand, and the interval can only be said "probably" to include the true population mean. The confidence level specifies our confidence that the interval in fact encloses the true population mean.

18.5 *Multiple Intervals and the Bonferroni Adjustment*

Bonferroni adjustment

When we construct many confidence intervals, we expect that some of them will fail to cover the true population parameter value, but we don't know which ones. This uncertainty is true whether the intervals estimate the same parameter or are completely unrelated, as long as the samples have been drawn independently. The *Bonferroni adjustment* lets us construct several intervals without increasing the likelihood of at least one erroneous interval.

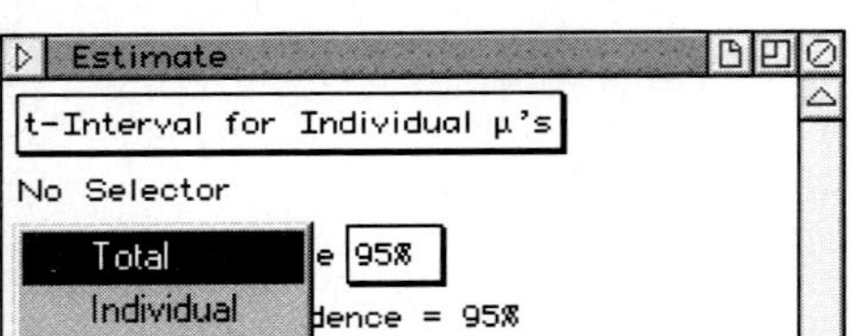

Figure 18-6. *Specifying Total versus Individual confidence level for multiple μ's.*

If we have selected several variables, the Estimate window (Fig. 18-6) offers the choice of a Total or Individual confidence levels. The Individual choice performs each test individually at the specified confidence level and thus increases the chances that some of the intervals are in error. Choosing Total applies the Bonferroni adjustment to the individual confidence levels so that the *total* probability of at least one erroneous interval equals the specified confidence level.

The Bonferroni adjustment considers the number of intervals requested and partitions the error probability equally among all the intervals. Thus a request for 3 intervals at a total 95% confidence level generates each interval at the (100 – 5/3)% confidence level. This adjustment makes each interval somewhat wider and thereby reduces the probability that it is in error. Because each of the intervals now has a 5/3% chance of being in error, there is a total of no more than 5/3% + 5/3% + 5/3% = 5% chance of at least one error, as we would want from a 95% confidence level.

multiple comparisons

The Bonferroni procedure is conservative. That is, it makes slightly more allowance for multiple intervals than is necessary in many situations. However, it applies to a wide variety of situations, and it is relatively easy to understand. The general problem of performing several inferential procedures together is called the problem of *multiple comparisons*.

18.6 *Testing Hypotheses*

Hypothesis tests are closely related to confidence intervals. Hypothesis tests require that you specify four things:

- The test statistic
- The null hypothesis, H_0
- The alternative hypothesis, H_A
- The probability of rejecting a true null hypothesis, usually called the α-level.

The {Calc} **Test** command opens a hypothesis test window. Pop-up menus in the hypothesis test window provide convenient ways to specify the components of hypothesis tests.

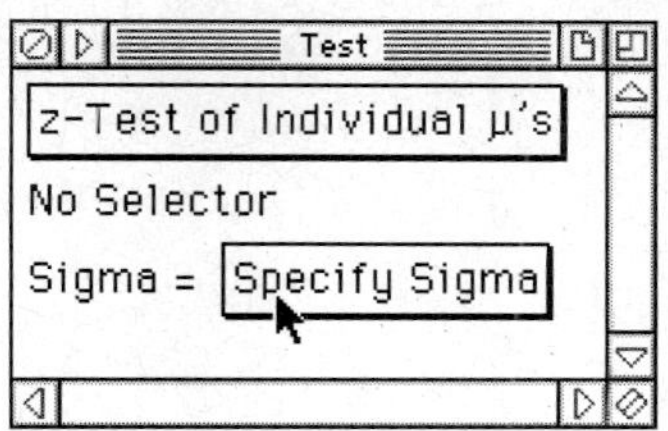

Figure 18-7. *Click the* ***Specify Sigma*** *button to type the value for population standard deviation.*

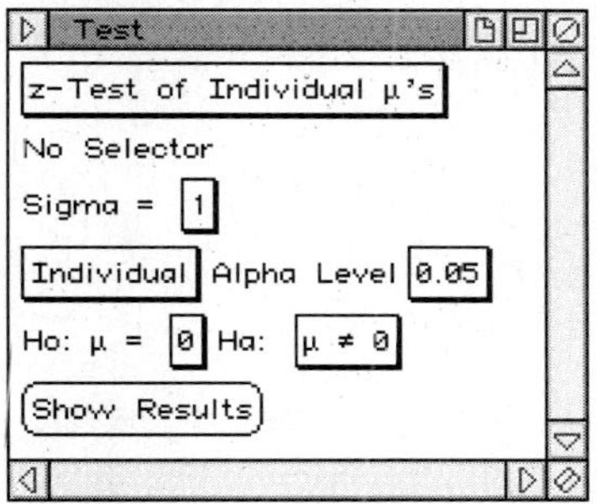

Figure 18-8. *A sample test window for* ***z-Test of Individual*** *μ's.*

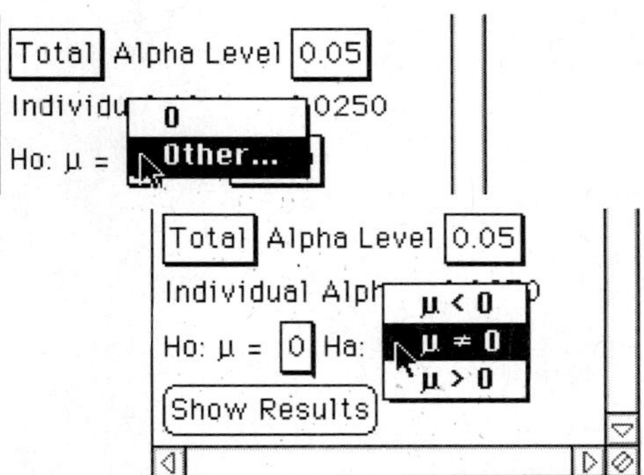

Figure 18-9*. Click the pop-up menu for* H_0 *to specify the null hypothesis. Click the* H_a *pop-up menu to select the alternative hypothesis.*

18.7 *Hypothesis Tests for μ When σ Is Known*

To test the null hypothesis that a population mean, μ, has some specified value, select a variable that contains a sample drawn from the population and choose {Calc} **Test**. If the population standard deviation, σ, is known, then select **z-Test of Individual** **μ's** from the topmost pop-up menu holding the different test selections.

Next, choose the **Specify Sigma** pop-up menu (Fig. 18-7), select Other..., enter the population standard deviation in the window provided and press **OK**. The window expands to look like that shown in Fig. 18-8.

Specify the appropriate confidence level in the **Alpha Level** pop-up menu, where 0.05 is offered as the default. An α-level of 0.05 means that, if we were to perform many independent repetitions of the experiment that generated the data and compute hypothesis tests *of a true null hypothesis* for each sample, we could expect that in the long run 5% of the tests would incorrectly reject the null hypothesis. Unlike the confidence level in the Estimate window, the α-level is *not* specified as a percent. In general, for a given α-level, the corresponding confidence level is $100(1 - \alpha)$%.

Next, specify the null and alternative hypotheses. The null hypothesis is specified in the $\mathbf{H_0}$ pop-up menu (Fig. 18-9). The default is $\mu = 0.0$, but you may specify any value.

The Test window offers three forms of alternative hypotheses. The alternative hypothesis is specified in the $\mathbf{H_a}$ pop-up menu. The default is a two-sided hypothesis test. Choosing a one-sided test improves your chance of rejecting the null hypothesis but introduces another subjective decision that must be documented and defended.

For example, a one-sided test of whether the average pay for women in a company was lower than the corresponding pay for men might be open to the challenge that the analysis was blind to the possibility that the company discriminated against men.

Data Desk computes the z-test statistic as

$$z = \frac{(\bar{y} - \mu_0)}{\sigma / \sqrt{n}}$$

where $\bar{y}$ is the sample mean, μ_0 is the value of the population mean specified in the null hypothesis, σ is the specified population standard deviation, and n is the number of numeric cases in the variable. The test compares the observed z-test statistic to the percentage point of a normal distribution that corresponds to the test's chosen α-level.

The pop-up menu to the left of the **Alpha Level** pop-up menu, holds the options Total and Individual. Use these options when you are testing hypotheses for two or more variables at once (see Section 18.9).

18.8 *Hypothesis Tests for μ When σ Is Unknown*

Usually, we don't know the standard deviation of the population and must estimate it from the sample. Therefore, we use a hypothesis test based on the t-distribution — a t-test.

To construct a t-test, choose {Calc} **Test**. Data Desk opens a Test window. Select **t-Test of Individual μ's** from the topmost pop-up menu. Define the test criteria using the remaining pop-up menus in the window, as described in Section 18.7.

From the **Alpha Level** pop-up menu, select the appropriate confidence level or choose Other... and type the confidence value in the window provided. Specify the null hypothesis from the $\mathbf{H_0}$ pop-up menu and the alternative hypothesis in the $\mathbf{H_a}$ pop-up menu. Select the **Show Results** button to compute the results.

Data Desk constructs the t-test statistic as

$$t_{(n-1)} = \frac{\bar{y} - \mu_0}{s/\sqrt{n}}$$

where $\bar{y}$ is the sample mean, μ_0 is the value of the population mean specified in the null hypothesis, s is the sample standard deviation, and n is the number of numeric values in the variable. The test compares the observed t-test statistic to the percentage point of a t-distribution that corresponds to the test's chosen α-level. The t-distribution's shape, and thus its percentage points, depends upon the degrees of freedom, $n - 1$, in this case.

18.9 *Multiple Hypothesis Tests and the Bonferroni Adjustment*

The Bonferroni procedure available for multiple confidence intervals also applies to hypothesis tests (see Section 18.5). It enables you to perform several tests without increasing the likelihood of rejecting at least one true null hypothesis. The Total confidence option performs a Bonferroni adjustment so that the probability of at least one erroneous test equals the α-level.

18.10 *Chi-Square Test of Individual Variances*

Data Desk also offers hypothesis tests for the variance. For samples drawn from a normal population, the statistic

$$(n - 1)\, s^2/\sigma^2$$

has a chi-square (χ^2) distribution with $(n - 1)$ degrees of freedom.

Choose **Chi-square Test of Individual Variances** from the topmost pop-up menu of the Test window and specify the confidence level value and the confidence level type from the appropriate pop-up menus. Select the **Specify Variance** button to enter the value for the null hypothesis; Data Desk automatically generates the term for the alternative hypothesis. You can still specify whether the test is to be two-sided, one-sided above the null value, or one-sided below the null value. Choose the **Show Results** button to compute the results.

APPENDIX 18A Example: Simulating Confidence Interval Performance

One way to get a better understanding of confidence intervals is to use Data Desk's ability to generate random values and simulate the collection of many samples from a known population. In this appendix we illustrate such an experiment.

Suppose that the true heights of the population of all women with soprano voices are normally distributed with a mean of 64 inches and a standard deviation of 2 inches. The experiment consists of drawing a sample of $n = 9$ women from this population. First, we choose {Manip} **Generate Random Numbers...**. To draw 20 independent samples of size 9 from a normal population with mean = 64 and standard deviation $\sigma = 2$, set the parameters in the Generate Random Data dialog as shown in Fig. 18-10.

```
Generate Random Data
Generate [20] variables with [9] cases.
Distribution:
( ) Uniform
(•) Normal mu = [64]   sigma = [2]
( ) Bernoulli trials: Prob(success) [ ]
( ) Binomial experiments:
      # Bernoulli trials / experiment [ ]
      Probability (success) = [ ]
( ) Poisson: lambda = [ ]
Seed = [ ]
Generator [Congruential]
[OK] [Cancel] [Help]
```

Figure 18-10. *To generate 20 random samples of* n *= 9 from a normal distribution with* $\mu = 64$ *and* $\sigma = 2$*, set the parameters in the* Generate Random Data *dialog.*

To construct a confidence interval for each of the 20 samples, Select all the variables (Ctrl-**A** is a shortcut on Windows, ⌘-**A** is a shortcut on Mac), choose {Calc} **Estimate**, specify **z-Interval of Individual μ's**, and enter the sigma value specified in the Generate Random Data dialog, in this case Sigma = 2 (Fig. 18-11).

For this experiment, choose **Individual confidence level**, each with a 90% confidence level. Accept the default two-sided interval form. Click the **Show Results** button to compute the calculations and open an output record of confidence intervals. Because this is a simulation, you should get different numbers than those displayed in Fig. 18-11 when you perform this experiment yourself.

```
z-Interval for Individual μ's
No Selector
Sigma = [2]
[Individual] Confidence [95%]
Bounds: [Lower Bound < μ < Upper Bound]
(Hide Results)
With 95% Confidence, 63.249064 < μ(Norm1) < 65.86235
With 95% Confidence, 63.409932 < μ(Norm2) < 66.023217
With 95% Confidence, 63.053121 < μ(Norm3) < 65.666406
With 95% Confidence, 62.299592 < μ(Norm4) < 64.912877
With 95% Confidence, 63.72244 < μ(Norm5) < 66.335725
With 95% Confidence, 61.797778 < μ(Norm6) < 64.411064
With 95% Confidence, 63.576476 < μ(Norm7) < 66.189761
With 95% Confidence, 63.142906 < μ(Norm8) < 65.756191
With 95% Confidence, 62.280193 < μ(Norm9) < 64.893478
With 95% Confidence, 63.08931 < μ(Norm10) < 65.702596
With 95% Confidence, 64.104303 < μ(Norm11) < 66.717588
With 95% Confidence, 62.479277 < μ(Norm12) < 65.092562
With 95% Confidence, 62.378715 < μ(Norm13) < 64.992
With 95% Confidence, 62.554792 < μ(Norm14) < 65.168077
With 95% Confidence, 62.651946 < μ(Norm15) < 65.265232
With 95% Confidence, 62.908758 < μ(Norm16) < 65.522044
With 95% Confidence, 62.440576 < μ(Norm17) < 65.053861
With 95% Confidence, 61.445949 < μ(Norm18) < 64.059235
With 95% Confidence, 63.783323 < μ(Norm19) < 66.396608
With 95% Confidence, 63.146932 < μ(Norm20) < 65.760218
```

Figure 18-11. *The 20 simulated confidence intervals.*

When we examine these confidence intervals we find that 1 of them fails to include the true mean of 64 inches. Because we computed the intervals at a 90% confidence level, we might have expected 10%, or 2, of them to fail to cover the true mean. This discrepancy illustrates that statistical inference only specifies how statistics will behave in the long run.

APPENDIX 18B Example: Simulating Hypothesis Test Performance

Suppose, as we did in the simulation of confidence intervals, that the true heights of the population of all women with soprano voices are normally distributed with a mean of 64 inches and a standard deviation of 2 inches. Let an experiment consist of drawing a sample of $n = 9$ women from this population. For convenience, we use the same samples generated for the confidence interval experiment in Appendix 18A. We could have generated 20 new samples.

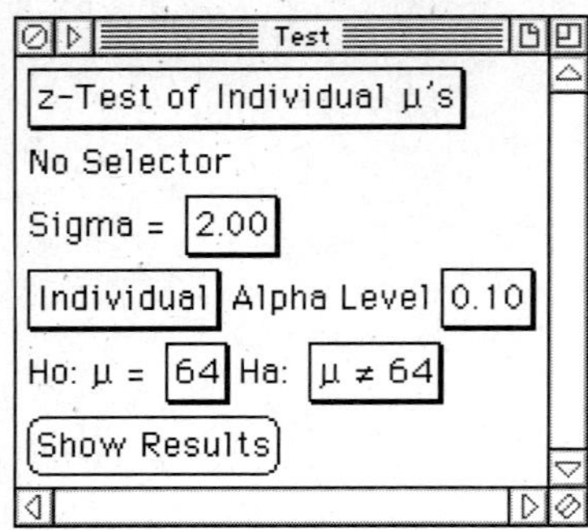

Figure 18-12. *Specifying z-test for 20 random normal samples.*

To perform a hypothesis test for each of the 20 samples, select the *Ran Data* relation icon (this automatically selects all 20 variables), choose {Calc} **Test**, specify **z-Test of Individual μ's**, and set Sigma = 2 (Fig. 18-12).

For this experiment, choose **Individual** confidence at an α-level of 0.10.

Specify a null hypothesis of μ = 64, and accept the default two-sided alternative hypothesis.

Click the **Show Results** button to display an output record of hypothesis tests. Because this is a simulation, you should get different numbers if you perform this experiment yourself. There isn't room to show all 20 tests, but the first four we obtained appear in Fig. 18-13.

```
Norm1 :
Test Ho: μ(Norm1) = 64 vs Ha: μ(Norm1) ≠ 64
Sample Mean = 64.016743 z-Statistic = 0.0251
Fail to reject Ho at Alpha = 0.10
p = 0.9800
Norm2 :
Test Ho: μ(Norm2) = 64 vs Ha: μ(Norm2) ≠ 64
Sample Mean = 63.684731 z-Statistic = -0.4729
Fail to reject Ho at Alpha = 0.10
p = 0.6363
Norm3 :
Test Ho: μ(Norm3) = 64 vs Ha: μ(Norm3) ≠ 64
Sample Mean = 64.312905 z-Statistic = 0.4694
Fail to reject Ho at Alpha = 0.10
p = 0.6388
Norm4 :
Test Ho: μ(Norm4) = 64 vs Ha: μ(Norm4) ≠ 64
Sample Mean = 63.312526 z-Statistic = -1.031
Fail to reject Ho at Alpha = 0.10
p = 0.3024
```

Figure 18-13. *The first four simulated hypothesis tests.*

Because we computed the tests at an α-level of 0.10, we expect, on average, that 10%, or 2, of the tests will reject the null hypothesis even though it is true.

EXERCISES

1. Work through the example in Appendix 18A, generating your own set of 20 confidence intervals. How many of the confidence intervals that you constructed contained the true population mean μ? How many would you have expected? Write the intervals you obtained (or print them) and circle the ones that don't contain the population parameter.

2. Suppose that tenors' heights are normally distributed with $\mu = 69$ and $\sigma = 3.2$. Repeat the experiment in Exercise 1 for tenors. (Save the random samples you generate for Exercise 3.)

(a) How many of the intervals contain μ?

(b) Are all the intervals of the same width? Should they be? Explain.

(c) Suppose that we had specified a 97% confidence level instead of 90% for the intervals we constructed in the example in Appendix 18A. Would you expect the intervals to be narrower or wider than before? Explain.

(d) Suppose that we had drawn samples of size $n = 49$ instead of 9. Would you expect the intervals computed to be narrower or wider than for $n = 9$? By how much?

(e) Suppose that we had thought that σ was 2 (rather than the true value of 3.2) and had calculated z-intervals accordingly. Would you expect more or fewer intervals to fail to cover μ? (Give it a try.) Why?

3. Repeat the experiment in Exercise 2 *for the same random samples* but compute t-intervals instead of z-intervals.

(a) How many of the intervals contain μ?

(b) Are all the intervals of the same width? Should they be? Explain.

(c) Suppose that we had specified a 97% confidence level instead of 90% for the intervals we constructed. Would you expect the intervals to be narrower or wider than before? Explain.

(d) Suppose that we had drawn samples of size $n = 49$ instead of 9. Would you expect the interval computed to be narrower or wider than for $n = 9$? Why?

(e) Compare the individual intervals in Exercises 2 and 3. How do the probability values from the tables compare? How do the estimated standard deviations compare to the standard deviation specified in Exercise 2?

4. When you construct a confidence interval for some population parameter, first select a *confidence level,* say, 95%. What is the correct interpretation of this number? (Circle the letters of all the statements that apply.)

(a) The population value has a 95% chance of falling within the constructed interval.
(b) If a very large number of confidence intervals were constructed, roughly 95% of them would contain the population value, μ.
(c) The population value equals 95.
(d) If a very large number of confidence intervals were constructed, roughly 5% of them would not contain the population value, μ.

5. Generate a random sample of 25 observations from a normal distribution with $\mu = 71$ and $\sigma = 2.5$. Construct a confidence interval for μ from the data, specifying a confidence level of 93%. Assume that the parent normal distribution is the true population that describes the heights of bass singers. Write the interval you obtained and interpret its meaning in both words and numbers.

6. To construct a confidence interval for μ when σ is unknown, you use the _______ distribution. This population is symmetric about its mean, but the peakedness varies according to the __________.

7. When constructing a hypothesis test, you specify the α-level. It is a number that ranges between __________ and __________. Give the definition of the α-level.

8. The general problem of performing several inferential procedures together is called the problem of multiple comparisons. You can apply a Bonferroni adjustment to guarantee that a set of independently constructed inferential statements (that is, confidence intervals) collectively yield a specified "total confidence level." If, for example, you request that a set of 5 intervals collectively yield a total confidence level of 95%, the Bonferroni adjustment would require that each interval be constructed according to a _____% level.

9. Repeat Exercise 3 but request a Bonferroni adjustment for the confidence intervals.

(a) How many contain the population mean?

(b) How many should you have expected?

10. Retrieve the Singers dataset. Compute a test of the null hypothesis that the true mean height of bass singers is 70 inches. Specify an alternative hypothesis of your choosing. Assume that the population of bass heights has a standard deviation of 3. Perform the test at a 5% confidence level.

(a) For this problem, should you perform a *z*-test or *t*-test? Explain your answer.

(b) Write the results of the test, as presented by Data Desk.

(c) Using both words and numbers, interpret what the test tells you about the heights of bass singers.

11. Test the hypothesis described in Exercise 10 but assume that the standard deviation of bass heights is unknown. In this case, you should perform a _______ test. Write the results of the test, as presented by Data Desk.

12. Test the null hypothesis that the population variance of soprano heights equals 4. Assume that soprano heights are normally distributed. For this problem, use the __________ distribution. Perform the test and write the results.

CHAPTER 19

Comparing Two Samples

MOST DATA ANALYSES deal with relationships. The comparison of two groups is one of the simplest relationships. The simplest comparison is a comparison of their centers. Such comparisons include questions such as "Are women paid less than men for the same work?" or "Is drug therapy A better than drug therapy B?"or "Will the Democratic or Republican candidate win more votes in the next election?"

Most of the methods in this chapter are strictly appropriate only when the underlying data are normally distributed. But they can be applied to data for which this assumption is only approximately true. Unlike the methods we discussed in some other chapters, some of these tests can compare unrelated groups of individuals and thus can apply to variables in different relations.

19.1 *Displaying Differences*

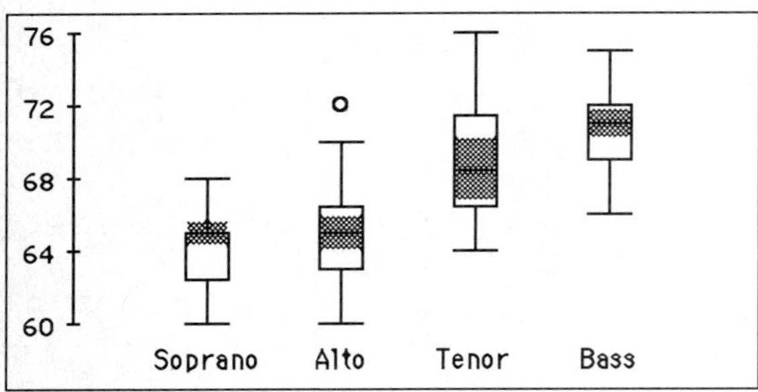

Figure 19-1. *Boxplots comparing the heights of singers by vocal part.*

Boxplots (see Section 8.7) are a useful way to display differences among variables because they focus on the features we most often compare. Boxplots show differences in the level or center in two ways — both as differences among medians (shown with a bar across the box) and as differences in the overall level of the boxes. They also show differences in spread through the size and extent of the boxes and of the whiskers. Finally, they explicitly exhibit outliers, which might affect numerical comparisons in unexpected ways.

The boxplots comparing the heights of singers in the Singers data provide a good example (Fig. 19-1).

19.2 *How to Set Up Your Data*

All Data Desk commands in the **Test** and **Estimate** menus expect the data values being compared to be in separate variables. If your data values are in one variable with a second variable holding the grouping data (the required format for ANOVA, discussed in Chapter 21), you need to perform a simple data manipulation step before you proceed with any of the commands discussed in Chapters 19 and 20. Select the variable holding the data as y and the variable holding the groups as x, and choose {Manip} **Split into Variables by Group**. Select the new variables and choose the required **Test** or **Estimate** command.

19.3 *Comparing Two Means When the Variances Are Assumed To Be Equal*

pooled variance

Often the two groups to be compared are similar in most respects, except that their means might be different. When we are willing to assume that the population variances of the two underlying populations are equal, procedures that use *pooled variance* estimates are appropriate.

The assumption of equal variances, like the assumption of normally distributed populations, isn't tested in the data; rather it is asserted by the data analyst. You should be prepared to justify this assertion from your knowledge of the population separate from the values in the samples at hand.

The pooled t-statistic combines, or pools, the data from both samples to get a single estimate of variance. Because t-statistics usually derive their degrees of freedom from the variance estimate, a pooled t-statistic is based on more degrees of freedom than the corresponding two-sample t-statistic (see Section 19.6). Thus the corresponding confidence intervals for $\mu 1 - \mu 2$ are somewhat smaller, and the corresponding tests for the difference between the means are more powerful *provided the assumption of equal variances is correct.*

To perform a pooled t-test, select the two variables to compare, choose {Calc} **Test** and select **pooled t-Test of μ_1 - μ_2.** from the topmost pop-up menu. Specify the alpha level, the H_0, and H_A values in the corresponding pop-up menus and click the **Show Results** button to display the results.

The pop-up menu **Total** is useful only when you are computing several hypothesis tests between means. (See Section 18.5 regarding the Bonferroni adjustment in the context of simple hypothesis tests.)

19.4 *An Example*

A glance at the boxplots in Fig. 19-1 confirms that the basses in this sample are taller than the sopranos. But do the basses and tenors differ in height? To investigate this question, we select the two variables and choose {Calc} **Test** (Fig. 19-2).

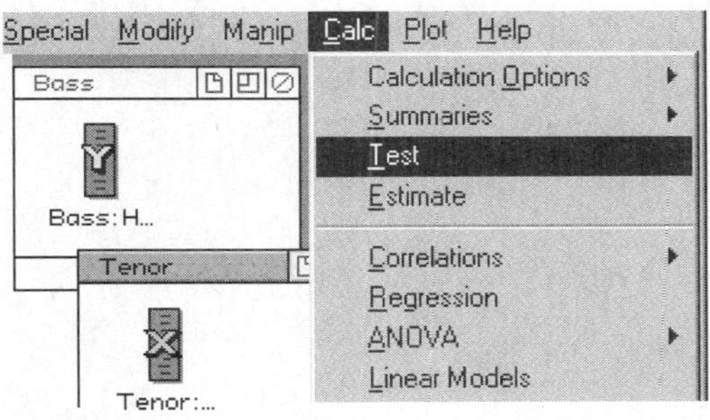

Figure 19-2. *Select* Tenor *and* Bass *and choose* **Test** *from the* **Calc** *menu.*

(The Singers dataset is unusual. Each vocal part has different singers, so variables reporting the heights of sopranos, altos, tenors, and basses must each be in their own relation. The dataset is organized so that the different relations are kept in a folder named *Relations,* but the variables that hold the heights are in a separate folder named *Heights.* Even though the variables have been placed in the same folder, they are still in separate relations. You can use them together only for those Data Desk operations that can work across relations.)

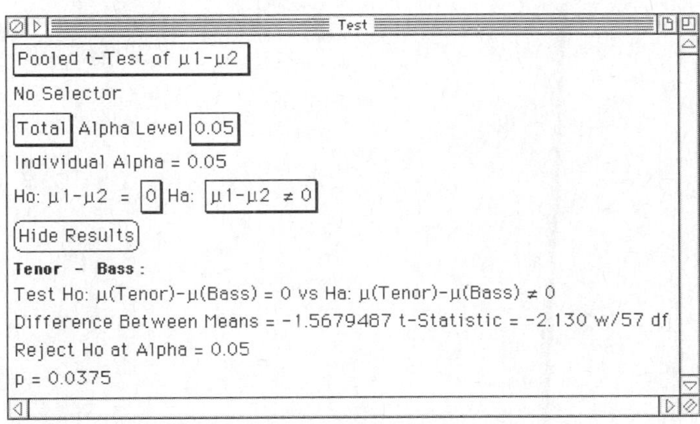

Figure 19-3. *The pooled* t-*test on heights of N.Y. Choral Society basses and tenors.*

We can assume that the tenors and basses in the N.Y. Choral Society are two independent samples from the population of men in the New York area and thus that the variances of their heights ought to be equal. We request a pooled estimate of the underlying population variance of height.

The null hypothesis of no difference in height ($\mu 1 - \mu 2 = 0$) is appropriate here, as is the default two-sided alternative ($\mu 1 - \mu 2 \neq 0$). That is, we didn't start out believing that either tenors or basses would be taller — a difference in either direction would be equally interesting.

The resulting test, in Fig. 19-3, shows that at the 0.05 α-level, we can indeed discern a difference in the heights of N.Y. Choral Society basses and tenors.

19.5 Formulas

The pooled estimate of variance is computed as

$$s_p^2 = \frac{(n_1 - 1)s_1^2 + (n_2 - 1)s_2^2}{n_1 + n_2 - 2}$$

where n_1 and n_2 are the sample sizes of the two groups and s_1^2 and s_2^2 are the sample variances of the two groups.

The pooled t-test statistic is

$$t = \frac{(\bar{y}_1 - \bar{y}_2)}{s_p\sqrt{1/n_1 + 1/n_2}}$$

where $\bar{y}_1$ and $\bar{y}_2$ are the sample means, $s_p = \sqrt{s_p^2}$ and n_1 and n_2 are the sample sizes. The t-statistic has $(n_1 + n_2 - 2)$ degrees of freedom.

19.6 Confidence Intervals for Pooled Variance

The **Estimate** command in the **Calc** menu offers confidence intervals for the difference in the population means, $\mu_1 - \mu_2$. Select **Pooled Interval of** $\boldsymbol{\mu_1 - \mu_2}$ from the topmost pop-up menu, specify the appropriate parameters in the other pop-up menus, and click the **Show Results** button. (Section 18.2 explains how to define the parameters.)

The confidence interval is computed as

$$(\bar{y}_1 - \bar{y}_2) \pm t^*_{df} s_p \sqrt{1/n_1 + 1/n_2}$$

where $\bar{y}_1$ and $\bar{y}_2$ are the sample means, $s_p = \sqrt{s_p^2}$ and n_1 and n_2 are the sample sizes, and t^*_{df} is the appropriate percentage point of the t-distribution with $(n_1 + n_2 - 2)$ degrees of freedom.

19.7 Comparing Two Means When the Variances Are Not Assumed To Be Equal

two-sample* t*-test

When we are unwilling to assume that the underlying population variances are equal but are still willing to believe that the populations are normally distributed, the *two-sample t* procedures are often appropriate. The difference between the two-sample t-procedures and the pooled t-procedures is that the former uses two estimates of variance — one from each sample — and has fewer degrees of freedom associated with the resulting t-statistic.

In the Test or the Estimate windows, select the **2-Sample t-Test of** $\boldsymbol{\mu_1 - \mu_2}$. The remaining steps are identical to those described in Sections 19.3 and 19.6.

The two-sample t-interval is computed as

$$(\bar{y}_1 - \bar{y}_2) \pm t^*_{df}\sqrt{s_1^2/n_1 + s_2^2/n_2}$$

where t^*_{df} is the appropriate percentage point from a t-distribution. The two-sample t-statistic is one of the few common statistics for which the calculation of degrees of freedom is complex. Data Desk approximates the degrees of freedom as

$$df = \frac{(s_1^2/n_1 + s_2^2/n_2)^2}{\dfrac{(s_1^2/n_1)^2}{n_1 - 1} + \dfrac{(s_2^2/n_2)^2}{n_2 - 1}}$$

The corresponding test statistic is

$$t_{df} = \frac{(\bar{y}_1 - \bar{y}_2)}{\sqrt{s_1^2/n_1 + s_2^2/n_2}}$$

19.8 *Paired Data*

paired* t-*statistics

When each case in the first group is paired naturally with the corresponding case in the second group, we can take advantage of the additional structure in the data and compute *paired t-statistics.* Typical pairings are pairs of twins, measurements on the same patient before and after medication, or pairs of judgements made by the same individuals.

Comparisons of paired groups operate on the pairs. Paired t-statistics find the pairwise differences and then construct a t-statistic based upon these differences by treating them as if they were a univariate collection of data values.

When data are naturally paired, paired t-procedures are likely to produce smaller confidence intervals and more powerful tests. If the data are not naturally paired, paired t-procedures are invalid.

Paired variables are typically in the same relation.

19.9 *An Example*

The Labor Force dataset contains the labor force participation rate (LFPR) of women in 19 cities in the United States in each of 2 years. These data might help us examine the growing presence of women in the labor force.

We can compute a pooled t-test to see if the LFPR in 1972 was different from the LFPR in 1968. Pooling seems reasonable because the cities in the United States didn't change much between 1968 and 1972. The hypothesis test shown in Fig. 19-4 doesn't discern any difference in the LFPR between 1968 and 1972.

pooled t-Test

1968 - 1972:
Test Ho: μ(1968)-μ(1972) = 0.00 vs Ha: μ(1968)-μ(1972) ≠ 0.00
Difference Between Means = -0.033684 t-Statistic = -1.496 w/36 df
Fail to reject Ho at Alpha = 0.05
p ≤ 0.14341

Figure 19-4. *Testing for a change in labor force participation rate among women with a pooled* t*-test.*

```
1968 - 1972:
Test Ho: μ(1968-1972) = 0.00 vs Ha: μ(1968-1972) ≠ 0.00
Mean of Paired Differences = -0.033684  t-Statistic = -2.458 w/18 df
Reject Ho at Alpha = 0.05
p ≤ 0.02435
```

Figure 19-5. The paired t*-test, contrary to the pooled* t*-test in Fig. 19-4, takes advantage of the natural pairing in the data and rejects the null hypothesis of no change in LFPR among women.*

However, these data are naturally paired because the measurements were made in the *same cities* for each of the 2 years. If some cities naturally have a high LFPR and others a low LFPR (which wouldn't be surprising), the variability across all cities might have swamped any changes over the 4-year period we are studying. Moreover, because cities with a high LFPR in 1968 typically have a high LFPR in 1972, we should try to look beyond the city-to-city differences so that we can concentrate on the year-to-year differences.

Thus to study changes in the LFPR, it is more appropriate to treat the data as paired, considering the change in each city between 1968 and 1972 and then looking at the collection of all these changes. The paired *t*-test shown in Fig. 19-5 rejects the null hypothesis of no difference.

19.10 *Comparing Multiple Means when the Variances Are Assumed To Be Equal*

F-*test*

There might be a situation where we want to test whether the means of more than two groups are equal. If we are willing to assume that the population variances of the underlying populations are equal, we can perform an *F*-test of multiple μ's. This test is the same test as a one-way Analysis of Variance (see Chapter 21). The decision to choose either command is based upon how the data are entered in Data Desk.

When the values for each group are stored in individual variables, the *F*-test of multiple μ's is most appropriate. When they are stored as values in a single variable with group names in a second variable, the ANOVA commands are more appropriate.

For example, we can compare the mean heights among the different singing parts in the Singers dataset. There are four parts — sopranos, altos, tenors and basses — each recorded in a separate variable. An *F*-test tests the hypothesis "The mean heights of singers in all four vocal parts are the same."

To perform an *F*-test, select the variables whose means you want to compare and choose {Calc} **Test**. Select **F-Test of Multiple μ's** from the top-most pop-up menu, specify the alpha level, and choose the **Show Results** button. Data Desk computes an *F*-ratio and a Prob value.

The *F*-ratio is the ratio of an estimate of the variance of the means based upon comparing the means of the different groups to an alternative estimate based upon a pooled estimate of variance. When the null hypothesis is true, both values estimate σ^2, the population variance, so the *F*-ratio will be near 1.0. The pooled variance estimates σ^2 even when the treatment means differ, but the numerator will grow as the group means vary. When the group means are different, the *F*-ratio grows.

The Prob value is the probability of observing an *F*-ratio as large as the one computed or larger, *if the null hypothesis were true.* The null hypothesis of equal treatment means can be rejected when the Prob value is smaller than the α-level you select for the test.

EXERCISES

1. Pooled t-procedures are appropriate when you can assume that the underlying population ______________________ are equal. A t-statistic based on a pooled estimate of variance has more ______________________ than a t-statistic based on separate estimates of variances.

2. Retrieve the Clouds dataset. The data represent rainfall measured for each of 52 clouds, 26 of which were chosen at random and seeded with silver iodide. Test the null hypothesis that the mean rainfall obtained from seeded clouds equals the mean rainfall obtained from unseeded clouds. Assume that the underlying population variances are unequal.

(a) Choose $\alpha = 0.05$ and test the null hypothesis against a two-sided alternative. Write the results of the test from the Data Desk output table.

(b) The scientist who conducted this experiment believed that seeding clouds increases rainfall and could not reduce it. For $\alpha = 0.05$, test the null hypothesis against this alternative. Write your results.

(c) Discuss any differences you observe between the results you obtained in parts (a) and (b).

3. (a) Repeat the test of Exercise 2(a) but choose $\alpha = 0.10$. Write your results.

(b) Explain how and why these results differ from those obtained in Exercise 2(a).

4. (a) Construct a confidence interval for the true mean difference between unseeded and seeded clouds. Request a 95% confidence level; assume that the population variances are unequal. Write the confidence interval.

(b) Explain in *words* what this interval tells you.

(c) How does the confidence interval relate to the hypothesis test performed in Exercise 2(a)?

(d) If you assumed that the underlying population variances were equal, how many degrees of freedom would the resulting t-statistic have?

5. Use the Singers dataset.

(a) Compute a 95% confidence interval for the difference between the true mean heights of tenor and bass singers. Write your results.

(b) Explain in *words* the meaning of the interval.

6. Use both a pooled t-hypothesis test and a pooled t-confidence interval to compare the heights of the sopranos and altos. Write your findings.

Does the interval tell you anything more than the hypothesis test? Why or why not?

7. (a) Assume that the true height of sopranos is 65 inches. Define a derived variable that computes the *t*-statistic value for the sopranos in the Singers dataset. Write the derived variable expression.

(b) Compute the value of the derived variable and compare it to the value produced by the **Test** command. Write these results.

(c) Assume that the underlying populations of tenors and sopranos are normally distributed. Test the hypothesis that the underlying variances are equal. Write your findings.

8. Use the Labor Force dataset.

(a) What are the individual cases in these data? What population(s) might they have been drawn from?

(b) Construct a 95% confidence interval for the difference between the labor force participation rates in 1968 and in 1972 both *without* and *with* pooled variance. Write the intervals and discuss how and why they differ.

(c) Does there appear to be a difference in the LFPR for these two years? How does this interval differ from the pooled variance interval? Explain your answers.

(d) Define a derived variable that, for each city, gives the difference between the 1968 and 1972 LFPRs. Construct a 90% confidence interval for its mean and compare it to a paired t-confidence interval computed for the same data.

9. Use the Hearing dataset.

(a) Test the null hypothesis that the first and fourth lists are equally difficult to understand in the presence of noise. Write your results.

(b) Compute a two-sample t-interval for the mean difference in hearing perception between list 1 and list 4. Write the interval.

(c) Use a paired t-procedure to compare hearing perception for list 1 and list 4. Write your results.

(d) Which of the three ways of comparing means is most appropriate for these data? Why?

10. Generate two samples of 35 cases from a normal distribution with $\mu = 10$ and $\sigma = 2$. Suppose that you want to compare these samples to test whether their underlying populations have the same mean.

(a) What is the appropriate null hypothesis? Is it true for these data? Explain your answer.

(b) If you perform a pooled t-test at $\alpha = 0.10$, what is the probability that you will reject the null hypothesis for these samples?

(c) Perform the test and write your result.

CHAPTER 20

Nonparametrics

THE TERM *NONPARAMETRIC* refers to statistical assumptions and hypotheses that do not specify parameters of an underlying distribution. For example, the null hypothesis

$$H_0: \mu = 0$$

is parametric because it specifies the population mean, μ. In contrast, the hypothesis

H_0: The population is symmetric

is nonparametric because no population parameters are mentioned.

The term *distribution-free* refers to tests that are valid regardless of the underlying distributions of the variables (except possibly for some very general assumptions, such as continuity).

nonparametric tests

Both terms (as well as some others such as *assumption-free*), although not synonyms, attempt to define a class of tests that are based upon few assumptions concerning the underlying populations. We follow the common custom of calling all such tests *nonparametric tests*.

The effective use of nonparametric tests is something of an art. We suggest that you read some of the many texts on this subject for a more complete discussion.

20.1 *Medians and Means*

Nonparametric tests often deal with characteristics of a population, such as continuity, symmetry, and quantiles that may not behave intuitively. For example, medians cannot be added and subtracted the way means can be added and subtracted.

That is, mean(x1 – x2) = mean(x1) – mean(x2), but in general the most common nonparametric alternative, the median, doesn't behave in the same way. In general,

$$\text{Median}(x1 - x2) \neq \text{Median}(x1) - \text{Median}(x2).$$

Thus, although the statement "variables X and Y have the same mean" is the same as "the variable X – Y has mean 0," the two statements aren't equivalent if we replace "mean" with "median."

Many two-sample nonparametric tests are tests of the median of a difference, testing whether med(x1 – x2) = 0. Even if the test concludes that the median difference isn't 0, we can't necessarily conclude that the populations have different medians.

20.2 *Ties*

bins

ranks

Many nonparametric tests sort data into ordered *bins*. For example, negative data values may be placed in one bin and positive values in another. Other nonparametric tests are based on *ranks*. Ranking can be viewed as placing the data in integer-valued bins with the lowest value in bin 1, the second lowest in bin 2, and so on. Values that are sorted into the same bin or assigned the same rank are said to be tied.

Binning procedures require that each data value be placed in a bin. Conversely, we would not expect a continuous variable to have two cases with exactly the same value, so in theory, no two values should have the same rank. However, real data aren't this simple. Even if the "true" data values are continuous, and thus different in perhaps the tenth decimal place, we can only record numbers with finite precision. As a result, our "bins" actually hold values that are very close but different. Data values placed in the same bin or given the same rank are called *ties.*

ties

Ties in the data change the significance level and power of nonparametric tests. Statisticians do not agree on the best way to handle them. Some advocate omitting tied data. This approach is the simplest and probably the most common. But ties can be included in nonparametric tests in several ways. For each nonparametric test, except the Wilcoxon signed rank test, Data Desk offers you the choice of including or omitting tied data. When alternative ways to include ties are available, Data Desk tries to favor the more conservative alternative, that is, the one that reduces the chance of a false positive result.

20.3 *One-Sample Sign Test*

one-sample sign test

The *one-sample sign test* tests whether the population median is equal to a specified value. The test is based on the binomial distribution, the distribution that describes the results of flipping a coin, or other two-outcome events.

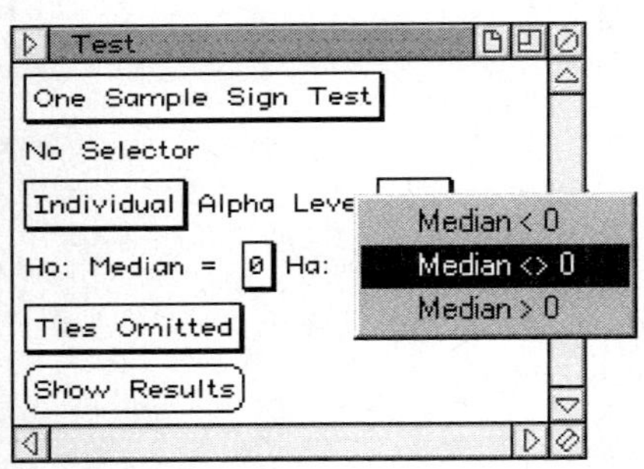

Figure 20-1. *Pop-up menus in the window provide a convenient way to specify details of the hypothesis test.*

To perform a one-sample sign test, select a variable and choose the {Calc} **Test** command. Choose **One Sample Sign Test** from the top pop-up menu. The pop-up menus in the window provide a convenient way to specify details of the hypothesis test (Fig. 20-1).

Specify the appropriate alpha level in the **Alpha Level** pop-up menu. Use the **H0** pop-up menu to specify the null hypothesis. The default is Median = 0, but you may specify any value by choosing Other....

Data Desk provides three alternative hypotheses. The **Ha** pop-up menu offers a choice of two-sided or one-sided to the left or right. The default is a two-sided alternative hypothesis. Choosing a one-sided alternative hypothesis improves your chance of rejecting the null hypothesis but introduces another subjective decision that must be defended. (See Section 18.7 for a discussion of one and two-sided tests.)

In Section 20.2 we discuss ties and their effects on nonparametric tests. In the one sample sign test, values equal to the hypothesized median are considered ties. If you decide to exclude ties from your test, choose Ties Omitted from the **Ties** pop-up menu.

If you are comparing more than one variable at once, you may want to perform a Bonferonni adjustment so that the total probability of at least one falsely positive test result equals the α–level. The default selection, *Total*, performs the Bonferonni adjustment. To perform the tests without the Bonferonni adjustment, change **Total** to **Individual**.

Once you have specified all the details of the test, the **Show Results** button becomes active. Choose the button to display the results.

```
MPG :
Test Ho: Median(MPG) = 20 vs Ha: Median(MPG) ≠ 20
Total Observations: 50
Observations MPG > 20: 42
Ties: 1
p ≤ 0.0001
Reject Ho at Alpha = 0.0500
```

Figure 20-2. *The result of the one-sample sign test for the MPG data.*

The first line of results restates the hypothesis using the variable names and hypothesized value. The Total Observations value is the number of nonmissing values in the selected variable. The test statistic is the number of cases that are greater than the hypothesized median. Because the median has half the data above it and half below it, we estimate the probability of the observed number of values above the median from the binomial distribution with probability, $p = .5$. If you choose to include ties, they are assigned to the bin (either above or below the hypothesized median) that has the fewest cases. This procedure makes the test more conservative by making rejection of the null hypothesis less likely.

Figure 20-2 displays the results for a two-tailed test with a hypothesis that the median miles per gallon value for a sample of cars is 20 mpg. The data comes from the Cars91 datafile.

20.4 *Paired Sign Test*

paired sign test

The *paired sign test* is the oldest nonparametric test, dating back to a 1710 study of the frequencies of male versus female births in London. It tests the median of the difference between two variables. It can be used to test a variety of hypotheses, but the possible interactions between the two populations and the variety of assumptions that can be made concerning the underlying distributions complicates its use. Thus we recommend that you consult a good reference text before using the paired sign test more generally.

Like the paired *t*-test (see Section 19.7), the paired sign test requires that the two variables being compared be naturally paired. That is, the first data value in one variable must match naturally with the first data value in the other variable. It isn't sufficient for the two variables simply to have the same number of data values; there must be an intrinsic match between them.

The paired sign test is based upon the assumption that the sample pairs are a random sample from the population of pairs. This assumption implies that the pairs are independent of each other. It doesn't imply that the two variables are independent. If you are willing to assume that the two variables are independent, you should choose the more powerful Mann–Whitney *U* test (see Section 20.6). Other assumptions are sometimes made in order to eliminate bias or achieve consistency. Examples of such assumptions are that both populations have symmetric distributions or that both populations have identical distributions except for location. Ties are cases in which the *x*- and *y*-values are equal.

The paired sign test is unbiased and is consistent for tests of the following hypotheses:

$$H_0: \text{Median}(x1-x2) = 0,\ H_a: \text{Median}(x1-x2) \neq 0 \text{ (2-sided test)}$$

$$H_0: \text{Median}(x1-x2) = 0,\ H_a: \text{Median}(x1-x2) < 0 \text{ (1-sided test)}$$

H_0: Median(x1–x2) = 0, H_a: Median(x1–x2) > 0 (1-sided test)

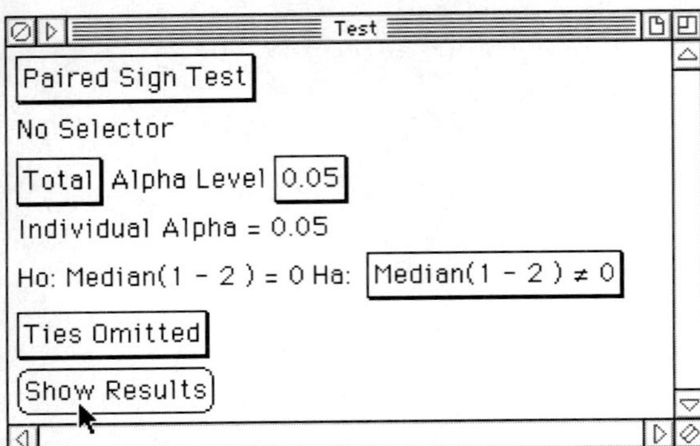

Figure 20-3. *The contents of the window specify details for the paired sign test.*

To perform a paired sign test, select two variables and choose the {Calc} **Test** command. Data Desk displays a test window with several pop-up menus (Fig. 20-3). Choose Paired Sign Test from the topmost pop-up menu. The details of the paired sign test are specified the same way as the one-sample sign test. When you are finished, press the **Show Results** button to display the results.

The first line of results restates the hypothesis, showing the variable names and test details. The Total Observations value is the number of nonmissing pairs in the selected variables. If either variable is missing, the entire case is removed from the computation. The test statistic is the number of cases for which the variable selected as y is greater than the variable selected as x. The critical region is found from the cumulative binomial distribution; B(n, x, 0.5) and the alternative hypothesis.

If you choose to include ties, they are assigned to the bin (either the difference greater than 0 or less than 0) that has the fewest cases, making the test more conservative by making nonrejection of the null hypothesis less likely.

Fig. 20-4 displays the results for a two-tailed test with a hypothesis that the labor force participation rate of women didn't change from 1968 to 1972. The data come from the Labor Force datafile.

1972 - 1968:
Test Ho: Median(1972-1968) = 0 vs Ha: Median(1972-1968) ≠ 0
Total Observations: 19
Observations 1972 > 1968: 13
Tied Values Between Samples: 4
p = 0.0074
Reject Ho at Alpha = 0.05

Figure 20-4. *The results of the paired sign test for the LFPR data reinforce the results obtained with the paired* t*-test in Section 19.8.*

20.5 *Wilcoxon Signed Rank Test*

Wilcoxon signed rank test

The Wilcoxon signed rank test is often applied to situations in which two treatments are tested by randomly assigning units to matched pairs, each unit of a pair receives one of the alternative treatments. This test is the nonparametric equivalent to the paired t-test (see Section 19.8). It would also be appropriate to apply the paired sign test to this situation. However, when we are willing to make certain assumptions about the data (for example, that the underlying error distribution is logistic) the Wilcoxon signed rank test is more powerful. Some analysts prefer to use the Wilcoxon signed rank test rather than the paired sign test when the data can be assumed to be symmetric, but it isn't clear whether this choice is well founded statistically.

An assumption of the Wilcoxon signed rank test is that the sample pairs are a random sample from the population of pairs and that the pairs are independent. This assumption doesn't mean that the two variables being compared are independent. If the two variables being compared can be assumed to be independent, the more powerful Mann-Whitney *U* test should be used instead. Commonly, the two variables being compared are assumed to come from populations that are either symmetric or identical (except, possibly, for location). This assumption ensures both lack of bias and consistency of the tests.

Like the paired sign test, the Wilcoxon signed rank test requires that the two variables being compared be naturally paired. That is, the first data value in one variable must match naturally with the first data value in the other variable. It isn't sufficient for the two variables simply to have the same number of data values; there must be an intrinsic match between them.

To perform a Wilcoxon signed rank test select two variables and choose {Calc}**Test**. From the topmost pop-up menu choose Wilcoxon Signed Rank. The details of the Wilcoxon signed rank test are specified the same way as in the other nonparametric tests (see Section 20.3). When you are finished specifying the test details, choose the **Show Results** button to display the results.

The Wilcoxon signed rank test calculates the absolute differences between the elements of each pair and ranks them. The variable selected as x is subtracted from the variable selected as y. If both variables are selected as y's or x's, the rightmost selected variable is subtracted from the leftmost selected variable. The sum of these ranks is calculated and displayed in the output table as the Rank Total for the Positive Ranks. The sum of the ranks for the cases where y is less than x is displayed in the Rank Total for Negative Ranks. The table also displays the number of cases and the Mean Rank for the Positive Rank and Negative Rank cases.

There are two kinds of ties in the Wilcoxon signed rank test. The first occurs if the two values of a pair are equal. This kind of tie is analogous to the ties in the paired sign test. Data Desk always excludes these ties from the test. The number of these ties, their rank total, and their mean rank are displayed in the Ties row of the output table.

The second kind of tie occurs if the absolute difference for one pair is equal to the absolute difference for another pair. Every pair that has the same absolute difference is assigned to the same tied differences group. The number of these tied groups is displayed in the Tied Differences row. The pairs in these tied groups are always included in the test and are assigned the average rank of the grouped pairs. However, the presence of grouped ties destroys the unconditional properties of the test and requires that the distribution of the statistic be approximated. Whenever ties of this kind are present, Data Desk displays the z-statistic, the variance, and the adjustment to the variance for the presence of ties.

1972 - 1968:

Test Ho: Median(1972-1968) = 0 vs Ha: Median(1972-1968) ≠ 0

	Rank Totals	Cases	Mean Rank
Positive Ranks	104	13	8
Negative Ranks	16	2	8
Ties	•	4	•
Total	120	15	8

Tied differences: 3
Variance: 310
Adjustment To Variance For Ties: -0.75000
Expected Value: 60
z-Statistic: 2.5021
p = 0.0123
Reject Ho at Alpha = 0.05

Figure 20-5. *Results table for a two-tailed Wilcoxon signed rank test comparing the difference between labor force participation rates in 1968 and 1972.*

The distribution of this statistic under the null hypothesis has been tabulated for small n and can be approximated by an appropriate normal distribution for large n. When the number of total paired cases is less than 33, Data Desk computes and displays an exact p-value. When the distribution is approximated, Data

Desk presents the z-statistic and variance in addition to the approximated p-value. Because Data Desk computes an exact p-value for analyses with small n and no tied differences, your answers might differ from results generated by software that computes approximations.

Fig. 20-5 displays results for a Wilcoxon sign rank test of the same Labor Force dataset used in the paired sign test example of Section 20.4. The formulas for the variance, adjustment for ties to variance, expected value, and z-value are given in Appendix 20A.

20.6 *Mann–Whitney* U *Test*

Mann-Whitney* U *Test

The Mann–Whitney U test is the most commonly applied nonparametric two-sample test. It is meant to test the equality of distributions of two populations, although with certain assumptions, it can be used as a test of the difference in location of the two populations. This test is the nonparametric equivalent to the two sample t-test (see Section 19.7).

The Mann–Whitney U test is based upon the assumption that the variables being compared are random samples from their respective populations. Other assumptions are that the two variables are independent and that the populations have continuous distributions. If we assume that the population distributions differ only in location, the test becomes a test for equality of location.

1972 - 1968:

Test Ho: Median(1972) = Median(1968) vs Ha: Median(1972) ≠ Median(1968)

	Rank Totals	Cases	Mean Rank
1972	124	10	12.40
1968	86	10	8.600
Total	210	20	10.50
Ties Between Groups	•	18	•

U-Statistic: 69
U-prime: 31
Sets of ties between all included observations: 5
Variance: 175
Adjustment To Variance For Ties: -0.65789
Expected Value: 50
z-Statistic: 1.4390
p = 0.1502
Fail to reject Ho at Alpha = 0.0250

Figure 20-6. *Results table for a two-tailed Mann–Whitney* U *test, comparing the difference between labor force participation rates in 1968 and 1972.*

To perform a Mann–Whitney U test select two variables and choose {Calc} **Test**. Data Desk displays a test window with several pop-up menus. Choose **Mann–Whitney U** from the top pop-up menu. The details of the Mann–Whitney test are specified the same way as the other nonparametric tests (see Section 20.3). When you are finished specifying the test details, press the **Show Results** button to display the results (Fig. 20-6).

The Mann–Whitney U test pools the two variables and computes a rank for each value of the combined set. It then finds, for each variable, the number of cases, the sum of the ranks of those cases, and the mean rank of those cases. Data Desk displays these results in the first two rows of the output table. The U- and U'-statistics are displayed in the lower part of the output table. They are computed from the formulas given in Appendix 20A. If no ties are present and the number of cases in the first variable times the number of cases in the second variable is less than 1001, an exact p-value is calculated. If ties are present or the dataset is large, an approximate p-value and an appropriate z-statistic are calculated. Because Data Desk computes an exact p-value for analyses with small n and no tied differences, your answers might differ from results generated by software that computes approximations.

Ties occur in the Mann–Whitney test because two sample points have the same rank in the combined sample. These tied ranks can occur between groups (that is, an x-value and a y-value are equal), within a group (that is, two x-values or two y-values are equal), or both.

Data Desk always includes ties that are strictly within a group in the test by assigning them average rank values. If you choose to include ties, the ties that are between groups are also assigned average rank values. The inclusion of either type of tie destroys unconditional properties of the test and requires that the distribution of the statistic be approximated.

APPENDIX 20A *Formulas*

The formulas for Wilcoxon signed rank test include

$$\text{Variance} = \frac{n_1 n_2 (n_1 + n_2 + 1)}{12}$$

$$\text{Adj. to Variance} = -\frac{n_1 n_2 \sum_j t_j (t_j^2 - 1)}{12(n_1 + n_2)(n_1 + n_2 - 1)}$$

where t_j is the number of tied ranks in the jth group, and j is the number of groups of tied differences, listed in the output table as Tied differences. Two other formulas are

$$\text{Expected Value} = \frac{n_1 n_2}{2}$$

$$z = \frac{U' - \text{Expected Value}}{\sqrt{\text{Variance} + \text{Adj. to Variance}}}$$

where T^+ is the sum of the positive ranks.

The formulas for Mann–Whitney U test include

$$U = R_1 - \frac{n_1(n_1 + 1)}{2}$$

where R_1 is the sum of the ranks for the variable selected as y, n_1 is the number of cases in y and n_2 is the number of cases in x. Also,

$$U' = n_1 n_2 - U$$

$$\text{Variance} = \frac{n_1 n_2 (n_1 + n_2 + 1)}{12}$$

$$\text{Adj. to Variance} = -\frac{n_1 n_2 \sum_j t_j (t_j^2 - 1)}{12(n_1 + n_2)(n_1 + n_2 - 1)}$$

where t_j is the number of tied ranks in the jth group and j is the number of tied groups, listed in the output table as Sets of ties between all included observations. Finally,

$$\text{Expected Value} = \frac{n_1 n_2}{2}$$

$$z = \frac{U' - \text{Expected Value}}{\sqrt{\text{Variance} + \text{Adj. to Variance}}}$$

CHAPTER 21

ANOVA

In Chapter 19 we described several methods for comparing the means of two groups. In this chapter we compare the means of several groups by using a technique called analysis of variance, usually abbreviated as ANOVA or AOV.

21.1 *An Example*

Michelson's measurements of the speed of light in air were collected in five runs of 20 trials each. Although the trials were performed on the same equipment, the equipment was continually adjusted and tuned, so we might reasonably wonder whether there were differences among the five runs. Data to be analyzed with ANOVA is organized as one variable holding the responses (in this case, measurements of speed) and one or more variables naming categories or groups (in this case, trial numbers).

21.2 *Comparing Several Groups Graphically*

Boxplots, which we discussed first in Chapter 8, compare several groups. Although boxplots show medians of the groups rather than means, they still make it easy to visualize the groups and compare their structures. In addition, boxplots reveal outliers, which might affect means and variances of the groups and thereby affect the analysis. The boxplots of the five runs in the Michelson dataset are shown in Fig. 21-1.

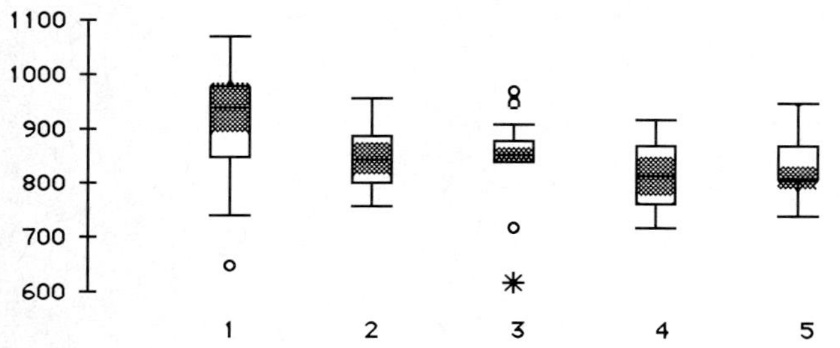

Figure 21-1. *Boxplots by group of Michelson's measurements of the speed of light.*

From the boxplots it looks as if the runs were similar, but the first and third run show additional within-group variability. Of course, in any experiment we expect some variability in results from trial to trial, so each run should show some within-run variability. The main question here is whether the variability of the means *between* runs is large relative to the variability of measurements *within* runs. If the answer is yes, we would conclude that there are differences due to the runs themselves.

21.3 *One-Way Analysis of Variance*

One-way ANOVA attempts to answer the question, "Do all the groups have the same mean?" Formally, to perform an ANOVA we are usually supposed to have random samples from normally distributed populations, and we must be willing to assume that the groups being compared have the same underlying variance even if they have different means. In practice, ANOVA works well even when the normality assumption is only roughly satisfied. The assumption of equal variance can also be violated, provided the groups are of similar size. When these assumptions are violated, it may be somewhat harder to discern differences among the means, but we are unlikely to falsely declare them different. The assumption of random sampling, however, is quite important.

A basic assumption in ANOVA is that each of the groups being compared has the same underlying variance. Therefore ANOVA estimates this variability with a generalization of the pooled estimate of variance discussed in Chapter 19. It then computes the means of the groups and compares *their* variance to the pooled variance. The comparison statistic follows an *F*-distribution — larger *F*-values suggest that the means differ more than we might have expected on the basis of the underlying sample-to-sample variability inherent among measurements within groups. Smaller *F*-values suggest that the means aren't discernably different.

To perform an ANOVA, Data Desk requires that the values being compared all reside in a single variable. A second variable supplies the category labels. If the measurements for each group are in separate variables, the **Append & Make Group Variable** command in the **Manip** menu will combine them into a single variable and create the required category variable, placing both in a new relation. The categories may be names or numbers. In Section 12.4 we discuss the **Append & Make Group Variable** command in more detail.

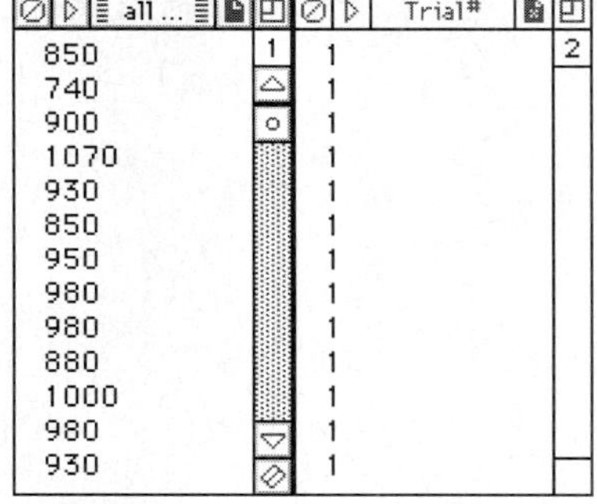

Figure 21-2. *The variable* Trial# *names the groups to be compared.*

For example, the Michelson measurements are in a single variable called *All Measurements*. The category variable is called *Trial#* and contains "1" for the 20 cases constituting the first run, "2" for the 20 cases of the second run, and so on (Fig. 21-2).

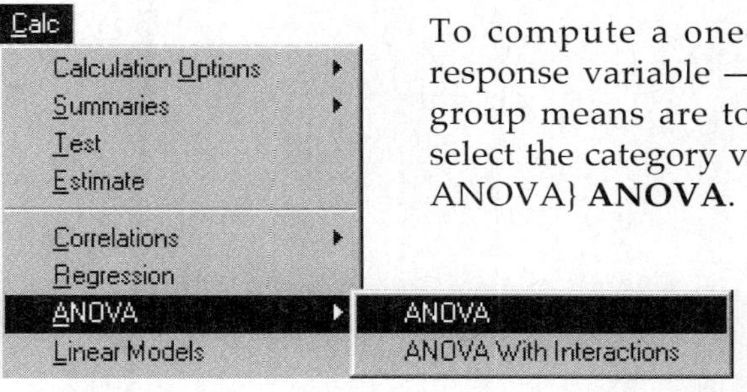

To compute a one-way ANOVA, select the response variable — the measurements whose group means are to be compared — as *y* and select the category variable as *x*. Choose {Calc ▶ ANOVA} **ANOVA**.

For the Michelson data, select *all measurements* as *y* and *Trial#* as *x*, and choose {Calc ▶ ANOVA} **ANOVA**. Analysis of variance output is almost always presented in a standard tabular form. Fig. 21-3 shows the ANOVA table for the Michelson data.

Analysis of Variance For all measurements
No Selector

Source	df	Sums of Squares	Mean Square	F-ratio	Prob
Const	1	72658576	72658576	13185	≤ 0.0001
Tr#	4	94514	23628.5	4.2878	0.0031
Error	95	523510	5510.63		
Total	99	618024			

Figure 21-3. *The ANOVA table for comparing Michelson's trials.*

The *F*-ratio tests the null hypothesis $\mu_1 = \mu_2 = \ldots = \mu_p$ against the alternative that at least one mean is not equal to the others. When the null hypothesis is true, the *F*-ratio has an expected value of 1.0. Larger *F*-ratios support rejecting the null hypothesis. The Prob value in the final column of the ANOVA table reports the probability of observing an *F*-ratio at least as large as the one observed if the null hypothesis is true. A small Prob value means that, although the observed *F*-ratio could be a result of chance fluctuation when the null hypothesis is true, it is very unlikely. In fact, it indicates exactly how unlikely it is. The Prob value is equivalent to the smallest α-level at which we would reject the null hypothesis of equal means for the observed data.

In this example, the ANOVA confirms our suspicion that the runs didn't all have the same mean. The *F*-ratio of 4.29 is sufficiently large to reject the null hypothesis of equal run means at any of the standard α-levels.

21.4 *The ANOVA Table*

Each column of an ANOVA table provides information about a different part of the analysis. The title of the table gives the name of the variable holding the measurements being analyzed — in this case, *All Measurements.* The Source column labels the major sources of variability under consideration — the differences in means of the groups defined by the category variable *Trial#* and the underlying measurement error. The row labeled Total holds values that refer to the data as a whole but also are the totals for their respective columns.

degrees of freedom

The df column holds the *degrees of freedom* associated with each row of the table. The first row, labeled Const, relates to the constant and is always equal to 1. The second row relates to the category variable. Its df value is equal to the number of categories in the category variable minus one. The next row, labeled Error, is equal to the number of numeric cases minus the df value for the category variable. The df value for the Total row is equal to NumNonNumeric – 1, or all the nonmissing cases less 1.

sums of squares

treatment

The Sums of Squares column holds *sums of squares*. For the category variable, the sum of squares is the sum of squared differences of the group means (usually called *treatment* means in this context) from the mean of all the measurements:

$$\sum_{i=1}^{\#\,groups} n_i(\bar{x}_i - \bar{\bar{x}})^2$$

Here, n_i is the number of observations in the *i*th group, $\bar{x}_i$ is the mean of the *i*th group, and $\bar{\bar{x}}$ is the mean of all the measurements. For the error term, the sum of squares is a pooled sum of individual sums of squared deviations from means found within each group:

$$\sum_i \sum_j (x_{ij} - \bar{x}_i)^2$$

where *j* goes from 1 to the number of observations in the group and *i* goes from 1 to the number of groups.

The Total sum of squares is the sum of squared deviations of each measurement from the overall mean:

$$\sum_i \sum_j (x_{ij} - \bar{\bar{x}})^2$$

The Total sum of squares is equal to the sum of the treatment sum of squares plus the Error sum of squares — a fact that underlies the

ANOVA calculations. In Fig. 21-3, we can confirm that the sum of squares for Trial# and the sum of squares for Error in the Michelson data sum to the Total sum of squares.

The row labeled Const displays the values for the constant term.

mean squares

The column labeled Mean Square contains *mean squares*. They are obtained by dividing the sum of squares values by the corresponding degrees of freedom. The mean square for Error is similar to the pooled estimate of σ^2 discussed in Chapter 19. It estimates the underlying variability of the data by combining data from different groups. Indeed, if there are only two groups, it is the same statistic.

The *F*-ratio is the ratio of the treatment mean square to the Error mean square. When the null hypothesis is true, both mean square values estimate σ^2, the population variance, so the *F*-ratio will tend to be near 1.0. The mean square for Error estimates σ^2 even when the treatment means differ, but the mean squares for treatments will grow as the treatment means vary. Thus, when the treatment means are different, the *F*-ratio will tend to be larger than 1.0.

The Prob value is the probability of observing an *F*-ratio as large as the one computed or larger, if the null hypothesis were true. The null hypothesis of equal treatment means can be rejected when the Prob value is smaller than the α–level for the test.

The row labeled Const displays information for the constant for the model. This row is sometimes thought of as a "test of the mean." The *F*-ratio tests the hypothesis that the mean of the y variable is 0. In many situations, the constant term isn't important and can be ignored. More information on constant terms in ANOVA models can be found in any good linear models book, including Searle (1971).

21.5 *Multiway ANOVA*

ANOVA is a general framework for analyzing experiments. In one-way ANOVA the groups whose means are compared are usually thought of as different categories of a single *factor* or *treatment*. Multiway ANOVA introduces more factors, each specified by its own variable. The factors might affect the response variable both individually and jointly through some interaction.

factor, treatment

Data Desk's ANOVA command works with any number of factors. Each factor is specified by a variable holding the names of the factor *levels* or categories. Factor categories are determined by the text rather than the numeric value of each case. Thus, for example, the factor levels "1" and "1.0" are different in Data Desk because their text is different, even though their values are equal.

levels

Two factors define a table with a row for each level of the first factor and a column for each level of the second. In Data Desk, the table they define may have any number of cases in each cell — that is, the analysis may be *unbalanced*. Cells may even be empty. The **Contingency Tables** command in the **Calc** menu can display a table that shows how many cases represent each factor-by-factor combination.

unbalanced

For example, the Eggs dataset reports the fat content of dried eggs. Two samples of dried eggs, labeled G and H, were drawn from a single well-mixed can of dried whole eggs and sent to six laboratories. At each laboratory, each sample was analyzed by two technicians. The measurements are recorded as percent fat minus 41.40. We are interested in differences among the laboratories, which (because they were given equivalent samples) should show no differences in their reported measurements.

Analysis of Variance For Fat Content
No Selector

Source	df	Sums of Squares	Mean Square	F-ratio	Prob
Const	1	7.20750	7.20750	513.33	≤ 0.0001
Lab	5	0.443025	0.088605	6.3106	0.0002
Tcn	1	0.004408	0.004408	0.31397	0.5783
Error	41	0.575667	0.014041		
Total	47	1.02310			

Figure 21-4. *The ANOVA table for the Eggs data.*

To compute the ANOVA, first select the response variable, *Fat Content*, then the two factor variables, *Lab* and *Technician* (we will ignore *Sample* for now), and choose {Calc ▶ANOVA} **ANOVA**. The response variable is the y-variable, branded with a "Y". The factors are x-variables, branded with an "X". Figure 21-4 shows the ANOVA table.

balanced design

This example has the same number of cases for each combination of levels of the two factors, so it is a *balanced* design.

The F-ratio for Lab is quite large (and its Prob value is correspondingly small), so we can conclude that there is a difference in the mean fat content reported by the different laboratories, indicating a difference in laboratories. The evidence of differences in the technicians (row labeled Tcn) is insufficient to reject the null hypothesis that they have measured the same values on average for fat content.

21.6 *Notation*

The algebraic notation that describes general ANOVA calculations is complex. Instead of presenting the most general form, in this section we present the notation for two-factor ANOVA. The formulas generalize naturally for more factors.

We denote the response variable y. The two factor variables are indicated by subscripts i and j, which count through the categories of the two factors, from 1 to I and from 1 to J, respectively. Each case has a response value and a level name for each factor. If there are K_{ij} observations for the ij cell of the design, they are indexed with the replication subscript, k, which runs from 1 to K_{ij}. Thus any response value may be denoted y_{ijk}, where i is the level of the first factor, j is the level of the second factor, and k is the replication count.

Factor levels are frequently nonnumeric. The values of i and j are integers assigned in an arbitrary order for notational convenience. Data Desk doesn't require factor-levels to be coded as numbers. The values of the factor variables are read as text and interpreted as factor level names.

We replace a subscript by a dot (•) to indicate that an average has been taken over all values of that subscript. Thus $y_{11\bullet}$ is the average of all of the response values for the first level of the first factor and the first level of the second factor, and $y_{1\bullet\bullet}$ is the average of all of the response values for the first level of the first factor regardless of the level of the second factor. The grand mean, $y_{\bullet\bullet\bullet}$, is the average of all of the response values.

The elements of the ANOVA table are defined with this notation. The sum of squares for the first factor, or treatment, is defined as

$$JK \sum_i (y_{i\bullet\bullet} - y_{\bullet\bullet\bullet})^2$$

and has $(I - 1)$ degrees of freedom. The sum of squares for the second factor is defined similarly as

$$IK \sum_j (y_{\bullet j\bullet} - y_{\bullet\bullet\bullet})^2$$

with $(J - 1)$ degrees of freedom. The Error sum of squares is defined as

$$\sum_i \sum_j \sum_k (y_{ijk} - y_{ij\bullet})^2$$

with $IJ(K - 1)$ degrees of freedom.

The Total sum of squares is

$$\sum_i \sum_j \sum_k (y_{ijk} - y_{\bullet\bullet\bullet})^2$$

with $IJK - 1$ degrees of freedom.

The mean squares are simply the sums of squares divided by their respective degrees of freedom. Each treatment's F-ratio is the ratio of the treatment mean square to the mean square for error.

21.7 *Interaction in ANOVA*

interaction

In ANOVA, *interaction* refers to that part of the combined effect of two or more factors that isn't accounted for by the effects of the individual factors. Interaction assesses whether the response variable, as measured for one of the factors, changes at different levels of the other factors. Data Desk's {Calc ▶ANOVA} **ANOVA With Interactions** command includes all possible two-factor interactions in the ANOVA model.

In the Eggs dataset, interaction might be present if the mean measured fat content in samples G and H depended on the laboratory. In a two-way table, interaction can be isolated only when there are at least two observations for some combinations of factor levels.

In the notation terms of Section 21.1, the Interaction sum of squares is defined as

$$K \sum_i \sum_j (y_{ij\bullet} - y_{i\bullet\bullet} - y_{\bullet j\bullet} + y_{\bullet\bullet\bullet})^2$$

with $(I - 1 \times J - 1)$ degrees of freedom.

When there is no interaction between factors, omitting interaction terms increases the power of the hypothesis tests. However, if you omit interaction terms when there is in fact some interaction, the resulting analysis loses power and the consequent tests and confidence intervals may be invalid.

21.8 *One Observation per Cell*

It isn't unusual to have only one observation for each cell of the design. In this case, it isn't possible to compute the variability within each cell of the data table and therefore to assess interaction. Instead, we predict a value for each combination of factor levels from the observed means for those factor levels (note that we now need only two subscripts because there are no replications):

$$y_{ij} = y_{\bullet\bullet} + (y_{i\bullet} - y_{\bullet\bullet}) + (y_{\bullet j} - y_{\bullet\bullet})$$

The error sum of squares is

$$SS_{\text{error}} = \Sigma_i \Sigma_j (y_{ij} - y_i)^2$$

For example, the Hearing dataset reports the percent of a list of 50 words understood correctly by each of 24 subjects when the words were spoken at low volume against a noise background. The word lists are ordinarily used to test hearing aids and are designed to be equally difficult to perceive when heard with no noise. The experimenter was interested in determining whether the lists were still equally difficult to perceive when noise was present.

We could perform a one-way ANOVA to compare the four lists; however, there is variability in the hearing acuity of the people who were tested that isn't relevant to the question being investigated. We might therefore prefer a two-way ANOVA with List and Subject as the two factors: List assesses the variability among the different lists, whereas Subject isolates the variability inherent among the people who were tested. In this design there is only one observation per cell. The resulting analysis appears in Fig. 21-5.

Analysis of Variance For Hearing
No Selector

Source	df	Sums of Squares	Mean Square	F-ratio	Prob
Const	1	76953.4	76953.4	2118.4	≤ 0.0001
SbD	23	3231.63	140.505	3.8678	≤ 0.0001
LsD	3	920.458	306.819	8.4461	≤ 0.0001
Error	69	2506.54	36.3267		
Total	95	6658.62			

Figure 21-5. *The two-way ANOVA for the Hearing dataset.*

The evidence is strong that the lists are not equally difficult to perceive when noise is present.

21.9 *Working with ANOVA Tables*

Data Desk's ANOVA views are interactive, offering associated plots from HyperView popup menus, the ability to add new factors to the model by grabbing icons and dragging them into the output window, and the ability to alter or correct the data and subsequently update the analysis.

The ANOVA HyperView menus offer a variety of plots and tools. The HyperView menu attached to the name of the response variable offers typical displays for a variable holding measured values. The HyperView menus attached to the factors offer typical displays for discrete or categorical variables and dotplots of the response variable against each factor (Fig. 21-6). The window's global HyperView menu offers overall diagnostic information and displays. **Compute Indicators** is a special command in the HyperView menu attached to each factor. Indicator

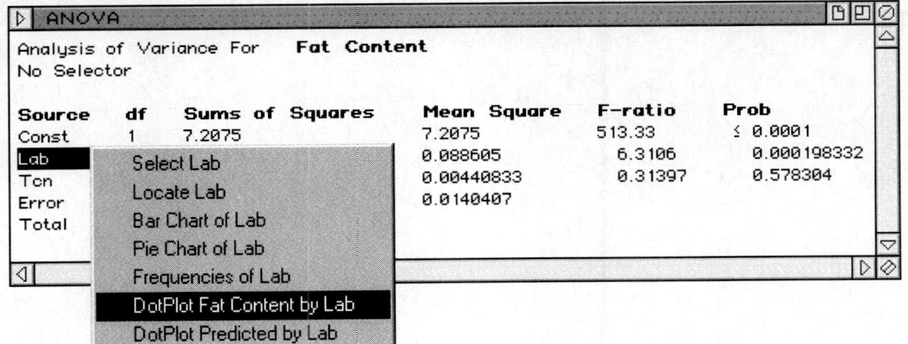

Figure 21-6. *The HyperView menus attached to each ANOVA factor offer displays that are appropriate for category variables and a dotplot of the response variable against the factor.*

variables use a combination of 0's, 1's and –1's to describe each level in the factor to the linear model. Statistically, sophisticated users will find the indicator variables useful for constructing special case analyses.

A dotplot of the response variable by the factor can be helpful in interpreting the ANOVA table. For example, in the Eggs data, a plot of *Fat Content* versus *Lab* shows that much of the difference among the labs may be attributable to Lab I, which has a higher mean and is more variable than the others (Fig. 21-7). The HyperView menu attached to the factor name Lab in the ANOVA table makes it easy to produce this dotplot.

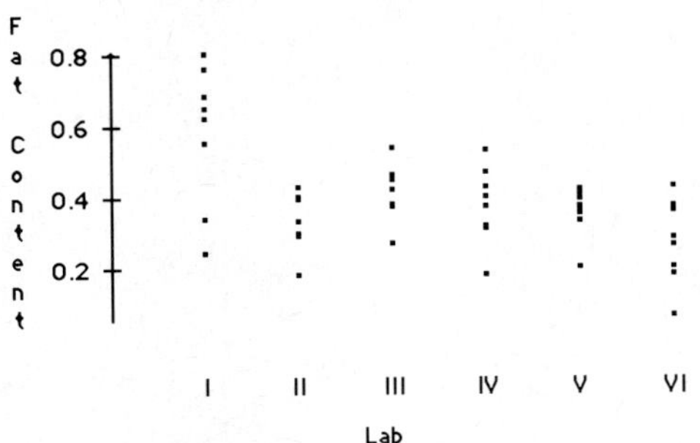

Figure 21-7*. A dotplot of* Fat Content *versus* Lab. *Here we can see that Lab I is different from the others, possibly accounting for much of the difference among the labs.*

Data Desk's plot modification abilities can help us look beneath the surface of the ANOVA. With the dotplot of *Fat Content* versus *Lab* frontmost, select the variable *Technician* and choose {Modify ▶ Symbols ▶ Add} **By Group**. Figure 21-8 shows that most of the difference among the labs is due to the results returned by Lab I, and that the two technicians in Lab I were entirely separate in their reported measurements. It is possible that a single technician in Lab I is responsible for most of the Laboratory effect in this analysis.

If you modify any of the data underlying an ANOVA, the ANOVA table will offer to update in place or recompute in a new window. A ❢ symbol appears in the window's HyperView menu in the upper left of the title bar whenever the underlying variables have been changed.

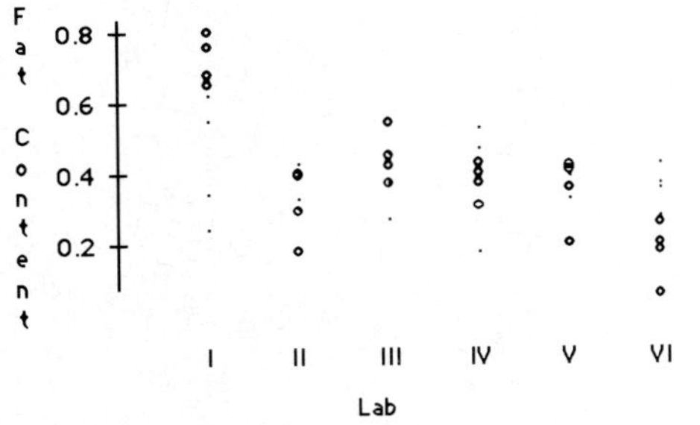

Figure 21-8. Fat Content *versus* Lab *with symbols added by group to show technician. Note that Lab I is different from the others and that the measurements of the two technicians there are entirely separate.*

21.10 Notes on Computing ANOVA

Analysis of Variance calculations can require more computer resources than many other Data Desk calculations. If you are using Mac, you may want to provide Data Desk with the maximum amount of memory possible to speed the calculations. If you are using Windows, you may want to quit any other active programs to free up memory. Interaction terms in multiway designs are especially demanding.

It is also possible that an ANOVA involving factors with many levels and using higher-order interactions will generate an intermediate structure that is too large for Data Desk to handle. Data Desk will alert you if this should happen. The only remedy for this problem is to provide Data Desk with more memory, simplify the design, reduce the number of levels of some factors, or omit higher-order interactions.

You can abort a lengthy ANOVA calculation by pressing the Esc key on Windows or ⌘-period on Mac whenever the rotating cursor is visible.

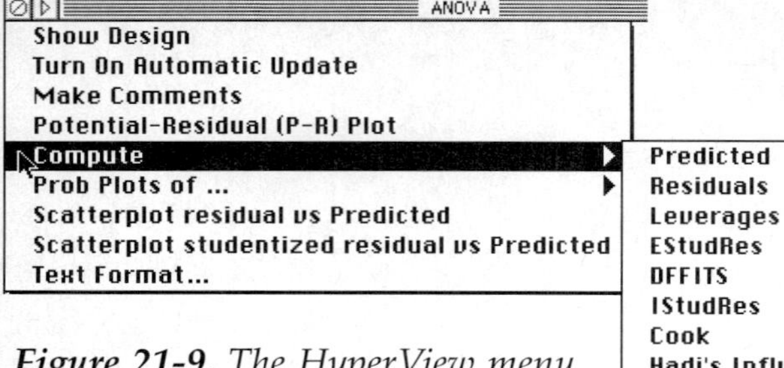

Figure 21-9. *The HyperView menu of the ANOVA table include commands for computing diagnostic statistics.*

21.11 ANOVA Options

Data Desk's ANOVA windows offer to compute statistics that can help you understand more about your data. The HyperView menus found in the ANOVA table window offer many helpful statistics and plots (Fig. 21-9). In this section we discuss some of them.

The ANOVA options are closely related to the regression options discussed in Chapters 24 and 25. For most ANOVAs, predicted values and residuals are the most useful.

Predicted Values

The ANOVA model predicts a value of the dependent (y) variable for each cell of the design. The prediction is the sum of an overall level plus contributions corresponding to the cell's level on each of the factors, plus contributions corresponding to each of the interaction terms. Data Desk computes the predicted values for each case and places them in a HotResult variable, *Predicted.*

Residuals

The difference between the dependent variable value for each case and the value predicted for its cell by the ANOVA model is the residual for that observation. Data Desk creates a HotResult variable to hold the residuals, *Residuals.*

Leverage Values

Leverage is a measure of the influence of a case on the analysis due to an extraordinary combination of factor variables. Designed experiments rarely have cases with extraordinary leverage; in balanced experiments, all cases have the same leverage. Leverage is thus likely to be interesting primarily for complex unbalanced designs.

Externally and Internally Studentized Residuals

The studentized residuals divide each residual by an estimate of its standard error. In Chapter 25 we describe the difference between internal and external studentizing and provides formulas. Histograms, boxplots, dotplots, and normal probability plots of the studentized residuals can help you identify outlying or extraordinary points. Cases with large residuals tend to reduce the value of the *F*-ratios in an ANOVA; you may want to consider omitting them from the analysis and dealing with them separately, though you must be careful to note what you have done when reporting your results.

Likelihood

Given the particular model, returns for each case the likelihood of observing the value in the dependent variable.

DFFits, Cook's Distance, and Hadi's Influence

These diagnostic statistics combine information about leverage and residuals. Any case with large DFFits, Cook's distance, or Hadi's Influence deserves special attention. You may want to remove it from the ANOVA and deal with it separately.

EXERCISES

1. The analysis of variance (ANOVA) procedure attempts to answer the question, "Do all of the groups have the same ______________?" To perform an ANOVA, you must have random samples drawn from ________________ distributed populations. You must also assume that the groups being compared have the same underlying ________________, even if they have different means. An ANOVA examines the ________________ among group means to determine whether this value is large relative to the variability inherent in the observations themselves.

(a) Write the null hypothesis appropriate for an ANOVA.

(b) Write the alternative hypothesis (words are sufficient).

(c) In an ANOVA, the test statistic follows an _______ distribution. When the null hypothesis is true, the test statistic has an expected value of _______.

(d) For the category variable, the ____________________ is the sum of squared differences among the group means from the overall mean of all the measurements.

(e) In the ANOVA table, the Mean Square column is obtained by dividing the ___________________ values by their corresponding ___________________.

(f) The _______________ for error behaves like the pooled estimate of variance by using all the observations, regardless of their level in the factor.

2. Retrieve the Michelson dataset and omit the first run. Perform an ANOVA.

(a) State the null hypothesis.

(b) What do you conclude from the test?

(c) Suggest a reason for what you found.

(d) The currently accepted value for the true speed of light in air is 299,792.5 km/sec. When this value is converted to one that corresponds to those in the dataset, it is 734.5. Perform a test of the hypothesis $\mu = 734.5$ for these data with and without the first trial. Write the results from both tests and discuss what you find.

3. Using the Graduation dataset:

(a) Investigate whether there is a difference in the rates of on-time graduation among the various colleges (in the variable *School*). First, state the null and alternative hypotheses.

(b) Perform the test and write your results.

(c) Explain in *words* what the test tells you.

(d) Investigate whether there has been a change in on-time graduation rates from year to year. How does the null hypothesis differ from the one you used in part (a)?

(e) Perform the test and write your results.

4. The Hearing dataset contains data from a study comparing the hearing perception among matched lists of words. These lists are used to test hearing aids and are matched to be equally difficult to understand when played on a tape player at low volume. The researcher played the tapes for subjects with normal hearing but added background noise. The question of interest is whether the lists retain the property of being equally hard to understand in the presence and absence of background noise. The data reported are the percentage of words understood by each of 24 subjects.

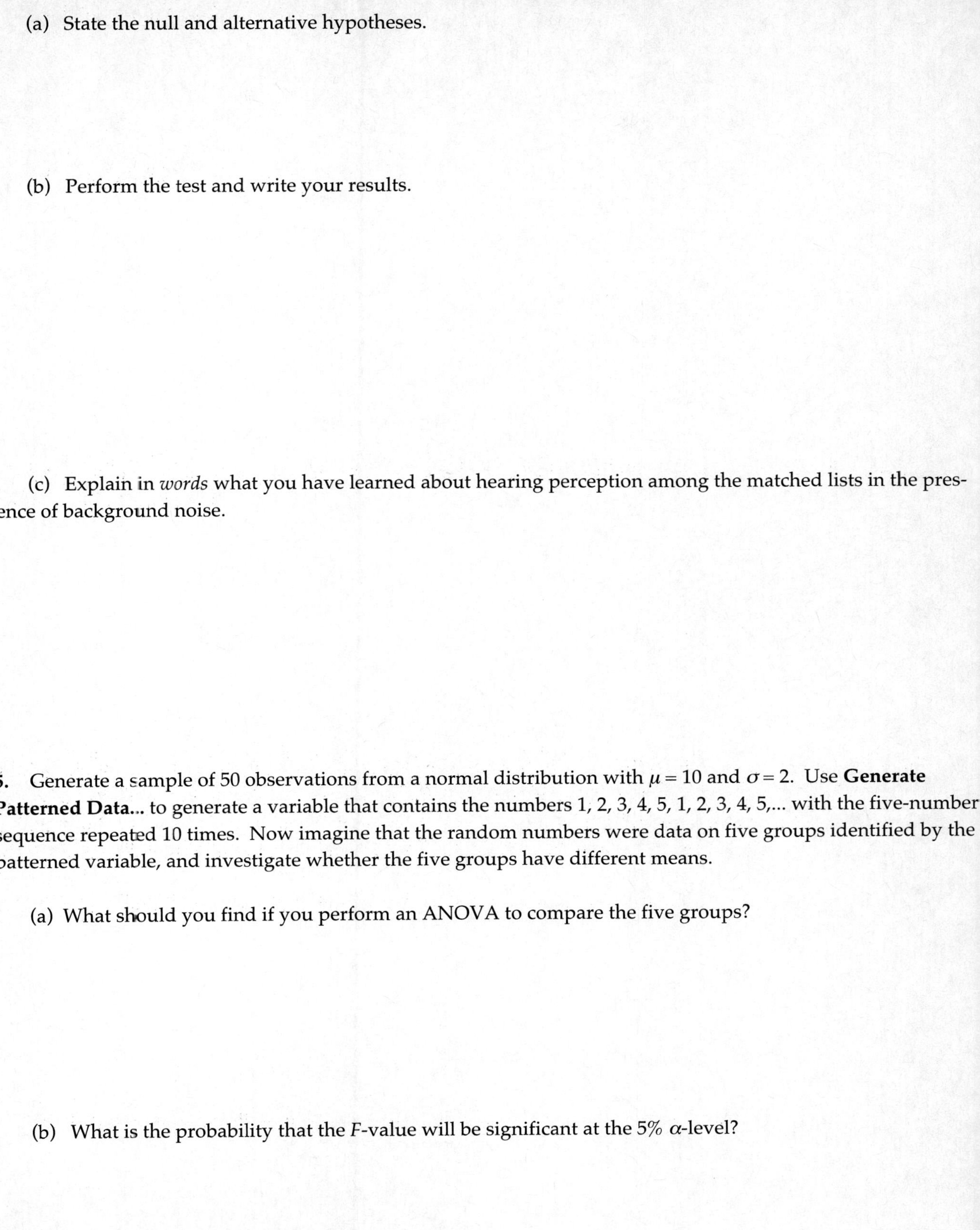

(a) State the null and alternative hypotheses.

(b) Perform the test and write your results.

(c) Explain in *words* what you have learned about hearing perception among the matched lists in the presence of background noise.

5. Generate a sample of 50 observations from a normal distribution with $\mu = 10$ and $\sigma = 2$. Use **Generate Patterned Data...** to generate a variable that contains the numbers 1, 2, 3, 4, 5, 1, 2, 3, 4, 5,... with the five-number sequence repeated 10 times. Now imagine that the random numbers were data on five groups identified by the patterned variable, and investigate whether the five groups have different means.

(a) What should you find if you perform an ANOVA to compare the five groups?

(b) What is the probability that the *F*-value will be significant at the 5% α-level?

(c) What three basic assumptions of the ANOVA procedure have been assured in this experiment?

(d) Perform the ANOVA and report what you find.

6. The one-way ANOVA compares the means of several groups, as represented by a single factor. The two-way ANOVA introduces a second factor. Typically, the two factors might affect the response variable both individually and jointly through some interaction. In a ____________________ ANOVA there are an equal number of measurements for every combination of levels of the two factors.

7. In a two-way ANOVA, the ____________________ mean square can be used to test whether the difference among the means of the response variable due to one of the factors changes at different levels of the other factor. This behavior can only be tested when at least ______ measurements have been recorded for each combination of factor levels.

8. Suppose that you have a balanced two-way ANOVA design. One factor (Treatment A) contains five levels and the second factor (Treatment B) contains four levels. Suppose that, for each combination of factor levels, four measurements were recorded. How many degrees of freedom are available for the following terms when interaction is included and when interaction isn't included?

Interaction Included		**Interaction Not Included**	
Treatment A	_________	Treatment A	_________
Treatment B	_________	Treatment B	_________
Interaction	_________		
Error	_________	Error	_________
Total	_________	Total	_________

9. Simulate the design of Exercise 8.

(a) Generate four random samples of size 20, each drawn from normal populations with different means and $\sigma = 1$. Generate side-by-side boxplots of the samples to check that you simulated the data correctly. Sketch the boxplots.

Use the **Append & Make Group Variable** command to append all four samples into a single response variable. (For convenience, name the appended data *Response* and the group variable *Treatment B*). Create the levels of Treatment A in the following way. First, use the **Generate Patterned Data...** command to create a variable consisting of "1, 1, 1, 1, 2, 2, 2, 2,..., 5, 5, 5, 5" repeated four times. Rename the variable *Treatment A*. To convince yourself that you have created a balanced two-way ANOVA, open all three variables: *Response, Treatment A,* and *Treatment B*. Note that for every combination of *Treatment A* and *Treatment B*, there are four measurements. You might also make a contingency table of *Treatment A* by *Treatment B* to verify that each cell count is 4.

(b) These data conform to the three basic assumptions of ANOVA. What are these assumptions?

(c) If you compute an ANOVA for the data created in part (a), do you expect to observe a treatment "effect"? If so, for which treatment? Why?

(d) Select {Calc ▶ANOVA} **ANOVA** for these data and write the results in the space provided.

(e) Check the degrees of freedom with the answers you gave in part (a). Explain the results of the test.

10. Select {Calc ▶ANOVA} **ANOVA with Interactions** for these data. Check the degrees of freedom with your answers to Exercise 8, and write the resulting ANOVA table.

11. For these simulated data, interaction would be present if measurements on levels of Treatment A depended upon Treatment B.

(a) Suppose that the first level of Treatment A and the first level of Treatment B behave differently from all other combinations. To demonstrate the effect on the ANOVA interaction term, open the response variable and add 10 to each response where Treatment A = 1 and Treatment B = 1. Recompute the ANOVA by using the HyperView menu **Redo in New Window** command on the ANOVA table. (Alternatively, select the variables as before and issue a new **ANOVA with Interactions** command.)

(b) Compare this table to the others computed in these exercises. Explain what you observe.

12. In the Graduation dataset, perform a two-way ANOVA of on-time graduation percentage with College and Year as the two factors.

(a) Write down your results.

(b) Is there evidence of differences among colleges? Explain your answer.

(c) Is there evidence of changes across years? Explain your answer.

(d) State the null and alternative hypotheses.

13. To perform a two-way ANOVA on the Michelson data, using Trial Number and Experiment Number as the two factors, might be tempting. Explain why doing so would be inappropriate.

14. In Exercise 4 you performed a one-way ANOVA, comparing the four-word lists in the Hearing dataset. Repeat the exercise by performing a two-way analysis.

(a) How do the results differ?

(b) Why do the results differ?

(c) Which analysis do you prefer for these data? Why?

CHAPTER 22

Simple Regression

SCATTERPLOTS LET US EXAMINE the relationship between two variables, a *response*, y, and a *predictor*, x. A more formal description of the way in which y is related to x — especially when we have some reason to believe that the value of y might depend on the value of x — comes from estimating an equation relating y and x. The simplest useful equation to try is a straight line, and the method most often used to find a line to summarize the x–y relationship is called *regression*.

regression

22.1 *Coefficients in Regression*

All points on any straight line fit an equation of the form

$$y = a + bx,$$

for the appropriate choice of a and b. Once we have a and b, every pair of numbers (x, y) for which the relationship $y = a + bx$ is true will lie on the same straight line when plotted.

constant coefficient

intercept coefficient

slope coefficient

The numbers represented by a and b are called the *coefficients* of the regression equation. The coefficient a is called the *constant coefficient* because it is a base constant added to the value found as bx. It is sometimes called the *intercept coefficient* because it specifies the value of y when $x = 0$, where the line intercepts the y-axis. The coefficient b is called the *slope coefficient* because it specifies the steepness and sign of the relationship between y and x.

The slope coefficient is best interpreted by noting the measurement units of y and x. The slope is measured in y-units per x-unit. Thus, for example, a regression of salary (in dollars) on experience (in years) has a slope estimated in dollars per year.

The intercept coefficient is measured in the same units as y, but may not be readily interpretable. Often the 0 value on the x-axis is not meaningful and thus can't serve as a basis for interpreting a. For example, the intercept of a regression of house price on number of rooms would, under a naive interpretation, represent the value of a house with no rooms. To avoid such nonsense, we often interpret the intercept simply as a base constant for the equation.

22.2 *Least Squares Regression*

The plotted points (x, y) on most real-data scatterplots don't ordinarily lie on a perfectly straight line, so the best we can do is to find a line that is close to the plotted points. The most common regression technique of closeness is *least squares regression*. We write the equation of the least squares regression as

least squares regression

$$\hat{y} = a + bx$$

where $\hat{y}$ denotes the predicted value of y for a specific value, x.

least squares criterion

In least squares regression, the coefficients are determined by the condition that the sum of squared differences between each observed value, y_i, and its corresponding predicted value, $\hat{y}_i$, be minimized — the *least squares criterion*. This criterion and its associated analysis are so common that the technique is almost always referred to simply as *regression*, which is how Data Desk refers to it.

The least squares criterion uniquely determines the values of a and b and provides useful related statistics and plots. However, it does produce an analysis that can be greatly influenced by extreme data values. Thus it is a good idea to look at plots of the data, as well as the summary table of the regression coefficients.

22.3 *Predicted Values and Residuals*

predicted values

Regression analysis estimates an equation that predicts a y value for any x-value. *Predicted values* are computed simply by substituting a value for x in the equation. As previously noted, predicted values are denoted $\hat{y}$, to differentiate them from observed y values. The regression options in Data Desk include saving a HotResult variable containing the predicted values for the regression. If a case has a missing value for x, Data Desk reports a missing value for its predicted value. However, if a case is missing in y but not in x, Data Desk can still compute a predicted value for it, so you can compute predictions at x-values for which you have no y-value observation.

residuals

The differences between the predicted values and the observed values are known as *residuals* and are denoted e_i. (The e represents the "error" the regression equation makes in describing each observed y-value.) There is one residual for each case, or

$$e_i = y_i - \hat{y}_i$$

In a successful regression analysis the residuals are small relative to the original y's. Regression options in Data Desk include creating a variable holding the residuals for the regression. It is often useful to plot them in a scatterplot against the predicted values or against the x-variable (Fig. 22-1). The regression summary table's global HyperView menu offers a scatterplot of residuals versus predicted values, $\hat{y}$. The HyperView menus associated with the t-ratio on the predictor's name offer the scatterplot of residuals versus the predictor, x.

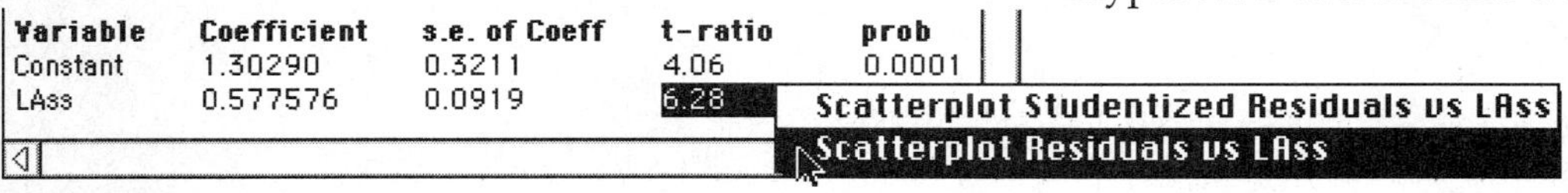

Variable	Coefficient	s.e. of Coeff	t-ratio	prob
Constant	1.30290	0.3211	4.06	0.0001
LAss	0.577576	0.0919	6.28	

Figure 22-1. *The HyperView menu of the regression table offers a scatterplot of residuals versus predicted values. The HyperView menu on the predictor variable offers a scatterplot of residuals versus that predictor.*

22.4 *Performing a Regression: An Example*

The Olympic Gold dataset contains the gold medal performance in the long jump for the Modern Olympic Games from 1900 through 1996. The

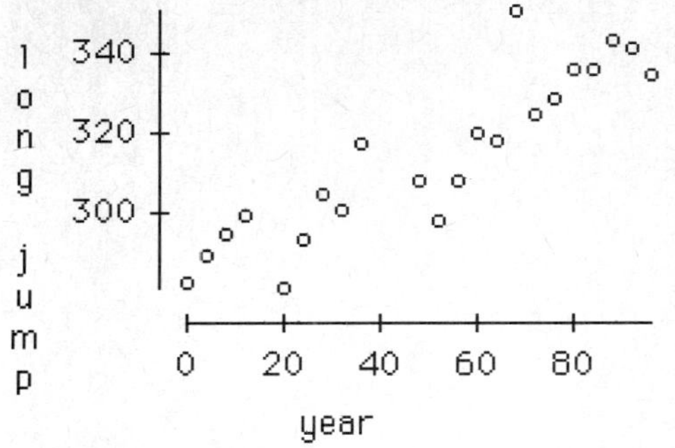

Figure 22-2. Olympic long jump gold medal performance shows a strong trend over the years of the Modern Olympic Games.

scatterplot shown in Fig. 22-2 clearly reveals that long jump gold medal performances have been improving over time.

But exactly how fast have they been improving? How long a jump might we predict will be required to take the gold medal at the next Olympic games?

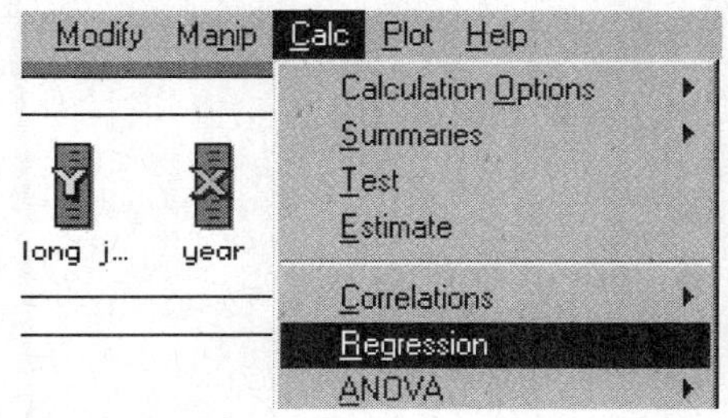

Figure 22-3. *Select the* y- *and* x-*variables, then choose {Calc}* ***Regression****.*

To perform the regression, select the response (*long jump*) as y and the predictor (*year*) as x, and choose {Calc} **Regression** (Fig. 22-3).

Figure 22-4 shows the regression results table. Note that *year* contains years since 1900.

The numbers in the column labeled Coefficient in the bottom part of the table are the values of a and b in the equation of the line. The constant coefficient, a, is about 283.6, and the slope coefficient, b, is about 0.61. Thus we write the regression equation as

$$y = 283.6 + 0.61x$$

Or, in words and numbers,

Predicted long jump distance = 283.6 + 0.61(years since 1900).

Long jumps are measured in inches, so the equation says that in 1900 (when $x = 0$) the long jump distance was about 283.6 inches. (In fact, it was 282.875 inches, but the line is an estimated fit for all the data.) The slope coefficient says that long jump gold medal performance has increased by about 0.61 *inch per year*.

Dependent variable is: **long jump**
No Selector
R squared = 81.0%   R squared (adjusted) = 80.0%
s = 9.257 with 22 - 2 = 20 degrees of freedom

Source	Sum of Squares	df	Mean Square	F-ratio
Regression	7289.12	1	7289.12	85.1
Residual	1714.00	20	85.6998	

Variable	Coefficient	s.e. of Coeff	t-ratio	prob
Constant	283.610	3.850	73.7	≤ 0.0001
year	0.609706	0.0661	9.22	≤ 0.0001

Figure 22-4. *The regression summary table for the regression of* long jump *on* year.

To see the predicted equation on the scatterplot with the original data choose **Add Regression Line** from the scatterplot's HyperView menu (Figs. 22-5 and 22-6). See Section 8.10 for adding regression lines to scatterplots.

lj/yr Plot
Regression of long jump vs year
Correlation of long jump vs year
Turn On Automatic Update
Freeze Scale
Show Plot Info
Add Regression Line
Add Color Regression Lines

Figure 22-5. *To add the best fit line to the scatterplot, choose* ***Add Regression Line*** *from the plot's HyperView menu.*

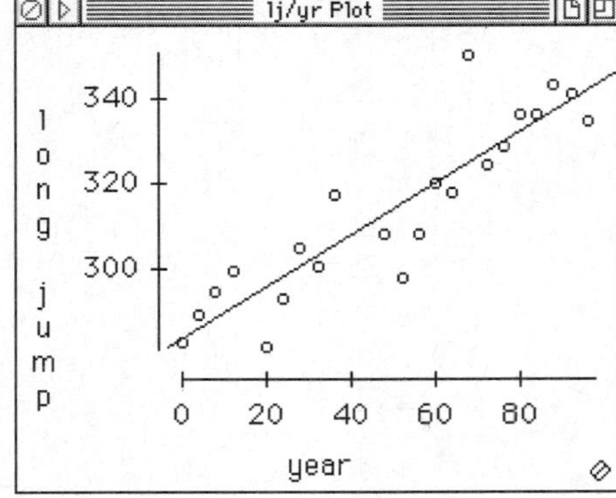

Figure 22-6. Long jump *versus* year *scatterplot with a regression line added as shown in Fig. 22-5.*

22.5 *Inference for Regression Coefficients*

The next column in the regression summary table, labeled s.e. of Coeff holds the standard deviation of the sampling distribution — the standard error — of each coefficient. Imagine drawing a multitude of random samples from the same underlying population, computing regressions for each sample, and collecting the coefficients. The standard error of the coefficient estimates the standard deviation of these collected coefficient estimates.

The statistical theory behind the estimate of the standard errors of the coefficients requires that the following conditions be at least approximately true:

- There is a true linear relationship between y and x in the underlying population. The equation of this line is usually written with Greek letters for the coefficients to indicate that they are the true population parameters:

  $$y = \alpha + \beta x + \varepsilon.$$

  This assumption doesn't assert a perfect linear relationship — only that there is a true underlying relationship with errors (denoted ε) in the measurement of y. The assumption that the underlying relationship between y and x is linear should be at least approximately true.

- The true residuals, ε, are mutually independent. This assumption is sometimes violated by data measured sequentially over time, when a residual is likely to resemble the immediately previous or immediately subsequent residual.

- The true residuals have the same variance, σ^2_ε, for all values of x. Equivalently, the population variance of y is the same for all values of x. The square root of this variance is called the standard deviation of y about the regression line, and its estimate is denoted s at the top fifth line of the regression summary table.

  This assumption is often the most difficult to satisfy. It is common, for example, for the variance of data values to increase as the value measured increases. If y grows with x, the variance of the values may grow as well. Note also that this is a property of the true residuals, ε, rather than the observed residuals, e.

- The true residuals follow a normal distribution with mean 0. This assumption is required only if we want to use statistical inference to interpret the t-ratios in terms of the t-distribution.

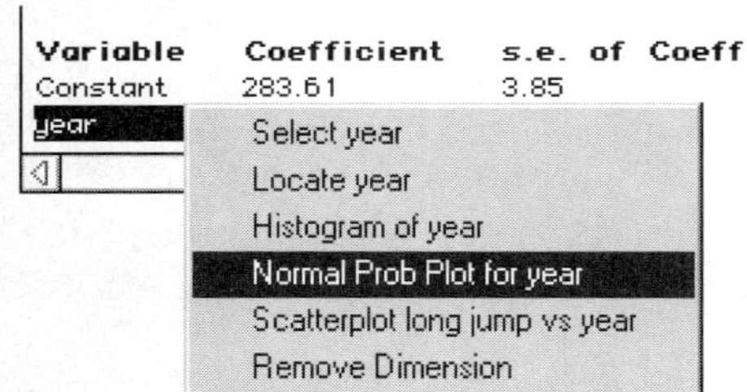

Figure 22-7. *The normal probability plot for the predictor can be created from the HyperView menu in the regression table.*

If all these assumptions are satisfied, the ratio of the difference between a coefficient and a contemplated value (usually 0) to its standard error is a t-statistic. This fact can be used to construct confidence intervals and hypothesis tests for the true population value of each coefficient. These ratios for contemplated value 0 are given in the column of the regression summary table labeled t-ratio. The HyperView menus attached to the predictors offer normal probability plots to look for extreme deviations from the normality assumption (Fig. 22-7).

Although the t-ratios can be used to test whether the true coefficients have any specified value, the most common null hypothesis states that the true slope coefficient value is 0. This hypothesis is roughly equivalent to claiming that knowledge of x isn't useful in linearly predicting y.

To find the value against which to compare the t-ratio, we need to select an α-level and to know the appropriate degrees of freedom to use. The regression summary table reports the degrees of freedom in the fifth line at the top of the table. If we test the hypothesis $\beta = 0$ versus the alternative $\beta \neq 0$ at an α-level of 0.05 for the Long Jump data, we reject the null hypothesis if t is greater than 2.110. The observed t-value is 9.22, so we can reject the null hypothesis. The corresponding confidence interval,

$$0.61 \pm (2.11 \times 0.0661) = (0.471, 0.749),$$

shows how precisely (or imprecisely) we have expressed the slope.

22.6 *The ANOVA Table for Regression*

The middle part of the regression output table is an Analysis of Variance table, much like the tables discussed in Chapter 21. The sums of squares here are defined as

$$SS_{Regression} = \Sigma(\hat{y}_i - \bar{y}_i)$$

$$SS_{Residual} = \Sigma(y_i - \hat{y}_i)$$

As we might expect, $SS_{Total} = SS_{Regression} + SS_{Residual}$.

The mean square values are the sums of squares divided by their respective degrees of freedom. The F-ratio is the ratio of the mean square for regression to the mean square residual.

The mean square for regression is related to the steepness of the regression line. The mean square residual estimates σ_ε^2, the variance of the distribution of the residuals. (Its square root is the value of s given in the fifth line of the regression output table.) The F-ratio is suitable for testing the hypothesis: "The true slope coefficient is 0." This hypothesis is the same as that tested by the t-ratio for the slope — in fact, the t-ratio for a regression with one predictor is the square root of the F-ratio. For regressions with more predictors (as described in Chapter 24), the F-ratio and t-ratio test different things.

22.7 R^2 *and Adjusted* R^2

R^2

The R^2 statistic, sometimes called the *coefficient of determination,* is an overall measure of the success of the regression in predicting y from x. The equation for R^2 is

$$R^2 = (SS_{Total} - SS_{Residual})/(SS_{Total}),$$

where R^2 measures the *fraction of the variability of* y *accounted for by its least squares linear regression on* x. Several of the words in this definition are important:

- R^2 is a *fraction* between 0 and 1. An R^2 value of 0 indicates that y isn't linearly predicted in any useful way by x. An R^2 value of 1 indicates that y is linearly predicted perfectly by x, so that each residual is 0.

- R^2 measures how successfully x *accounts for* or describes y.
- R^2 is most appropriate for *least squares linear regression*. It is usually not appropriate for other fitting criteria or for other functions relating y and x.

correlation coefficient

The square root of the R^2 statistic is the *correlation coefficient* for y and x. In Chapter 23 we discuss correlation and its relationship to regression.

***adjusted* R²**

The *adjusted* R^2 statistic is defined as

$$R^2(\text{Adjusted}) = (MS_{Total} - MS_{Residual})/(MS_{Total})$$

mean square

where MS, or *mean squares*, are defined as

$$MS_{Residual} = SS_{Residual} / df_{Residual}$$

and

$$MS_{Total} = SS_{Total} / df_{Total}$$

Adjusted R^2 is most often used in multiple regression (see Chapter 24), where there are several predictors. In that case it helps to account for the number of predictors in the equation.

22.8 *Examining Residuals*

A regression equation rarely accounts for all the variability in the data, so you should examine the residuals — that part of y not accounted for by the regression. Removing the regression line from the x–y relationship often exposes less prominent patterns in the residuals. A scatterplot of the residuals against the predicted values is almost always useful, and the easiest way to make one is with the global HyperView menu on the regression summary table (see Fig. 22-1).

The scatterplot of residuals versus predicted values for the Long Jump data is shown in Fig. 22-8.

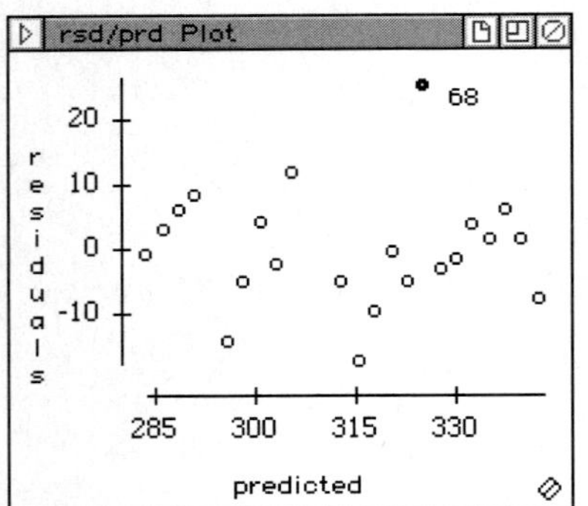

Figure 22-8. *The scatterplot of residuals versus predicted values for long jumps shows an extreme value.*

Here, the largest residual (roughly 25) stands out. It corresponds to Bob Beamon's record long jump performance at the 1968 Mexico City Olympics. You can confirm this by opening the *Year* variable and clicking the extreme point with the **?** tool.

It is often useful to plot the residuals against the x-variable to see the part of the relationship between y and x not accounted for by the regression line. The HyperView menu attached to the t-ratio in the regression summary table offers the plot directly (see Fig. 22-1). In this example, it also helps to rescale the plot to emphasize the time sequence. Here we can see a second pattern. The 1916, 1940, and 1944 Olympics were cancelled because of world wars. In the periods before World War I, between the two world wars, and after World War II, the residuals show an increasing trend (Fig. 22-9). It seems that each world war set back long jump performances, perhaps by interrupting training and by killing many fine athletes. Between the wars, long jump performance advanced more rapidly.

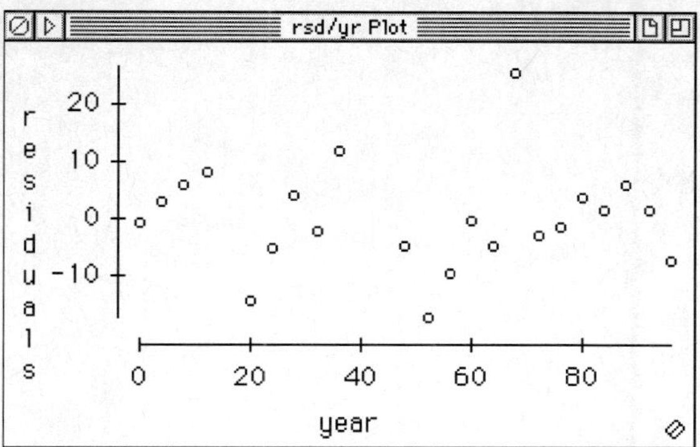

Figure 22-9. The scatterplot of residual versus year shows three distinct time periods separated by the two world wars.

It isn't at all unusual for the residuals to reveal something new about the data. This example shows two of the kinds of things we might find; an outlying point and a pattern that was hidden in the overall trend (Fig. 22-9). If we planned to use the regression equation for predicting future long jump performance, we would do better to take Beamon's extraordinary jump and the world wars into account.

22.9 *Checking Assumptions*

The scatterplot of residuals against predicted values is often an effective way to check whether the residuals seem to have constant variance as required by the regression assumptions.

A normal probability plot or histogram of the residuals can be used to check the assumption that they are normally distributed (Fig. 22-10).

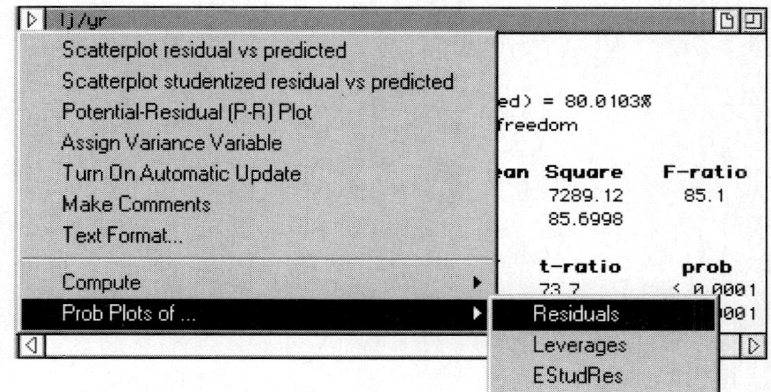

*Figure 22-10. Choose **Prob Plots of... ▸ Residuals** from the regression table's HyperView menu to check on the assumption that the residuals are normally distributed.*

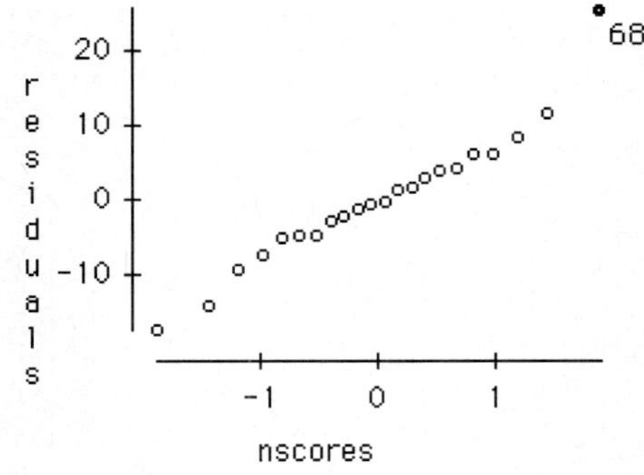

Figure 22-11. A normal probability plot of regression residuals for the Long Jump data shows that the largest residual is larger than would be expected if the residuals were truly normal.

For example, the normal probability plot of the residuals shown in Fig. 22-11, shows a distribution that seems reasonably normal except for Beamon's jump in 1968. (See Section 8.13 for a discussion of normal probability plots.)

EXERCISES

1. In the regression equation $\hat{y} = a + bx$ the coefficient a describes the regression line's ____________________.
The coefficient b describes the line's ____________________________.

2. Create a variable x containing the integers in order from –10 to 20. (Use the **Generate Patterned Data...** command in the **Manip** menu). Use the following expressions to create derived variables and plot them against x. Resize the scatterplots so that the y-axes are comparable. Sketch the plots.

(a) x

(b) $-x$

(c) $3 + x$

(d) $3 + 2 * x$

(e) $3 - 3 * x$

3. The most common statistical criterion for fitting a regression line is called the *least squares criterion*. Give its definition.

4. In 1975, an estimated 60,000 deaths in the United States were attributable to lung cancer. One 1985 study estimated an annual increase of 5000 lung cancer deaths during the decade.

(a) Write the equation of the line that describes this trend, using both *words* and *numbers*.

(b) Based upon this prediction equation, what were the expected number of deaths in 1980?

(c) If, in fact, there were 90,000 lung cancer deaths in 1980, find the residual value for the year 1980.

(d) Suppose that smoking had become decidedly unpopular during the decade so that the prediction changed to an annual *decrease* of 5000 deaths from lung cancer. Write the new regression equation, using both *words* and *numbers*.

(e) Based upon the new equation, what would be the expected number of deaths in 1980? In 1995?

(f) Why is the prediction for 1995 in part (e) meaningless? What does this reason tell you about the use of regression equations for predicting real events?

5. Use the Nuclear Plants dataset to define a new derived variable, *Date67* with the expression *'Date' - 67*. This variable is measured in years since 1967. Plot *Cost* versus *Date67*.

(a) Print the plot and draw a line on the plot *by hand* to describes the relationship. Sketch the plot.

(b) Compute the slope and intercept of your line. Write them.

(c) Define a derived variable that would compute the residuals from your line. Write its equation.

(d) Modify the derived variable in (c) to compute the sum of squared residuals from your line. *(Hint:* You may find the *SSQ* function useful.) Evaluate the sum of squared residuals with the **Evaluate Derived Variable** command. Write the equation you are using and the resulting sum.

(e) Compute the regression of *Cost* on *Date67*. Write the regression equation and compare it to your fit by eye.

(f) Find the sum of squared residuals from the regression. *(Hint:* You can find it on the regression summary table or compute it from the saved residuals.) Compare this sum to the sum of squared residuals for your fit by eye and report how they compare.

(g) Write a brief sentence that describes the meaning of the slope and intercept of the regression equation as you might report it to someone who knew no statistics.

6. As with other statistics, the least squares regression coefficients have known sampling distributions provided certain conditions hold. These conditions are:

(a) The underlying relationship between the dependent variable, y, and the independent variable, x, is ________________________.

(b) The true residuals are mutually ________________________. This assumption is sometimes violated if the data are measured over time.

(c) The true residuals have the same ________________________ for all values of the independent variable, x. This statement is equivalent to the statement that the variance of the population from which values of the dependent variable y are sampled is the same for all values of x.

(d) The true residuals follow a __________________ distribution with mean ______ and variance σ^2.

7. If all the assumptions in Exercise 6 are satisfied, the ratio of the regression coefficient to its standard deviation has a ________ distribution.

8. (a) The R^2 statistic is an overall measure of the success of the regression in predicting y from x. R^2 measures the ______________ of the variability of y accounted for by ____.

(b) R^2 is always between 0 and 1. A value of 0 indicates that ____________________. A value of 1 indicates that ______________________________.

(c) The square root of R^2 is the __________________________ coefficient.

9. Use the Olympic Gold dataset. The Modern Olympic Games series actually started in 1896. In that year the gold medal in the long jump was awarded for a jump of 249.75 inches.

(a) Compute the residual corresponding to this jump by using the regression model of the example in this chapter either by hand or with a derived variable.

(b) Discuss what you find: Is the residual large or small? Was the jump particularly short, long, or about as expected? Can you offer any explanation of why?

10. Use the regression equation in the text to predict how long a long jump will have to be to win the gold medal in the Olympics of the year 2000. Show your work or explain how you used derived variables.

11. Omit Beamon's 1968 performance and predict long jump distance from Olympic year. (To omit this point, open the *year* variable, click just in front of "68", and type any nonnumeric character, such as a *.)

(a) Write the new regression equation. How does it differ from the equation based on the full dataset?

(b) What prediction would you make from this regression for the gold medal performance in 2000?

(c) Which of the two equations do you think would provide the best prediction? Why?

12. Some people have suggested that one factor contributing to Beamon's remarkable performance in 1968 is that Mexico City is at such a high altitude that the force of gravity may have been slightly less. Do you see any evidence of improved performance in the high jump in 1968? (*Hint:* It is probably better to examine the trend in the residuals rather than in the original data. Why?) Report your findings, along with the analyses you performed or sketches of plots you made.

13. Use the Cars dataset and compute the regression of *MPG* versus *Weight*.

(a) Write a sentence describing the relationship, using the coefficients in the regression.

(b) Make a histogram of the residuals and plot them against the predicted values and sketch it.

(c) Do these residuals seem to satisfy the regression assumptions? Explain your answer. Be specific.

(d) Write a brief sentence describing what the R^2 value means.

14. Create the variable x containing the integers from 1 to 30. Generate a random sample of 30 values from a normal population with $\mu = 0$ and $\sigma = 10$ (creating the variable *Norm1*). Define the derived variable y as 3 + 2*x + '*Norm1*'.

(a) Plot y versus x. Sketch the plot.

(b) How do y and x relate to the regression model assumptions?

(c) Perform the regression of y on x. How close do the estimated coefficients come to the true values?

(d) Repeat the experiment four more times for new random samples. How much do the estimated coefficients vary? (*Note:* The easiest way to do this task is to generate four samples from the normal (0, 10) distribution and then edit the definition of y in the derived variable to refer to *Norm2, Norm3,* and so on. Renaming the random samples to *Norm1* won't work because the derived variable identifies its underlying variables when it is defined. Editing the derived variable makes it reevaluate the variable names.) Discuss what you find.

(e) Suppose that the random numbers had been generated with $\mu = 0$ and $\sigma = 50$. How would you expect each of the following statistics to change from those obtained in the first experiment? Should it get larger, smaller, or not change?

R^2	________________	F	________________
$SS_{Residual}$	________________	s	________________
a	________________	b	________________

By performing the experiment, you can check your answers.

(f) Suppose that the random numbers had been generated with $\mu = 10$ and $\sigma = 1$. How would you expect each of the following statistics to change from those obtained in the first experiment? Should it get larger, smaller, or not change?

R^2	________________	F	________________
$SS_{Residual}$	________________	s	________________
a	________________	b	________________

By performing the experiment, you can check your answers.

CHAPTER 23

Correlation

CORRELATION COEFFICIENTS MEASURE the degree of association between two variables. Data Desk computes three kinds of correlation: Pearson product–moment correlation, Spearman rank correlation, and Kendall's tau. Each measures association differently and emphasizes different aspects of the relationship between variables. Data Desk also computes covariance, another measure of association between variables. All of these statistics are found in the {Calc} **Correlations** submenu.

The Pearson product–moment correlation is the statistic commonly called *correlation*. It is a multifaceted statistic that shows up in a variety of apparently unrelated places.

23.1 *Pearson Product–Moment Correlation*

The product–moment correlation of the variables x and y is

$$r = \frac{(x_i - \bar{x})(y_i - \bar{y})}{\sqrt{(x_i - \bar{x})^2 \quad (y_i - \bar{y})^2}}$$

To compute the product–moment correlation between two variables, select both variables and choose {Calc ▸ Correlations} **Pearson Product-Moment.**

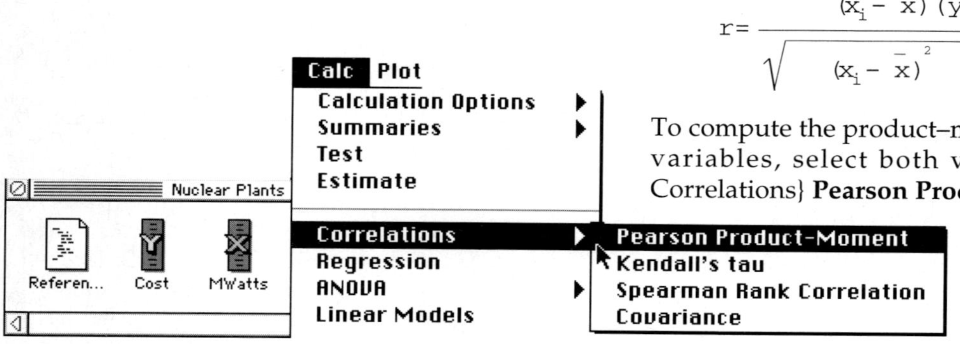

Figure 23-1. *To compute Pearson correlation, select two or more variables and choose {Calc ▸ Correlations}* ***Pearson Product–Moment.*** *The submenu may drop down to the left of the menu bar on smaller screens.*

Data Desk creates a table of correlations. The correlation coefficient in the row for *MWatts* and the column for *Cost* is the correlation of those two variables (Fig. 23-1).

Pearson Product-Moment Correlation

	Cost	MWatts
Cost	1.000	
MWatts	0.472	1.000

Figure 23-2. *The Pearson correlation of* Cost *and* MWatts *for the Nuclear Plants dataset.*

Because the correlation of any variable with itself is always 1, the diagonal entries of the table are always 1.000. Here the correlation of *Cost* and *MWatts* is 0.472.

23.2 *Linear Association*

Correlation measures *linear* association. Variables can be closely related by some nonlinear function and still have a small or even a zero correlation. The correlation coefficient can have any value between –1 and +1. Negative values indicate a negative slope in the x–y scatterplot (that is, y decreases as x increases). Positive values indicate that x and y increase or decrease together. A value near 0 means that any relationship between x and y is nonlinear. A value near +1 or –1 means that there is a nearly perfect linear relationship between x and y.

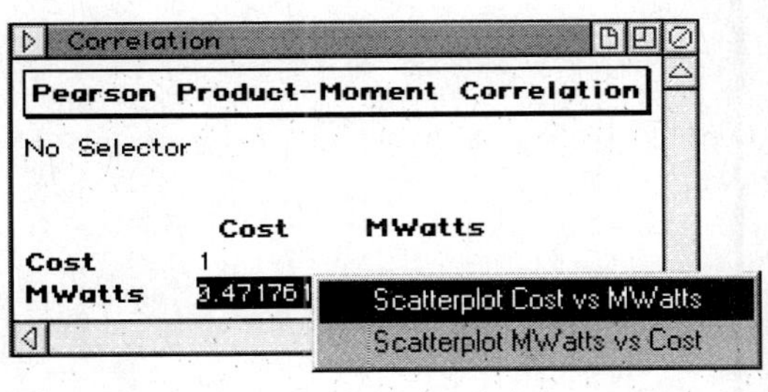

Figure 23-3. *The HyperView menu attached to each correlation coefficient offers the corresponding scatterplots. Correlation is symmetric, so either scatterplot is appropriate.*

Because product–moment correlation measures only linear association, it is possible for two variables to be closely related but have a small or even a zero correlation. For example, if $y = x^2$ for values of x equally spaced between –1 and 1, there is clearly a relationship between y and x, but their correlation is zero. Similarly, a single extraordinary datapoint can make any correlation either large or small (depending upon its location). It is always a good idea to look at a scatterplot of y versus x before placing too much trust in a correlation value. The HyperView menus attached to correlation coefficients in Data Desk offer to draw the associated scatterplots (Fig. 23-3).

23.3 *Correlation and Simple Regression*

Product–moment correlation and least squares regression are closely related. The R^2 statistic of the regression of y on x is the square of the correlation of y and x. This relationship suggests another way to interpret the correlation coefficient: the squared correlation coefficient is the fraction of the variability of y accounted for by its least squares linear regression on x.

Regression treats y and x differently, but correlation treats them symmetrically. That is, whereas the regression of x on y is different from the regression of y on x, the correlation of x with y is the same as the correlation of y with x. Thus the square of the correlation between y and x is also the fraction of the variability of x that would be accounted for by its least squares linear regression on y.

The correlation of y and x is also the correlation of the regression's predicted values, $\hat{y}$, and the observed values, y. Thus correlation measures the success of a regression. In this sense, behind every correlation coefficient is a regression analysis that might provide additional information about the relationship between y and x. Whenever a correlation is of particular importance, it is a good idea to make the corresponding scatterplot to check for linearity and to perform the corresponding regression. HyperView menus make following this path easy.

23.4 *Correlation and Standard Scores*

Regression slopes are in y-units *per* x-unit, but correlation has no units.

Sometimes that can be an advantage if the original units of the data are meaningless or if there is some reason to hide them (such as a promise not to report incomes or ages.)

For example, in a study relating income and age, a researcher might promise respondents that both numbers would be kept confidential. To establish alternative units to work with, the researcher might standardize the values as

(Income - Mean(Income))/Standard Deviation(Income)

(Age - Mean(Age))/Standard Deviation(Age).

The resulting variables preserve information about the overall relationship of income and age, but report each individual in terms of standard deviation units above or below the mean. As long as the standard deviation isn't reported, the original values are hidden.

Dependent variable is: **StdCost**
No Selector
R squared = 22.3% R squared (adjusted) = 19.7%
s = 0.8963 with 32 - 2 = 30 degrees of freedom

Source	Sum of Squares	df	Mean Square	F-ratio
Regression	6.89931	1	6.89931	8.59
Residual	24.1007	30	0.803356	

Variable	Coefficient	s.e. of Coeff	t-ratio	prob
Constant	-4.03266e-17	0.1584	0.000	1.0000
StdMW	0.471761	0.1610	2.93	0.0064

Figure 23-4. *The regression on standardized scores has a slope coefficient equal to the correlation.*

The regression slope of *Standardized Income* on *Standardized Age* is the same as the correlation between the original income and age variables, so we can avoid standardizing and just use the correlation coefficient.

Returning to the Nuclear Plants dataset, we construct the following standardized derived variables:

Cost/StDev(Cost)

MWatts/StDev(MWatts)

The regression of one on the other (Fig. 23-4) has a regression coefficient of 0.472, which is the correlation between *Cost* and *MWatts*.

23.5 *Correlation Tables*

To find all the pairwise correlations among a collection of variables, select the variables and choose {Calc} **Pearson Product-Moment**. Data Desk computes the correlations between each pair of variables and places them in a table. Because correlation is symmetric, the numbers in this table are symmetric around the diagonal from upper left to lower right, so Data Desk prints only the lower half of the table. Because the correlation of any variable with itself is always 1, the diagonal elements of the table are 1.000.

For example, a correlation table for several variables from the Cars dataset is shown in Fig. 23-5.

TIP

You can add variables to a correlation table simply by dragging their icons into the table. The correlation table recomputes automatically.

Pearson Product-Moment Correlation
No Selector

	MPG	Weight	Drive R	Horsepo	Displace
MPG	1.000				
Weight	-0.903	1.000			
Drive Ratio	0.417	-0.688	1.000		
Horsepower	-0.871	0.917	-0.589	1.000	
Displacement	-0.786	0.951	-0.798	0.872	1.000

Figure 23-5. *Correlation table for the cars data.*

The correlation between any two variables is at the intersection of the row and column labeled with their names.

23.6 *Spearman Rank Correlation (Rho)*

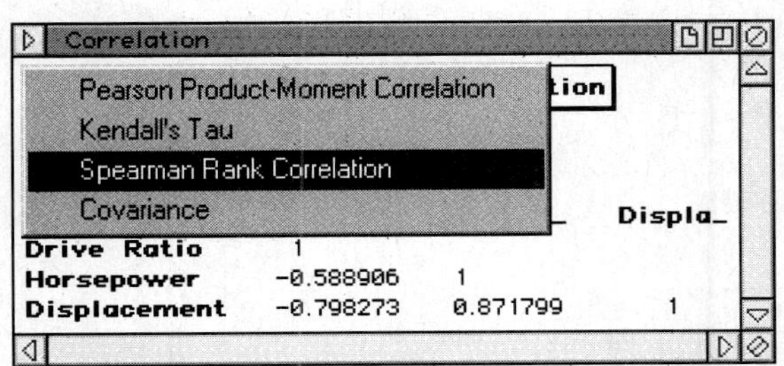

When x and y aren't linearly related but show a consistently increasing or decreasing trend, a nonparametric correlation such as *Spearman's rho* is appropriate. Spearman's rho is simply the correlation between the *ranks* of the two variables. To compute rho in Data Desk, choose {Calc ▸Correlations} **Spearman Rank Correlation**. Alternatively, click on the correlation table title to pop up a menu offering each of the correlation computations.

Because Spearman's rho is based upon ranks, it has two special properties.

- It is not changed when either x or y is transformed by a *monotone* function. Monotone functions don't alter the order of values. The log, square root, and squaring functions are monotone for positive values. Because monotone functions preserve order, the ranks of *log(income)* will be the same as the ranks of *income*, so Spearman's rho will also be the same.
- It is less affected by outliers or extraordinary values than product–moment correlation. This too, can be attributed to using ranks. If the largest value in one variable is extraordinarily large, its correlation with another variable is likely to be strongly affected. However, the rank of the largest value depends only upon the sample size and not on the magnitude of that value, so the value can be arbitrarily large without altering rho.

Rho can take on values between –1 and 1. If the value of rho is near 1 or –1, we conclude only that there is a *monotone* relationship between x and y, rather than that there is a *linear* relationship between them. In a monotone relationship x and y are in the same order or are in exactly reversed orders relative to each other.

Conversely, if rho is near 0, we conclude that there is no evidence for a monotone relationship. For many types of data, a monotone (but not linear) relationship exists between x and y. In such cases, rho is a more appropriate statistic than the product–moment correlation.

For example, the scatterplot of *MPG* versus *Displacement* in the Cars dataset shows that the relationship isn't linear. Therefore Spearman's rho is a more appropriate statistic (Fig. 23-6).

Spearman Rank Correlation
No Selector

	MPG	Displace...
MPG	1.000	
Displacement	-0.838	1.000

Figure 23-6. *Spearman's rho of* MPG *and* Displacement.

Transforming *MPG* to "Gallons per 100 miles" as –100/MPG makes the relationship more linear. Spearman's rho, however, isn't affected by such monotone transformations (Fig. 23-7).

Spearman Rank Correlation
No Selector

	-1/MPG	**Displace...**
-1/MPG	1.000	
Displacement	-0.838	1.000

Figure 23-7. *The Spearman correlation is unaffected by monotone transformations such as the negative reciprocal.*

23.7 *Kendall's Tau*

Kendall's Tau

Kendall's tau is similar to Spearman's rho in that it is based upon the ranks of the data and is thus a nonparametric method. Kendall's tau measures the degree of monotonicity in the relationship between x and y by considering all *pairs* of datapoints in the scatterplot of y versus x. The slope between each pair of points is positive, negative, or zero. Kendall's tau is the difference between the number of positive slopes and the number of negative slopes, divided by the total number of pairwise slopes.

Tau ranges between –1 and 1. If it is near –1, nearly all the pairwise slopes are negative, indicating a generally decreasing relationship between x and y. If tau is near 1, nearly all the pairwise slopes are positive, indicating a generally increasing relationship. If tau is near 0, the number of positive slopes is roughly equal to the number of negative slopes, indicating that x and y are not ordered similarly.

To compute Kendall's tau in Data Desk, select the variables and choose {Calc ▸ Correlations} **Kendall's tau**.

23.8 *Covariance*

The covariance of x and y is computed as

$$\frac{\sum_{i=1}^{n}(x_i-\bar{x})(y_i-\bar{y})}{n-1}$$

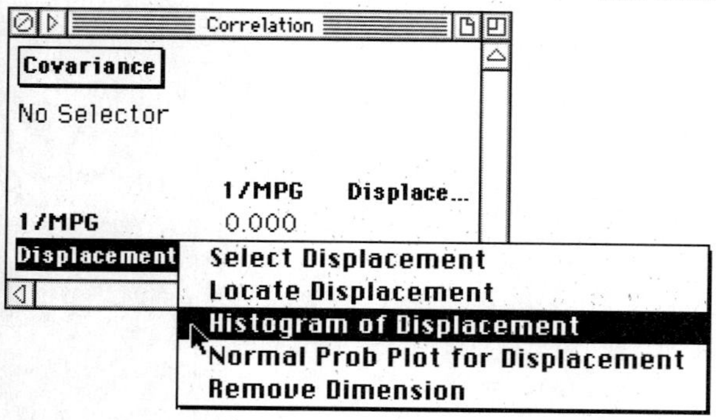

Correlation

Covariance

No Selector

	1/MPG	Displace...
1/MPG	0.000	
Displacement		

Select Displacement
Locate Displacement
Histogram of Displacement
Normal Prob Plot for Displacement
Remove Dimension

Figure 23-8. *The HyperView menu attached to the variable name lets you create a histogram plot of the variable to examine its distribution and range.*

Covariance is a common measure of association that can be used in calculations such as principal components. Data Desk computes and displays covariances in the same manner as correlations. Large covariance values indicate a strong relationship among variables being compared. Unlike correlation, covariance isn't bounded by –1 and +1 but can take on any value. Like correlation, a covariance of 0 indicates a lack of association between the variables.

The covariance measure is greatly influenced by the spread of the data, so variables with large ranges of values produce large covariance values. A histogram plot helps you examine the spread of your data before accepting a large covariance measure.

23.9 *Missing Values and Correlation*

When Data Desk computes the correlation between two variables, x and y, it omits any cases that are missing on either x or y. That is, Data Desk omits cases in a *pairwise* manner. Data Desk thus regards a table of correlations as a table of two-variable statistics rather than as a part of a multivariate analysis for which cases missing on *any* of the variables included would be omitted.

This procedure guarantees that any correlation in a table of correlations corresponds to the scatterplot of its component variables and doesn't change as variables are added to or removed from the correlation table. However, the correlations displayed in a correlation table of several variables may not be the same as the correlations Data Desk computes for some multivariate analyses. In a multivariate analysis, such as principal components analysis, Data Desk omits all cases with missing values on *any* variable.

23.10 *Extracting Values from Correlation Tables*

Some statistics calculations use correlations or covariances as parameters. You can extract correlations from a Data Desk correlation table with the following steps.

- Compute the correlation table.
- With the Table window frontmost, choose {Edit} **Copy Window** and select the **Text only** option.
- Open a ScratchPad window and paste the table into it.

The text in the ScratchPad window is now tab-delimited text containing the correlation table. You can select any correlation, copy it, and paste it in a derived variable expression, variable editing window, or program outside Data Desk.

If you delete the table title and labels, you can copy the body of the table, click on a folder window, and {Edit} **Paste Variables** to make each column of the table a variable. You can then select and reorder columns by selecting the variables and using {Edit} **Copy Variables**.

EXERCISES

1. Define a variable, x, containing the integers from –10 to 10. (Use the **Generate Patterned Data...** command in the **Manip** menu.) Define derived variables for the following functions. For each one, make a scatterplot against x and compute its correlation with x. Sketch each plot and write the correlation next to the plot.

(a) x^2

(b) abs(x)

(c) sqrt $(100 - x^2)$

(d) sign(x – 5) + sign(x + 5)

(e) cos($\pi * x/30$)

2. The correlation coefficient measures the degree of ______________ association between two variables, x and y. Its value ranges from ________ to ________. A positive value indicates that y ___________ as x increases. A negative value indicates that y ____________ as x increases. A value of 0 indicates that ________________________. A value of +1 or –1 indicates that there is a ______________ relationship between y and x. The correlation of any variable with itself equals ________.

3. Generate 21 random numbers from the normal (0, 1) distribution and rename the variable *Normals*. Use x from Exercise 1 and construct derived variables for the following functions. For each one, make a scatterplot against x and find its correlation with x. Sketch each plot and report the correlation coefficient.
(Alternatively, create a slider, name it p, and construct the derived variable $x + p$**normals*. Then move the slider rather than editing the expression.)

(a) x + normals

(b) x + 4 * normals

(c) x + 8 * normals

(d) x + 16 * normals

4. The correlation of y and x is also the correlation of the ________________ and ________________ values obtained from the regression of y on x.

5. Use the Nuclear Plants dataset to show that the correlation of *Cost* and *Date* is the same as the slope coefficient of the regression of *Cost*/*Std*(*Cost*) on *Date*/*Std*(*Date*). Write your results.

6. Correlation tables can be dangerous because each of the correlations carries the assumption of ____________. It is easy to compute many correlations without checking the correctness of this assumption.

7. Spearman's rho is the correlation between the ______________ of two variables. If the value of this statistic is near –1 or +1, you can assume that the underlying variables are ____________________________ . Spearman's rho is less affected by ______________ than is the Pearson correlation coefficient.

8. Generate 10 variables of 20 observations each from a normal distribution. Compute the correlation table for these variables. Write or paste it in the space provided.

(a) What is the underlying "true" value of these correlations? Why?

(b) Do the values you observe differ much from what you expected? Why should they differ at all?

9. In the Olympic Gold dataset, compute the correlation table for the three gold medal performance variables both with and without Beamon's 1968 long jump. Write your results and explain any differences that you observe between the two tables.

10. Use the Cars dataset.

(a) Sketch a scatterplot of *MPG* versus *Displacement*.

(b) Compute the correlation coefficient and Spearman's rho for these two variables.

Correlation value _________

Spearman's rho value _________

(c) Which statistic is more appropriate for this relationship? Why?

CHAPTER 24

Multiple Regression

SIMPLE LINEAR REGRESSION (see Chapter 22) describes the relationship between a response variable, y, and a predictor variable, x. Multiple regression extends simple regression to include more predictors in the prediction equation. Multiple regression describes data measured on several variables with a simple expression. The relative simplicity of the description, along with its usefulness as a basis for many other multivariate analysis methods, make multiple regression one of the most widely used statistical analyses.

24.1 *The Nature of Multiple Regression*

Multiple regression describes the linear relationship between one dependent variable, y, and several predictor variables with a linear equation. In general, the regression equation for p predictors is written as

$$\hat{y} = b_0 + b_1x_1 + b_2x_2 + \ldots + b_px_p$$

where the b_j are estimates of the true population parameters, denoted β_j. If $p = 2$ and we were to substitute random numbers for x_1 and x_2 and specify y as a derived variable, a rotating plot would show a flat surface — the generalization of a straight line to three dimensions. Of course, if $p = 1$, the equation is the same as for simple regression and the points that satisfy it fall on a straight line.

In Data Desk, multiple regression is specified in the same way as simple regression. Select the y-variable (response) first and then extend the selection to include the x-variables (predictors). To select the variables in any order, Option-click (Ctrl-click on Windows) the y-variable and Shift-click the x-variables. You can add additional x-variables to the analysis by dragging their icons into the center of the regression summary table. You can replace an x-variable by dragging the icon of the new variable over the label of the x-variable to be replaced. You can replace the y-variable by dragging the icon of the new variable over the label of the current y-variable.

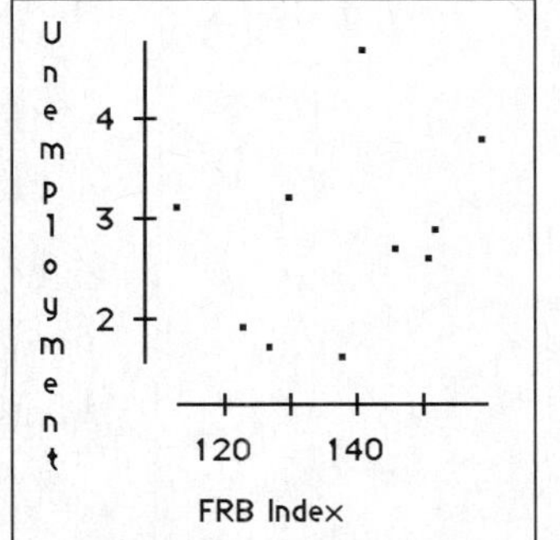

Figure 24-1*. The scatterplot of* Unemployment *versus the* FRB Index.

24.2 *An Example*

An example illustrates the similarities and differences between simple and multiple regression and points out some of the complexities of multiple regression. The Unemployment dataset, in the Data Desk *Datafiles* folder, contains the U.S. unemployment rate, Federal Reserve Board index of industrial production, and year for 1950–1959. The scatterplot shown in Fig. 24-1 depicts the relationship of *Unemployment* to the *FRB Index*.

Dependent variable is: Unemployment
No Selector
R squared = 9.8% R squared (adjusted) = -1.5%
s = 0.9719 with 10 - 2 = 8 degrees of freedom

Source	Sum of Squares	df	Mean Square	F-ratio
Regression	0.819310	1	0.819310	0.867
Residual	7.55669	8	0.944586	

Variable	Coefficient	s.e. of Coeff	t-ratio	prob
Constant	-0.035172	3.081	-0.011	0.9912
FRB Index	0.020690	0.0222	0.931	0.3789

Figure 24-2*. The simple regression of* Unemployment *on* FRB Index.

The simple regression of *Unemployment* on *FRB Index* shows two surprising results (Fig. 24-2).

From the positive sign of the *FRB Index* coefficient, we might at first think that, as industrial production rose during the 1950s, unemployment rose. (Rising industrial production would usually be expected to increase employment and reduce unemployment.) However, the t-ratio for this coefficient is quite small, which suggests that the coefficient's value isn't reliably different from 0. Of course, even a value of 0 could be surprising; the *FRB Index* and unemployment rate should be related. The R^2 for the regression shows that only 9.8% of the variability in unemployment is accounted for by its linear relationship to the FRB index, so the overall regression is rather unsuccessful.

Many aspects of the U.S. economy changed during the decade of the 1950s. The simple regression of unemployment on FRB index must ignore the impact of these changes because it is limited to a single predictor. Multiple regression introduces more predictors to account for some of the changes.

Dependent variable is: Unemployment
No Selector
R squared = 86.6% R squared (adjusted) = 82.7%
s = 0.4011 with 10 - 3 = 7 degrees of freedom

Source	Sum of Squares	df	Mean Square	F-ratio
Regression	7.24976	2	3.62488	22.5
Residual	1.12624	7	0.160891	

Variable	Coefficient	s.e. of Coeff	t-ratio	prob
Constant	13.4539	2.484	5.42	0.0010
FRB Index	-0.103339	0.0217	-4.77	0.0020
year	0.659417	0.1043	6.32	0.0004

Figure 24-3*. The multiple regression of* Unemployment *on* FRB Index *and* Year.

We can try to represent some of these changes with the variable *Year,* which simply records the year of the decade. Select the icon of *Year* and drag it into the middle of the regression table to include it as a predictor in the regression. The resulting regression summary table will recompute to look like that shown in Fig. 24-3.

This regression is much more successful. The R^2 is now 86.6%, and the absolute value of all of the t-ratios are fairly large. After allowing for the changes during the decade represented by year, the coefficient associated with the *FRB Index* is now negative, indicating decreasing unemployment with increasing industrial production.

24.3 *Interpreting the Regression Table*

Most of the multiple regression summary table is interpreted in the same way as the simple regression summary table discussed in Chapter 22, with the following exceptions.

- The null hypothesis tested with the F-ratio is now

  $$H_0: \beta_1 = \beta_2 = \ldots = \beta_p = 0$$

  which is a general hypothesis stating that the true coefficients are all 0. (Note that the constant coefficient, β_0, isn't included in the hypothesis.) If the F-ratio is sufficiently large, we reject this null hypothesis.

- Multiple regression coefficients must be interpreted more carefully than simple regression coefficients. Each coefficient is still measured in y-units per unit of its associated x-variable, but all the coefficients are now tied together and must be interpreted as a group. One way to describe this relationship in words is to say that a coefficient measures the change in y for a one-unit change in its associated x-variable *after removing the linear effects of all the other* x*-variables.* In Section 25.2 we discuss partial regression plots, which depict the basis for each regression coefficient.

- The t-ratios for the regression coefficients are interpreted as in simple regression, except that now they have, in general, $n - (p + 1)$ degrees of freedom, where n is the number of cases and p is the number of predictor variables. The third line of the regression table reports degrees of freedom.

- Adjusted R^2 is useful in multiple regressions because the adjustment accounts for the number of predictors in the regression equation. As new predictors are added to a regression equation, the value of R^2 can only increase, so even the addition of a predictor filled with random numbers can increase R^2. Adjusted R^2 accounts for this effect so that it doesn't generally improve if you add a useless predictor. Adjusted R^2 is more appropriate in a multiple regression, especially when alternative regression equations are compared.

24.4 *Predicted Values and Residuals*

HOW-TO

To compute predicted values for new datapoints:

- Add the new cases to the variables, marking the y-values as missing.
- Compute a regression, requesting predicted values.
- Data Desk finds predicted values for the new cases.

Every regression table offers to compute *predicted values, residuals,* and other diagnostic variables with the **Compute** command located in the global HyperView menu of the regression summary table. Data Desk saves the new variable as a HotResult variable and places its icon at the end of the current relation. Any changes made to the underlying data or to the model will reflect immediately in the diagnostic HotResult variable and any table or display built with that variable.

The predicted values, denoted $\hat{y}$, estimate the observed values of y from a linear equation in terms of the predictors. There is a predicted value for each case that isn't missing any of its predictor variables. The HotResult variable created for predicted values is named *Predicted*.

Real data are almost never so structured as to fit a model as simple as the linear multiple regression equation. We expect the predicted values and the observed values to differ, although we hope that they differ relatively slightly. The differences between the observed and predicted values are the residuals. As for predicted values, there is one residual for each case. The HotResult variable created for residuals is named *Residuals*.

Least squares multiple regression minimizes the sum of the squared residuals, so we expect them to be small compared to the original data. For that reason, it is usually better to plot residuals directly rather than as part of a plot showing the original data. A scatterplot of residuals versus predicted values is often useful for assessing the success of the regression. The regression window's HyperView menu offers this plot (see Section 22.8).

24.5 *Missing Values in Regression*

casewise deletion

Whenever the response variable or any of the predictor variables in a regression has a nonnumeric or infinite value for any case, that case is omitted from the regression. This omission is sometimes called *casewise deletion*. To omit a case from the regression, mark the value for that case as missing in any of the variables included in the regression. Alternatively, use a selector variable (see Chapter 13). If you make the case missing in the dependent variable, a predicted value will still be computed for that case, based upon the remaining points.

This feature provides a convenient way to compute predicted values for new datapoints. Enter the values of the predictors for the new points and mark the dependent variable missing. Then recompute the regression and examine the predicted values.

Data Desk tries to compute all requested statistics, even for cases that are omitted. Omitting cases with a selector variable results in estimates for those cases based upon the regression computed without them.

24.6 *Regression Options*

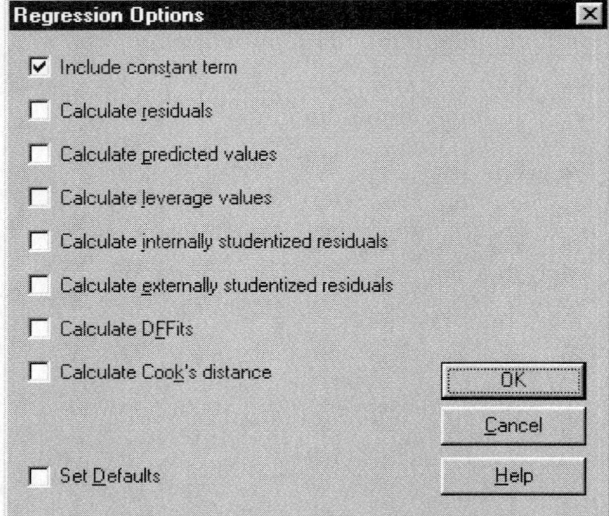

Figure 24-4. *The Regression Options dialog.*

The {Calc ▶ Calculation Options} **Set Regression Options...** command allows for specific diagnostic variables to be calculated each time a regression is computed (Fig. 24-4). Unlike the commands accessed from the table's global HyperView menu, the HotResult variables computed from this dialog are placed in the *Regression* folder in the *Results* folder. Chapter 25 is devoted to the discussion of regression diagnostics. All the diagnostics available from the Regression Options dialog are discussed in detail in that chapter, so the discussion is not repeated here.

The Include constant term selection in the Regression Options dialog provides an opportunity to compute a regression without a constant or intercept term. Because most relationships don't naturally fall through the origin, the default is to include the constant term. The constant term should be excluded if your model already includes a constant predictor or you want to compute a regression through the origin.

The regression options affect the computing of all subsequent regressions, but don't alter any that have already been computed. Data Desk will remember the options you set if you click on the Set Defaults box.

24.7 *Working with Regression Summary Tables*

Data Desk summary tables are interactive in much the same way as Data Desk plots. They provide ways to alter and learn more about your analysis.

The simplest source of additional information is in the HyperView menus attached to the regression summary table. Many parts of the regression summary table have HyperView menus attached to them. You can tell when a HyperView menu is available because the cursor changes to ☝ when the mouse is over a HyperView menu. Press the mouse button to pop up the HyperView menu. Regression HyperView menus offer plots to help you view important aspects of the regression analysis.

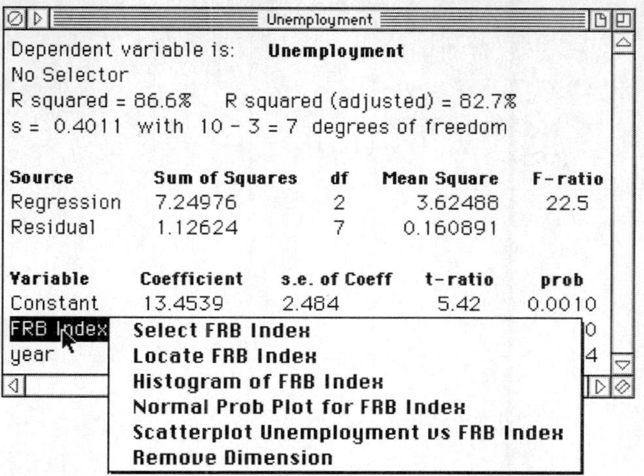

Figure 24-5. *The HyperView menu attached to the name of a predictor in a regression summary table.*

Some of these plots are basic background displays, such as histograms of the variables in the regression or scatterplots of y against one of the x-variables. It is always a good idea to examine such plots. Others offer more sophisticated views of the regression and are discussed in Chapter 25.

In addition to HyperView menus, you can use the regression summary table to add new predictors to the regression model, remove predictors from the model, and update the regression calculation to reflect changes, corrections, or "what if?" alterations in the data (Fig. 24-5).

The HyperView menu attached to the name of each predictor offers to remove that predictor from the model and recompute the regression. This provides a tool that can be useful in building regression models. Removing a predictor recomputes the regression, recomputes any diagnostic variables tied to this regression table, and offers to update any plots created from this regression table.

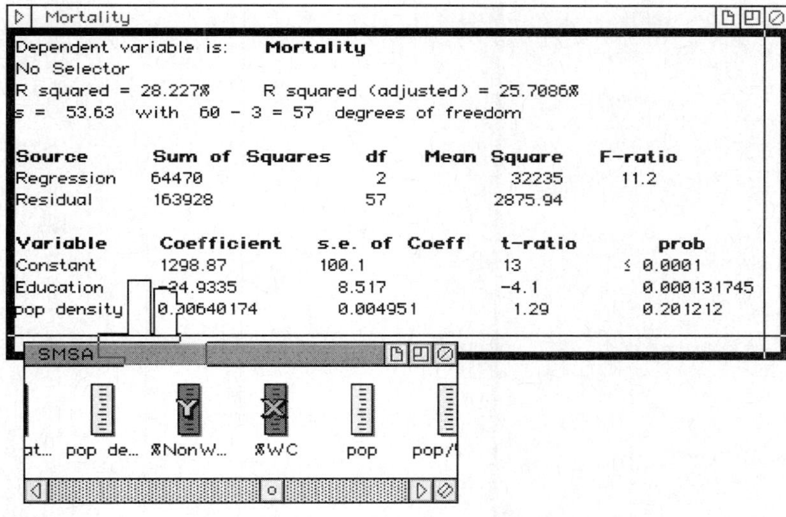

Figure 24-6. *Drag additional predictors into the regression summary table to add them to the regression model. The window border becomes darker to acknowledge the drag.*

To add new predictors to an existing regression analysis, select the icons of the new predictors and drag them into the regression summary table. The border of the summary table highlights to acknowledge the new predictors. Drop the icons inside the table to initiate the new regression (Fig. 24-6).

Data Desk also provides facilities for adjusting cases. If you modify any of the data underlying the regression or the expression in any derived variable in the regression, the regression summary table immediately offers to update in place or recompute in a new window. A symbol replaces the window's HyperView menu at the left of the window's title bar whenever the underlying variables have been changed. The menu offers to update the regression in place or redo it in a new window.

Often it is better to recompute the regression in a new window so that you can compare the "before" and "after" versions of the analysis. Regression analyses can change in subtle ways even when you make changes that seem trivial. Data Desk's updating capabilities also ensure that you know immediately if the analysis you are using was computed from data values that have since been changed.

EXERCISES

1. Use the Nuclear Plants dataset to compute a regression to predict *Cost* in terms of *Date* and *MWatts*.

(a) Consider the statistics in the first three lines of the regression summary table. For each of these statistics, give its value and write a sentence interpreting it. How do these statistics compare to the corresponding statistics in the regression of *Cost* on *Date* from Chapter 22?

R^2

Adjusted R^2

s

(b) Consider the table of regression coefficients in the last four lines of the regression summary table. For each of the statistics listed, give its value and write a sentence interpreting it.

Intercept coefficient

Regression coefficient for *MWatts*

s.e. of the regression coefficient for *MWatts*

t-statistic for the regression coefficient for *MWatts*

2. Generate five random samples of 30 numbers from a normal distribution (with any mean and standard deviation you want). Compute the regression to predict one of them from the other four.

(a) What is the "true" value of the underlying coefficients? Why?

(b) Compare R^2 and adjusted R^2. Which describes the success of the regression more accurately?

(c) What value did you compute for F? ________

(d) Examine the residuals to see if they seem to satisfy the regression assumptions. Sketch an appropriate display. Knowing how the data were generated, would you say that the regression assumptions are satisfied? Explain.

(e) If you were to generate 20 rather than 5 random samples of 30 and compute the regression of one on the others, how would you expect the following regression statistics to change?

R^2

Adjusted R^2

s

3. Use the Cars dataset and compute the regression of *MPG* on *Weight* and *Horsepower.*

(a) What are the units of these three variables?

(b) Write a few sentences describing what the following coefficients mean.

Weight coefficient:

Horsepower coefficient:

4. Now compute the regression of *MPG* on *Weight, Horsepower,* and *#Cylinders.* Does this regression appear to be more or less useful than the one in Exercise 3? Why?

5. Compute the regression of *MPG* on *Weight* and *Displacement.* Compare the regressions of Exercises 3 and 4 with this one. Which appears to be the most useful regression? Why?

6. (a) Consider the regression of *MPG* on *Weight* and *Displacement* computed in Exercise 5. Report the regression coefficients and any useful associated statistics.

(b) The coefficient of *Displacement* in this regression is positive and has a large t-statistic. Does this result suggest that bigger engines (with larger displacement) get better gas mileage? If so, how can you account for that? If not, what does it mean?

(c) Compute the regression of *MPG* on *Displacement*. Discuss the relationship of the two regression models.

(d) Construct a partial regression plot for *Displacement* by removing the linear effects of *Weight*. (Use the HyperView menu on the regression summary table under the *Displacement* coefficient.) Compare it to a scatterplot of *MPG* versus *Displacement*. Sketch both plots. Discuss their differences and what they tell you.

7. (a) Examine the residuals from the regression of *MPG* on *Weight* and *Displacement* computed in Exercise 5 by plotting residuals against predicted values. (The global HyperView menu of the summary table makes this task easy.) Sketch the scatterplot.

(b) The curved pattern indicates that the linearity assumption may have been violated. Define a derived variable named *GPM* as *–100/MPG.* (Multiplying by 100 gives numbers that are of convenient size, computing "gallons per 100 miles." The negative sign preserves the order so that larger numbers still represent better gas mileage.) Now compute the regression of *GPM* on *Weight* and *Displacement* and sketch the scatterplot of residuals against predicted values.

(c) What other differences do you notice between the two regressions? (You should expect the coefficients to change because of the transformation. What other statistics have changed?)

8. (a) Perform a regression of *MPG* on *Weight, Drive Ratio, Horsepower,* and *Displacement.* Make a histogram of the DFFits or Cook's distance values by using the appropriate command in the global HyperView menu of the summary table. Sketch the histogram.

(b) Identify the extraordinary car. Find its name by opening the *Car* variable, selecting the extraordinary point in the plot, and finding the selected car. Which car is it?

(c) Now omit the extraordinary car and repeat the regression. (Open *MPG* and edit the value to be missing — for example, by typing an * next to its value.) How do each of the following statistics change? Why?

R^2

Adjusted R^2

s

Coefficient of *Weight*

t-statistic for the coefficient of *Weight*

F

CHAPTER 25

Regression Diagnostics

MULTIPLE REGRESSION ANALYSIS provides a deceptively simple description of multivariate data. The regression model is an effective basis both for understanding relationships among many variables and for predicting values of the dependent variable for new cases. But regression coefficients are more subtle than they may appear at first, and regression computations can be sensitive to anomalies in the data and to violations of the assumptions underlying regression analysis.

Even though the principles of regression analysis date back to the 19th century, statistics and plots for diagnosing the effects of individual cases on a regression are quite recent. Data Desk provides a wide range of plots and statistics designed to help you identify patterns in the data and individual data values that might unduly influence the regression analysis.

The diagnostic statistics discussed in this chapter can be requested with the {Calc ▶ Calc Options} **Set Regression Options...** command or from HyperView menus. Diagnostics requested from the Options dialog are placed in HotResult variables in the *Regression* folder inside the *Results* folder. Diagnostic statistics requested from an output table's HyperView menu are placed in the data relation.

A Note on Notation

Some of the diagnostic statistics defined in this chapter are best defined algebraically with matrix equations. But you need not know matrix algebra to understand how to interpret and use these statistics. We provide the equations to define the statistics.

Throughout our discussions of regression we denote the number of cases in the regression (after excluding any cases due to missing values or selector variables) by n and the number of predictor variables (not counting the constant term) by p. The predictors are sometimes gathered column by column into a matrix, $\mathbf{X}$. Values representing population parameters are denoted with Greek letters, and data-based estimates are denoted by placing a ^ over a term or with Roman letters. The notation (i) is read "not i" and denotes omitting the ith case from the calculation.

The examples in this chapter are based upon an analysis of the SMSAs dataset and are set aside by printing in italics so that you can follow the story told by the analysis more easily. These data report properties of 60 Standard Metropolitan Statistical Areas (the standard Census Bureau designation of a major city and the region around it) in the United States, collected from a variety of sources. The data include information on the social and economic conditions in these areas, on their climate, and geographic location, and some indices of air pollution potentials. The dependent variable of interest is Age-Adjusted Mortality. We will illustrate diagnostic methods by working with the regression analysis shown in Fig. 25-1.

Dependent variable is: Mortality
No Selector
R squared = 60.4% R squared (adjusted) = 56.7%
s = 40.94 with 60 - 6 = 54 degrees of freedom

Source	Sum of Squares	df	Mean Square	F-ratio
Regression	137880	5	27576.0	16.5
Residual	90518.2	54	1676.26	

Variable	Coefficient	s.e. of Coeff	t-ratio	prob
Constant	1081.73	96.74	11.2	≤ 0.0001
Education	-21 9230	7.417	-2.96	0.0046
pop density	7.93091e-3	0.0039	2.02	0.0482
%NonWhite	3.82884	0.6434	5.95	≤ 0.0001
Rain	0.601016	0.6042	0.995	0.3243
NOx	-2.97740e-3	0.1359	-0.022	0.9826

Figure 25-1. *The regression of* Age-Adjusted Mortality *on* Median Education, Population Density, %Nonwhite, Mean Annual Rainfall, *and* Nitrous Oxide *pollution potential for 60 U.S. Standard Metropolitan Statistical Areas.*

25.1 *Checking Basic Assumptions*

Most statistics texts recommend that you examine simple plots to ascertain that the variables in a regression do not have any wild values and that the relationships between the *y*-variable and each of the *x*-variables are essentially linear. Most data analysts will admit (if they are honest) that they often overlook this step because it can be difficult and time-consuming.

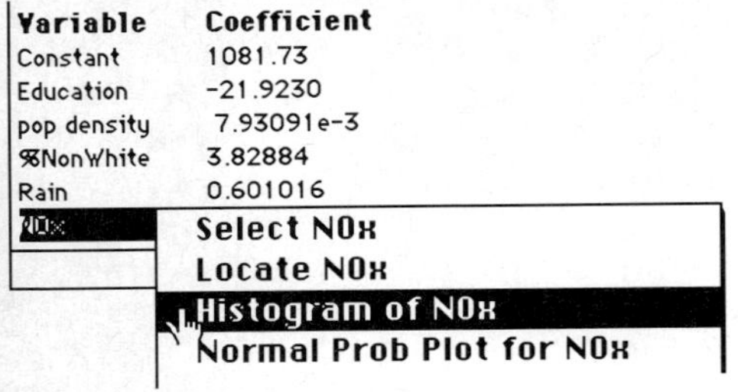

Figure 25-2. *Choose* ***Histogram of NOx*** *from the HyperView menu in the regression table.*

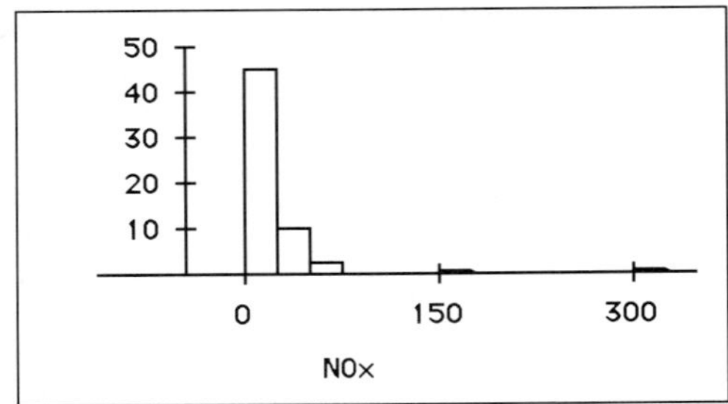

Figure 25-3. *A histogram of nitrous oxide pollution potential (NOx) reveals two extreme cases that may deserve special attention.*

Data Desk makes it easy to examine these plots by providing HyperView menu commands to create them (Fig. 25-2). Histograms of each of the variables in the analysis let us see at a glance any data value that is extraordinary (Fig. 25-3). We can also check for bimodal distributions, which suggest that we separate the data into two groups and analyze each separately, and for variables with skewed distributions, which suggest that we transform the variable to improve its symmetry.

Scatterplots of the *y*-variable versus each *x*-variable let us check for linear relationships — a basic assumption of regression analysis. Nonlinear relationships can sometimes be improved by transforming one or both of the variables. Some nonlinear relationships suggest including a quadratic or cubic term in the model.

Dependent variable is: Mortality
No Selector
R squared = 64.7% R squared (adjusted) = 61.4%
s = 38.65 with 60 - 6 = 54 degrees of freedom

Source	Sum of Squares	df	Mean Square	F-ratio
Regression	147753	5	29550.6	19.8
Residual	80645.6	54	1493.44	

Variable	Coefficient	s.e. of Coeff	t-ratio	prob
Constant	1031.73	93.36	11.1	≤ 0.0001
Education	-20.6236	6.992	-2.95	0.0047
pop density	3.20934e-3	0.0040	0.799	0.4275
%NonWhite	3.16133	0.6481	4.88	≤ 0.0001
Rain	1.38444	0.5939	2.33	0.0235
LNOx	31.8577	12.39	2.57	0.0129

Figure 25-4. *Substituting* log(NOx) *for* NOx *improves the regression in several ways. Note the higher* R^2*, and several improved* t*-ratios.*

The extreme NOx *values belong to Los Angeles and San Francisco. They might be telling us that air pollution in California is different from that in the rest of the U.S. However, the rest of the distribution is skewed, so we should first try to reexpress the variable. A histogram of* log(NOx) *is symmetric and unimodal, so there is no reason to treat the California cities separately. We perform a new regression, using* log(NOx) *instead of* NOx*. The regression summary table is shown in Fig. 25-4.*

25.2 Partial Regression Plots

partial regression plot

A good interpretation of the *j*th multiple regression coefficient, b_j, is that it reports the relationship between y and x_j *after the linear effects of the other x-variables have been removed from both.* One advantage of this description is that we can depict it with a *partial regression plot.* Partial regression plots are particularly useful because they provide a simple and intuitive way to see the influences of individual cases on the estimation of a multiple regression coefficient. Any intuition you might have about a simple slope in a scatterplot applies in the same way to the partial regression plot.

Although it is now considered a modern computer-oriented method, partial regression plots and other plots related to them were widely used when regression was first developed — decades before computers were available to perform the calculations. They are given different names by different statisticians, including *added variable plot, adjusted-variable plot,* and *individual coefficient plot.*

Each coefficient in a multiple regression can be depicted in its own partial regression plot. A partial regression plot graphs y *with the linear effects of the other* x*-variables removed* against x *with the linear effects of the other* x*-variables removed.* To remove the linear effects of the other x-variables from our chosen x, we perform another regression "on the side" and keep the residuals.

partial correlation

This extra regression estimates the linear effects of the other x-variables, and the residuals are what is left after removing these effects. The *partial correlation* of y and x is the correlation between the y and x adjusted in this way for the other x-variables. Some authors write of "partialing out" the linear effects of the other x-variables.

Coefficient	s.e. of Cceff	t-ratio	prob
1031.73	93.36	11.1	<0.0001
-20.6236	[illegible]	[illegible]	[illegible]
0.003209	0.0040	0.799	≤0.4275
3.16133	0.6481	4.88	<0.0001
1.38444	0.5939	2.33	≤0.0235
31.8577	12.39	2.57	≤0.0129

Partial regression plot of Education

Thus, to construct a partial regression plot of y and a particular predictor, x_j, we compute the regression of x_j on the other x-variables and save the residuals, compute the regression of y on the same x-variables (that is, all the predictors except x_j) and save those residuals, and then plot the y-residuals against the x-residuals. Data Desk provides a simple HyperView menu command to do all this work. The HyperView menu attached to each regression coefficient in the regression summary table offers the partial regression plot for that coefficient.

The partial regression plot has several useful properties:

- The least squares slope of the partial regression plot of y and x_j is b_j, the least squares coefficient associated with x_j in the full multiple regression of y on all the x-variables.
- The residuals from the least squares line in the partial regression plot are the same as the *final* residuals for the full multiple regression. (We have removed from y the linear effects of all of the predictors except x_j to obtain the ordinate for this plot. If we now remove the linear effects of x_j we obtain the final residuals.)
- The influence of each individual data point, as depicted in the partial regression plot for x_j, accurately reflects its influence on the regression coefficient b_j in the full regression model. Thus, for example, if one point is far from the others and evidently pulling the least squares line away from the slope indicated by the others, that case is exerting a similar influence on the coefficient of x_j in the multiple regression.

TIP

It is often useful to add a regression line to a partial regression plot.

Choose **Add Regression Line** from the plot's HyperView menu.

In short, you can transfer your intuition for how simple least squares regression relates to the standard y versus x scatterplot to how a multiple regression coefficient relates to its partial regression plot.

For example, the partial regression plot for Education *in Fig. 25-5 depicts the relationship between* Mortality *and* Education *in the full model given in Fig.*

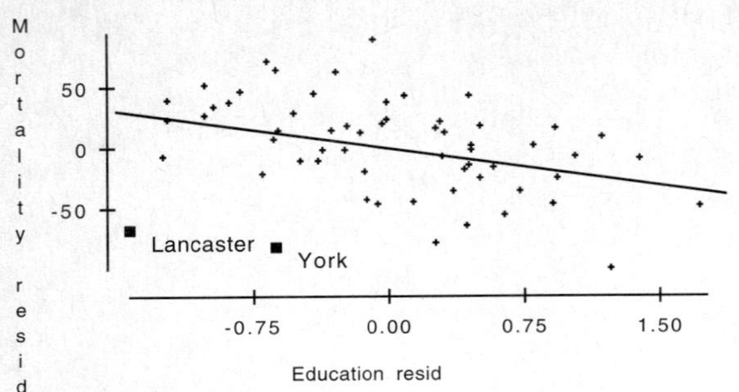

25-4. The plot shows a generally consistent trend with two points away from the body of the data.

The two extraordinary points can easily be identified as York and Lancaster — SMSAs that are adjacent to each other geographically in the Pennsylvania Dutch country and that have a local culture that might lead to an unusually low median education level. Intuition from the partial regression plot suggests that these two points are forcing the coefficient of Education *closer to 0 than it might otherwise have been.*

Figure 25-5. *The partial regression plot for* Education *shows a consistent negative trend and two points away from the others, indicated here by plotting them with an* x.

25.3 Leverage

Regression diagnostic statistics provide tools for assessing the influence of individual cases on a regression analysis. Regression analyses can be strongly affected by even a single extreme value, so it is wise to be aware of any cases exerting such an influence. Influential cases may be in error, but they are more likely to be extraordinary for some other reason. Whatever the reason, you can often learn more about your data by identifying the influential cases and giving them special attention.

leverage

The *leverage* of a data point measures how extreme it is on its x-variables and, consequently, how much influence it can exert on the regression. The leverage of the ith case, h_i, is the amount by which the ith predicted value, y_i, would change if the ith observed dependent variable value, y_i, were incremented by one and all other values in the regression data were unchanged.

Each h_i lies between 0.0 and 1.0. A leverage of 0 indicates a data point with no influence on the regression — for example a value observed at $x = 0$ for a regression constrained to pass through the origin. A leverage of 1 indicates a data point guaranteed to have a 0 residual.

In general, a case has higher leverage when it is farther from the center of the x-values. The appropriate physical model is a lever in which force applied farther from the fulcrum can move the lever more easily than force applied near the fulcrum. In least squares regression each point can be thought of as "pulling" on the line to try to make its residual as small as possible. Those farther from the center of the data can exert a stronger pull.

Leverage and residuals are related by the relationship

$$h_i + \frac{e_i^2}{\sum e_i^2} < 1.0$$

In a simple regression of y on a single x-variable, the leverage of the ith case is

$$\frac{(x_i - \bar{x})^2}{\sum (x_i - \bar{x})^2}$$

In a multiple regression, the expression is more complex and requires matrix algebra.

For the regression of the vector **y** on the matrix of predictor variables, **X**, the leverage of the *i*th case is the *i*th diagonal element of the matrix:

$$\mathbf{H} = \mathbf{X}\,(\mathbf{X}^T\mathbf{X})^{-1}\,\mathbf{X}^T$$

hat matrix

The matrix **H** is sometimes called the *hat matrix* because

$$\hat{y} = Hy$$

so **H** "puts a hat on **y**." Some authors call **H** the prediction or the projection matrix (because it projects any vector into the space of the **X**-vectors) and denote it **P**.

Cases with high leverage can be extraordinary, either because they have an extreme value on one of the predictors or because the combination of values on some set of predictors is unusual. For example, the subject in a medical study who is 6′3″ tall isn't extraordinary. Nor is the subject who weighs 97 pounds. But a subject who exhibits both these measurements is extraordinarily thin for his or her height.

Leverage values are fundamental building blocks of many regression statistics. For example, the variance of the *i*th predicted value is

$$Var(\hat{y}_i) = \sigma_\varepsilon^2 h_i$$

where σ_ε^2 is the variance of the regression residuals and the variance of the *i*th residual is

$$Var(\hat{e}_i) = \sigma_\varepsilon^2\,(1 - h_i)$$

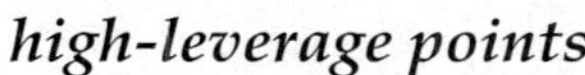

There are several rules of thumb for deciding that the leverage of a case is large enough for the case to deserve special attention. Some authors recommend that cases with leverage exceeding *2p/n* or *3p/n* be considered *high-leverage points.* Others have proposed that leverages above 0.5 deserve attention. We have found that using a histogram, dotplot, or boxplot of the leverage values is often better than relying on inflexible rules. Any case whose leverage sticks out in such a plot deserves a second look.

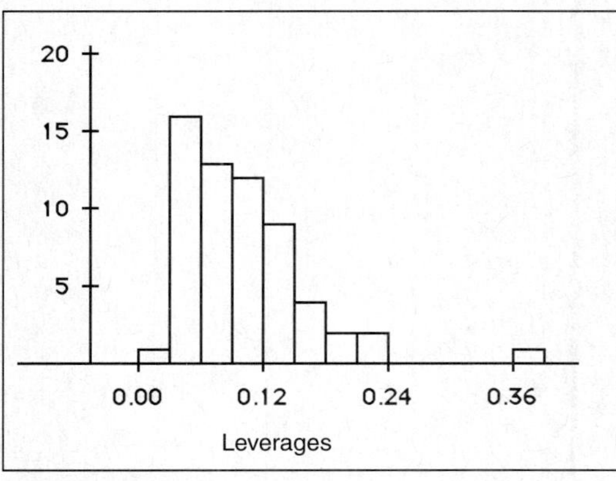

Figure 25-6. *A histogram of the leverages reveals a high-leverage point.*

You can make a histogram of the leverages by choosing **Compute ▶ Leverages** from the regression table's global HyperView menu and then choosing {Plot} **Histogram.** Fig. 25-6 displays the leverages of the regression given in Fig. 25-4 as a histogram. They reveal a high-leverage point.

The leverages are saved as a HotResult variable named *Leverages* in the same relation with other variables. You can locate its icon conveniently with the HyperView menu under the name *Leverages* on the axis of the plot.

We can illustrate the principles of leverage by using Data Desk's plots. Make a dotplot of the leverage values and a rotating plot of *Education, Pop Density,* and *Rain.* Slice up and down the dotplot with the tool and watch the rotating plot to see where the points with highest and lowest leverage fall.

You can also assign a different plotting symbol to the high-leverage points or color the points according to their leverage or to the rank of their leverage.

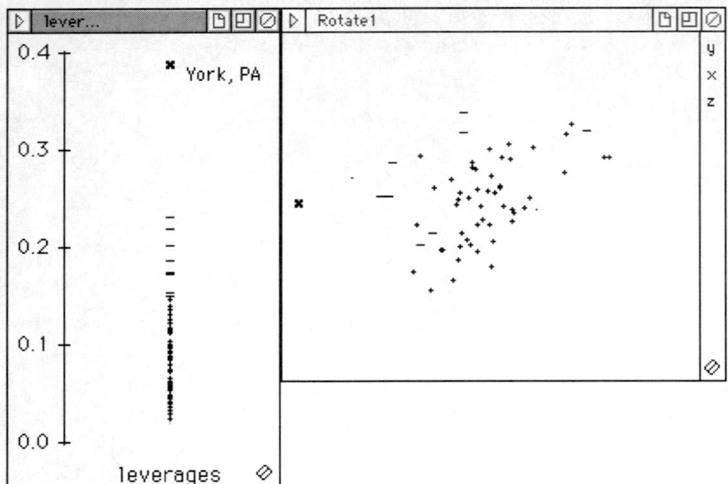

Figure 25-7. *Cases with higher leverage values correspond to those around the outside of the rotating plot of* Education, Pop Density, *and* Rain. *The point with highest leverage is York, which is plotted here with an* x.

Dependent variable is: Mortality
No Selector
R squared = 71.2% R squared (adjusted) = 67.9%
s = 35.25 with 60 - 7 = 53 degrees of freedom

Source	Sum of Squares	df	Mean Square	F-ratio
Regression	162551	6	27091.8	21.8
Residual	65847.3	53	1242.40	

Variable	Coefficient	s.e. of Coeff	t-ratio	prob
Constant	1040.19	85.19	12.2	≤ 0.0001
Education	-23.8313	6.445	-3.70	0.0005
pop density	0.010461	0.0042	2.48	0.0164
%NonWhite	2.82729	0.5990	4.72	≤ 0.0001
Rain	1.64921	0.5471	3.01	0.0039
LNOx	26.8664	11.39	2.36	0.0221
York	-155.443	45.04	-3.45	0.0011

Figure 25-8. *Isolating York by including a 0/1 variable improves the regression.*

You can rotate the plot to see the points from several angles. From some points of view the high-leverage points may not seem extreme, but by rotating the plot you can easily see that they are around the edges of the point cloud. Fig. 25-7 shows one view.

It is important to remember that leverage is a property only of the predictors. It takes no account of the *y*-values at all. That is why the rotating plot in Fig. 25-7 plots only predictor variables. Rotating plots of other predictors will also work for this exercise, although we admit to selecting one for this example in which the pattern is clearest.

We have now shown in a few ways that York is a high-leverage point for this analysis. Along with the partial regression plot in Fig. 25-5, we have substantial evidence that York is an extraordinary point that might be best analyzed separately from the other cases. We can isolate York from the analysis in a variety of ways. We choose here to generate an indicator variable that is 1 only for York and 0 elsewhere, and add it to the regression model.

To do so, select York alone in any plot, choose {Modify ▸Selection} ***Record As Indicators****, and drag the resulting icon into the regression summary table. If your label variable is open, in this case* City*, the indicator variable will be named correctly. Fig. 25-8 shows the results. The* t-ratio *associated with the indicator variable for York provides a test of whether York is an outlier for this analysis; the large* t-ratio *confirms that the datapoint is extraordinary.*

A Note on Removing Cases

The question of when a case may be treated specially, such as we have done above with York, has been discussed by many authors but there doesn't seem to be any consensus of opinion. Certainly, you shouldn't simply discard cases unless you have confirmed that they are wrong and beyond correcting. Nevertheless, often it is possible to obtain a very good fit to 90% or more of the data and deal specially with the remaining cases.

Dealing specially with selected cases means examining how they differ from the *pattern* described by the analysis, and reporting them as part of the analysis. In our experience, the occasional extraordinary case often can be understood best in terms of its deviation from a model or equation determined by the remaining cases, and this understanding can inform the entire analysis.

One response to an extraordinary case is to sample more data for similar situations. If the new data resemble the extraordinary case, you have probably learned something new and important. If not, you may be able to correct or better understand the original extraordinary value. Unfortunately, you often won't have the luxury of being able to gather additional data.

25.4 Studentized Residuals

The residuals in a regression are the differences between the observed and predicted y-values:

$$e_i = y_i - \hat{y}_i$$

It is always a good idea to examine the residuals. The regression table's HyperView menu offers several appropriate plots including a probability plot of the residuals, scatterplots of the residuals and studentized residuals versus the predicted values (an effective way to check for some kinds of nonlinear structure in the data). Context-sensitive HyperView menus on each predictor's t-ratio value in the table offers scatterplots of the residuals and studentized residuals versus the predictor.

However, as we noted in Section 25.3, the residuals don't all have the same variance. Residuals for x-values near the mean of the x's are more variable than those for more extreme x-values. This result follows from the earlier observation that the variance of the ith residual, e_i, depends, in part, upon the leverage of the ith data point:

$$Var(\hat{e}_i) = \sigma_\varepsilon^2(1 - h_i)$$

This equation suggests that the raw residuals may be misleading, especially for assessing whether the residuals have constant variance.

A useful alternative is to standardize the residuals by dividing each by an estimate of its own standard deviation:

$$r_i = \frac{e_i}{\sqrt{Var(\hat{e}_i)}} = \frac{e_i}{\hat{\sigma}_\varepsilon \sqrt{1 - h_i}}$$

Residuals so standardized are called *studentized residuals* after the pseudonym of W. S. Gosset, the originator of Student's t.

internally studentized residual

To compute a studentized residual, we must estimate the standard error of the residuals, σ_ε, from the data. If we estimate the standard error by the residual standard deviation, s, we obtain the *internally studentized residual*. Internally studentized residuals have unit standard deviation. However, the ith residual participates in estimating the residual standard error, so the numerator and denominator aren't statistically independent.

externally studentized residual

The *externally studentized residual* estimates the residual standard deviation in the regression that omits the ith case, so its numerator and denominator are statistically independent. We write the residual standard deviation omitting the ith case as $s(i)$. Note that it isn't simply the standard deviation of all the residuals except the ith, but rather is the residual standard deviation from a regression that omits the ith case. Data Desk uses a calculation method that does not require a new regression calculation to obtain $s(i)$.

Although the two kinds of studentized residuals are almost always very similar, some authors, including the authors of Data Desk, prefer the externally studentized residuals because they have several pleasant properties:

- The ith externally studentized residual is distributed as Student's t on $(n - p - 1)$ degrees of freedom — a distribution for which tables are readily available. By contrast, the internally studentized residuals follow a Beta[1/2, $(n - p - 1)/2$] distribution. Of course, the studentized residuals in either form aren't mutually independent.
- The ith externally studentized residual can be interpreted as a t-statistic for testing whether the ith case is an outlier in the regression.
- The estimate $s(i)$ isn't inflated by gross errors in the ith residual.
- The externally studentized residuals are monotonic transformations of the residuals that may be arbitrarily large. They thus tend to exhibit outliers more dramatically.
- The ith externally studentized residual is the same as the regression coefficient of the indicator variable constructed to isolate the ith case, as we did with York in Fig. 25-8.

The regression table's global HyperView menu offers probability plots of both the externally and internally studentized residuals and a scatterplot of the externally studentized residuals versus the predicted values. Context-sensitive HyperView menus on each predictor's t-ratio value in the table offers a scatterplot of the externally studentized residuals versus the predictor.

A Note on Usage

The terms *standardized residual* and *studentized residual* are used in different ways by different statistics packages. Standardized residuals, in particular, are defined by some packages simply as e_i/s and in others as

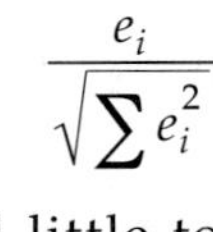

$$\frac{e_i}{\sqrt{\sum e_i^2}}$$

These adjustments add little to the usefulness of residuals because the residuals still have different variances. It is always wise to determine exactly what is meant by these terms. The terminology used in Data Desk agrees with the most prominent recent books and articles on regression and regression diagnostics.

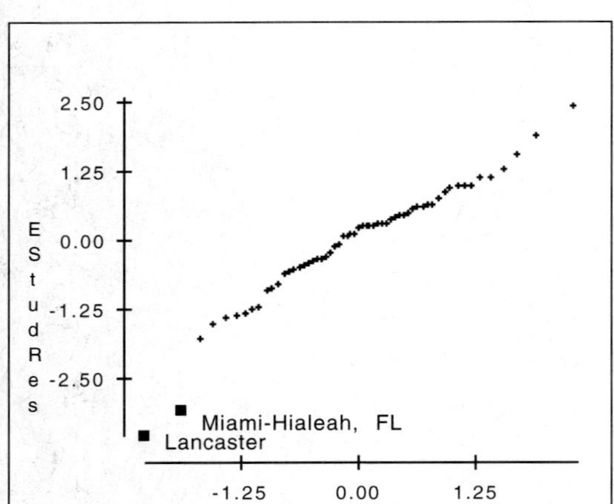

Figure 25-9. *A normal probability plot of the externally studentized residuals from the regression given in Fig. 25-8 is straight but for two cities, Lancaster and Miami.*

Working from the global HyperView menu for the regression in Fig. 25-8, we can make a normal probability plot of the externally studentized residuals. When (n – p – 1) *is large, the externally studentized residuals should be approximately normal. The plot shows a generally normal distribution except for two points. These points turn out to be Lancaster and Miami (Fig. 25-9).*

This result suggests that these two cities may deserve special attention. The partial regression plot for Education *shown in Fig. 25-5 provided a good explanation for why Lancaster should be influential and why it should be isolated from a regression intended to describe cities in general. We isolate it from the analysis here by creating a 0/1 indicator variable and adding it to the model (Fig. 25-10).*

```
Dependent variable is:    Mortality
No Selector
R squared = 76.7%    R squared (adjusted) = 73.6%
s = 31.98  with  60 - 8 = 52  degrees of freedom
```

Source	Sum of Squares	df	Mean Square	F-ratio
Regression	175209	7	25029.8	24.5
Residual	53189.7	52	1022.88	

Variable	Coefficient	s.e. of Coeff	t-ratio	prob
Constant	1113.33	80.04	13.9	≤ 0.0001
Education	-29.7017	6.081	-4.88	≤ 0.0001
pop density	9.12979e-3	0.0038	2.37	0.0214
%NonWhite	2.42814	0.5552	4.37	≤ 0.0001
Rain	1.68544	0.4965	3.39	0.0013
LNOx	28.8218	10.35	2.78	0.0075
York	-164.927	40.96	-4.03	0.0002
Lancaster	-120.331	34.21	-3.52	0.0009

Figure 25-10. *The regression model with a 0/1 indicator variable to isolate Lancaster. The large* t*-statistic for Lancaster confirms that it is an outlier relative to the remaining cases in this regression.*

25.5 Distance Measures

Leverage measures how extreme a case is in the predictors. Residuals and studentized residuals measure how extreme a case is in the dependent variable. Distance measures combine both of these concepts to measure the overall influence of a case on the regression.

DFFITS

The diagnostic statistic *DFFITS* is defined as the change that would occur in the *i*th predicted value were the *i*th data point to be deleted, divided by the standard error of the *i*th predicted value:

$$DFFITS_i = \frac{\hat{y}_i - \hat{y}_i(i)}{s(i)\sqrt{h_i}} = \sqrt{\frac{h_i}{1-h_i}}\frac{e_i}{s(i)\sqrt{1-h_i}}$$

The calculation form of *DFFITS* shows it to be a product of a leverage-based term and the externally studentized residual. Although *DFFITS* doesn't generally follow a *t*-distribution, it is a *t*-like statistic, so cases with values of *DFFITS* greater than 1 or 2 may deserve special attention. Histograms, boxplots, and dotplots of the *DFFITS* values can highlight cases with extraordinary values regardless of the absolute magnitude of the *DFFITS* value.

Cook's distance

Cook's distance is similar to *DFFITS,* except that it uses the internally studentized residual and is squared relative to *DFFITS*. Specifically, Cook's distance is defined as

$$D_i = \frac{(\hat{y} - \hat{y}(i))^T(\hat{y} - \hat{y}(i))}{(p+1)\hat{\sigma}^2} = \frac{1}{p+1}\frac{h_i}{1-h_i}\frac{e_i^2}{s\sqrt{1-h_i}}$$

where the (i) subscript indicates values from a regression omitting the *i*th case. Cook originally proposed this statistic in an equivalent form that emphasizes its interpretation as a scaled change in the coefficients due to the omission of the *i*th case:

$$D_i = \frac{(\hat{\beta} - \hat{\beta}_{(i)})^T X^T X (\hat{\beta} - \hat{\beta}_{(i)})}{(p+1)\hat{\sigma}^2}$$

Cook suggests that D_i be compared to the percentiles of the F-distribution with $(p + 1)$ and $(n - p - 1)$ degrees of freedom and interpreted relative to the confidence ellipsoids for β. Thus a D_i value that is approximately at the 95% point of its F-distribution can be interpreted to mean that removing the ith case would move the coefficient vector to the edge of its original 95% confidence ellipsoid.

Hadi's Influence

Hadi's influence measure is a new diagnostic statistic that often makes it easy to identify influential datapoints. Most influence statistics look at the effect on the slope and intercept of the regression line. Hadi's influence measure looks at these effects plus the effect of any points on the variability of the model. Points that influence the variance may not affect the regression line, but they do affect the standard errors of the coefficients. If the point increases these standard errors, the t-values of the coefficients will become smaller and their null hypotheses harder to reject. To generate a variable holding Hadi's influence choose {Compute} **Hadi's Influence** from the global HyperView menu of any regression or ANOVA table.

Hadi's influence measure is computed as

$$H_i^2 = \frac{p}{1-h_i}\frac{d_i^2}{1-d_i^2} + \frac{h_i}{1-h_i}$$

where p is a number of predictors, h_i is the leverage of the ith case, and

$$d_i = \frac{e_i^2}{\sum_{i=1}^{n} e_i^2}$$

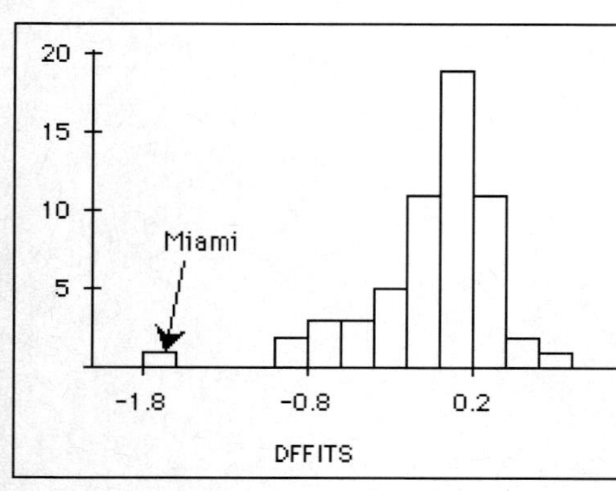

Figure 25-11. *A histogram of DFFITS for the regression in Fig. 25-10 shows one influential point — Miami.*

Hadi's influence thus combines the information about the size of the ith residual with information about the leverage of the ith datapoint. The leverage information is a separate term and can be thought of as measuring the potential of the case to influence the regression. Cases far from the center of the data have a greater potential to harm the regression. It can also be thought of as the ratio of the variance of the ith predicted value to the variance of its residual.

The first part of the expression is a function of the ith residual weighted by the ith leverage value. The **Potential-Residual** plot is a scatterplot of these two parts of H_i, the potential versus the residual (Fig. 25-11). You can generate a **Potential-Residual** plot from the global HyperView menu of any regression or ANOVA table.

The potential-residual plot for the regression shown in Fig. 25-10 reveals that Miami is influential in the regression.

*Having seen that Miami has a large studentized residual, we should not be surprised to find it influential according to this plot. We might want to identify the way in which Miami influences the regression so that we can better understand whether it is reasonable to treat Miami specially. One way to do so is to make Miami missing in one of the variables (for example, by typing an * in front of one of its data values) and compare the regression that includes Miami to the one that omits it (Fig. 25-12).*

Variable	t-ratio Miami	t-ratio no Miami
Constant	13.9	13.9
Education	-4.88	-4.47
pop density	2.37	3.30
%NonWhite	4.37	4.89
Rain	3.39	4.32
LNOx	2.78	2.21
York	-4.03	-4.83
Lancaster	-3.52	-3.71

It is easy to understand that Miami should have a climate different from other

Figure 25-12. *Comparing the coefficient* t-ratios *with and without Miami shows that coefficients associated with population density and mean annual rainfall seem to have been affected most.*

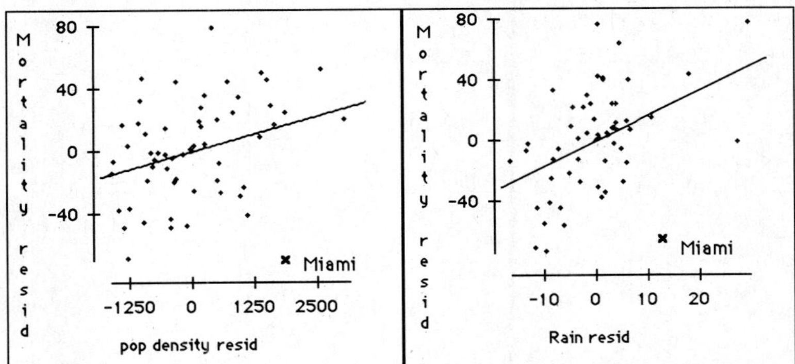

Figure 25-13. *Partial regression plots of* Pop Density *and* Rain *show that Miami influences both of these regression coefficients.*

cities — Miami is classified as having a subtropical climate. It is harder to understand why Miami should be influential on the coefficient for population density (Fig. 25-13).

To pursue the analysis further, we create a 0/1 indicator variable for Miami and add it to the regression model, obtaining the regression shown in Fig. 25-14.

A look at the potential–residual plot for this model suggests that Worcester, MA, and

Dependent variable is: Mortality
No Selector
R squared = 80.8% R squared (adjusted) = 77.8%
s = 29.32 with 60 - 9 = 51 degrees of freedom

Source	Sum of Squares	df	Mean Square	F-ratio
Regression	184550	8	23068.8	26.8
Residual	43848.3	51	859.770	

Variable	Coefficient	s.e. of Coeff	t-ratio	prob
Constant	1052.78	75.65	13.9	≤ 0.0001
Education	-25.5607	5.715	-4.47	≤ 0.0001
pop density	0.012006	0.0036	3.30	0.0018
%NonWhite	2.48953	0.5094	4.89	≤ 0.0001
Rain	2.01293	0.4659	4.32	≤ 0.0001
LNOx	21.5207	9.746	2.21	0.0318
York	-183.546	37.97	-4.83	≤ 0.0001
Lancaster	-116.452	31.38	-3.71	0.0005
Miami	-107.687	32.67	-3.30	0.0018

Figure 25-14. *The regression model with three cities isolated.*

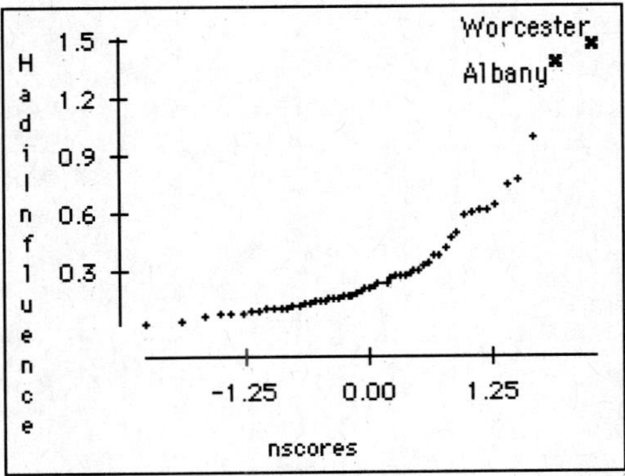

Figure 25-15. *A normal probability plot of Hadi's influence for the regression in Fig. 25-14 shows that Worcester and Albany might also be extreme.*

Albany, NY, might also be extreme.

Diagnosis of the regression in Fig. 25-16 reveals no additional extraordinary cases and general adherence to the regression assumptions. The studentized residuals appear close to normal when plotted in histograms and normal probability plots. They show no pattern when plotted against predicted values or individual predictors. The adjusted R^2 is large and the coefficients t-ratios are all significantly different from 0.

Dependent variable is: Mortality
No Selector
R squared = 85.3% R squared (adjusted) = 82.3%
s = 26.20 with 60 - 11 = 49 degrees of freedom

Source	Sum of Squares	df	Mean Square	F-ratio
Regression	194764	10	19476.4	28.4
Residual	33634.0	49	686.409	

Variable	Coefficient	s.e. of Coeff	t-ratio	prob
Constant	1003.67	69.67	14.4	≤ 0.0001
Education	-22.7724	5.189	-4.39	≤ 0.0001
pop density	0.011784	0.0033	3.62	0.0007
%NonWhite	2.25352	0.4850	4.65	≤ 0.0001
Rain	2.55044	0.4682	5.45	≤ 0.0001
LNOx	23.4569	8.743	2.68	0.0099
York	-191.321	34.46	-5.55	≤ 0.0001
Lancaster	-117.185	28.11	-4.17	0.0001
Miami	-118.676	29.60	-4.01	0.0002
Worcester	-77.7631	30.41	-2.56	0.0137
Albany	73.6381	26.76	2.75	0.0083

Figure 25-16. *The regression with Worcester and Albany also isolated.*

25.6 Regression Options

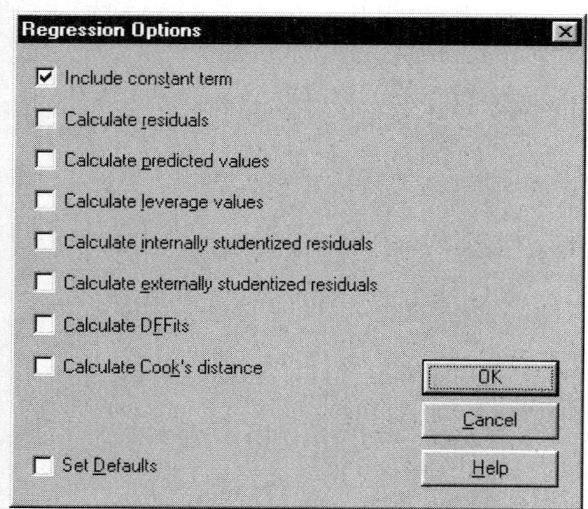

Figure 25-17. *The Regression Options dialog.*

The {Calc ▶ Calculation Options} **Regression Options...** command offers each of the diagnostic statistics discussed in this chapter (Fig. 25-17). The diagnostic statistics selected in this dialog are created for all subsequent {Calc} **Regression** commands. All diagnostic statistics, whether they are requested from the Options dialog or the table's HyperView menu, are saved as HotResult variables. Any change to the regression due to editing the underlying data, dragging in a new variable, or removing a variable from a HyperView menu, causes all diagnostic HotResult variables to update automatically. Any plot created with a diagnostic variable indicates its out-of-date status with a ! in the upper left corner. Diagnostic plots can be updated without updating the regression table, but we do not recommend doing so because trying to work with an out-of-date regression and up-to-date diagnostic plots can be confusing.

We discussed the first three regression options in Chapter 24. The remaining options calculate diagnostic statistics.

CALCULATE LEVERAGE VALUES

When this option is checked, all subsequent regressions create a HotResult variable, *Leverages.* It contains a leverage value for each case in the regression and places it in the *Regression* folder.

Calculate Studentized Residuals

The options "Calculate internally studentized residuals" and "Calculate externally studentized residuals" each create a new HotResult variable in the *Regression* folder containing one appropriately studentized residual for each case. The created HotResult variables are named *Ext Stud Res* or *Int Stud Res,* according to the kind of studentized residual requested.

Distance Measures

The options to calculate *DFFITS,* Cook's distance and Hadi's Influence each create a new HotResult variable in the *Regression* folder that contains one value for each case. The variables are named *DFFITS, Cook's Distance,* or *HadiInfluence.*

25.7 *A Note on Identifying Cases*

Regressions can be computed from a table of correlation coefficients. In the past, some statistics packages used this method because it is fast and requires relatively little computer memory. Modern regression methods, however, require that the individual cases be available for examination and correction during a regression analysis.

The diagnostic statistics discussed in this chapter are *casewise* diagnostics. That is, they generate an entire variable full of values, one for each case. The HotResult variables holding diagnostics are in the same relation as the data because they hold a value for each case. The easiest way to use them is to simply make probability plots, histograms, or dotplots of them and identify any cases with extraordinarily large diagnostic values. A large diagnostic value typically means that the case in question is influential in the regression. The case might be entirely correct, but you will want to know that it is influential anyway.

Because all Data Desk plots are linked, you can identify extraordinary points with the **?** tool. Alternatively, you can select them and see where they lie in other plots. Plotting several diagnostic statistics together as the variables making up a scatterplot or rotating plot can help you to identify extraordinary or influential cases.

25.8 *Collinearity*

A multiple regression in which two or more predictors are highly correlated is said to be *collinear*. Data Desk checks for severe collinearity and aborts the regression computation before the rounding errors that collinearity causes can ruin the value of the regression output.

Sometimes a case can be influential because it is the only point that stands between your analysis and collinearity. For example, in a regression of y on two predictors, if the predictors are collinear but for one point, the regression analysis is balancing the regression plane like a table top on a knife edge and one other point. That point will have leverage very near 1.0; if it is moved up or down, the table top will follow. If you omit the point from the regression, the underlying collinearity shows through and the table top is no longer stable.

One way to assess collinearity is to perform a partial regression of one predictor on the others. The R^2 for this regression measures the collinearity of the multiple regression model as it affects the coefficient of that predictor; R^2 values near 1.0 indicate strong collinearity.

Bibliography

Andrews, D. F., and Herzberg, A. M. *Data: A Collection of Problems from Many Fields for the Student and Research Worker*. New York: Springer-Verlag, 1985.

Becker, R. A., and Cleveland, W. S. "Brushing Scatterplots." *Technometrics,* 1987, 29: 127-142.

Belsely, D., Kuh, E. and Welsch, R. E. *Regression Diagnostics*. New York: John Wiley & Sons, 1980.

Box, G. E. P., and Cox, D. R. "An Analysis of Transformation." *JRSS,* 1964, B26: 211-243.

Catton, W. R., Smircich, R., and Smircich, R. J. "A Comparison of Mathematical Models for the Effect of Residential Propinquity on Mate Selection." *American Sociological Review*, 1964, 29(4): 522-529.

Chambers, J. M., Cleveland, W. S., Kleiner, B., and Tukey, P. A. *Graphical Methods for Data Analysis*. Belmont, CA: Wadsworth, 1983.

Chaterjee, S., and Hadi, A. *Sensitivity Analysis in Linear Regression*. New York: John Wiley & Sons, 1988.

Cleveland, W. S. *The Elements of Graphing Data*. Monterey, CA: Wadsworth, 1985.

Conover, W. J. *Practical Nonparametric Statistics*. 2nd edition, New York: John Wiley & Sons, 1980.

Cook, R. D. "Detection of Influential Observations in Linear Regression." *Technometrics*, 1977, 19: 15-18.

Dongarra, J. J., Moler, C. B., Bunch, J. R., and Stewart, G. W. *LINPACK User's Guide*. Philadelphia: Society for Industrial and Applied Mathematics, 1979.

Draper, D., Hodges, J., Mallows, C., Pregibon, D. "Exchangeability and Data Analysis." *Journal of the Royal Statistical Society,* Series A, 1993, 156: 9-37.

Ezekial, M. "A method of handling curvilinear correlation for any number of variables." *Journal of the American Statistical Association*, 1924, 19: 431-453.

Gnanadesikan, R. *Methods for Statistical Data Analysis of Multivariate Observations,* New York: John Wiley & Sons, 1977.

Gibbons, J. D., and Chakraborti, S. *Nonparametric Statistical Inference,* 3rd edition. New York: Marcel Dekker, 1992.

Henderson, H., and Velleman, P. F. "Building Multiple Regression Models Interactively." *Biometrics*, 1981, 37: 391–411.

Hoaglin, D. C. "Transformations in Everyday Experience." *Chance,* 1988, 1(4): 40-45.

Hoaglin, D. C., and Moore, D. S. *Perspectives on Contemporary Statistics*. Washington, DC: Mathematical Association of America, 1992.

Hoaglin, D. C, Mosteller, F., and Tukey, J. W. *Understanding Robust and Exploratory Data Analysis*. New York: John Wiley & Sons, 1983.

Hoaglin, D. C, Mosteller, F., and Tukey, J. W. *Exploring Data Tables, Trends and Shapes*. New York: John Wiley & Sons, 1985.

Hoaglin, D. C, Mosteller, F., and Tukey, J. W. *Fundamentals of Exploratory Analysis of Variance*. New York: John Wiley & Sons, 1991.

Hoaglin, D. C., and Welsch, R. E. "The hat matrix in regression and ANOVA." *The American Statistician*, 1978, 32: 17-22.

Huff, D. *How to Lie with Statistics*. New York: W. W. Norton, 1954.

Joiner, B. L. "Lurking Variables: Some Examples." *The American Statistician*, 1981, 35, 227-233.

Jones, L. V. (ed.) *The Collected Works of John W. Tukey, Volume III: Philosophy and Principles of Data Analysis: 1949–1964.* Monterey, CA: Wadsworth & Brooks/Cole Advanced Books & Software, 1986.

Kennedy, W. J., and Gentle J. E. *Statistical Computing*. New York: Marcel Dekker, 1980.

Larsen, W. A., and McCleary, S. J. "The use of Partial Residual Plots in Regression Analysis." *Technometrics*, 1971, 14: 781-790.

McKeon, F. "F approximations to the Distribution of Hotellings T^2." *Biometrica*, 1974, 61: 381-383.

Moore, D. S., and McCabe, G. P. *Introduction to the Practice of Statistics.* New York: W. H. Freeman, 1993.

Mosteller, F., and Tukey, J. *Data Analysis and Regression.* Reading, MA: Addison-Wesley, 1977.

Neter, J., Wasserman, W., and Kutner, M. H. *Applied Linear Statistical Methods,* 3rd edition. Homewood, IL: Irwin, 1980.

Norman, D. A. *The Design of Everyday Things*. New York: Basic Books, 1988.

Ott, R. Lyman. *An Introduction to Statistical Methods and Data Analysis.* Belmont, CA: Wadsworth, 1993.

Pratt, J. W., and Gibbons, J. D. *Concepts of Nonparametric Theory.* New York: Springer-Verlag, 1989.

Searle, S. *Linear Models.* New York: John Wiley & Sons, 1971.

Sprent, P. *Applied Nonparametric Statistical Methods*. New York: Chapman & Hall, 1989.

Stigler, Stephen M. "Do Robust Estimators Work with Real Data?" *The Annals of Statistics,* 1977, 5(4): 1075.

Thisted, R. A. *Elements of Statistical Computing*. New York: Chapman & Hall, 1988.

Tufte, E. R. *The Visual Display of Quantitative Information*. Cheshire, CT: Graphics Press, 1983.

Tukey, J. W. "The Future of Data Analysis." *Annals of Mathematical Statistics,* 1962, 33: 1-67, 812.

Tukey, J. W. *Exploratory Data Analysis*. Reading, MA: Addison-Wesley, 1977.

Velleman, P. F., and Hoaglin, D. C. *Applications, Basics, and Computing of Exploratory Data Analysis.* Boston: Duxbury Press, 1981.

Velleman, P, F., and Welsch, R. E. "Efficient Computing of Regression Diagnostics." *The American Statistician,* 1982, 36.

Weisberg, S. *Applied Linear Regression*. New York: John Wiley & Sons, 1980.

Weisberg, S. *Applied Linear Regression,* 2nd edition. New York: John Wiley & Sons, 1985.

Wilkinson, L., and Velleman, P. F. "Nominal, Ordinal, Interval, and Ratio Typology Is Misleading." *The American Statistician,* 1993, 47.

Index

B

C

D

I

J K

L

P

Q R

T

U

V

W

X Y Z